THE CRUSADER KINGDOM
OF VALENCIA

VOLUME TWO

THE CRUSADER KINGDOM OF

VALENCIA

RECONSTRUCTION ON A THIRTEENTH-CENTURY FRONTIER

Robert Ignatius Burns, S.J.

VOLUME TWO

HARVARD UNIVERSITY PRESS

CAMBRIDGE, MASSACHUSETTS

1967

CONTENTS

v

THE CRUSADER KINGDOM
OF VALENCIA

APPENDIXES

APPENDIX I

∽∾

CIVIL AND MILITARY
CHRONOLOGY

1212   Almohad power crippled by Hispanic states at battle of Las Navas de Tolosa.

1213   Peter I "the Catholic" of Aragon killed at Muret battle; waning of Aragonese hold on Languedoc. James I, minor of five years, is king; reigns from 1217.

1225   Abortive attempt on Valencia kingdom; Peñíscola siege.

1229   Balearics crusade; Majorca city falls. Pact with Saʿīd of Valencia.

1232   Valencia crusade begins; Morella taken.

1233   Burriana sieged, falls on July 28; much of northern Valencia kingdom follows.

1235   Tarragona metropolitan conquers Ibiza in Balearics.

1236   Monzón general parliament gives new life to Valencia crusade; James begins use of title "King of Valencia."

1237   Pitched battle and Christian victory at Puig, just above Valencia city.

1238   Valencia city sieged, falls (September 28).

1242   Alcira falls.

1244   Játiva sieged, taken. Almizra treaty with Castile.

1245   Biar falls, Murcia border reached; end of crusade.

1248   Valencian Moslems rebel under al-Yazraȳī. In west, Seville falls to Ferdinand.

1258   Corbeil treaty with France, loss of Languedoc claims. Second al-Yazraȳī war.

1262   Prince Peter (b. 1240) marries Constance, Hohenstaufen heir; by now associated in governmental affairs.

1263   Moslem revolts in Andalusia, Murcia, possibly Valencia. Castilians ask Aragonese help.

1265   Expeditions by Prince Peter into Murcia; conquest completed by James I (Murcia city falls, 1266).

1269   Abortive crusade to Holy Land by James I.

1274   James I at ecumenical council of Lyons. Returns to find revolt by Catalan-Aragonese nobles, civil disturbances in Valencia city.

1275   Great Moslem revolt in Valencia kingdom.

1276   King James dies at Valencia city (June 27), aged 68. Peter III "the Great" succeeds; Montpellier, Balearics, Roussillon to brother James as separate kingdom.

1277   King Peter pacifies the Valencian Moslem rebels.

1280   Catalan barons revolt; subdued.

1282   "Sicilian Vespers"; King Peter clears Sicily of Angevin-papal forces, is excommunicated.

1285   French crusade invades Aragon; eventually repulsed. Peter III dies (November 11). Alphonse III "the Liberal" (b. 1267) succeeds.
1287   King Alphonse definitively conquers Minorca island.
1291   Alphonse III dies (June 18). Succeeded by his brother, then king of Sicily, James II.

APPENDIX II

ରୈ

SAINTS ON THE VALENCIAN FRONTIER

St. Peter Pascual is a figure of mystery. The evidence for most of his story is a mare's-nest of surmise and critical problems; but no Valencian would forgive the omission of his story. The son of Mozarabs in Valencia, he left that city, shortly before the Christians attacked it, to study at the university of Paris. Some say he held a canonry at the cathedral of Valencia until 1250, resigning it at Rome to join (perhaps) the Mercedarians. He had a varied career as tutor to King James's son Sancho; then as assistant for nine years to the latter, who had become primate of Toledo; as writer of theologico-controversial tracts; and as preacher throughout the western Mediterranean from Tuscany to Andalusia. He was named bishop of Jaén in 1296, was snatched by the Moors into three years' captivity, and was beheaded at Granada. A careful reading of his works (assuming that they are genuine, and assuming also that he is not two different persons under the same name) yields no information on religious conditions in early Valencia.*

St. Bernard Calvó is quite another case. His life is well documented and his connection with Valencia clear. Of knightly family, a jurist and a civil functionary at the episcopal curia of Tarragona, he became a Cistercian monk at Holy Crosses (1214) and subsequently abbot. He was elected bishop of Vich in 1233, went on crusade with his household in 1238, materially aided at the sieges of Burriana and Valencia, and was present with his troops at the first Mass in the central mosque of the fallen capital. He traveled again to Valencia in 1242, owned substantial grants in the new kingdom, and helped publish the *Furs*. He died in 1243.†

The Franciscan martyrs John and Peter, who came down from Teruel to die at Valencia city shortly before the crusade, were mentioned in Chapter XI.‡ Another

---

* The available information is summed up by Ventura Pascual y Beltrán, though less critically than one might wish, in his "Recuerdos de un insigne mozárabe valenciano, su estatua, su casa, sus libros," *ACCV*, XII (1944), 82–97. See too R. Menéndez Pidal, "Sobre la bibliografía de San Pedro Pascual," *BRAH*, XLVI (1905), 259–266; Fidel Fita, "San Pedro Pascual, incidente bibliográfico," *ibid.*, pp. 266–269; *idem*, "Once bulas de Bonifacio VIII inéditas y biográficas de San Pedro Pascual," *BRAH*, XX (1892), 32–61. There is a very complete though piously naïve biography of him by Pedro Armengol Valenzuela, *Vida de S. Pedro Pascual, religioso de la Merced, obispo de Jaén, y mártir glorioso de Cristo* (Rome, 1901); and another life by Ramón Rodríguez de Gálvez, *San Pedro Pascual, obispo de Jaén y mártir, estudios críticos* (Jaén, 1903). Pedro Armengol Valenzuela has edited the works attributed to the saint, *Obras de S. Pedro Pascual, mártir, obispo de Jaén, y religioso de la Merced, en su lengua original, con la traducción latina y algunas anotaciones*, 4 vols. (Rome, 1905–1908).

† *Diplomatari de Sant Bernat Calvó*, with bibliography. *Acta sanctorum*, October, XII, 21–102. Honorio García, "Un santo en la conquista de Valencia," *BSCC*, XXV (1949), 69–75. J. M. Canivez, "Bernard Calvo," *DHGE*, VIII, cols. 766–767. José Ricart, *San Bernardo Calvo* (Barcelona, 1943), a brief biography.

‡ See Chapter XI, note 3.

set of pre-crusade martyrs, who also seem to have been venerated by the settlers of Valencia, were Bernard of Alcira, Mary, and Grace (Gracia). Bernard is supposed to have been a Moslem ambassador to King Alphonse II of Aragon, later becoming a Christian and a monk of Poblet. There is really very little reason for believing this story. What evidence can be gathered, suggesting some vague substance underlying the legend, has been enthusiastically but not too convincingly elaborated in the biography by Andrés Monzó Nogués.* In 1262, a legacy of 21 solidi was left for the support of "St. Bernard of Alcira," by the son of the converted ex-king of Moslem Valencia. Today St. Bernard is venerated along the Júcar River, especially in Benifairó de Valldigna, and as the patron of Alcira and Carlet.

The Dominican Michael of Fabra, who was prominent at the Majorcan crusade, and who came on the Valencian crusade, was a founder of the influential Dominican community in Valencia city.† He passed the preliminary phase of the canonization process, but is today relatively neglected. After his death, because of his reputation for holiness and because of luminous phenomena above his grave, his body was removed from the Dominican cemetery into the church, with due solemnities.

Jordán and other Augustinian authors tend on slender evidence to exalt the sanctity of the Augustinian Salelles or Serelles; it is difficult to take this sort of exercise seriously today. St. Raymond Nolasco, whose connections with Valencia were recounted in Chapter XIII, is a universally known figure.‡ A Catalan whose ideas were a powerful force in thirteenth-century Valencia was the celebrated St. Raymond of Penyafort. The same may be said perhaps for Blessed Raymond Lull; and it seems likely that Lull traveled in the new kingdom as a youngster.

King James, though surrounded by saintly in-laws (St. Ferdinand III of Castile, St. Louis IX of France), and proud of his relation to the recently deceased and canonized St. Elizabeth of Hungary, and of his granddaughter St. Elizabeth of Portugal,§ was unhappily far from being a saint himself—though he had the privilege of being lengthily rebuked by one for that circumstance (the pope, Blessed Gregory X). A naïve descendant of the king was later (1634) to propagandize for the canonization of the old sinner. The king's abandoned wife, "the holy queen" Teresa, enjoyed a reputation for sanctity in the new kingdom of Valencia, where she lived and died.||

---

* *La Vall d'Alcalá y sus egregias figuras Ahmet ben Almançor, Çaida, y Çoraida* (Carlet, Valencia, 1954), with full bibliography. Pedro Antonio Pérez Ruiz has a popular biography in his *Glorias de Valencia, biografías de hijos inmortales del reino* [series 2] (Valencia, 1955), pp. 25–37. There is a long dissertation on St. Bernard in Finestres, *Poblet*, II, 93–112.

† See Chapter XI, notes 43, 44.

‡ See Chapter XIII, notes 82–84 and text. For Serelles see Chapter XI, note 94.

§ James married the sister of St. Elizabeth (†1231) a few months after the canonization (1235); Elizabeth had been the wife of Ludwig, landgrave of Thuringia. St. Elizabeth of Portugal was the daughter of James's son, Prince Peter. She became queen of Portugal at the age of twelve; James I is said to have considered her a precocious saint even as a small child, and liked to keep her near him.

|| See Chapter XII, section 4, "Cistercian Nuns."

APPENDIX III

ᴨᴨ

CHURCHES OF THE VALENCIA DIOCESE, 1279–1280 DISTRIBUTION AND INCOME

A. DIOCESE OF VALENCIA , 1279*	Solidi	denarii
Pro redditibus ecclesie sancti Salvatoris	85	9
Item a quodam alio beneficium ibidem habente		8
Item pro ecclesia sancti Martini	133	−3
Item pro ecclesia de Torres torres	23	
Item pro ecclesia de Alfusar	37	6
Item pro ecclesia de sancta Catarina	154	6
Item pro ecclesia de Sullana	68	2
Item pro ecclesia de sancto Petro Maioricarum	112	1
Item pro ecclesia de sancto Thoma	32	3
Item pro ecclesia de sancto Laurentio	99	2
Item pro ecclesia de Muntcada	37	
Item pro ecclesia de Xilvella	88	7
Item pro ecclesia de sancto Johanne	85	4
Item pro ecclesia de Algemesi	65	7
Item pro dominabus monialibus de Algesira	306	7
Item pro ecclesia de Ruçafa	35	−1
Item pro ecclesia de Turris	38	9
Item pro ecclesia de Museros	28	1
Item pro ecclesia de sancto Stephano	152	3
Item pro ecclesia de sancto Georgio	60	9
Item pro ecclesia de Albal	72	5
Item pro ecclesia de Torrento	86	2
Item pro ecclesia de Madrona	75	6
Item pro ecclesia de Carpesta	100	11
Item pro ecclesia de Foyes	105	5
Item pro ecclesia de Sancto Bartholomeo	110	5
Item pro ecclesia de Paterna	16	2
Item pro ecclesia de Alto Ponte	82	4
Item pro ecclesia de Almonesir	18	9
Item pro ecclesia de Arcubus	37	4
Item a capellano sancti Lazari	39	7
Item pro ecclesia maiori de Muro veteri	600	
Item a quodam inibi beneficium habente	5	8
Item pro ecclesia sancte Tecla	39	
Item a rectore de Toro	60	8

* *Rationes decimarum*, I, 256–259, and 262–267, adapted with omission of those exempt, of expenses, and of like details. Odd spellings and errors, of scribe or transcriber, are retained. The figures represent less than 10 percent of each income (see above, Chapter V, pp. 79 ff., esp. note 51).

A. DIOCESE OF VALENCIA, 1279 (continued)	Solidi	denarii
Item a rectore sancti Johannis de Muroveteri	155	− 1
Item a rectore de Carleto	80	1
Item a capellano de sancta Trinitate	44	− 1
Item a quodam habente alibi beneficium		13
Item a rectore de Vilamerxant	94	
Item a rectore ecclesie de Pina, quia crucesignatus est	nichil.	
Item a rectore de Algesira	144	7
Item a rectore de Binalgesir	37	4
Item a rectore de Spyoca	54	8
Item a rectore de Alboraya	62	4
Item a rectore de Albalato	98	5
Item a rectore de Maçamagrello	98	− 3
Item a preposito Terrachonen., pro quibusdam reddiditibus Valentin.	15	6
Item ab abbate de Balneolis	2	6
Item a capellano Regalis	53	
Item a capellano de Aris	26	4
Item a rectore de Xuella	20	7
Item ab archiepiscopo Terrachone	51	6

Ecclesie ultra Xucarum

Item a rectore de Xaxona	26	7
Item a rectore de Corbera	240	6
Item a capellano altaris Jesu Christi	58	7
Item a rectore de Alfandech	38	− 2
Item a rectore de Releu	19	6
Item a rectore de Unxen	89	7
Item a rectore de Godaquaquer	25	9
Item a rectore de Carcel	43	9
Item a rectore de Castilione	74	2
Item a rectore de Rogat	38	6
Item a rectore den Centya	29	6
Item a capellano de Albayda, quia crucesignatus est	nichil.	
Item a capellano de Tarvils	57	9
Item a rectore de Ollaria	17	4
Item a rectore de Xella	25	6
Item a rectore sancti Petri Xative	5	6
Item a rectore de Palma	60	6
Item a rectore de Reboleto	48	3
Item a rectore de Canalibus	180	
Item a rectore de Gorga	29	5
Item a rectore de Luxen	29	5
Item a rectore de Godalest	21	5
Item a rectore de Denya	50	7
Item a rectore de Alcoy	67	2
Item a rectore de Gandia	223	2
Item a rectore de Bocayren	51	5
Item a rectore de Perpunxen	25	4
Item a rectore de Carricola	30	− 2
Item a rectore de Carbonera	19	7

A. DIOCESE OF VALENCIA, 1279 (continued)	Solidi	denarii
Item a rectore de Concantaina	143	5
Item a rectore de Planes	35	5
Item a rectore de Xalocum cum Parcaciis	18	−2
Item a rectore de Navarres	38	3
Item a rectore de Castel	18	5
Item a rectore de Enova	30	8
Item a rectore de vicario de Xativa habente beneficium de Parcaciis	5	
Item a capellano castri de Xativa	31	3

De sede Valentina

	Solidi	denarii
Item pro pasturis et quibusdam denariis sacriste Valentini, de V° et VI° annis	201	
Item de portione Sancii Bertrandi	40	
Item de portione sancti Spiritus	38	
Item de ebdomodaria Francisci	11	3
Item de capellania Amore	40	4
Item de capellania sancti Pauli	38	9
Item de capellania sancti Michaelis	37	6
Item a Raimundo Calandri, succentore	38	3
Item de duobus portionibus episcopi Oscensis	90	
Item a capellano sancti Petri Sedis	54	2
Item de capellania Octoviani	64	
Item ab Ar.° Busqueti, canonico	151	−2
Item a Benedicto, canonico	90	3
Item a Petro Lagestera, subdiachono sedis	19	8
Item de Bartholomeo, epdomodario	44	1
Item de prepositura Decembris	265	2
Item de prepositura Septembris	249	7
Item de prepositura Octubris	261	
Item de prepositura Novembris	282	6
Item de prepositura Januarii	291	6
Item ab arrhidiacono Valentino, pro archidiaconatu	252	7
Item pro canonia Petri Cambrer	70	8
Item pro canonia Guiraldi de Albalat	48	
Item pro portione sacriste Valentini	49	4
Item pro altare sancti Vincentii	55	3
Item pro capellania sancti Petri Mayoricarum	31	−1
Item pro censuali scolarium magistri Vincentii	18	6
Item de portione Berengarii Mironis	39	4
Item a Johanne, subdiacono sedis	19	8
Item a prepositura magistri Radulfi	159	3
Item a precentore Valentino	415	5
Item a prepositura sacriste	156	9
Item a precentore de oblitis, pro P. de Albalato	30	
Item pro portione Oliverii, canonici	66	
Item pro capellania den Saragossa	15	3
Item de capellania Palacii episcopi	22	4
Item de capellano Nicholay d'Ungaria	32	2
Item pro portione magistri Rudulfi	51	

A. DIOCESE OF VALENCIA, 1279 (continued)	Solidi	denarii
Item a Bertrando de Coscolola	48	4
Item pro portione Dominici Mathei	47	5
Item pro portione Vilarii et censu fossariorum	119	
Item pro redditibus magistri Petri de Briva	47	−1
Item a sacrista Valentino	400	
Item pro capellania Guillelmi de Arenes	36	6
Item pro capellania sancti Jacobi	50	−2
Item a prepositura Julii quam tenet Andreas	218	4
Item a portione Petri Petri et vestiario	55	9
Item pro censu cuiusdam orti capituli	10	
Item pro prepositura domini Benedicti	366	
Item a domino episcopo, pro decima suorum reddituum	5,500	
Item pro capellania Petri Sancii	36	6
Item pro portione archidiaconi Valentini, de medio anno	23	7
Item pro capellania Amaldani, quia crucesignatus est	nichil.	

Total

Summa	6,979	2
Summa totius collectionis	17,056	9

B. DIOCESE OF VALENCIA, 1280		
Primo, videlicet, a rectore ecclesie de Archubus	26	5
Item a rectore ecclesie de sancto Bartholomeo	46	−1
Item a rectore sancti Laurentii	132	6
Item a rectore sancti Salvatoris	93	9
Item a rectore de Ans	36	3
Item a rectore de sancto Martino	126	−2
Item a rectore de Albalato	102	6
Item a rectore de Carpesia	92	6
Item a rectore de Muntcada	36	8
Item a rectore sancti Petri martiris	140	7
Item a rectore sancti Iohannis de Buatella	117	−2
Item a rectore de Xilvella	83	3
Item a rectore de sancto Stephano	173	−2
Item a rectore de Albal	54	−3
Item a rectore Maçamagrel	69	3
Item a rectore de Alfufar	34	1
Item pro capellania Octaviani	60	
Item pro capellania Garcie de Olito	30	
Item pro capellania Sancii Bertrandi	38	9
Item a rectore ecclesie de Torres Torres	19	3
Item a rectore ecclesie de Turis	34	6
Item a rectore de sancta Caterina	141	4
Item a rectore de Gorga	25	−3
Item a rectore de Museros	21	2
Item a rectore de Almonezir	46	−1
Item a rectore de Algemezi	53	3
Item a dominabus monialibus de Algesira	248	6
Item a rectore de Madrona	51	2
Item a rectore de Torrent	101	2

B. DIOCESE OF VALENCIA, 1280 (continued)	Solidi	denarii
Item a rectore novo sancti Andree	10	−2
Item ab antiquo rectore sancti Andree crucesignato, defuncto, pro toto tempore quo fuerat crucesignatus	500	
Item a rectore sancti Jacobi Buatelle	19	
Item a rectore de Foyos	77	
Item pro beneficio Sancii Muyoz	41	6
Item a rectore sancti Johannis de Muro veteri	76	8
Item a rectore de Valmarxant	116	8
Item a rectore de sancto Thoma	59	3
Item a rectore de Ruzaffa	31	9
Item a rectore de sancta Tecla	41	−1
Item a rectore de Carleto	64	
Item a rectore de Algesira	508	
Item a rectore de Salana	77	3
Item a rectore de Spiocha	51	
Item a rectore sancto Georgio	36	3
Item a rectore de Alborraya	76	2
Item a rectore de Xulella	26	8
Item a rectore de Paterna	119	2
Item a rectore de sancto Lazaro	36	8
Item a rectore de Altoponte	64	2
Item a rectore de Binalgosir	37	
Item a rectore de Xiva	21	1
Item a rectore de sancta Trinitate	41	6
Item a rectore de Toro	87	2
Item capellanus Amaldani, crucesignatus est.		
Item de capellano noviter constituto	22	3
Item a rectore de Senentries de Parataciis	22	4
Item a rectore de Constantina	91	3
Item a rectore de Muro veteri	600	
Item de dominabus sancte Marie Magdalene	165	
Item pro stabilimento B. de Rosanis	35	6
Item a preposito Terrachonen	56	
Item ab abbate de Baucellis	2	
Item a quodam habente alibi beneficium	11	8

Capitulum et ecclesia sedis Valentine

Item a domino episcopo Valentino	2,750	
Item ab eodem, alia	2,750	
Item a precentore	334	6
Item ab eodem pro portione	45	5
Item a Raymundi Calandri	40	
Item a Benedicto pro portione et capellania	88	9
Item a capellano sancti Spiritus	38	
Item a capellano sancti Petri	52	9
Item a capellano Amore	41	2
Item a capellano de sancto Vincencio	51	6
Item a capellano de sancto Petro Maioricarum	32	2
Item a redditibus scolarium magistri Vincencii	16	8
Item a capellano sancti Pauli	38	10

B. DIOCESE OF VALENCIA, 1280 (continued)	Solidi	denarii
Item a capellano sancti Michaelis	38	2
Item a Br. de Muro	39	3
Item pro portione sacriste Valentine, et pro sacristia	450	7
Item a Garcia Petri subdiachono	23	1
Item a Rovira, dyachono	23	1
Item a rectore castri de Xulella	53	−4
Item ab archidiachono Valentino	248	1
Item pro portione Dominici Mathei	50	6
Item pro portione et redditibus magistri Petri de Briva	45	2
Item pro portione Andree, canonici	50	−3
Item pro portione Petri, camararii	70	3
Item pro portione B. Figara, subdiachono	22	8
Item pro portione Geraldi de Albalato	48	2
Item pro portionibus episcopi Oscensis	53	1
Item pro portione archidiachoni Valentini, quia non fuit continue	23	3
Item pro portione Olivarii canonici	67	5
Item pro portione Ferrarii de Avenis	43	7
Item a quodam habente beneficium alibi	9	8
Item pro capellania Guillelmi de Arenys	36	7
Item pro portione Petri, quondam canonici	19	−1
Item pro portione Petri de Lacustaria, dyachoni	22	5
Item pro portione B. de Coscolola et partaciis	47	9
Item pro portione den Saragossa	14	9
Item pro portione Francisci	8	9
Item a capellano Palacii episcopi	24	6
Item pro portione Bartholomei	42	6
Item pro portione magistri Radulphi	52	3
Item pro portione Ar. Busqueti, canonici	67	3
Item pro portione Ar. de Raxacho	16	9
Item pro portione Molleti	16	9
Item pro portione Villarii	16	6
Item a B. de Moraria	6	9
Item a Jacobo de na Mura	6	−2
Item pro capellania N. de Ungaria	31	5
Item pro prepositura Archidiaconi Valentini	260	9
Item pro prepositura Dominici Mathei	273	2
Item pro prepositura Geraldi de Albalato	244	5
Item pro prepositura Vilarii	267	3
Item pro censu fossariorum	62	2
Item pro prepositura Arnaldi de Rachaco	190	7
Item a prepositura Andree	293	4
Item pro prepositura Benedicti	278	2
Item pro prepositura Pontiliani	7	1
Item pro prepositura magistri Radulphi	184	4
Item pro prepositura sacriste	208	5

Ultra Xucarum

Item a rectore de Sera	20	7
Item a rectore de Godalest	51	−1

B. DIOCESE OF VALENCIA, 1280 (continued)	Solidi	denarii
Item a rectore de Palma et Racuna	50	3
Item pro capellania den Sentiu	23	−1
Item a rectore de Luxen	46	5
Item a rectore de Godacequer	25	−1
Item a rectore de Villanova de Rogat	47	4
Item a rectore de Alfandech	37	4
Item a rectore de Albayda, crucesignatus est.		
Item a rectore de Vinxen	82	−1
Item a rectore de Carricola	31	−1
Item a rectore de Nonarres	30	8
Item a rectore de Castelo	67	−2
Item a rectore de Corbera	188	3
Item a capellano Jesu Christi	59	−2
Item a rectore de Gandia	183	4
Item a rectore de Perpunxen	25	
Item a rectore de Rebolet	69	−3
Item pro capellania rectoris de Rebolet	36	7
Item a rectore ecclesie de Cartel	41	5
Item a rectore de Tarnils	84	−3
Item a rectore de Bocayren	45	2
Item a rectore de Xella	23	
Item a quodam habente alibi beneficium	5	1
Item a rectore de Cascala	29	−1
Item a rectore de Canalibus	180	
Item a rectore de Saxona	18	3
Item a vicario de Xativa		18
Item a capellano de Alfufar		12
Item a rectore de Releu	19	8
Item a Raymundo Mathei	25	
Item a Bertrando pro tribus preposituris	5	
Item a rectore de Calp	16	
Item pro ecclesie de Xativa	100	
Item a rectore de Perpunxen	28	
Item dixerunt se recepisse pro portionibus episcopi Oscen. et pro capellania s. Jacobi, et pro ecclesia de Xericha et pro capella de sancta Margarita de Xativa et pro castro de Xulella et pro capellania Garsie de Olito, et pro quibusdam aliis minuciis	409	2
sic in summa de quinto et sexto anno.		
Item de compositione Posolii, pro sexto anno	33	4
Item a domina Alda pro quibusdam redditibus ecclesiasticis quos ocupaverat, pro sex annis	1,000	
Item a Petro Lupi, rectore ecclesiarum Rivi de Milariis, pro sex annis	1,000	
Item a precentore de Morariis et de emendis de Foxos	27	6
Item ab episcopo Vici	34	4
Item a Berengario de Lansolis, pro quibusdam redditibus ecclesiasticis	200	
Item a sacrista de Morariis, laudimiis et emendis	54	5
Item a precentore de Villalonga		20

B. DIOCESE OF VALENCIA, 1280 (continued)	Solidi	denarii
Item a capitulo de Rivomilariis et pro castro de Gargio et de Alfandech	112	6
Item pro restitunionibus factis domino episcopo defuncto	210	
Item a quibusdam qui minus integre extimaverant redditus suos, ut eis videbatur	100	
Item a rectore de Alcoy	50	6
Item a rectore de Enova	20	
Item a rectore de Xerichan	125	
Item a dominabus de Algesira, pro quibusdam redditibus additis	12	7
Item a quodam habente alibi beneficium	10	
Item a priore sancte Trinitatis pro quodam legato de quo dubitabatur	7	3
Item a rectore de Picacen pro annis transactis	92	6
Item a quodam habente alibi officium	30	6
Summa collectionis decime non exemptorum Valentin. de sexto anno	17,858	
Summa maior quod deductis expensis restant de dicta decima Valentina non exemptorum	17,793	
Dixerunt etiam dicti collectores se recepisse de annis transactis post computum videlicet:		
Ab archidiachono Xative	62	7
A rectore de Albayda	35	
A rectore de Carricola	17	3
A rectore de sancti Andree	96	9
A comendatore sancti Georgii	10	
Item ab archidiachono Valentino, pro quarto anno	269	7
Item a Francisco		13
Item a capellano sancti Johannis de Muroveteri	131	9
Item a precentore	41	6
Item a capellano de Regali	20	
Item a Petro Petri	2	5
Item a dominabus de Algesira	250	
Item a Cardona	106	
Item ab archidiachono Valentino, pro prepositura tertii anni	40	5
Item	18	7
Item ab archidiachonatu Valentino	200	
Item a Guillelmo de Castro	7	
Summa de istis additionibus supra proximo scriptis de sexto anno et aliis precedentibus	4,688	7

Total

Et sic est summa de toto sexto anno cum prescriptis additionibus	22,481	7

C. SEGORBE*

D. TORTOSA HOLDINGS IN THE KINGDOM OF VALENCIA†

* No lists have survived for Segorbe-Albarracín, but some incomplete, generalized returns are given for 1278, 1279, and 1280, *ibid.*, pp. 271–272.

† These are mixed into the Tortosa lists, and are identified in Chapter V, pp. 86–87; cf. also *ibid.*, pp. 84–86 *passim*.

BIBLIOGRAPHY

BIBLIOGRAPHY

ಬಚಿ

This is largely a bibliography of works cited (though over fifty citations of minor interest are omitted). It includes all the direct sources of importance, primary and secondary, with a sampling of titles supplying background or incidental information. A number of cross references are included to facilitate the checking of short-title citations. One vexing question is the division of primary from secondary materials. A number of books consist of documents in substantial part, or are equipped with large and important documentary appendixes. Also, many articles appearing in technical reviews in Spain supply a small appendix of several documents, a practice rendered necessary by the deficiencies of the few general collections. To the heading "Secondary Sources" therefore, the sub-title, "And Secondary-with-Primary," has been added.

There has been a heartening renaissance of historical studies in Spain during the last two or three decades, and admirable work is being produced in quantity. At last, from 1953–1954, we have an adequate bibliographical tool, the *Índice histórico español*, issued three times a year by the Centro de estudios históricos internacionales at the University of Barcelona; bound and retitled as *Bibliografía histórica de España e Hispanoamérica*, it is commonly referred to as the *Índice*. The ecclesiastical history of the realms of Aragon is fortunate in being the subject of an able review, *Analecta sacra tarraconensia*; regular, meticulous bibliographies appear as supplements to this from 1928 on, the *Bibliografía hispánica de ciencias histórico-eclesiásticas*. More general coverage of ecclesiastical history in all countries is supplied by the elaborate bibliographies of the *Revue d'histoire ecclésiastique*. *Al-Andalus*, journal of the Escuelas de estudios árabes de Madrid y Granada, calls attention to works touching its own specialty, the history and literature of Moslem Spain. *Sefarad* does the same office for the history of Spanish Jews.

For the period before the appearance of the *Índice*, the bibliographies in the *Estudis universitaris catalans* are especially helpful. Frequently of use, too, are the extensive bibliographical surveys which appear in the *Estudios de edad media de la corona de Aragón*, published irregularly by the Consejo superior de investigaciones científicas since 1945 at Zaragoza. The standard work of Benito Sánchez Alonso should not be overlooked, *Fuentes de la historia española e hispano-americana, ensayo de bibliografía sistemática* (3rd ed. revised; 3 vols., Madrid, 1952). For the kingdom of Valencia the bibliographies of Vicente Ximeno and Francisco Almarche y Vázquez are important (see below under secondary sources).

The careful reader of Valencian provincial historical reviews will have his attention called to out-of-the-way items. *Saitabi* is the organ of the faculty of philosophy and letters at the University of Valencia; the *Anales del centro de cultura valenciana* and the excellent *Boletín de la sociedad castellonense de cultura* represent respectively the modern provinces of Valencia and Castellón. Further bibliographical tools are suggested in the apposite sections of Sánchez Alonso and of the *Índice*. The reader should note that Spanish authors often reprint their articles as books, so that one commonly finds such works cited under different forms; thus, a number of booklets often separately cited are given in the present bibliography as parts of the volume *Congrés I*.

Spanish names can be an embarrassment for the bibliographer. Behind a deceptively simple patronymic, there often lurks a formidable longer name. This may coexist in a Catalan and a Castilian form, with or without a linking y (Catalan i) or a hyphen. No logic governs the deployment of these elements, and a single name can sometimes metamorphose in several different combinations. Personality, whim, pride of family or of native province, democratic humility or chaste simplicity, a regard for space on the printed page, the nature of the occasion, or the basic need of distinguishing oneself from colleagues similarly named—all conspire to produce vagaries of form which confound the foreign bibliographer.

Many historians habitually dispense with their second or maternal surname, as do Soldevila and Llorente; others dress up their names only on more formal occasions, so that Roque Chabás (Roc Chavàs) can acquire "(y) Lloréns." Others remain determinedly formal during their literary appearances: "Miret" does not venture forth without his "Sans." Only a confirmed antiquarian would burden the laconic Flórez (of *España sagrada* fame) with his cumbrous addition "de Setién y Huidobro." Certain names are frankly eccentric. Sáenz de Aguirre is customarily known as Aguirre, while both Pérez Miedes and Gómez Miedes are merely Miedes; Matheu y Sanz displays one t or two, according to one's taste; Ramón de María and Lamberto de Zaragoza are complete names, deriving from the religious life; Joseph may emerge as José, Josep, Josef, or even Josephus. And when a splendidly Spanish name is unfurled like Doña Consuelo Gutiérrez del Arroyo de Vázquez de Parga (chronicler of the Santiago knights' privileges), the Anglo-Saxon bibliographer recoils before its complexities.

Any attempt to cope with this multiple problem consistently—to Castilianize all names, for example, or to follow Antonio Palau's *Manual del librero* (16 volumes to date, Barcelona, 1948-[1964])—eventually involves one in absurdities. The only general rule adopted, therefore, was to Castilianize except where, on balance, it seemed best to leave a name in Catalan, and usually to give the surname in full even when that form is less familiar. This was also done, though not always, in each first citation of the notes.

Treatment of any topic is influenced, and in many ways limited, by the nature of the surviving sources. The Valencia diocesan archives, for example, were destroyed partly by fire during an attack on the diocesan buildings in the late Civil War, and partly by subsequent vandalism. There are no contemporary parish lists, visitation records, and the like. The regional archives for the kingdom of Valencia itself have been twice devastated by fire—in 1423 and in 1586; of unpublished documents, not very much remains here for our purposes. Nor was history kind to the metropolitan archives at Tarragona, where the troops of Napoleon worked much damage; these too are disappointing for our story. On the other hand, the Valencia cathedral archives have a splendid run of parchments (almost a thousand for the sixty years of Valencian history in the thirteenth century), as well as synodal records and other codices. These have all been gone through, piece by piece.

At Rome, the Vatican archives have the invaluable tax lists of 1279-1280 for the clergy of the kingdom of Valencia, and an alternate version of the trial record used in Chapter XIV. Especially they have thirty or more bulky registers filled with papal documents of this period; most papal documents were not registered, making those which survive very valuable. At Madrid, the national archives are rich in documentation on the religious and military Orders. At Paris, both the national archives and the national library furnished useful manuscripts. Ecclesiastical archives at Tortosa, Huesca, and Toledo made contributions, as did the municipal archives at Valencia and the university manuscripts at Valencia and Barcelona. At Barcelona, above all, the great collection of royal documents at the crown archives proved to be a treasure-house. Besides many hundreds of individual parchments, and such special records as the papal or the Templar manuscripts, there are close to fifty large volumes of registers which provide a wealth of documentation bearing upon the subjects in this book. Of all these documents, the larger number seem to center upon property acquisition and crown privileges—which explains the circumstance of their preservation. But these glint with the gold of names, places, and deeds which would not otherwise have been known. And they make it possible to place the economic resources of a group, and its popularity, where further penetration is impossible.

None of these archives could have been properly exploited were it not for the dedicated labors of the cataloguers. Sometimes their products are feeble instruments, as with the incomplete and confusing Garampi *schedario* at the Vatican. Sometimes they are models of compilation, like the volumes of Martínez Ferrando and of Olmos y Canalda.* Collections of published source materials, monumental or modest, are not lacking. A real debt is owing to compilers such as Huici, Vincke, Bofarull y Mascaró, Villanueva, Aguirre, Flórez, Canivez, Teulet, and others. There are important collections of the laws, municipal privileges, and land distribution for Valencia; and general collections of documentation relating to synods, councils, Dominicans, Cistercians, guilds, church-state relations, royal affairs, and the like. There are a number of chronicles or histories by contemporaries, some of them of great value, and useful bits of information from Moslem writers.

In working with original materials, I have cited the published form as well, where one exists. The latter are widely scattered, and searching for them represents a reflexive and time-consuming activity; no guarantee is offered the reader that a given document has not appeared somewhere in print. However, most of the manuscripts cited from Valencia, Barcelona, Tortosa, Madrid, and Paris have never been published. Vatican documents affecting Spain are often left unpublished, or are only partially published, in the *Registres* of the Bibliothèque des écoles françaises d'Athènes et de Rome. In a number of cases, adverted to in the footnotes, serious misreadings have crept into the published form of documents.

There is no history of the church in Valencia. But in exploring the subject, one

* The most useful of the published aids are: J. E. Martínez Ferrando, *Catálogo de los documentos del antiguo reino de Valencia*, 2 vols. (Madrid, 1934), for the Archivo de la corona de Aragón; F. J. Miquel Rosell, *Regesta de letras pontificias del archivo de la corona de Aragón, sección cancillería real, pergaminos* (Madrid, 1948); Elías Olmos y Canalda, *Pergaminos de la catedral de Valencia* (Valencia, 1961); and his *Códices de la catedral de Valencia* (Madrid, 1943); César T. Laguía, *Catálogo de la sección de pergaminos del archivo de la catedral de Albarracín* (Teruel, 1955); Aurea L. Javierre Mur, *Privilegios reales de la orden de Montesa en la edad media, catálogo de la serie existente en el archivo histórico nacional* (Madrid, 1956); C. Gutiérrez del Arroyo de Vázquez de Parga, *Privilegios reales de la orden de Santiago en la edad media, catálogo de la serie existente en el archivo histórico nacional* (Madrid, 1946); Francisco Rafael de Uhagón, "Índice de los documentos de la orden militar de Calatrava," *Boletín de la real academia de la historia*, XXXV (1899), 5–167; Manuel Magallón, "Los templarios de la corona de Aragón, índice de su cartulario del siglo xiii," *ibid.*, XXXII (1898), 451–463; Marcelino Gutiérrez del Caño, *Catálogo de los manuscritos existentes en la biblioteca universitaria de Valencia*, 3 vols. (Valencia, 1913); Julián Paz, *Documentos relativos a España existentes en los archivos nacionales de París*, 3 vols. (Madrid, 1934); Jean Regné, "Catalogue des actes de Jaime I, Pedro III, et Alfonso III, rois d'Aragon, concernant les juifs (1213–1327)", *Revue des études juives*, LX (1910), 161–201, LXI (1911), 38–73, LXIII (1912), 245–276. There is a fine series of articles by Felipe Mateu y Llopis describing various archives, or parts of archives, in the city and realm of Valencia; representative of these are his studies in the *Revista de archivos, bibliotecas y museos*, LVI (1950), 5–35, LVIII (1952), 23–52, LIX (1953), 7–37, and LXII (1956), 699–737.

does not walk alone. Several men of impressive talent have gone on ahead—here mapping out a piece of land, there marking off a wilderness trace, and elsewhere laboriously effecting clearings. Foremost among the pioneers is the great, eighteenth-century antiquarian, the Dominican Josef Teixidor. His two-volume *Antigüedades de Valencia* is an old-curiosity-shop of documents now lost, archaeological rummagings, fierce tilts at local legend, extended critical essays, and excursions into secular and ecclesiastical byways. Canon Roque Chabás y Lloréns, nineteenth-century archivist at Valencia cathedral, was his worthy successor. Chabás copied documents and wrote articles with an indefatigable energy; he also managed to found and sustain, almost singlehandedly, *El archivo*, a short-lived technical journal devoted to Valencian researches. His *Episcopologio valentino* unfortunately never went beyond one volume; and it is rather sketchy for the thirteenth century. José Sanchís y Sivera continued the work of Chabás, both as archivist and as researcher. A number of Sanchís Sivera's disparate essays were gathered into two volumes under the generic title *La diócesis valentina*; eight more volumes were projected but never done. Even more valuable and original was his *Nomenclátor*, identifying place-names in diocesan documentation, and his monograph on the parish of St. Thomas.

There are a number of sixteenth-to-eighteenth century historians—such as Beuter, Diago, Escolano, Esclapés, Ribera, and Viciana—of poor quality; occasional items in these, on secular or ecclesiastical history, have their uses; but, as Sanchís Sivera says, "hardly anything in them can be accepted without careful examination." One or other Valencian topic has been elaborated by modern authors—the history of the Mercedarians by Gazulla, for example, and that of the Hospitallers and Templars by Miret y Sans. The debt owed to such authors has become evident from the citations.

Much material is scattered and incidental. The bibliography as a whole is still, as Sanchís Sivera remarked of it sadly in 1920, "deficientísima y casi sin valor." Extrinsic bibliography, on the other hand, is enormous. This book crosses many areas of interest—such as schools, ecclesiastical offices, economic developments, and so on, and each might be made to trail its bibliographical glory. The accumulated writings on certain religious Orders alone is formidable. One oddity, writings on the Valencia Mozarabic community in the thirteenth century, I have not bothered to include; in common with a number of other students of the area I do not believe the Mozarabic community had survived here.

Finally, the autobiography of King James I is so unusual a document for medieval times that doubts as to its authenticity naturally arise. Long controversy has settled the issue, however, and the reader may accept the document as substantially genuine. King James did not of course pen it in its entirety; he seems rather to have dictated much of it, somewhat after the modern custom of entrusting one's reflections and reminiscences to a "ghost" who then presents them in more polished form. As the king's best modern biographer, Tourtoulon, remarks in concluding his summary of arguments, "the author of the work is none other than the king himself."

Martín de Riquer discusses the manner in which James and his collaborators probably worked, the stages of their labor, the inclusion of contemporary poems, and the origin of the present texts. The recent comments of Ferran Soldevila, dean of Catalan historians, who is preparing a critical edition of the king's memoirs, run along the same lines. Manuel de Montoliu goes into the subject at analytical length in the best treatment to date. Part one of the chronicle seems to have been done at Játiva in 1244, part two at Barcelona in 1274. Though the king's words require careful weighing and criticism, they are universally employed by historians of Aragon as James's own. It sometimes seemed convenient to adopt Forster's clumsy translation; at other times I have made my own translation.*

The whole problem of Moslem Valencia and the relation of the conquered Moslems to the Christians has been left to a book I am now preparing. Bibliography touching this subject therefore has been generally omitted; nevertheless, the present book owes a certain debt, a kind of dimension, to authors like Halperin Donghi and Lapeyre who are absent from this bibliography.

Local town histories were diligently studied but failed to help much; a sampling of the more useful works is included here. Readers interested in a given locality may consult the comprehensive bibliography of Francisco Almela y Vives, *Bibliografía de historias locales relativas al reino de Valencia* (Valencia, 1952). Municipal archives of the old Valencia kingdom are similarly unrewarding in matters ecclesiastical. A document here or there has incidental relevance—like the two Templar privileges at Vinaroz or the late tithe document at Villafranca del Cid. A good idea of the kind of materials available may be had from J. M. Ibarra Folgada's "Los archivos municipales, eclesiásticos, y notariales de la provincia de Castellón" (*Saitabi*, VIII, 1950–1951, 123–45).

The Alcira documentation is introduced in detail by J. M. Parra Ballester's *Catálogo del archivo municipal de la ciudad de Alcira* (part 1, Alcira, 1961). The recent spate of works on early Alicante (which lies just beyond our horizon of interest in the present book), and Vicente Martínez Morella's four-volume guide to its archives, suggest that little material useful for this book is there. A final disappointment: my visit to the Castellón archives coincided with their lengthy closure for rebuilding; the register of José Sánchez Adell indicates a few parchments here of peripheral interest to us: *Catálogo de pergaminos del archivo municipal de Castellón* (Castellón de la Plana, 1950).

Parish records are especially barren for our period and purpose. The present state of parish antiquities and archives in the Valencia diocese is carefully surveyed by Salvador Pallarés Ciscar and his staff in the excellent *Guía de iglesia en la diócesis de Valencia* (Valencia, 1963). Ramón d'Alós, in his "L'arxiu capitular de Tortosa" (*Butlletí de la biblioteca de Catalunya*, V, 1920, 103–119), offers an overview of the surviving documentation in the northern diocese as it was organized before the losses of the civil war.

Some manuscript depositories are missing from the bibliography as having supplied nothing relevant—the Barcelona municipal archives and the central library, for example, or the seminary museum at Lérida. One kind of depository, though it yielded little to a patient search, has been included, with no contents indicated beyond a reference to this essay. These are the cathedral archives of King James's non-Valencian bishoprics, and the diocesan collections of his collaborators in southern France. Since these bishops sent aid and in many cases led contingents to the crusade, and were rewarded with properties on the new frontier, their archives cannot be omitted.

But at Barcelona neither the diocesan property documents nor the cathedral archives have anything on the bishop's Valencian holdings. (Cathedral archives in general held out some promise for the themes of this book, where diocesan archives had too often been made barren by wars and mischance.) Vich does not retain a manuscript memory of its prelate's role as fighter and landlord in Valencia. The massive cartularies of Lérida, Gerona, and Zaragoza likewise offer nothing—

---

* Manuel de Montoliu, *Les quatre grans cròniques* (Barcelona, 1959). Martín de Riquer, *Resumen de literatura catalana* (Barcelona, 1947), pp. 33–37; M. de Riquer and Antoni Comas, *Història de la literatura catalana*, 2 vols. (Barcelona, 1964), I, 394–429. See bibliography for Tourtoulon, Soldevila, and editions of chronicle (James).

though the d'Espés manuscript history at the latter cathedral has a section on the crusade. Albarracín still has a few pertinent parchments, and Huesca boasts a fine set of materials for the Valencia story. In southern France, dioceses like Elne, Agde, Maguelone, Arles, Aix, and Marseilles proved to be almost uniformly silent. Still, there are some echoes of the Valencia crusade itself, especially at Perpignan.

These bleak results contrast with the riches garnered in the other cities discussed above. Such archives are included then for their useful "negative" result; and the search did broaden the background for this book. If documentation has been lost, and sections of some cathedral archives so disorganized from war and movement as to be useless for a long time to come, we may repose more confidence in the rich materials available elsewhere. The central data, insofar as they still exist, have been assembled in this bibliography in as complete a way as is currently possible.

PRIMARY SOURCES

MANUSCRIPT

Albarracín
Archivo Catedral. See introduction to bibliography.

Barcelona
Archivo de la Corona de Aragón.
    Cancillería Real.
        Pergaminos de Jaime I. (A collection of many hundreds of individual documents on parchment.)
        Pergaminos de Pedro el Grande (I of Valencia, II of Catalonia, III of Aragon).

    Cancillería Real. Registros de Jaime I (28 regs. in 33 vols.).
        Reg. 5. Annis 1237–1252. Donationum regni Valentiae.
        Reg. 6. Annis 1234–1252. Super diversis.
        Reg. 7. Anno 1239. De domibus Valentiae.
        Reg. 8. Annis 1252–1265. Speciale.
        Reg. 9. Annis 1257–1259. (Untitled).
        Reg. 10. Annis 1257–1259.
        Reg. 11. Annis 1259–1261.
        Reg. 12. Annis 1262–1265.
        Reg. 13. Annis 1262–1265.
        Reg. 14. Annis 1262–1272.
        Reg. 15. Annis 1265–1268.
        Reg. 16. Annis 1268–1276.
        Reg. 17. Annis 1265–1275. Speciale promiscuum.
        Reg. 18. Annis 1270–1274.
        Reg. 19. Annis 1270–1274.
        Reg. 20. Annis 1274–1276.
        Reg. 21. Annis 1271–1273.
        Reg. 22. Annis 1273–1278. Promiscuum.
        Reg. 23. Annis 1274–1276. Diversorum.
        Reg. 24. Annis variis. Diversorum.
        Reg. 25. Annis variis. Diversorum.
        Reg. 26. Anno 1230. Particio regni Maioricarum.

Reg. 27. Anno 1258. Diversorum.
Reg. 28. Annis 1263–1274. Super pecuniis.
Reg. 29. Anno 1260. (Accounts.)
Reg. 30. Annis 1265–1266. (Household accounts.)
Reg. 31. Annis 1266–1267. (Household accounts.)
Reg. 32. Annis 1267–1268. (Household accounts.)
Reg. 33. Annis 1267–1276.
Reg. 34. Anno 1268. Super quitacione famuli domus sue [Petri] et super ordinacione eiusdem domus.
Reg. 35. Annis 1268–1276.
Reg. 36. Annis 1269–1270. Libre de mesió de casa del . . . Pere fill del rey En Jaume.
Reg. 37. Annis 1269–1276. Speciale.

Cancillería Real. Registros de Pedro el Grande. (18 regs. in 24 vols.)
Reg. 38. Annis 1276–1277. Speciale.
Reg. 39. Annis 1276–1277. Speciale.
Reg. 40. Annis 1277–1278. (Untitled.)
Reg. 41. Annis 1278–1280. Speciale.
Reg. 42. Annis 1278–1280. Speciale.
Reg. 43. Annis 1278–1284.
Reg. 44. Annis 1278–1284.
Reg. 45. Annis 1278–1284. Super feudis Cathaloniae.
Reg. 46. Annis 1278–1284. Gratiarum.
Reg. 47. Annis 1278–1285. Gratiarum.
Reg. 48. Anno 1280. Super negotiis justitiae.
Reg. 49. Annis 1280–1281.
Reg. 50. Annis 1280–1281.
Reg. 51. Annis 1281–1284. Exercituum et redemptionibus eorumdem.
Reg. 52. Annis 1281–1284. Donationibus de cenariis, equitatum, vestibus et aliis mobilibus.
Reg. 53. Annis 1282–1283. De rebus regni Siciliae.
Reg. 54. Annis 1282–1283. De rebus regni Siciliae.
Reg. 55. Annis 1282–1306. Promiscuum regum. Alphonsi II at Jacobi II exercituum.
Reg. 56. Annis 1284–1285. Speciale.
Reg. 57. Annis 1284–1285. Speciale.
Reg. 58. Annis 1284–1285. Pecuniae.
Reg. 59. Anno 1282. Speciale.
Reg. 60. Annis 1282–1283.
Reg. 61. Annis 1282–1283.
Reg. 62. Annis 1283–1285.

Cancillería. Cartularia.
Reg. 309. Liber privilegiorum templariorum.
Reg. 310. Privilegia templariorum.

Cancillería. Códices.
Casa Real, no. 9. Privilegios concedidos a la ciudad de Valencia, 1238–1301.
Liber patrimonii regni Valentiae, índice alfabético y libro de engañaciones del real patrimonio en Valencia [survey by royal commission of patrimony documents in the archives of the crown, of the *magister rationalis*, and of the *bailliae generalis*].

Bulas Pontificias.
  Legajo V, no. 10 through legajo XVI, no. 5 (thirteenth-century pontificates).
Clero Regular y Secular.
  Merced (other groups proved disappointing).
Gran Priorato de Cataluña (Hospitallers).
Real Patrimonio, Real Casa, extra series (Jaime I).

Archivo Catedral. See introduction to bibliography.

Biblioteca Universitaria.
  MS, Pablo Vidal, Anales de la orden de predicadores, 1172–1624.
  MS, Pere Marsili, Cronica ill. regis Aragoniae (1314).
  MS, Lluís Pons de Icart, Catálogo dels archebisbes de Tarragona (1572).
  MS, Jaume I, Crònica del rei En Jacme (1343).

Gerona
Archivo Catedral. See introduction to bibliography.

Huesca
Archivo Catedral.
  Pergaminos, annis 1230–1250.
  Códices.

Lérida
Archivo Catedral. See introduction to bibliography.

Madrid
Archivo Histórico Nacional.
  Clero secular y regular.
    Alcira: S. Agostín. Pergaminos, legajos.
    Castellón: Benifasá. Pergaminos, legajos.
    Puig: N. S. de los Ángeles. Pergaminos and legajos.
    Valencia: S. Vicente, Zaidia, S. Domingo, N. S. de la Merced. Pergaminos
      and legajos for each.
    Valldigna: Bernardos.

  Códices.
    Privilegia et scripta S. Vincentii Valencie; and the Repertori de tots los privi-
      legis y gracies reals, ê indults ô bulles apostolics, i demes escriptures y
      papers que se encontren en lo arxiu de este real priorat de San Vicent
      (comp. P. F. Lluch, 1763).
    Llibre de la fundació del monestir i convent de nostra señora de Benifiçá de la
      ordre de Cistel y tenença de aquell (comp. Miquel Joan Gisbert, 1586;
      various copies).
    Cartulario de Poblet (B-1220).
    Poblaciones i privilegios de los lugares de la orden de Montesa, 1234–1426.
    Cartulario del temple (sig. mod. 1,032; 1,241).
    Becerro II de la catedral de Toledo.

  Ordenes Militares.
    Calatrava (Privilegios reales; Documentos particulares).
    Montesa (Documentos reales).
    Santiago (Arch. Uclés).
  Sigilografía.

Biblioteca Nacional.
Manuscritos, nos. 11,592; 13,028: Dd47; 13,028: D47; 13,029: Dd98.

Real Academia de la Historia.
Ms: C-20, Miguel Eugenio Muñoz, Descripciones de los pueblos, yglesias, y parrochias pertenecientes al arzobispado de Valencia fuera de su capital, sacadas de sus archivos.
(Many late copies of our documents are also on file here.)

Marseilles
Archives Départementales, Bouches-du-Rhône.
Archives of Aix metropolitanate; of Arles metropolitanate; of Marseilles diocese. See introduction to bibliography.

Montpellier
Archives Départementales, Hérault.
Cartularies, dioceses of Agde, Maguelone.

Perpignan
Archives Départementales, Pyrénées-Orientales.
(References to Valencia crusade, properties. See introduction to bibliography.)

Padua
Biblioteca Antoniana.
Miscellaneo, Codice No. 79.

Paris
Archives Nationales.
J. 587. Fasc. Aragon I.
J. 589. Fasc. Aragon II.
J. 696. Bulles. Mélanges.
Bibliothèque Nationale.
MSS Latin, no. 5455: Chartae monasterii S. Mariae Crassensis.
MSS Latin, no. 9189: Cartulaire de l'abbaye de Lazat, XIII siècle.
Collection Doat (Collection de Languedoc): vols. 55, 67.

Rome
Archivio Segreto Vaticano.
Registra Vaticana. Regs. 9–43 (Registra Honorii III, Gregorii IX, Celestini IV, Innocentis IV, Alexandris IV, Urbani IV, Clementis IV, Gregorii X, Innocentis V, Hadriani V, Johannis XXI, Nicolai III, Martini IV, Honorii IV).
Archivum Arcis (Archivio di Castel San Angelo). Armaria Inferiora, arm. I–XVIII, 2222. Processus causae vertentis inter archiepiscopos toletanum et terraconensem super subiectione ecclesiae valentinae tempore Gregorii IX.
Codex Arm. XXXI, t. 2. Version of Marinus, as below.
Camera Apostolica. Collectoria, no 25. Rationes collectoriae decimarii [Aragoniae et Navarrae].
Archivio della Biblioteca Apostolica Vaticana.
Codices Vat. Lat. 3975 and 3976. Magister Marinus de Ebolo, Collectio diversarum litterarum et formarum ac processuum secundum stylum romanae curiae.
Capitular Archives of St. Peter's. Codex C-117, version of Marinus (see last entry).

Segorbe
Archivo Catedral. See introduction to bibliography.

Tarragona
Archivo Catedral. See introduction to bibliography.

Toledo
Archivo Catedral.
  Liber instrumentorum ecclesie toletane.
  Becerro 2 (roll).

Tortosa
Archivo Catedral.
  Pergaminos y legajos.
  Cajón Alcalatén.
  Cajón Arcediano mayor.
  Cajón Benifasá, Rafalgari, y Sasalfori.
  Cajón Concesiones apostólicas.
  Cajón Común de cabildo.
  Cajón Deán.
  Cajón Diezmos.
  Cajón Donaciones y privilegios reales.
  Cajón Mas de Barbaráns.
  Cajón Obispo.
  Cajón Obispo-Cabildo.
  Cajón Subtesorería.
  Cajón Templarios.
  Cajón Testamentos.
  Diversos:
    Índice alfabético (parishes).
    Llibre de les baroníes.
  Cartularios: Códices 2, 3, 4, 5, 6, 8, 9, 9A, 10, 12.

Valencia
Biblioteca Universitaria.
  Códice, Privilegia regum (pergaminos; all the royal documents in fifteenth-
    century municipal archives).
  Códice, 799: Varia, I.
  Códice, 145: Bulas, reales órdenes, y concordias sobre diezmos.
Archivo Catedral.
  Pergaminos. (All those pertaining to the thirteenth century, about 900 docu-
    ments.)
  Legajo 32. Fasc. 24. Papeles pertenecientes a la canonización del S. Pedro
    Pascual.
  Legajo 35. Fasc. 1. Reals privilegis y donacións, sobre els delmes del arquebisbat
    de Valencia.
  Fasciculos 2, 3, 4, 5, 6, 9, 13. (Individual parchments from James I and from the
    chapter, 1241–1276.)
  Legajo 40. Fasc. 23. (Copies of Vatican documents.)
  Legajo 60. Fasc. 1. (Pergamino of 1260 establishing episcopal chaplaincy.)
  Legajo 661. Fasc. 1. (Fols. 1–3 are documents relating to the organization of
    diocesan revenues.)

Códice 98. Constituciones synodales ecclesiae valentinae.
Códice 162. Liber instrumentorum.
Códice 146.
Códice 163. Sínodos valentinos y constituciones tarraconenses.
Códice 307. Liber de la bisbalía vulgariter nuncupatus quam plura continens instrumenta, episcopo et capitulo valentinae ecclesiae concernantia.
Archivo General del Reino.
Sección clero: parroquias y conventos.
Arch. de la bailía; y real justicia.
Archivo Municipal.
MS: Pedro Sucías Aparicio, Los monasterios del reino de Valencia, 3 vols. (1907).
Idem, Los conventos del reino de Valencia, 3 vols. (1906).
Idem, Templos a la Santísima Virgen en el reino de Valencia (n.d.).

Vich
Archivo Catedral. See introduction to bibliography.

Zaragoza
Archivo Catedral.
MS: Diego d'Espés, Historia ecclesiastica caesaraugustana, 3 vols. (16th century).
Diputación del Reino de Aragón.
Papeles procedentes de Zurita: Donationes factae in feudum per regem Iacobum.

PUBLISHED

'Abd al-Mun'im, al-Ḥimyarī. See Al-Ḥimyarī.
'Abd al-Wāḥid (Abū Muḥammad), al-Marrākušī. *Kitāb al-mu'ẏib fī taljīṣ ajbār al-Magrib. Lo admirable en el resumen de las noticias del Magrib.* Translator and editor, Ambrosio Huici Miranda. *Colección de crónicas árabes de la reconquista (q.v.),* no. 4. Tetuán: Instituto General Franco de estudios e investigación hispano-árabe, 1955.
Acta capitulorum generalium ordinis praedicatorum (1220–1303). Monumenta ordinis fratrum praedicatorum historica, no. 3. Editor, B. M. Reichert. Rome: Congregatio de propaganda fide, 1898.
Acta capitulorum provincialium ordinis fratrum praedicatorum. Première province de Provence, province romaine, province d'Espagne (1239–1302). Editor, P. Douais. Toulouse: Ed. Privat, 1894.
Acta sanctorum. Editors, the Bollandists (Jean Bolland, D. Papebroch, *et alii*). 67 vols. to date. Paris *et alibi*: Victor Palmé *et alii*, 1863– .
Actas del capítulo general de 1317 celebrada en Valencia, en que fué elegido maestro general el Ven. Raimundo Albert. Editor, Guillermo Vázquez Núñez. Rome: Colegio Pio Generalicio, 1930.
Aguirre, José Sáenz de. See *Collectio maxima conciliorum.*
Aḥmad ibn Muḥammad ibn Mūsā al-Rāzī. "Description de l'Espagne," translator E. Lévi-Provençal, *Al-Andalus,* XVIII (1953), 50–108.
Albanès. See *Gallia christiana.*
Alexander IV, Pope. *Les registres d'Alexandre IV, recueil des bulles de ce pape publiées ou analysées d'après les manuscrits originaux des archives du Vatican.* Editors, C. Bourel de la Roncière *et alii.* 3 vols. Paris: Bibliothèque des écoles françaises d'Athènes et de Rome, 1902–1953.

Al-Ḥimyarī, Muḥammad Ibn ʿAbd al-Munʿim. *La péninsule ibérique au moyen-âge d'après le Kitāb ar-Rawḍ al-miʿṭār fī ḫabar al-akṭār d'Ibn ʿAbd al-Munʿim al-Ḥimyarī. Texte arabe des notices relatives à l'Espagne, au Portugal et au sud-ouest de la France, publié avec une introduction, un répertoire analytique, une traduction annotée, un glossaire et une carte.* Editor and translator, E. Lévi-Provençal. Publications de la fondation de Goeje, no. 12. Leiden: E. J. Brill, 1938.

"*Al-Ḥulal al-Mawšiyya.*" *Crónica árabe de las dinastías almorávide, almohade y benimerín.* Translator, Ambrosio Huici Miranda. *Colección de crónicas árabes de la reconquista (q.v.)*, no. 1. Tetuán: Instituto General Franco de estudios e investigación hispano-árabe, 1952.

Al-Marrākušī. See Ibn ʿIḏārī, al-Marrākušī; see also ʿAbd al-Wāḥid.

Alphonse X the Learned (Wise), King. *Primera crónica general. Estoria de España que mandó componer Alfonso el Sabio y se continuaba bajo Sancho IV en 1289.* Editor, Ramón Menéndez Pidal. Nueva biblioteca de autores españoles, no. 5. Madrid: Bailly-Baillière e Hijos, 1906.

Al-Šaqundī (Abū-l-Walīd Ismāʿīl Ibn Muḥammad). *Elogio del Islam español (Risāla fī faḍl al-Andalus).* Translator, Emilio García Gómez. Escuelas de estudios árabes de Madrid y Granada, serie B, no. 2. Madrid: E. Maestre, 1934.

Anales toledanos I. In *España sagrada (q.v.)*, XXIII, 358–362, 381–400.

Anales toledanos II. In *España sagrada (q.v.)*, XXIII, 363–364, 401–409.

Annales compostellani. In *España sagrada (q.v.)*, XXIII, 317–324.

(Anónimo). *El anónimo de Madrid y Copenhague.* Editor and translator, A. Huici Miranda. Anales del instituto, no. 2. Valencia: Instituto general y técnico de Valencia, 1917.

Armengol Valenzuela, Pedro. See Pascual, S. Pedro; see also secondary sources.

Aureum opus regalium priuilegiorum ciuitatis et regni Valentie cum historia cristianissimi regis Jacobi ipsius primi conquistatoris. Editor, Luis de Alanya. Valencia: Diego de Gumiel, 1515.

Auvray. See Gregory IX.

Barcinonense. See *Chronicon barcinonense.*

Berger. See Innocent IV.

Bernardus Guidonis. *E floribus chronicorum.* In *Recueil des historiens des Gaules et de la France (q.v.)*, XXI, 690–734.

Bofarull y Mascaró, Próspero de. See *Repartimiento de Mallorca; Repartimiento de Valencia; Censo de Catalunya;* and *De domibus Valentiae.*

Bofarull y Sans. See *Judíos.*

Bullarium coelestis ac regalis ordinis B. Mariae Virginis de Mercede redemptionis captivorum. . . . Editor, José Llinás y Aznar, Barcelona: Rafael Figuero, 1696.

Bullarium equestris ordinis S. Iacobi de Spatha. . . . Editors, Antonio Francisco Aguado de Córdova and José López Agurleta. Madrid: J. de Ariztia, 1719.

Bullarium franciscanum romanorum pontificum. . . . Editors, J. H. Sbaraleus *et alii.* 7 vols. Rome: Congregatio de propaganda fide, 1759–1904.

Bullarium ordinis ff. praedicatorum. . . . Editors, Thomas Ripoll and Antonine Brémond. 8 vols. Rome: Hieronymus Mainard, 1729–1740.

Bullarium ordinis militiae de Calatrava. Editor, I. J. de Ortega y Cotes. Madrid: M. Antonio Marín, 1761.

Calvó, Bernat. *Diplomatari de Sant Bernat Calvó, abat de Santes Creus, bisbe de Vich.* Editor, Eduardo Junyent. Reus: Asociación de estudios reusenses, 1956.

Cartoral dels templers de les comandes de Gardeny y Barbens. Editor, J. Miret y Sans. Barcelona: Tipografía L'Avenç, 1899.

Cartulaire général de l'ordre des hospitaliers de S. Jean de Jerusalem (1100–1310). Editor, J. Delaville Le Roulx. 4 vols. Paris: E. Leroux, 1894–1901.

Cartulaire général de l'ordre du temple. Editor, Marquis d'Albon. Paris: H. Champion, 1913.

Cartulari de Poblet, edició del manuscrit de Tarragona. Editor, Joan Pons i Marqués. Barcelona: Institut d'estudis catalans, 1938.

"Cartulario de Monroyo (Aragón)," editor Santiago Vidiella, *Congrés I,* 172–189.

Cartulario de "Sant Cugat" del Vallés. Editor, José Rius Serra. Textos y estudios de la corona de Aragón, no. 5. 3 vols. Barcelona: Consejo superior de investigaciones científicas, 1946–1947.

Catalonia monastica, recull de documents i estudis referents a monestirs catalans. Editors, anon. 2 vols. Montserrat: Abadía de Montserrat, 1927–1929.

Censo de Catalunya ordenada en tiempo del rey Don Pedro el Ceremonioso. Editor, Próspero de Bofarull y Mascaró. In *Colección de documentos inéditos del archivo general de la corona de Aragón (q.v.),* vol. XII. Barcelona: Imprenta del archivo, 1856.

Chronicon. See also *Crónica.*

Chronicon barcinonense. In *Marca hispanica (q.v.),* cols. 754–758; also in *Collectio maxima conciliorum (q.v.),* V, 231–232 (excerpted).

Chronicon ecclesiae Sancti Pauli Narbonensis. In Vic and Vaissète, *Histoire générale de Languedoc (q.v.),* V, cols. 37–49.

Chronicon mundi. See Lucas of Tuy.

Chronicon ordinis praedicatorum ab anno MCCIII ad annum MCCLIV. In Peñafort, *Summa (q.v.),* pp. xlvi–xlvii.

Chronicon Sancti Saturnini Tolosae. In Vic and Vaissète, *Histoire générale de Languedoc (q.v.),* V, cols. 49–54.

Cláusulas testamentarias relativas a la iglesia de San Nicolás, de Alicante, siglo xiv. Editor, Vicente Martínez Morellá. Alicante: Artes gráficas, 1954.

Clement IV, Pope. *Les registres de Clement IV (1265–1268), recueil des bulles de ce pape.* Editor, E. Jordan. 1 vol. Paris: Bibliothèque des écoles françaises d'Athènes et de Rome, 1893–1945.

Clement V, Pope. *Regestum Clementis Papae V.* Editors, Benedictine monks. 12 vols. Rome: Typis vaticanis, 1885–1957.

Codex regularum monasticarum et canonicarum. Editor, Lucas Holstenius [Holstein]. 6 vols. in 3. Graz: Akademische Druck- und Verlagsanstalt, [1759] 1957–1958.

Colección de cánones y de todos los concilios de la iglesia de España y de América. Editor, Juan Tejada y Ramiro. 7 vols. Madrid: Imprenta de Pedro Montero, 1859–1863.

"Colección de cartas pueblas," series issued irregularly in *Boletín de la sociedad castellonense de cultura.* I (1920), 122–124, 187–188; II (1921), 23–24, 183–185, 297–300; III (1922), 390–393; IV (1923), 189–195; V (1924), 283–285; IX (1928), 166–168; X (1929), 85–87; XI (1930), 36–38, 88–89, 354–357; XII (1931), 132–138; XIII (1932), 168–170, 190–192, 395–404; XIV (1933), 169–173, 200–202, 339–341, 433–436; XV (1934), 68–69, 287; XVI (1935), 289–292, 385–389; XVIII (1943), 30–32, 159–160, 267–270; XX (1944), 103–104; XXI (1945), 232; XXII (1946), 13–17; XXIII (1947), 88–89, 279–282, 389–390; XXIV (1948), 65–66, 226–230; XXVI (1950), 15–16, 88–89; XXXVII (1961), 127–129, 268–269.

Colección de crónicas árabes de la reconquista. Editor and translator, Ambrosio Huici Miranda. 4 vols. to date. Tetuán: Instituto General Franco de estudios e investigación hispano-árabe, 1952–   .

Colección diplomática. Citation used here only for the collection by Huici, immediately below.

Colección diplomática de Jaime I, el Conquistador. Editor, Ambrosio Huici Miranda. 3 vols. Valencia: Hijo de F. Vives Mora, 1916–1920; Renovación tipográfica, 1922.

Colección diplomática de los documentos a que se refiere la disertación del feudalismo particular e irredimible de los pueblos del reino de Valencia, de donde salieron expulsos los moriscos en el año 1609. Editors, Miguel Salvá and Pedro Sáinz de Baranda. In *Colección de documentos inéditos para la historia* (q.v.), vol. XVIII.

Colección diplomática de Pedro I de Aragón y Navarra. Editor, Antonio Ubieto Arteta. Escuela de estudios medievales, textos, no. 19. Zaragoza: Consejo superior de investigaciones científicas, 1951.

Colección de documentos inéditos del archivo general de la corona de Aragón. Editors, Próspero de Bofarull y Mascaró *et alii.* 41 vols. Barcelona: Imprenta del archivo, 1847–1910.

Colección de documentos inéditos para la historia de España. Editors, Martín Fernández Navarrete, Miguel Salvá, Pedro Sáinz de Baranda *et alii.* 112 vols. Madrid: Viuda de Calera *et alibi,* 1842–1896.

Coleccíon de fueros municipales y cartas pueblas de los reinos de Castilla, León, corona de Aragón y Navarra coordinada y anotada. Editor, Tomás Muñoz y Romero. (Vol. I, *unicum*). Madrid: J. M. Alonso, 1847.

"Collecció diplomàtica de l'església de Tarragona, en el pontificat d'En Benet de Rocabertí (1251–1268)," editor Sanç Capdevila, *Boletín arqueológico* [Tarragona], LII (1952), 182–185.

Collectio maxima conciliorum omnis Hispaniae et novi orbis, epistolarumque decretalium celebriorum, necnon plurium monumentorum veterum ad illam spectantium, cum notis et dissertationibus, quibus sacri canones, historia ac disciplina ecclesiastica, et chronologia, accurate illustrantur. Editors, José Sáenz de Aguirre and Giuseppe Catalani. 6 vols. Rome: A. Fulganius, 1753–1755.

"Concilios tarraconenses en 1248, 1249 y 1250," editor Fidel Fita y Colomé, *Boletín de la real academia de la historia,* XL (1902), 444–460.

Congrés. See secondary sources.

Constitutiones sive ordinationes insignis metropolitanae ecclesiae valentinae ab eius primaeva fundatione et origine. . . . In quibus breviter ea omnia continentur quaecunque ad cultum divinum, optimumque statum, ac circunspectam administrationem: necnon ad officium quorumcunque ministrorum eiusdem spectant. Quae summa fidelitate ad veterum exemplarium collationem comprobate, ac veritate amusi correctae. Ad haec e dispersis hinc inde collectae, inque decentissimum ordinem redactae: adiecto copiosissimo indice: de mandato reverendorum dominorum canonicorum praefatae ecclesiae prodeunt in lucem. Editor, Miguel Pérez de Miedes. Valencia: Ioannes Mey Flandro, 1546.

"Constitutiones synodales valentinae diocesis." See *Collectio maxima conciliorum.*

Constituciones synodales ecclesiae valentinae. See primary sources: Manuscript, Valencia cathedral codices.

Corpus iuris canonici. Editors, Emil Friedberg and E. L. Richter. Second edition. 2 vols. Leipzig: B. Tauchnitz, 1879–1881.

Cortes de los antiguos reinos de Aragón y de Valencia y principado de Cataluña. 26 vols. in 27. Madrid: Real academia de la historia, 1896–1922.

Crónica. See also *Chronicon;* Desclot; James; Muntaner.

Crónica del moro Rasis. See Aḥmad.

Crónica de San Juan de la Peña [Latin text only]. Editor, Antonio Ubieto Arteta.

Textos medievales, no. 4. Valencia: Gráficas Bautista, 1961. (See also *Historia de la corona; Crónica general*.)

Crónica del santo rey Ferdinando III. Seville, 1516; Medina del Campo, 1657. Same as Rodrigo Jiménez de Rada, *De rebus Hispaniae* (*q.v.*).

Crònica general de Pere III el Cerimoniòs, dita comunament crònica de Sant Joan de la Penya [old Catalan text]. Editor, Amadeu J. Soberanas Lleó. Barcelona: Alpha, 1961. See also *Historia; Crónica de San Juan*.

De domibus Valentiae. Editor, Próspero de Bofarull y Mascaró. In *Repartimiento de Valencia* (*q.v.*), pp. 515–656.

De rebus Hispaniae. See Rodrigo.

Desclot, Bernat. *Crònica*. Editor, Miguel Coll y Alentorn. 4 vols. Barcelona: Editorial Barcino, 1949–1950.

——— *Chronicle of the Reign of King Pedro III of Aragon*. Translator, F. L. Critchlow. 2 vols. Princeton, N.J.: Princeton University, 1928–1934 (vol. II preceding vol. I).

"División de la conquista de la España mora entre Aragón y Castilla," editor Roque Chabás y Lloréns, *Congrés I* (*q.v.*), pp. 139–141.

La documentación pontificia hasta Inocencio III, 965–1216. Editor, Demetrio Mansilla Reoyo. Monumenta Hispaniae vaticana, no. 1. Rome: Instituto español de estudios eclesiásticos, 1955.

Documenta selecta mutuas civitatis arago-cathalaunicae et ecclesiae relationes illustrantia. Editor, Johannes Vincke. Biblioteca histórica de la biblioteca Balmes, series II, no. 15. Barcelona: Biblioteca Balmes, 1936.

"Documento curioso de Onteniente," editor Roque Chabás y Lloréns, *El archivo*, VI (1892), 374–376.

"Un documento inédito de D. Jaime el Conquistador, la concesión á la sede barcelonesa de las iglesias de Mallorca, Menorca, Ibiza, Denia y Orihuela," editor José de Peray y March, *Congrés I* (*q.v.*), pp. 444–456.

Documentos inéditos. See *Colección de*.

"Documentos para el estudio de la reconquista y repoblación del valle del Ebro," editor José M. Lacarra, *Estudios de edad media de la corona de Aragón*, III (1947–1948), 499–727.

[Documents], in irregular series, editor Roque Chabás y Lloréns, *El archivo*, I (1886), 120, 127–128, 135–136, 144, 183–184, 199–200, 207–208, 215–216, 223–224, 231–233, 239–240, 247–248, 255–256, 264, 319–320; II (1887–1888), 20–21, 204–205, 321–328, 336–337, 339–340, 350–351, 354, 365, 390–392, 400–408; IV (1890), 214–238, 264–282, 289–318, 373–388; V (1891), 408–409.

Donationum regni Valentiae. See *Repartimiento de Valencia*.

Ecclesiae S. Pauli. See *Chronicon ecclesiae*.

Elogio del Islam español. See Al-Šaqundī.

Epistolae saeculi xiii e registris pontificum romanorum. Editors, Charles Rodenberg and G. Pertz. In *Monumenta Germaniae historica* (*q.v.*), section III, epistolae, no. 2.

Epitome, sive compendium constitutionum sanctae metropolitanae ecclesiae valentinae. Editor, Bernadino Gómez Miedes. Valencia: Pedro Patricio Mey, 1582.

España sagrada, teatro geográfico-histórico de la iglesia de España. Origen, divisiones y límites de todas sus provincias. Antigüedad, traslaciones y estado antiguo y presente de sus sillas, en todos los dominios de España y Portugal. Con varias disertaciones críticas, para ilustrar la historia eclesiástica de España. Editor, Henrique Flórez et alii. 58 vols. Madrid: A. Marín et alibi, 1747–[1879] 1918.

Febrèr, Jaume. *Trobes*. See secondary sources.

Fori regni Valentiae. Monzón: Impressi imperiali, 1548.

Die Formularsammlung des Marinus von Eboli. Editor, Fritz Schillman. Bibliotek des preussischen historischen Instituts in Rom, bd. XVI. Rome: W. Regenberg, 1929.

"Fragmentos inéditos de la 'Ordinatio ecclesiae valentinae,'" editor F. Martorell, *Cuadernos de trabajos,* Escuela española de arqueología e historia en Roma, I (1912), 81–127.

Furs. Short title for edition *Fori* (*q.v.*); cf. *Furs* below.

Furs e ordinacions fetes per los gloriosos reys de Aragò als regnícols del regne de València. Valencia: Lambert Palmart, 1482.

Gallia christiana novissima, histoire des archevêchés, évêchés et abbayes de France d'après les documents authentiques. Editors, J. H. Albanès and U. Chevalier. 7 vols. Montbéliard: P. Hoffman, and Valence: Imprimerie valentinoise, 1899–1920.

Gesta comitum barcinonensium. Textos llatí i català. Editors, L. Barrau Dihigo and J. Massó i Torrents. Cròniques catalanes, no. 2. Barcelona: Institut d'estudis catalans, 1925. Also in *Marca hispanica* (*q.v.*), cols. 538–595.

Gonzáles, J. See *Repartimiento de Sevilla.*

Gregory IX, Pope. *Les registres de Gregoire IX, recueil des bulles de ce pape, publiées ou analysées d'après les manuscrits originaux du vatican.* Editor, Lucien Auvray. 3 vols. Paris: Bibliothèque des écoles françaises d'Athènes et de Rome, 1896–1955.

Gregory X, Pope. *Les registres de Gregoire X (1272–1276), recueil des bulles de ce pape publiées ou analysées d'après les manuscrits originaux du vatican.* Editor, Jean Guiraud. (1 vol.). Paris: Bibliothèque des écoles françaises d'Athènes et de Rome, 1892–1906.

Gremios y cofradías de la antigua corona de Aragón. Editor, Manuel de Bofarull y de Sartorio. 2 vols. In *Colección de documentos inéditos del archivo general de la corona de Aragón* (*q.v.*), vols. XL–XLI.

Guillaume de Nangis. *Chronicon.* In *Recueil des historiens des Gaules et de la France* (*q.v.*), XX, 342–382.

—— *Gesta sanctae memoriae Ludovoci regis Franciae.* In *Recueil des historiens des Gaules et de la France* (*q.v.*), XX, 309–465.

Guiraud. See Gregory X.

Hispaniae illustratae seu rerum urbiumq[ue] Hispaniae, Lusitaniae, Aethiopiae, et Indiae, scriptores varii, partim editi nunc primi, partim aucti atque emendati. Editor, Andreas Schott. 4 vols. Frankfort: Apud Claudium Marnium et haeredes Johannis Aubrii, 1603–1608.

Historia de la corona de Aragón (la más antigua de que se tiene noticia) conocida generalmente con el nombre de crónica de San Juan de la Peña. Editor, Tomás Ximénez de Embún. Biblioteca de escritores aragoneses, sección histórico-doctrinal, no. 1. Zaragoza: Diputación provincial de Zaragoza, 1876. (See also *Crónica de San Juan; Crónica general.*)

Honorius III, Pope. *La documentación pontificia de Honorio III (1216–1227).* Editor, Demetrio Mansilla Reoyo. Monumenta Hispaniae vaticana, no. 2. Rome: Instituto español de historia eclesiástica, 1965.

—— *Regesta Honorii papae III.* Editor, P. Pressutti. 2 vols. Rome: Bibliothèque des écoles françaises d'Athènes et de Rome, 1888–1895.

Honorius IV, Pope. *Les registres d'Honorius IV, publiées d'après le manuscrit des archives du Vatican.* Editor, Maurice Prou. (1 vol.). Paris: Bibliothèque des écoles françaises d'Athènes et de Rome, 1886–1888.

Hoveden, Roger of. See Roger.

Huici. See *Anónimo; Colección diplomática; Colección de crónicas árabes*, and individual volumes thereof ('Abd al-Wāḥid; Al-Ḥulal; Ibn ʿIdārī).

Ibn 'Abd al-Munʿim al-Ḥimyarī. See Al-Ḥimyarī.

(Ibn al-Abbār). "Un traité inédit d'Ibn al-Abbār à tendance chiite," editor A. Ghedira, *Al-Andalus*, XXII (1957), 31–54.

Ibn Adari al-Marracochi. See Ibn 'Idārī.

Ibn 'Idārī, al-Marrākušī. *Al-Bayān al-Mugrib fī-ijtiṣār ajbār muluk al-Andalus wa al-Magrib. Los almohades*. Translator, Ambrosio Huici Miranda. In *Colección de crónicas árabes de la reconquista (q.v.)*, nos. 2, 3. 2 vols. Tetuán: Instituto General Franco de estudios e investigación hispano-árabe, 1953–1954.

Innocent IV, Pope. *Les registres d'Innocent IV publiées ou analysées d'après les manuscrits originaux du Vatican*. Editor, Élie Berger. 4 vols. Paris: Bibliothèque des écoles françaises d'Athènes et de Rome, 1884–1921.

"Inventaris de les cases del temple de la corona d'Aragó en 1289," editor J. Miret y Sans, *Boletín de la real academia de buenas letras de Barcelona*, VI (1911), 61–75.

"Inventaris inèdits de l'ordre del temple a Catalunya," editors Jordi Rubió, Ramón d'Alós, and F. Martorell, Institut d'estudis catalans, *Anuari*, I (1907), 385–407.

James I, King (Sp. Jaime; Cat. Jaume, Jacme). *Chronica ó comentaris del gloriosissim é invictissim rey En Jacme primer, rey Daragó, de Mallorques é de Valencia, compte de Barcelona é de Montpesler*. Editor, Mariano Aguiló y Fúster. Biblioteca catalana. Barcelona: Alvar Verdaguer, [1873] 1905.

────── *Crònica*. Editor, Joseph M. de Casacuberta. Collecció popular barcino, nos. 15, 21, 185, 186, 196, 197, 199, 200, 9 vols. in 2. Barcelona: Editorial Barcino, 1926–1962.

────── *The Chronicle of James I, King of Aragon, Surnamed the Conqueror (Written by Himself)*. Translator, John Forster; introduction, notes, appendix and glossary by Pascual de Gayangos. 2 vols. London: Chapman and Hall, 1883.

────── *Libre de saviesa del rey en Jacme I d'Aragó*. Editor, Gabriel Llabrés y Quintana. Santander: Imp. de Propaganda Católica, 1908. Also ed. J. M. Castro y Calvó; Barcelona: Consejo superior de investigaciones científicas, 1946.

────── *Llibre dels feyts*. See James I, *Crónica*.

────── *Versión literal del fuero I, lib. IV, rub. 24 de los del reyno de Valencia sobre diezmos, primicias, y derechos parroquiales, que es la sentencia arbitral del señor rey Don Jayme I de Aragón el Conquistador, contenida en el privilegio 77; la qual se aprobó en las cortes por los tres estamentos eclesiástico, militar, y real, y en consecuencia se incluyó en el cuerpo de los fueros o leyes municipales de dicho reyno*. Valencia: Benito Monfort, 1797.

Jiménez de Rada, Rodrigo. See Rodrigo.

John XXI, Pope. *Le registre de Jean XXI (1276–1277), recueil des bulles de ce pape publiées ou analysées d'après les manuscrits originaux du Vatican*. Editor, E. Cadier. Paris: Bibliothèque des écoles françaises d'Athènes et de Rome, 1906.

John XXII, Pope. *Lettres communes de Jean XXII, 1316–1334*. Editor, G. Mollat. 16 vols. Paris: Bibliothèque des écoles françaises d'Athènes et de Rome, 1921–1946.

Die Juden im christlichen Spanien, Urkunden und Regesten. Editor, F. Baer. Akademie für die Wissenschaft des Judentums, historische Sektion, bd. 4. 2 vols. (Bd. I: *Aragonien und Navarra*). Berlin: Akademie, 1929–1936.

Los judíos en el territorio de Barcelona (siglos x al xiii). Reinado de Jaime I, 1213–76. Editor, Francisco de Bofarull y Sans. Barcelona: F. J. Altés, 1910. Also in *Congrés* I (*q.v.*), II, 819–913.

Kitāb al-muʿyib fi taljīṣ. See ʿAbd al-Wāḥid.

Kitāb ar-Rawḍ al-miʿṭār. See Al Ḥimyarī.

Layettes du trésor des chartes, séries inventaires et documents. Editor, [J. B.] Alexandre Teulet. 5 vols. Paris: H. Plon *et alibi*, 1863–1909.

Letterae encyclicae magistrorum ordinis praedicatorum ab anno 1233 usque ad annum 1376. Editor, B. M. Reichert. Rome: Sacra congregatio de propaganda fide, 1900.

"Lettere 'secretae' d'Innocenzo IV e altri documenti in una raccolta inedita del secolo xiii (regesto)," compiler Giuseppe Abate, *Miscellanea franciscana*, LV (1955), 317–373.

Lévi-Provençal, E., ed. *La péninsule ibérique.* See Al-Ḥimyarī. See also Aḥmad.

Le Liber censuum de l'église romaine. Editors, Louis Duchesne and Paul Fabre. 3 vols. Paris: Bibliothèque des écoles françaises d'Athènes et de Rome, 1901–1952.

Liber feudorum maior. Cartulario real que se conserva en el archivo de la corona de Aragón. Editor, Francisco Miquel Rosell. Textos y estudios de la corona de Aragón, no. 2. 2 vols. Barcelona: Consejo superior de investigaciones científicas, 1945.

A Life of Ramón Lull, Written by an Unknown Hand About 1311. Editor and translator, E. A. Peers. London: Burns, Oates and Washbourne, 1927.

Llibre de ordinacions de la vila de Castelló de la Plana. Estudio preliminar, edición, notas y glosario. Editor, Luis Revest y Corzo. Libros raros y curiosos, no. 13. Castellón de la Plana: Consejo superior de investigaciones científicas, 1957.

Llibre de privilegis de Ulldecona. See secondary sources, Bayerri.

Llibre dels feyts del rei En Jacme. See James I, *Crònica.*

Lorenzana, F. de. See *SS. Patrum.*

Luca d'Acherio. *Chronicon barcinonense.* In *Collectio maxima conciliorum* (*q.v.*), V, 231–232.

Lucas (Tudensis, diaconus) of Tuy. *Chronicon mundi.* In *Acta sanctorum* (*q.v.*), May, VII.

Lull [Llull], Ramón. *Blanquerna: A Thirteenth-Century Romance.* Translator, Edgar Allison Peers. London: Jarrolds Publishers, *ca.* 1925.

—— *Obres de Ramon Lull, edició original feta en vista dels millors i més antics manuscrits.* Editors, Mateo Obrador y Bennássar, Salvador Galmés *et alii.* 21 vols. to date. Palma de Mallorca: Comissio editora lulliana, for Institut d'estudis catalans, 1906.

—— See *Life.*

Mansi. See *Sacrorum conciliorum.*

Mansilla Reoyo. See *Documentación*; Honorius III.

Marca hispanica sive limes hispanicus, hoc est, geographica et historica descriptio Cataloniae, Ruscinonis, et circumiacentium populorum. Compiler, Pierre de Marca; editor, E. Baluze. Paris: F. Muguet, 1688.

Marinus de Eboli. See *Formularsammlung.*

Marsilio, Pedro. "Commentarium de gestis Jacobi I," in Peñafort, *Summa* (*q.v.*), pp. xlvii–li.

Martorell. See "Fragmentos inéditos."

Matthew Paris. *Chronica maiora.* Editor, Henry R. Luard. 7 vols. London: 1872–1883. In *Rerum brittanicarum medii aevi scriptores* (*q.v.*).

—— *Historia anglorum sive ut vulgo dicitur historia minor. Item, eiusdem abbrevi-*

atio chronicorum Angliae. Editor, Sir Frederic Madden. 3 vols. London: 1866–1869. In *Rerum brittanicarum medii aevi scriptores (q.v.)*.

Memorial histórico español: colección de documentos, opúsculos y antigüedades. 48 vols. Madrid: Real academia de la historia, 1851–1918.

Miedes, Bernadino [Gómez]. See *Epitome*.

Miedes, Miguel [Pérez]. See *Constitutiones sive ordinationes*.

Monumenta Germaniae historica. Editors, George Heinrich Pertz *et alii*. 200 vols. to date. Hanover and Berlin: Hahn *et alibi*, 1826– .

Muntaner, Ramón. *Crònica*. Editor, Enrique Bagué. 9 vols. in 2. Collecció popular barcino, nos. 19, 141–148. Barcelona: Editorial Barcino, 1927–1952.

—— *Crònica*. Editor, José Coroleu e Inglada. Barcelona: Imprenta La Renaixensa, 1886.

—— *Crònica catalana*. Editor, Antonio de Bofarull y Brocá. Barcelona: Imprenta de Jaime Jepús, 1860.

—— *The Chronicle of Muntaner Translated from the Catalan*. Translator, Lady Henrietta Margaret Goodenough. Hakluyt Society publications, series 2, nos. 47, 50. 2 vols. London: Hakluyt Society, 1920–1921.

Nangis, G. de. See Guillaume.

Nicholas III, Pope. *Les registres de Nicholas III (1277–1280), recueil des bulles de ce pape publiées ou analysées d'après les manuscrits originaux des archives du Vatican*. Editors, Jules Gay and Suzanne Vitte. 1 vol. Paris: Bibliothèque des écoles françaises d'Athènes et de Rome, 1898–1938.

"Once bulas de Bonifacio VIII, inéditas y biográficas, de San Pedro Pascual, obispo de Jaén y mártir," editor F. Fita y Colomé, *Boletín de la real academia de la historia*, XX (1892), 32–61.

"La orden franciscana en el antiguo reino de Aragón, colección diplomática," editor Ambrosio de Saldes, *Revista de estudios franciscanos*, I (1907), 88–92, 148–151, 219–222, 354–358, 414–417, 478–482, 537–540, 608–612, 753–757.

Ordinatio ecclesiae valentinae. In Sanchís y Sivera, *Diócesis valentina, nuevos estudios históricos (q.v.,* secondary sources), pp. 191–412.

"Para la historia del derecho eclesiástico valenciano," editor José Sanchís y Sivera, *Analecta sacra tarraconensia*, IX (1933), 137–147.

Paris, Matthew. See Matthew.

Pascual, San Pedro. *Obras de S. Pedro Pascual, mártir, obispo de Jaén, y religioso de la Merced, en su lengua original, con la traducción latina y algunas anotaciones*. Editor, Pedro Armengol Valenzuela. 4 vols. Rome: Tipografia della Pace di F. Cuggiani, and Imprenta Salustiana, 1905–1908.

Peñafort [Penyafort], Ramón de. *Decretals*. See *Corpus iuris canonici*.

—— *Sancti Raymundi de Pennafort ordinis praedicatorum summa ad manuscriptorum fidem recognita et emendata, sacrorumque canonum, qui in codicibus et anterioribus editionibus tantummodo allegantur, testimoniis aucta, iuxta editionem anni MDCCXX, quam P. Honoratus Vincentius Laget eiusdem ordinis, sacrae theologiae professor, procuravit*. Verona: Ex typographia seminarii, apud Augustinum Carattonium, 1744.

—— *Raymundiana seu documenta quae pertinent ad S. Raymundi de Pennaforti vitam et scripta*. Editors, Franciscus Balme, Ceslaus Paban, and Joachim Collomb. Rome: In domo generalitia [O.P.], 1898–1901.

La péninsule ibérique. See Al-Ḥimyarī.

"Un pergamino [1251] y un sello de Jaime I del archivo histórico nacional," editor Miguel Gómez del Campillo, *Boletín de la sociedad castellonense de cultura*, XXVIII (1952), 167–172.

Pressutti. See Honorius III.

"Primera contribución conocida impuesta a los moros del reino de Valencia," editor Roque Chabás y Lloréns, *El archivo*, I (1886), 255–256.

Primera crónica general. See Alphonse X the Learned.

Privilegios reales de Montesa. See introductory essay to bibl., note 1.

Prou. See Honorius IV.

Rada, Rodrigo Jiménez de. See Rodrigo.

Ramón Lull. See Lull.

Ramón de María. See *"Repartiment"* de Burriana.

Ramón de Peñafort. See Peñafort.

Rasis. See Aḥmad.

Rationes decimarum Hispaniae (1279–1280). Editor, José Rius Serra. (Vol. I: *Cataluña, Mallorca y Valencia.* Vol. II: *Aragón y Navarra*). Textos y estudios de la corona de Aragón, nos. 7, 8. Barcelona: Consejo superior de investigaciones científicas, 1946–1947.

Rationes decimarum Italiae nei secoli xiii e xiv. Tuscia, la decima degli anni 1274–1280. Editor, Pietro Guidi. Studi e testi, no. 58. Rome: Tipografia vaticana, 1932.

Raymundiana. See Peñafort.

Recueil des historiens des Gaules et de la France. Editors, M. Bouquet *et alii.* 24 vols. Paris: Imprimerie nationale *et alibi*, 1737–1904 (incl. new series in progress).

El "Repartiment" de Burriana y Villarreal. Editor, Ramón de María. Valencia: J. Nácher, 1935.

Repartiment de Valencia. Edición fotocópica. Editor, Julián Ribera y Tarragó. Valencia: Centro de cultura valenciana, 1939.

Repartimiento de Mallorca. Editor, Próspero de Bofarull y Mascaró. In *Colección de documentos inéditos del archivo general de la corona de Aragón (q.v.),* vol. XIII, 1–141.

Repartimiento de Murcia. Editor, Juan Torres Fontes. Escuela de estudios medievales, textos, no. 31. Madrid: Consejo superior de investigaciones científicas, 1960.

Repartimiento de Sevilla. Estudio y edición. Editor, Julio González. Escuela de estudios medievales, textos, nos. 15, 16. 2 vols. Madrid: Consejo superior de investigaciones científicas, 1951.

Repartimiento de Valencia. Editor, Próspero de Bofarull y Mascaró. In *Colección de documentos inéditos del archivo general de la corona de Aragón (q.v.),* vol. XI, 143–656.

"Repàs d'un manual notarial del temps del rey En Jaume I," editor Joan Segura, *Congrés I (q.v.),* pp. 300–326.

Rerum brittanicarum medii aevi scriptores, or Chronicles and Memorials of Great Britain and Ireland during the Middle Ages. 244 vols. London: Longman and Co. *et alibi*, 1858–1896.

Rerum italicarum scriptores, raccolta degli storici italiani dal cinquecento al millecinquecento da L. A. Muratori. Revised edition. Directors, Giosué Carducci, Vittorio Fiorini, and Pietro Fedele. 344 fasc. to date. Città di Castello: S. Lapi, and Bologna: N. Zanichelli, 1900–   .

Rius Serra. See *Rationes decimarum; Cartulario de "Sant Cugat."*

Roderick Simon of Rada. See Rodrigo.

Rodrigo Jiménez de Rada. *De rebus Hispaniae libri ix emendatiores et auctiores.* In *Hispaniae illustratae (q.v.),* II, 2–148. Also in SS. *Patrum toletanorum (q.v.),* III, 5–208.

Roger of Hoveden. *Chronica magistri Rogeri de Houdene*. Editor, William Stubbs. 4 vols. In *Rerum brittanicarum medii aevi scriptores* (*q.v.*).

Sacrorum conciliorum nova et amplissima collectio. Editors, J. D. Mansi *et alii*. 53 vols. (plus those irregularly numbered). Leipzig: H. Walter, 1903–1927.

Sáenz de Aguirre (for Aguirre, Sáenz de). See *Collectio maxima conciliorum*.

Sancti Saturnini. See *Chronicon Sancti Saturnini*.

SS. Patrum toletanorum quotquot extant opera. Editor, Francisco Antonio [Cardinal] de Lorenzana y Buitrón. 3 vols. Madrid: Vidua Ioachimi Ibarra, 1782–1793.

Segura. See "Rapàs."

Statuta capitulorum generalium ordinis cisterciensis ab anno 1116 ad annum 1786. Editor, Joseph M. Canivez. Bibliothèque de la *Revue d'histoire ecclésiastique*, fascs. 9 to 14b. 8 vols. Louvain: La Revue, 1933–1941.

"Super officiis Aragonum," editor J. E. Martínez Ferrando, *Hispania* [Paris], IV (1944), 499–535.

Tejada y Ramiro. See *Colección de cánones*.

Teulet. See *Layettes*.

Thesaurus novus anecdotorum. Editors, E. Martène and U. Durand. 5 vols. Paris: F. Delaulne, 1717.

Tratados de legislación musulmana. Editor, Içe de Gebir. *Memorial histórico español* (*q.v.*), vol. V.

Urban IV, Pope. *Les registres d'Urbain IV (1261–1264), recueil des bulles de ce pape publiées ou analysées d'après les manuscrits originaux du Vatican*. Editor, Jean Guiraud. 4 vols. Paris: Bibliothèque des écoles françaises d'Athènes et de Rome, 1900–1903.

Vic and Vaissète. See secondary sources.

Villanueva. See secondary sources.

Voragine [Varazze], Jacobus da. *The Golden Legend of Jacobus de Voragine*. Translators, Granger Ryan and Helmut Ripperger. 2 vols. London: Longmans, Green and Co., 1941.

Wadding. See secondary sources.

SECONDARY SOURCES

(and Secondary-with-Primary)

Abadal y de Vinyals, Ramón de. "Origen y proceso de consolidación de la sede ribargorzana de Roda," *Estudios de edad media de la corona de Aragón*, V (1952), 7–82.

Aguilar y Serrat, F. de Asís (reorganized from manuscript by Juan Bautista Pérez [1537–1597]). *Episcopologium segobricense*. Segorbe: F. Romaní y Suay, 1883.

⸺ *Noticias de Segorbe y de su obispado*. 2 vols. Segorbe: F. Romaní y Suay, 1890.

Ajo G. y Sáinz de Zúñiga, C. María. *Historia de las universidades hispánicas. Orígenes y desarrollo desde su aparición a nuestros días*. 3 vols. to date. Avila: Centro de estudios e investigaciones, and Madrid: Consejo superior de investigaciones científicas, 1957–1959.

Almagro Basch, Martín *et alii*. *Historia de Albarracín y su sierra*. 3 vols. to date. Teruel: Instituto de estudios turolenses, 1959.

Almarche y Vázquez, Francisco. *Historiografía valenciana. Catálogo bibliográfico de dietarios, libros de memorias, diarios, relaciones, autobiografías, etc., inéditas, y referentes a la historia del antiguo reino de Valencia*. Anales del instituto general y técnico de Valencia. Valencia: La Voz valenciana, 1919–1920.

Almela y Vives, Francisco. *La catedral de Valencia*. Colecció Sant Jordi, series 2, no. 5. Barcelona: Editorial Barcino, 1927.

——— "El 'Llibre del mustaçaf' y la vida en la ciudad de Valencia a mediados del siglo xvi," *Boletín de la sociedad castellonense de cultura*, XXV (1949), 1–24.

Amorós Payá, León. "Los santos mártires franciscanos B. Juan de Perusa y B. Pedro de Saxoferrato en la historia de Teruel," *Teruel*, XV (1956), 5–142.

Aragón, Josephus de. *Propugnaculum juris precedendi vener. provinciae valentinae ordinis B. N. de Mercede redemptionis captivorum contra vener. provincias Franciae et Andalusiae*. Rome: Camera apostolica, 1689–1690.

El archivo. Revista literaria semanal. [Subtitle varies]. 7 vols. Denia: Imprenta de Pedro Botella, 1886–1893. (II: 1887–1888; III: 1888–1889). See also Chabás, and above in primary sources, Documents.

Arco y Garay, Ricardo del. "El famoso jurisperito del siglo xiii, Vidal de Cañellas, obispo de Huesca (noticias y documentos inéditos)," *Boletín de la real academia de buenas letras de Barcelona*, VIII (1916), 464–480, 508–521, 546–550.

——— *Sepulcros de la casa real de Aragón*. Madrid: Consejo superior de investigaciones científicas, 1945.

——— "El jurisperito Vidal de Cañellas, obispo de Huesca," *Jerónimo Zurita*, I (1951), 23–113.

——— "Nuevas noticias biográficas del famoso jurisperito del siglo xiii, Vidal de Cañellas, obispo de Huesca," *Boletín de la real academia de buenas letras de Barcelona*, IX (1917), 221–249; X (1921), 83–113.

——— "El obispo Don Jaime Sarroca, consejero y gran privado del rey Don Jaime el Conquistador (noticias y documentos inéditos)," *Boletín de la real academia de buenas letras de Barcelona*, VIII (1916), 463–480, 508–521; IX (1917), 65–91.

Armengol Valenzuela, Pedro. *Vida de S. Pedro Pascual, religioso de la Merced, obispo de Jaén, y mártir glorioso de Cristo*. Rome: Federico Setth, 1901.

——— See primary sources, Pascual.

Asín Palacios, Miguel. *Contribución a la toponomía árabe de España*. Second edition. Madrid: Consejo superior de investigaciones científicas, 1944.

Aunós Pérez, Antonio. *El derecho catalán en el siglo xiii*. Barcelona: Ediciones Helios, 1926.

Aymerich, Mateo. *Nomina et acta episcoporum barcinonensium, binis libris comprehensa, atque ad historiae, et chronologiae rationem revocata*. Barcelona: P. Nadal, 1760.

Ballesteros Gaibrois, Manuel. *Don Rodrigo Jiménez de Rada*. Colección pro ecclesia et patria. Barcelona: Editorial Labor, 1936.

Barberá Sentamáns, Antonio. *El derecho canónico valentino comparado con el general de la iglesia*. Valencia: Tipografía Doménech, 1928.

Baron, Bonaventure. *Annales ordinis Ssmae. Trinitatis redemptionis captivorum fundatoribus SS. Joanne de Matha et Faelice de Valois, 1198–1297*. Rome: A. Bernabò, 1684.

Barraclough, Geoffrey. *Papal Provisions. Aspects of Church History Constitutional, Legal and Administrative in the Later Middle Ages*. Oxford: B. Blackwell, 1935.

Bayerri y Bertoméu, Enrique. *Llibre de privilegis de la vila de Ulldecona, cartulario de la militar y soberana orden de San Juan de Jerusalén (ahora de Malta) en su comendadoría de Ulldecona desde mediados del siglo xii hasta finales del xvi*. Archivo histórico de la Ulldecona medieval. Tortosa: Imprenta Blanch, 1951.

—— *Historia de Tortosa y su comarca.* 8 vols. to date. Tortosa: Algueró y Baíges, 1933–[1960].

Beazley, C. Raymond. *James the First of Aragon.* Oxford: B. H. Blackwell, 1890.

Bellini, Albano. "San Pedro Pascual, nuevos datos biográficos," *Boletín de la real academia de la historia,* XLI (1902), 345–347.

Beltrán de Heredia, V. "La formación intelectual del clero en España durante los siglos xii, xiii y xiv," *Revista española de teología,* VI (1946), 313–357.

Beneyto Pérez, Juan. "Sobre siervos cristianos bajo el dominio musulmán," *Boletín de la sociedad castellonense de cultura,* XIII (1932), 361–365.

—— "Sobre la territorialización del código de Valencia," *Boletín de la sociedad castellonense de cultura,* XII (1931), 187–197.

Betí Bonfill, Manuel. "Ares y su carta puebla," *Boletín de la sociedad castellonense de cultura,* I (1920), 189–191.

—— "Çilla y su carta puebla," *Boletín de la sociedad castellonense de cultura,* II (1921), 25–28.

—— "Fundación del real monasterio de monjes cistercienses de Santa María de Benifazá," *Congrés I (q.v.),* pp. 408–421.

—— "Primeros señores de Castellón," *Boletín de la sociedad castellonense de cultura,* VII (1926), 113–114, 181–191.

—— *Ros[s]ell, pleito que por su dominio sostuvieron en el siglo xiii la orden de San Juan de Jerusalén y el real monasterio de Benifazá.* Castellón de la Plana: Hijos de J. Armengot, 1920.

Beuter, Pedro Antonio. *La coronica general de toda España y especialmente del reyno de Valencia.* 2 vols. [*Primera parte de la . . .; Segunda parte . . .*] Valencia: Pedro Patricio Mey, [1538–1551] 1604.

Bibliotheca hagiographica latina antiquae et mediae aetatis. Editors, the Bollandists. 2 vols. Brussels: Societas bollandiana, 1898–1901.

Bidagor, Ramón. *La "iglesia propia" en España, estudio histórico-canónico.* Analecta gregoriana, no. 4. Rome: Gregorian University, 1933.

Bishko, Charles Julian. "The Castilian as Plainsman: the Medieval Ranching Frontier in La Mancha and Extremadura," *New World Looks at its History (q.v.),* pp. 47–69.

Blanch, Josep. *Arxiepiscopologi de la santa església metropolitana i primada de Tarragona.* Editor, Joaquín Icart. 2 vols. Tarragona: Agrupació de bibliòfils de Tarragona, 1951.

Boix y Ricarte, Vicente. *Apuntes históricos sobre los fueros del antiguo reino de Valencia.* Valencia: Mariano de Cabrerizo, 1855.

—— *Historia de la ciudad y reino de Valencia.* 3 vols. Valencia: Benito Monfort, 1845–1847.

Bonduelle, J. "Convers," *Dictionnaire de droit canonique,* IV, cols. 562–588.

Botet y Sisó, Joaquín. "Nota sobre la encunyació de monedes aràbigues pêl rey Don Jaume," *Congrés I (q.v.),* pp. 944–963.

Boyd, Catherine E. *Tithes and Parishes in Medieval Italy. The Historical Roots of a Modern Problem.* Ithaca, N.Y.: Cornell University, for the American Historical Association, 1952.

Boyl, Francisco. *N[uestra] S[eñora] del Puche, camara angelical de María santissima, patrona de la insigne ciudad, y reyno de Valencia, monasterio real del orden de redentores de Nuestra Señora de la Merced, fundación de los reyes de Aragón.* Zaragoza: S. Esparsa, 1631.

Branchát, Vicente. *Tratado de los derechos y regalías que corresponden al real patrimonio en el reyno de Valencia y de la jurisdicción del intendente como subrogado en lugar del antiguo bayle general.* 3 vols. Valencia: José y Tomás de Orga, 1784–1786.

Burns, Robert Ignatius. "The Friars of the Sack in Valencia," *Speculum,* XXXVI (1961), 435–438.

———— "Los hospitales del reino de Valencia en el siglo xiii," *Anuario de estudios medievales,* II (1965), 135–154.

———— "Journey From Islam, Incipient Cultural Transition in the Conquered Kingdom of Valencia (1240–1280)," *Speculum,* XXXV (1960), 337–356.

———— "A Mediaeval Income Tax: the Tithe in the Thirteenth-Century Kingdom of Valencia," *Speculum,* XLI (1966), 438–452.

———— "Un monasterio-hospital del siglo xiii: San Vicente de Valencia," *Anuario de estudios medievales,* III (1966).

———— "The Organization of a Mediaeval Cathedral Community: the Chapter of Valencia (1238–1280)," *Church History,* XXXI (1962), 14–23.

———— "The Parish as a Frontier Institution in Thirteenth-Century Valencia," *Speculum,* XXXVII (1962), 244–251.

———— "Social Riots on the Christian-Moslem Frontier, Thirteenth-Century Valencia," *American Historical Review,* LXVI (1961), 378–400.

Cagigas, Isidro de las. *Los mozárabes.* Minorías étnico-religiosas de la edad media española, nos. 1, 2. 2 vols. Madrid: Instituto de estudios africanos, Consejo superior de investigaciones científicas, 1947–1948.

———— *Los mudéjares.* Minorías étnico-religiosas de la edad media española, nos. 3, 4. 2 vols. Madrid: Instituto de estudios africanos, Consejo superior de investigaciones científicas, 1948–1949.

Canivez, J. M. "Bernard Calvo," *Dictionnaire d'histoire et de géographie ecclésiastiques (q.v.),* VIII, cols. 766–767.

Capeille, J. "Albalat (Pierre d'), *"Dictionnaire d'histoire et de géographie ecclésiastiques (q.v.),* I, col. 1364.

Carboneres, Manuel. *Picaronas y alcahuetes ó la mancebía de Valencia. Apuntes para la historia de la prostitución desde principios del siglo xiv hasta poco antes de la abolición de los fueros, con profusión de notas y copias de varios documentos oficiales.* Valencia: El Mercantil, 1876.

Carot y García, José. *Origen y vicisitudes del templo catedral de Segorbe a través de los tiempos.* Castellón de la Plana: Diputación provincial, 1949. In *Efemérides (q.v.).*

Carreras y Candi, Francisco. *Miscelánea histórica catalana.* 2 vols. Barcelona: Casa provincial de caridad, 1905–1918.

———— "Notes dotzecentistes d'Ausona," *Boletín de la real academia de buenas letras de Barcelona,* V (1910), 430–479; VI (1911), 6–32. Also in his *Miscelánea (q.v.),* II, 361–464.

———— See *Geografía.*

Caruana Tomás, Carmen. *Estudio histórico y jurídico de la Albufera de Valencia. Su régimen y aprovechamientos desde la reconquista hasta nuestros días.* Valencia: Academia valenciana de jurisprudencia y legislación, 1954.

Casas Torres, José Manuel. *La vivienda y los nucleos de población rurales de la huerta de Valencia.* Madrid: Consejo superior de investigaciones científicas, 1944.

Castañeda y Alcover, Vicente. "Relaciones geográficas, topográficas e históricas del reino de Valencia hechas en el siglo xviii a ruego de Don Tomás López," *Revista da archivos, bibliotecas, y museos,* XXXV (1916), 352–383; XXXVI (1917), 43–59, 224–248; XXXVII (1917, pt. 2), 56–74, 270–323; XXXVIII (1918), 234–251, 392–410; XXXIX (1918, pt. 2), 68–88, 324–353; XL (1919),

281–302; XLI (1920), 89–118, 275–293, 394–416, 574–592; XLII (1921), 85–110, 247–275, 445–467, 641–665; XLIII (1922), 118–133, 281–296, 434–452; XLIV (1923), 99–131, 265–272, 363–388; XLV (1924), 244–267, 336–351. Offprint as a book, 2 vols., Madrid: La Revista, 1919–1922.

Castell Maiques, Vicente. See Chapter XIV, note 1.

Castro, Américo. *The Structure of Spanish History*. Translator, E. L. King. Princeton, N.J.: Princeton University, 1954.

Cavanilles, Antonio J. *Observaciones sobre la historia natural, geografía, agricultura, población y frutos del reyno de Valencia*. 2 vols. Madrid: Imprenta Real, 1795–1797. (Second printing, much reduced in size and maps, 2 vols. Zaragoza: Consejo superior de investigaciones científicas, 1958.)

Cebrián Ibor, Santiago. "Los fueros de Valencia," *Congrés III* (*q.v.*), I, 605–665.

Chabás y Lloréns, Roque. *El archivo metropolitano de Valencia*. Barcelona: Tipografía L'Avenç, 1903.

——— See above, *El archivo. Revista*.

——— "El archivo municipal de Alcira," *El archivo*, II (1887–1888), 36–41.

——— "El aureum opus de Játiva," *El archivo*, V (1891), 304–306.

——— "El capitán Carroz," *El archivo*, II (1887–1888), 30–36, 77–84.

——— "La carta puebla de Sueca," *El archivo*, II (1887–1888), 205–208, 386–390.

——— "Çeid Abu Çeid," *El archivo*, V (1891), 143–166, 288–304, 362–376.

——— "La cosecha del azúcar en el reino de Valencia (Jaime I)," *El archivo*, I (1886), 43–44.

——— "Doña Teresa Gil de Vidaure," *El archivo*, VI (1892), 22–35.

——— "El Edrisí y sus noticias sobre Denia," *El archivo*, I (1886), 373–374.

——— *Episcopologio valentino. Investigaciones históricas sobre el cristianismo en Valencia y su archidiócesis, siglos i á xiii*. (Vol. I, *unicum*.) Valencia: Francisco Vives Mora, 1909.

——— *Génesis del derecho foral de Valencia*. Valencia: Francisco Vives Mora, 1902.

——— "Glosario de algunas voces oscuras usadas en el derecho foral valenciano," *Anales del centro de cultura valenciana*, XII (1944), 3–27, 76–79, 128–150. Offprint as a book, Valencia: Imprenta Diana, 1946.

——— *Historia de la ciudad de Denia*. Second edition. Editor, F. Figueras Pacheco. Instituto de estudios alicantinos, nos. 3, 4. 2 vols. Alicante: Diputación provincial, 1958–1960.

——— "El libro del repartimiento de la ciudad y reino de Valencia," *El archivo*, VI (1892), 240–250, VII (1893), 365–372.

——— "El libro de las ordenanzas municipales de Alcira," *El archivo*, VII (1893), 302–318.

——— "Liquidación de notas," *El archivo*, VII (1893), 335–355.

——— "Los mozárabes valencianos," *El archivo*, V (1891), 6–28.

——— "Notas cronológicas del reinado de Don Jaime I de Aragón," *El archivo*, VII (1893), 238–248.

——— "Obispo de Denia en el siglo xii," *El archivo*, VII (1893), 140.

——— "Orígines de Gandía," *El archivo*, I (1886), 185–187.

——— "Orígines de Gandía, el anverso," *El archivo*, I (1886), 281–283, 289–291, 322–323, 330–331.

——— "Valldigna, excursión arqueológico-geográfica," *El archivo*, III (1888–1889), 289–296.

——— "Viaje literario al archivo general de la corona de Aragón," *El archivo*, I (1886), 187–190.

346 THE CRUSADER KINGDOM OF VALENCIA

Chabás y Lloréns, Roque. "Zahen y los moros de Uxó y Eslida," *El archivo*, I (1886), 262–263.

—— See primary sources, "División"; "Documento"; Documents; "Primera."

Chaytor, Henry John. *A History of Aragon and Catalonia*. London: Methuen and Co., 1933.

Claeys-Bouuaert, F. "Cure," and "Curé," *Dictionnaire de droit canonique*, IV, cols. 889–900, 900–942.

Coll, José M. "La crónica de Fr. Pedro Marsili y la 'Vita anonymi' de S. Ramón de Penyafort, su historicidad," *Analecta sacra tarraconensia*, XXII (1949), 21–50.

—— "Escuelas de lenguas orientales en los siglos xiii–xiv," *Analecta sacra tarraconensia*, XVII (1944), 115–38; XVIII (1945), 59–90; XIX (1946), 217–240.

Condé, José Antonio. *Historia de la dominación de los árabes en España, sacada de varios manuscritos y memorias arábigas*. Madrid: Marín y Compañía, 1874.

Congrés I. See entry immediately following.

Congrés d'història de la corona d'Aragó, dedicat al rey En Jaume I y a la seua época. 2 vols. but paginated to form one. Barcelona: Ayuntamiento de Barcelona, 1909–1913.

III Congrés d'història de la corona d'Aragó, dedicat al període compres entre la mort de Jaume I i la proclamació del rey Don Ferrán d'Antequera. 2 vols. Valencia: Diputación provincial, and Ayuntamiento de Valencia, 1923.

"Consideraciones." See Mateu y Llopis.

Constable, Giles. *Monastic Tithes from their Origins to the Twelfth Century*. Cambridge Studies in Medieval Life and Thought, new series, no. 10. Cambridge: Cambridge University Press, 1964.

—— "Resistance to Tithes in the Middle Ages," *Journal of Ecclesiastical History*, XIII (1962), 172–185.

Cortés Muñoz, Fermín. "Aportación al estudio de las instituciones mercantiles de la Valencia foral, la condición jurídica de los mercaderes," *Boletín de la sociedad castellonense de cultura*, XXIV (1948), 218–225.

Cruilles, El Marqués de [Vicente Salvador y Montserrat]. *Los gremios de Valencia. Memoria sobre su origen, vicisitudes y organización*. Valencia: Casa de beneficencia, 1883.

Deslandres, Paul. *L'ordre des trinitaires pour le rachat des captifs*. 2 vols. Paris: Plon, Nourrit et Compagnie, 1903.

Devic. See Vic.

Diago, Francisco. *Historia de la provincia de Aragón de la orden de predicadores, desde su origen y principio hasta el año de mil y seyscientos*. Barcelona: Jaume Cendrat, 1599.

Díaz Cassou, Pedro. *Serie de los obispos de Cartagena, sus hechos y su tiempo*. Madrid: Tip. de Fortanet, 1895.

Diccionario de historia de España. 2 vols. Madrid: Revista de occidente, 1952.

Dictionnaire de droit canonique. Directors, R. Naz, A. Villien, E. Magnin. 6 vols. to date. Paris: Letouzey et Ané, 1924– .

Dictionnaire d'histoire et de géographie ecclésiastiques. Directors, A. Baudrillart, A. de Meyer, and E. Van Cauwenbergh. 15 vols. to date. Paris: Letouzey et Ané, 1912– .

Dictionnaire des ordres religieux ou histoire des ordres monastiques, religieux, et militaires. Comp., Pierre (Hippolyt) Hélyot; editor, M. L. Badiche. 4 vols. Paris: [*Encyclopédie théologique* (*q.v.*)], 1847–1859.

Dictionnaire historique, géographique, et biographique des croisades. Editor, M. D'Ault-Dumesnil. Paris: [*Encyclopédie théologique (q.v.)*], 1852.

Diócesis valentina. See Sanchís y Sivera.

Donovan, Richard B. *The Liturgical Drama in Medieval Spain.* Pontifical Institute of Mediaeval Studies, Studies and Texts, no. 4. Toronto: Pontifical Institute, 1958.

Duart Alabarta, Luis. *Obispados godos de Levante, aportación a la historia eclesiástica del reino de Valencia.* Madrid: Ed. Morata, 1961.

Durán Gudiol, Antonio. "El derecho capitular de la catedral de Huesca desde el siglo xii al xvi," *Revista española del derecho canónico,* VII (1952), 447–515.

Durand, H. "Confrérie," *Dictionnaire de droit canonique (q.v.),* IV, cols. 128–176.

Efemérides gloriosas para la historia de Segorbe. Compilación de los discursos y trabajos científico-literarios del primer certamen celebrado con motivo de la entrega oficial de la S.I.C. de Segorbe. Castellón de la Plana: Diputación provincial, 1949.

Emery, Richard W. *The Friars in Medieval France; a Catalogue of French Mendicant Convents, 1200–1550.* New York: Columbia University Press, 1962.

—— "The Friars of the Sack," *Speculum,* XVIII (1943), 323–334.

—— *Heresy and Inquisition in Narbonne.* Studies in History, Economics and Public Law, no. 480. New York: Columbia University, 1941.

—— "A Note on the Friars of the Sack," *Speculum,* XXXV (1960), 591–595.

—— "Notes on the Early History of the Augustinian Order in Southern France," *Augustiniana* [Louvain], VI (1956), 336–345.

Encyclopédie théologique ou série de dictionnaires. Editor, J. P. Migne. 168 vols. in 170, in 3 sets. Paris: Chez l'éditeur, 1845–1873.

Esclapés de Guilló, Pascual. *Resumen historial, de la fundación, i antigüedad de la ciudad de Valencia de los Edetanos, vulgò del Cid. Sus progressos, ampliación, i fábricas insignes, con notables particularidades.* Valencia: Antonio Bordazar de Artazú, 1738.

Escolano, Gaspar. *Décadas de la historia de la insigne y coronada ciudad y reino de Valencia.* Editor, Juan B. Perales. 3 vols. Valencia: Terraza, Aliena y Compañía, [1610–1611] 1878–1880.

Estapé Rodríguez, Fabián. "Diezmo," *Diccionario de historia de España (q.v.),* I, 891–893.

Esteban Abad, Rafael. *Estudio histórico-político sobre la ciudad y comunidad de Daroca.* Teruel: Instituto de estudios turolenses, 1959.

Esteve, Antonio. "El castillo de Rebollet," *El archivo,* I (1886), 69–71.

Eubel, Conrad *et alii. Hierarchia catholica medii aevi sive summorum pontificum, s.r.e. cardinalium, ecclesiarum antistitum series ab anno 1198.* Second edition. 3 vols. Münster: Libreria Regensbergiana, 1913–1914.

Febrèr, Jaume. *Trobes de Mosen Jaume Febrèr, caballer, en que tracta dels llinatges de la conquista de la ciutat de Valencia e son regne.* Valencia: Imprenta del Diari, 1796–1797.

Fernández y Domingo, Daniel. *Anales o historia de Tortosa desde su fundación hasta nuestras dias.* Second edition. Barcelona: Jepús, 1867.

Fernández y González, Francisco. "Ampliación sobre los mozárabes valencianos," *El archivo,* V (1891), 28–30.

—— *Estado social y político de los mudéjares de Castilla, considerados en sí mismos y respecto de la civilización española.* Madrid: Joaquín Muñoz, 1866.

Ferrer Flórez, Miguel. "Mallorca y la teocracia pontificia," *Analecta sacra tarraconensia,* XXIII (1950), 16–30.

Ferrer Salvador, Vicente. "El real monasterio cisterciense de Gratia Dei (Zaidia) en Valencia, aportación a su historia," *Anales del centro de cultura valenciana*, XXII (1961), 60–108.

Finestres y de Monsalvo, Jaime. *Historia del real monasterio de Poblet*. 6 vols. Barcelona: Editorial Orbis, [1746] 1947–1955.

Fita y Colomé, Fidel. "Don Pedro de Albalat, arzobispo de Tarragona, y Don Ferrer Pallarés, obispo de Valencia, cuestiones cronológicas," *Boletín de la real academia de la historia*, XL (1902), 335–352.

—— "San Pedro Pascual, incidente bibliográfico," *Boletín de la real academia de la historia*, XLVI (1905), 266–269.

—— See primary sources, "Concilios"; "Once bulas."

Flórez. See primary sources, *España sagrada*.

Font y Rius, José M. *Instituciones medievales españolas. La organización política, económica y social de los reinos cristianos de la Reconquista*. Madrid: Consejo superior de investigaciones científicas, 1949.

—— "Orígenes del régimen municipal de Cataluña," *Anuario de historia del derecho español*, XVI (1945), 389–529; and XVII (1946), 229–585.

—— "La reconquista y repoblación de Levante y Murcia," in J. M. Font y Rius *et alii*, *La reconquista española y la repoblación del país*, Escuela de estudios medievales, no. 15, Zaragoza: Consejo superior de investigaciones científicas, 1951, pp. 85–126.

Fontavella González, Vicente. *La huerta de Gandía*. Zaragoza: Consejo superior de investigaciones científicas, 1950.

Foran, E. A. *The Augustinians from St. Augustine to the Union, 1256*. London: Burns, Oates, and Washbourne, 1938.

Fuente, Vicente de la. *Historia eclesiástica de España*. Second edition, revised. 6 vols. Madrid: Compañía de Impresores del reino, 1873–1875.

Galmés de Fuentes, Álvaro. "El mozárabe levantino en los 'Libros de los repartimientos de Mallorca y Valencia,'" *Nueva revista de filología hispánica*, IV (1950), 313–346.

Gams, Pius Bonifacius. *Series episcoporum ecclesiae catholicae quotquot innotuerunt a beato Petro apostolo*. Graz: Akademische Druck- und Verlagsanstalt, [1873] 1957.

—— *Die Kirchengeschichte von Spanien*. 3 vols. in 5. Ratisbon: 1863–1879; reprint Graz: Akademische Druck- und Verlagsanstalt, 1956.

García y García, Honorio. "El alcadiazgo de Eslida," *Boletín de la sociedad castellonense de cultura*, XVIII (1943), 161–165.

—— "La Aldea, su carta puebla y venta al monasterio de Benifazá," *Boletín de la sociedad castellonense de cultura*, XV (1934), 292–295.

—— "El derecho romano en los 'Furs' (estudios de derecho foral valenciano)," *Boletín de la sociedad castellonense de cultura*, XXX (1954), 177–182.

—— "Los elementos germánico y musulmán en los 'Furs' (estudios de derecho foral valenciano)," *Boletín de la sociedad castellonense de cultura*, XXXI (1955), 80–85.

—— "La iglesia del monasterio de Nuestra Señora de Benifazá," *Anales del centro de cultura valenciana*, XX (1952), 184–191.

—— "El 'Libre del Repartiment' y la práctica notarial de su tiempo," *Boletín de la sociedad castellonense de cultura*, XXV (1949), 493–499.

—— *Notas para la historia de Vall de Uxó*. Vall de Uxó: Ayuntamiento, and Instituto laboral, 1962.

—— "La parroquial del Santo Ángel de la Vall de Uxó," *Boletín de la sociedad castellonense de cultura*, XXII (1946), 318–330.

—— "Posibilidad de un elemento consuetudinario en el código de Jaume I (estudios de derecho foral valenciano)," *Boletín de la sociedad castellonense de cultura*, XXIII (1947), 428–450, and XXIV (1948), 5–14.

García y García, Honorio. "Problemática acerca de los 'Furs' (estudios de derecho foral valenciano)," *Boletín de la sociedad castellonense de cultura*, XXX (1954), 89–105.

———— "Real monasterio de Santa María de Benifazá," *Boletín de la sociedad castellonense de cultura*, XXVI (1950), 19–35.

———— "Un santo [Bernard Calvó] en la conquista de Valencia," *Boletín de la sociedad castellonense de cultura*, XXV (1949), 69–75.

———— "Sobre el fondo consuetudinario del derecho de Valencia (estudios de derecho foral valenciano)," *Boletín de la sociedad castellonense de cultura*, XVIII (1943), 17–29.

———— "La tinença de Benifaçá," *Boletín de la sociedad castellonense de cultura*, XIII (1932), 405–406.

García Gómez. See primary sources, Al-Šaqundī.

García Larragueta, Santos A. "El carácter de los primeros establecimientos de la orden de San Juan en el reino de Navarra," *Annales de l'ordre souverain militaire de Malte*, XIX (1961), 18–23.

———— *El gran priorado de Navarra de la orden de San Juan de Jerusalén. Siglos xii–xiii*. 2 vols. Pamplona: Diputación foral de Navarra, 1957.

Garciá Sanz, A. "Mudéjares y moriscos en Castellón," *Boletín de la sociedad castellonense de cultura*, XXVIII (1952), 94–114.

Garciá Villada, Zacarías. *Historia eclesiástica de España*. 3 vols. as 5. Madrid: Editorial Razón y Fe, 1929–1936.

Gazulla, Faustino D. "Don Jaime de Aragón y la orden de Nuestra Señora de la Merced," *Congrés I (q.v.)*, pp. 327–388.

———— "Los mercedarios en Arguines y Algar (siglo xiii)," *Boletín de la sociedad castellonense de cultura*, VI (1925), 64–77.

———— "Los mercedarios en Játiva durante el siglo xiii," *Boletín de la sociedad castellonense de cultura*, IV (1923), 129–43.

———— "Moros y cristianos, algo sobre cautivos," *Boletín de la sociedad castellonense de cultura*, VI (1925), 209–217, 195–209, 266–272, 317–320; XI (1930), 94–107, 202–210.

———— *La orden de Nuestra Señora de la Merced, estudios histórico-críticos (1218–1317)*. Barcelona: Luis Gili, 1934.

———— "El puig de Santa María," *Congrés III (q.v.)*, II, 593–654.

———— "Los religiosos de la Merced en la ciudad de Valencia (siglo xiii)" *Boletín de la sociedad castellonense de cultura*, VI (1925), 1–12.

Geografía general del reino de Valencia. Editor, F. Carreras y Candi. 5 vols. Barcelona: Alberto Martín, 1920–1927.

Giacomozzi, Gabriele G. "L'ordine della penitenza di Gesù Cristo, contributo alla storia della spiritualità del secolo xiii," *Studi storici dell' ordine dei servi di Maria*, VIII (1957–1958), 3–60.

Gibert y Sánchez de la Vega, Rafael. "Los contratos agrarios en el derecho medieval," *Boletín de la universidad de Granada*, XXII (1950), 305–330.

Giméno Michavila, Vicente. "El antiguo hospital municipal de Castellón," *Boletín de la sociedad castellonense de cultura*, XIII (1932), 208–213.

Goñi Gaztambide, J. *Historia de la bula de la cruzada en España*. Victoriensia, no. 4. Vitoria: Editorial del seminario, 1958.

———— "Los obispos de Pamplona del siglo xiii," *Príncipe de Viana*, XVIII (1957), 41–237.

González, Julio. *El reino de Castilla en la época de Alfonso VIII*. Escuela de estudios medievales, textos, no. 25. 3 vols. Madrid: Consejo superior de investigaciones científicas, 1960.

González, Julio. See primary sources, *Repartimiento de Sevilla*.

Gorosterratzu, Javier. *Don Rodrigo Jiménez de Rada, gran estadista, escritor y prelado. Estudio documentado de su vida, de los cuarenta años de su primacía en la iglesia de España y su cancillerato en Castilla*. . . . Pamplona: T. Bescansa, 1925.

Gottlob, Adolf. *Die päpstlichen Kreuzzugs-Steuern des 13 Jahrhunderts, ihre rechtliche Grundlage, politische Geschichte und technische Verwaltung*. Heiligenstadt: F. W. Cordier, 1892.

Gual Camarena, Miguel. "Contribución al estudio de la territorialidad de los fueros de Valencia," *Estudios de edad media de la corona de Aragón*, III (1947–48), 262–289.

―――― "Mudéjares valencianos, aportaciones para su estudio," *Saitabi*, VII (1949), 165–199.

―――― "Precedentes de la reconquista valenciana," *Estudios medievales* [Valencia], I (1952), 167–246.

―――― "Reconquista de la zona castellonense," *Boletín de la sociedad castellonense de cultura*, XXV (1949), 417–441.

Guillemain, Bernard. "Chiffres et statistiques pour l'histoire ecclésiastique du moyen âge," *Moyen âge*, LXIX (1953), 340–363.

Gutton, Francis. *L'ordre de Calatrava, la chevalerie militaire en Espagne*. Commission d'histoire de l'ordre de Citeaux, no. 4. Paris: P. Lethielleux, 1955.

Hebrera y Esmir, José Antonio de. *Chronica real seráfica del reyno y santa provincia de Aragón de la regular observancia de nuestro padre San Francisco*. Zaragoza: Diego de Larumbe, 1703–1705.

Hefele, Charles Joseph. *Histoire des conciles d'après les documents originaux*. Revised and translated by H. Leclerq. 10 vols. (each a double volume). Paris: Letouzey et Ané, 1907–1938.

Heimbucher, Max. *Die Orden und Kongregationen der katholischen Kirche*. Third edition, revised. 2 vols. Paderborn: F. Schöningh, 1933–1934.

Heintschel, D. E. *The Mediaeval Concept of an Ecclesiastical Office. An Analytical Study of the Concept of an Ecclesiastical Office in the Major Sources and Printed Commentaries from 1140–1300*. Canon Law Studies, no. 363. Washington, D.C.: Catholic University of America, 1956.

Hélyot. See *Dictionnaire des ordres*.

Hill, Rosalind. "Bishop Sutton and His Archives: A Study in the Keeping of Records in the Thirteenth Century," *Journal of Ecclesiastical History*, II (1951), 43–53.

Hofmeister, Philipp. "Die Verfassung der ehemaligen claustralen Benediktinerkongregation in Katalonien und Aragon," *Studien und Mitteilungen zur Geschichte des Benediktiner-Ordens und seiner Zweige*, LXX (1959), 206–235.

Hoyos, Manuel M. de los. *Registro documental, material inédito dominicano español*. Madrid: Selecciones gráficas, 1961.

Imbert, Jean. *Les hôpitaux en droit canonique du décret de Gratien à la sécularisation de l'Hotel-Dieu a Paris en 1565*. L'église et l'état au moyen âge, no. 8. Paris: J. Vrin, 1947.

Itinerari. See Miret y Sans.

Ivars Cardona, Andrés. "Año de fundación y diferentes advocaciones que ha tenido el monasterio de la Puridad o Purísima Concepción de Valencia," *Archivo ibero-americano*, XIX (1932), 435–464. Offprint as a book, Vich: Editorial Seráfica, 1933.

Janer, Florencio. *Condición social de los moriscos de España, causas de su expulsión y consecuencias que este produjo en el orden económico y político*. Madrid: Real academia de la historia, 1857.

Javierre Mur. See introductory essay to bibl., n. 1.

Johnstone, Hilda. "Poor Relief in the Royal Households of Thirteenth-Century England," *Speculum*, IV (1929), 149–157.

Jordán, Jayme. *Historia de la provincia de la corona de Aragón de la sagrada orden de los ermitaños de nuestro gran padre San Augustín compuestos de quatro reynos, Valencia, Aragón, Cataluña, y las islas de Mallorca y Menorca*. 3 vols. Valencia: J. García *et alibi*, 1704–1712.

Kantorowicz, Ernst. *The King's Two Bodies, A Study in Mediaeval Political Theology*. Princeton, N.J.: Princeton University, 1957.

Kehr, Paul. *Das Papsttum und die Königreiche Navarra und Aragon bis zur Mitte des XII Jahrhunderts*. Berlin: Abhandlungen der preussischen Akademie der Wissenschaften, 1928.

Klein, Julius. *The Mesta, a Study in Spanish Economic History, 1273–1836*. Harvard Economic Studies, no. 21. Cambridge, Mass.: Harvard University, 1920.

Lacarra, José M. "La restauración eclesiástica en las tierras conquistadas por Alfonso el Batallador (1118–1134)," *Revista portuguesa de historia*, IV (1948–1949), 263–286.

La Fuente. See Fuente.

Laguía, César Tomás. "La erección de la diócesis de Albarracín," *Teruel*, X (1953), 201–230.

Lalinde Abadía, Jesús. *La gobernación general en la corona de Aragón*. Zaragoza: Consejo superior de investigaciones científicas, 1963.

Lambert, A. "Aragon, royaume d'," *Dictionnaire d'histoire et de géographie ecclésiastiques (q.v.)* III, cols. 1347–1386.

——— "Arnauld de Gurb," *Dictionnaire d'histoire et de géographie ecclésiastiques (q.v.)*, IV, cols. 509–514.

——— "Arnauld de Peralta," *Dictionnaire d'histoire et de géographie ecclésiastiques (q.v.)*, IV, cols. 518–523.

——— "Barcelone," *Dictionnaire d'histoire et de géographie ecclésiastiques (q.v.)*, VI, cols. 671–747.

Lamberto de Zaragoza, and Ramón de Huesca. *Teatro histórico de las iglesias del reyno de Aragón*. 9 vols. Pamplona: J. M. Ezquerro, 1780–1807.

Laurent, M. H. *Le bienheureux Innocent V (Pierre de Tarentaise) et son temps* [1276]. Studi e testi, no. 129. Rome: Biblioteca apostolica vaticana, 1947.

Lavedan, Pierre. *L'architecture gothique religieuse en Catalogne, Valence et Baléares*. Paris: Henri Laurens, 1935.

Legendre, M. "Albarrazin," *Dictionnaire d'histoire et de géographie ecclésiastiques (q.v.)*, I, cols. 1383–1386.

Lepointe, G. "Dîme," "Dîmier," "Décimateur," *Dictionnaire de droit canonique*, IV, cols. 1231–1244, 1059.

Llorca, Fernando. *Una fundación del siglo xiii, San Juan del Hospital de Valencia*. Valencia: Editorial Prometeo, 1930.

Lloréns y Raga, Peregrín L. "El deanato de la catedral de Valencia," *Anales del centro de cultura valenciana*, XXII (1954), 8–21.

——— *Presencia histórica de la sede de Segorbe en el reino de Valencia*. Biblioteca de estudios de Segorbe y su comarca, no. 15. Segorbe: Departamento de Publicaciones del Instituto Laboral de Segorbe, 1960.

——— *Episcopologio segobricense*. See Chapter III, note 44.

Llorente y Olivares, Teodoro. *Valencia.* España, sus monumentos y artes, naturaleza e historia, nos. 24, 25. 2 vols. Barcelona: Daniel Cortezo, 1887–1889.

Lluch Arnal, Emilio. *Compendio de historia del antiguo reino de Valencia.* Valencia: Sucesor de Vives Mora, Artes gráficas, 1953.

López, Anastasio. "Confesores de la familia real de Aragón," *Archivo iberoamericano,* XVI (1929), 145–240.

López, Tomás. See Castañeda y Alcover.

López Rodó, Laureano. *El patrimonio nacional.* Madrid: Consejo superior de investigaciones científicas, 1954.

Loscertales, Pilar. "Exáricos," *Diccionario de historia de España (q.v.),* I, 1059–1060.

Lot, Ferdinand. *L'art militaire et les armées au moyen âge en Europe et dans le proche orient.* 2 vols. Paris: Payot, 1946.

Lunt, William E. *Papal Revenues in the Middle Ages.* Records of Civilization, Sources and Studies, no. 19. 2 vols. New York: Columbia University, 1934.

Luttrell, Anthony, "The Aragonese Crown and the Knights Hospitallers of Rhodes: 1291–1310," *English Historical Review,* LXXVI (1961), 1–19.

Macabich Llobet, Isidoro. "Es feudalisme a Ivissa (anotacions històriques)," *Congrés I (q.v.),* pp. 457–482.

Madurell y Marimón, José M. "Las escuelas de la seo de Barcelona (notas para su historia)," *Hispania sacra,* I (1948), 389–401.

Magallón, Manuel. "Templarios y hospitalarios, primer cartulario en el archivo histórico nacional," *Boletín de la real academia de la historia,* XXXIII (1898, part 2), 257–266.

—— See introductory essay to bibl., note 1.

Mann, H. K. *The Lives of the Popes in the Middle Ages.* 18 vols. London: K. Paul, Trench, Trübner and Co., 1906–1932.

Manrique, Ángel. *Cisterciensium seu verius ecclesiasticorum annalium a condito cistercio . . .* 4 vols. Lyons: G. Boissat and L. Anisson, 1642–1659.

Mansilla Reoyo, Demetrio. "Disputas diocesanas entre Toledo, Braga y Compostela en los siglos xii a xv," *Anthologica annua* [Rome], III (1955), 89–143.

—— *Iglesia castellano-leonesa y curia romana en los tiempos del rey San Fernando.* Estudio documental sacado de los registros vaticanos. Madrid: Consejo superior de investigaciones científicas, 1945.

—— "Episcopologio de Burgos, siglo xiii," *Hispania sacra,* IV (1951), 313–333.

—— See primary sources, *Documentación.*

Marchal, Jean. *Le "droit d'oblat,"* essai sur une variété de pensionnés monastiques. Archives de la France monastique, no. 49. Ligugé (Vienne): A. Picard, 1955.

María, Ramón de. See Ramón de María.

Mariana, Juan de. "Memoria de las concesiones que el rey D. Jayme I de Aragón hizo á los prelados, ricos hombres, caballeros y demas soldados que le servieron en la conquista de la ciudad y reyno de Valencia," *Historia general de España,* 9 vols. Valencia: Benito Monfort, 1783–1796, IV, app. 2.

Martínez Aloy, José. *La diputación de la generalidad del reino de Valencia.* Valencia: Diputación provincial de Valencia, 1930.

—— *Los prelados de Valencia. Sigilografía.* Valencia: Imprenta Doménech, 1887.

Martínez Colomer, Vicente. *Historia de la provincia de Valencia de la regular observancia de San Francisco.* Vol. I (*unicum*). Valencia: Salvador Fauli, [1803] 1901.

Martínez Díez, Gonzalo. *El patrimonio eclesiástico en la España visigoda. Estudio histórico-jurídico.* Miscelánea Comillas, no. 32. Palencia: Comillas University, 1959.

Martínez Ferrando, Jesús Ernesto. "Castellón de la Plana en la baja edad media (noticias sobre documentación de este período como propriedad de la corona real)," *Boletín de la sociedad castellonense de cultura*, XXV (1949), 351–360.

————— See introductory essay to bibl., note 1.

————— See primary sources, "Super officiis."

Martínez y Martínez, Francisco. "Pego, su población y primeros señores," *Congrés I (q.v.)*, pp. 63–69.

Martínez Morellá, Vicente. *La iglesia de San Nicolás de Alicante*. Instituto de estudios alicantinos, no. 23. Alicante: Diputación provincial, 1960.

————— See primary sources, *Cláusulas*.

Mas, Josep. *Antigüetat d'algunes esglésies del bisbat de Barcelona*. Notes històriques del bisbat de Barcelona, no. 13. Barcelona: Tipografía Católica pontificia, 1921.

Más y Gil, Luis. "La orden de San Jorge de Alfama, sus maestres, y la cofradía de Mossén Sent Jordi," *Hidalguía*, X (1963), 247–256.

Mateu Ibars, Josefina. *Los virreyes de Valencia. Fuentes para su estudio*. Publicaciones del archivo municipal de Valencia, series III, no. 2. Valencia: Ayuntamiento, 1963.

Mateu y Llopis, Felipe. "La circulación monetaria en las diócesis de Tortosa y Segorbe-Albarracín en el reino de Valencia, segun la décima de 1279–1280," *Boletín de la sociedad castellonense de cultura*, XXII (1946), 494–501.

————— "Consideraciones sobre nuestra reconquista," *Hispania*, XI (1951), 3–46.

————— *Glosario hispánico de numismática*. Barcelona: Consejo superior de investigaciones científicas, 1946.

————— "Lérida y sus relaciones con Valencia" [running title for "Datos y documentos para la historia monetaria de Lérida, siglos xiii a xvii"], *Ilerda*, V (1945), 8–55.

————— "Materiales para un glosario de diplomática hispánica. Corona de Aragón. Reino de Valencia." *Boletín de la sociedad castellonense de cultura*, XXXII (1956), 257–292 [cont.].

————— *El país valencià*. Valencia: Centro de cultura valenciana, 1933.

————— "Los privilegios de los monederos en la organización foral del reino del Valencia," *Anuario de historia del derecho español*, XX (1950), 70–135.

————— "Les relacions monetàries entre Catalunya i València des de 1276 a 1376," *Boletín de la sociedad castellonense de cultura*, XII (1931), 27–39.

————— "La repoblación musulmana del reino de Valencia en el siglo xiii y las monedas de tipo almohade," *Boletín de la sociedad castellonense de cultura*, XXVIII (1952), 29–43.

————— "Sobre la política monetaria de Jaime I y las acuñaciones valencianas de 1247 y 1271," *Anales del centro de cultura valenciana*, XV (1947), 233–261.

————— "Valores monetarios valencianos," *Boletín de la sociedad castellonense de cultura*, VII (1926), 287–294.

————— See introductory essay to bibl., note 1.

Matheu y Sanz, Lorenzo. *Tractatus de regimine urbis et regni Valentiae sive selectarum interpretationum ad principaliores foros eiusdem*. Valencia: Bernardo Nogués, 1654.

Matthaeu y Sanz. See Matheu.

Mayer, Ernesto. *Historia de las instituciones sociales y políticas de España y Portugal durante los siglos v a xiv*. 2 vols. Madrid: Anuario de historia del derecho español, 1925–1926.

Meersseman, G. G. *Dossier de l'ordre de la pénitence au xiie siècle*. Spicilegium friburgense, no. 7. Fribourg: Fribourg University, 1961.

Menéndez Pidal, Ramón. *La España del Cid.* Fourth edition, revised. 2 vols. Madrid: Espasa-Calpe, 1947. (See also first edition, 2 vols., Madrid: Editorial Plutarco, 1929.)

—— "Sobre la bibliografía de San Pedro Pascual," *Boletín de la real academia de la historia*, XLVI (1905), 259–266.

—— "Sobre los limites del valenciano," *Primer congrés internacional de la llengua catalana*, Barcelona: Joaquim Horta, 1908, pp. 340–344.

Mestre y Noé, Francisco. "Notes tortosines," *Congrés I (q.v.)*, pp. 422–428.

Michavila y Vila, Antonio. "Apuntes para el estudio de la vida social del reino de Valencia en la época de los reyes de la casa de Aragón," *III Congrés (q.v.)*, II, 113–168.

Milián Boix, Manuel. "Tasas y sobreprecios en el siglo xiv por tierras de Morella," *Boletín de la sociedad castellonense de cultura*, XXV (1949), 787–798.

Miquel Parellada, José M., and José Sánchez Real. *Los hospitales de Tarragona.* Tarragona: Instituto de estudios tarraconenses, 1959.

Miret y Sans, Joaquín. *Les cases de templers y hospitalers en Catalunya, aplech de noves y documents històrichs.* Barcelona: Casa provincial de caritat, 1910.

—— "La esclavitud en Cataluña en los ultimos tiempos de la edad media," *Revue hispanique*, XLI (1917), 1–109.

—— "Escolars catalans al estudi de Bolonia en la xiiia centuria," *Boletín de la real academia de buenas letras de Barcelona*, VIII (1915), 137–155.

—— *Itinerari de Jaume I "el Conqueridor."* Barcelona: Institut d'estudis catalans, 1918.

—— See primary sources, "Inventaris"; *Cartoral.*

Miscellanea historica in honorem Alberti de Meyer. Louvain: Louvain University, 1946.

Molin, Nicolaus. *Historia cartusiana ab origine ordinis usque ad tempus auctoris 1638.* 3 vols. Tournai: A. Baudechon, 1903–1906.

Mollat, G. "Bénéfices ecclésiastiques en occident," *Dictionnaire de droit canonique (q.v.)*, II, cols. 405–448.

Momblanch y Gonzálbez, Francisco de P. *Historia de la Albufera de Valencia.* Publicaciones del archivo municipal. Valencia: Ayuntamiento, 1960.

Moncada, Juan Luis de. *Episcopologio de Vich, escrito a mediados del siglo xvii.* Editor, Jaime Collell. 2 vols. Biblioteca histórica de la diócesis de Vich, nos. 1, 3. Vich: Viuda de R. Anglada, 1891–1894. (Supplementary vol. III, not in series, by Luis B. Nadal, Vich: *idem*, 1904.)

Monumentos españoles, catálogo de los declarados histórico-artísticos. Editor, J. M. de Azcárate. 3 vols. Madrid: Consejo superior de investigaciones científicas, 1953–1954.

Monzó Nogués, Andrés. *La Vall d'Alcalá y sus egregias figuras Ahmet ben Almançor, Çaida, y Çoraida.* Carlet, Valencia: Centro de cultura valenciana, 1954.

Moorman, John R. H. *Church Life in England in the Thirteenth Century.* Cambridge: Cambridge University, 1946.

Moragues, Miguel, Joaquín María Bover de Rosselló *et alii. Historia general del reino de Mallorca.* 3 vols. Palma: J. Guasp y Pascual, 1840.

Moreau, Edouard de. *Histoire de l'église en Belgique.* Museum lessianum, section historique, nos. 1, 2, 3, 12, 13. 6 vols. (vos. I, II, second edition, revised, 1945). Brussels: Edition universelle, 1941–1952.

Morera y Llauradó, Emilio. *Tarragona cristiana. Historia del arzobispado de Tarragona y del territorio de su provincia (Cataluña La Nueva).* 2 vols. Tarragona: F. Asís e Hijo, 1889–1899.

Morgades, Bernardo. *Historia de Poblet.* Barcelona: Talleres Gráficos rex, 1948.

Moscardó Cervera, Frederic. *Breu compendi de la història del regne de València*. Valencia: V. Cortell, 1953.

Mundy, J. H. *Liberty and Political Power in Toulouse, 1050-1230*. New York: Columbia University, 1954.

———— "Hospitals and Leprosaries of Twelfth and Early Thirteenth-Century Toulouse," *Essays in Medieval Life and Thought Presented in Honor of Austin Patterson Evans*, ed. J. H. Mundy *et alii*, New York: Columbia University, 1955, pp. 181-205.

Nadal. See Moncada.

Nanni, Luigi. *La parrocchia studiata nei documenti lucchesi dei secoli viii-xiii*. Analecta gregoriana, no. 47. Rome: Gregorian University, 1948.

The New World Looks at its History. Editors, A. R. Lewis and T. F. McGann. International Congress of Historians of the United States and Mexico, *Proceedings*, 2. Austin: University of Texas, 1963.

Nicolau y d'Olwer, Lluís. "Jaume I y los trovadors provensals," *Congrés I (q.v.)*, pp. 389-407.

Nomenclátor. See Sanchís Sivera; see also Pujol.

O'Callaghan, Joseph F. "The Affiliation of the Order of Calatrava with the Order of Citeaux," *Analecta sacra ordinis cisterciensis*, XV (1959), 163-193, XVI (1960), 3-59.

Oliver, Bienvenido. *Historia del derecho en Cataluña, Mallorca y Valencia. Código de las costumbres de Tortosa*. 4 vols. Madrid: Miguel Ginesta, 1876-1881.

Olmos y Canalda, Elías. *Los prelados valentinos*. Madrid: Consejo superior de investigaciones científicas, 1949.

———— See introductory essay to bibl., note 1.

Orellana, Marcos Antonio de. *Valencia antigua y moderna*. 3 vols. Valencia: Acción bibliográfica valenciana, 1923-1924.

Oriola-Cortada, E. Antonio de. "La couronne d'Aragon et les Hafsides au xiiie siècle (1229-1301)," *Analecta sacra tarraconensia*, XXV (1952), 51-115.

Orlandis Rovira, J. "Traditio corporis et animae: la 'familiaritas' en las iglesias y monasterios," *Anuario de historia del derecho español*, XXIV (1954), 95-279.

Pallarés y Gil, Matías. "Don Blasco de Alagón, señor de Morella," *Congrés I (q.v.)*, pp. 218-233.

Palomeque Torres, Antonio. "Contribución al estudio del ejército en los estados de la reconquista," *Anuario de historia del derecho español*, XV (1944), 205-351.

Pascual y Beltrán, Ventura. "La conquista de Játiva por Jaime I no pudo ser en 1249," *Anales del centro de cultura valenciana*, XVII (1949), 41-50.

———— "Recuerdos de un insigne mozárabe valenciano [S. Pedro Pascual], su estatua, su casa, sus libros," *Anales del centro de cultura valenciana*, XII (1944), 82-97.

Pelufo, Vicente. "Topografía de Alcira árabe," *Anales del centro de cultura valenciana*, VII (1934), 21-31.

Pérez, Juan Bautista. See Aguilar.

Pérez de Urbel, Justo. *Los monjes españoles en la edad media*. 2 vols. Madrid: Instituto de Valencia de Don Juan, 1930-1934 [revised edition, 1945].

Pérez Ruiz, Pedro Antonio. *La fe, la historia y el arte en el antiguo convento de predicadores de Valencia*. Valencia: Publicaciones verdad y belleza, 1952.

Pétiet, René. *Contribution à l'histoire de l'ordre de St-Lazare de Jérusalem en France*. Paris: E. Champion, 1914.

Piles Ibars, A. *Historia de Cullera*. Sueca: Ricardo Benedito, 1893.

Piles Ros, Leopoldo. "La judería de Burriana, apuntes para su estudio," *Sefarad*, XII (1952), 105–124.

——— "Los judíos valencianos y la autoridad real," *Sefarad*, VIII (1948), 78–96.

——— *Estudio sobre el gremio de zapateros.* Publicaciones del archivo municipal de Valencia. Valencia: Ayuntamiento, 1959.

Plöchl, Willibald M. *Geschichte des Kirchenrechts.* 3 vols. Vienna: Verlag Herold, c. 1959–1960.

Pons y Fábregues, Benito. "Les franqueses concedides a Mallorca per Jaume I," *Congrés I (q.v.)*, pp. 52–60.

Pou y Martí, José M. "Conflictos entre el pontificado y los reyes de Aragón en el siglo xiii," *Sacerdozio e regno da Gregorio VII a Bonifacio VIII*, Miscellanea historiae pontificiae, no. 18, Rome: Gregorian University, 1954, pp. 139–160.

Privilegios reales de Montesa. See introductory essay to bibl., note 1.

Puig y Puig, Juan. "Capbreu d'algunes persones distingides d'Ares del Maestre," *Boletín de la sociedad castellonense de cultura*, XIII (1932), 432–443.

——— "Iglesia arciprestal de San Mateo, su construcción, modificaciones impertinentes, su restauración," *Boletín de la sociedad castellonense de cultura*, XXX (1954), 70–84.

——— "Senyors de Morella durant el segle xiiiè," *Boletín de la sociedad castellonense de cultura*, XXXI (1955), 89–105.

Puig y Puig, Sebastián. *Episcopologio de la sede barcinonense. Apuntes para la historia de la iglesia de Barcelona y de sus prelados.* Biblioteca histórica de la biblioteca Balmes, series I, no. 1. Barcelona: Biblioteca Balmes, 1929.

Pujol y Camps, Celestino, and Pedro Alsius y Torrent. *Nomenclátor geográfico-histórico de la provincia de Gerona desde la más remota antigüedad hasta el siglo xv.* Gerona: Paciano Torres, 1883.

Rades y Andrada, Francisco de. *Chrónica de las tres órdenes y cavallerías de Sanctiago, Calatraua y Alcántara: en la qual se trata de su orígen y suceso, y notables hechos en armas. . . .* Toledo: Juan de Ayala, 1572.

Ramón de María. "Don Poncio de Torrella y el asedio de Peñíscola," *Boletín de la sociedad castellonense de cultura*, XVIII (1943), 271–274.

——— "Fadrell, Almazora y Castellón, para la catedral de Tortosa," *Boletín de la sociedad castellonense de cultura*, XVI (1935), 390–397.

——— "Jaime I dedica Peñíscola a Santa María y dota su culto," *Boletín de la sociedad castellonense de cultura*, XXI (1945), 233–235.

——— "Oropesa, por donación y cambio, para la orden de San Juan del Hospital," *Boletín de la sociedad castellonense de cultura*, XXIII (1947), 283–286.

——— "Un regalo que en realidad es una restitución," *Boletín de la sociedad castellonense de cultura*, XVIII (1943), 33–36.

——— See primary sources, "*Repartiment*" de Burriana.

Regné, Jean. See introductory essay to bibl., note 1.

Reino de Valencia. In *Geografía general del reino (q.v.)*.

Répertoire topo-bibliographique des abbayes et prieurés. Editor, L. H. Cottineau. 2 vols. Mâcon: Protat frères, 1939.

Revest Corzo, Luis. *Hospitales y pobres en el Castellón de otros tiempos.* Obras de investigación histórica, no. 24. Castellón de la Plana: Sociedad castellonense de cultura, 1947.

Ribera, Manuel Mariano. *Centuria primera del real y militar instituto de la ínclita religión de Nuestra Señora de la Merced redempción de cautivos cristianos.* (Part 1, *unicum*). Barcelona: Pablo Campins, 1726.

——— *Real patronato de los serenísimos señores reyes de España en el real, y militar orden de Nuestra Señora de la Merced, redención de cautivos.* 2 vols. Barcelona: Pablo Campins, 1725.

Ribera y Tarragó, Julián. "Enterramientos moros en Valencia," *El archivo,* I (1886), 209–212.

―――― *Opúsculos dispersos.* Tetuán: Instituto General Franco de estudios e investigación hispano-árabe, 1952.

―――― "Los tribus árabes en el reino de Valencia," *El archivo,* I (1886), 83–85.

―――― See primary sources, *Repartiment de Valencia.*

Rivera Recio, Juan Francisco. "El 'Liber privilegiorum' de la catedral de Toledo y los documentos reales en él contenidos," *Hispania sacra,* I (1948), 163–181.

―――― "La erección del obispado de Albarracín," *Hispania,* XIV (1954), 27–52.

―――― "Personajes hispanos asistentes en 1215 al iv concilio de Letrán: revisión y aportación nueva de documentos, datos biográficos," *Hispania sacra,* IV (1951), 335–355.

―――― "La provincia eclesiástica de Toledo en el siglo xii," *Anthologica annua* [Rome], VII (1959), 95–145.

Roca y Alcayde, Francisco. *Historia de Burriana.* Castellón de la Plana: Hijo de J. Armengot, 1932.

Roca Traver, Francisco A. "La gobernación foral del reino de Valencia: una cuestión de competencia," *Estudios de edad media de la corona de Aragón,* IV (1951), 177–214.

―――― "El gremio de curtidores de Castellón: unas ordenanzas desconocidas del siglo xiv," *Boletín de la sociedad castellonense de cultura,* XXVI (1950), 195–215.

―――― "Interpretación de la 'cofradía' valenciana: la real cofradía de San Jaime," *Estudios medievales* [Valencia], II (1957), 37–83.

―――― "Un siglo de vida mudéjar en la Valencia medieval (1238–1338)," *Estudios de edad media de la corona de Aragón,* V (1952), 115–208.

Rodrigo y Pertegás, José. "La morería de Valencia, ensayo de descripción topográfico-histórica de la misma," *Boletín de la real academia de la historia,* LXXXVI (1925), 229–251.

―――― "La urbe valenciana en el siglo xiv," *Congrés III* (*q.v.*), II, 279–374.

Rodríguez de Gálvez, Ramón. *San Pedro Pascual, obispo de Jaén y mártir. Estudios críticos.* Jaén: Establecimiento tipográfico de la unión, 1903.

―――― *San Pedro Pascual, obispo de Jaén y mártir. Informe histórico-crítico sobre su vida, escritos y pontificado.* Jaén: T. Rubio y Campos, 1900.

Romano, David. "El reparto del subsidio de 1282 entre las aljamas catalanas," *Sefarad,* XIII (1953), 75–76.

Rotger y Capllonch, Mateo. *Historia de Pollensa.* 3 vols. Palma de Mallorca: Armengual y Muntaner, 1897–1906.

Ruano, Eloy Benito. "España y las cruzadas," *Anales de historia antigua y medieval* [Buenos Aires], V (1951–1952), 92–120.

Rubió y Lluch, Antonio. "Algunes consideracions sobre la oratoria política de Catalunya en l'edat mitjana," *Estudis universitaris catalans,* III (1909), 213–214.

Ruiz, S. "Bérenger de Castelbisbal," *Dictionnaire d'histoire et de géographie ecclésiastiques* (*q.v.*), VIII, col. 371.

Ruiz-Moreno, Aníbal. "Los baños públicos en los fueros municipales españoles," *Cuadernos de historia de España* [Buenos Aires], III (1945), 152–157.

Rumeu de Armas, Antonio. *Historia de la previsión social en España, cofradías, gremios, hermandades, montepíos.* Madrid: Editorial Revista de derecho privado, 1944.

358   THE CRUSADER KINGDOM OF VALENCIA

Russell, J. C. "The Medieval Monedatge of Aragon and Valencia," *Proceedings of the American Philosophical Society*, CVI (1962), 483–504.

Sagarra y de Siscar, Fernando de. "Segells del temps de Jaume I," *Congrés I (q.v.)*, pp. 978–1040.

Salcedo Ferrándiz, Salvador. "Estudio histórico-jurídico de la Albufera de Valencia y de sus aprovechamientos," *Boletín de la sociedad castellonense de cultura*, XXXII (1956), 77–86, 232–244 [cont.].

Saldes. See primary sources, "Orden."

Sales y Alcalá, Agustín. *Historia del real monasterio de la Ssma. Trinidad, religiosas de Santa Clara, de la regular observancia, fuera los muros de la ciudad de Valencia, sacada de los originales de su archivo.* Valencia: Josef Estevan Dolz, 1761.

———— *Memorias históricas del antiguo santuario del santo sepulcro de Valencia.* Valencia: Josef Estevan Dolz, 1746.

Salvador. See Ferrer Salvador.

Salvat y Bové, Juan. *Tarragona y el gran rey Jaime I de Aragón (estudio histórico crítico literario), 1228–1929.* Tarragona: Diputación provincial, 1957.

Samper, Hipólito (de). *Montesa ilustrada. Origen, fundación, principios, institutos, casos, progresos, jurisdicción, derechos, privilegios, preeminencias, dignidades, oficios, beneficios, héroes y varones ilustres de la real, ínclita y nobilissima religión militar de N.S. Santa María de Montesa y San George de Alfama.* 2 vols. Valencia: Jerónimo Vilagrasa, 1669.

San Martín Payo, Jesús. *El diezmo eclesiástico en España hasta el siglo xii.* Palencia, Spain (for Gregorian University, Rome), 1940.

Sanahuja, Pedro. *Historia de la seráfica provincia de Cataluña.* Barcelona: Editorial Seráfica, 1959.

Sánchez Adell, José. "Carta puebla de Borriol, por Pedro Ximénez, señor de la misma villa," *Boletín de la sociedad castellonense de cultura*, XXV (1949), 155–156.

———— "Colección de documentos para la historia de Castellón," *Boletín de la sociedad castellonense de cultura*, XXVIII (1952), 405–410.

———— "Las murallas medievales de Castellón," *Boletín de la sociedad castellonense de cultura*, XXVIII (1952), 44–59.

Sánchez Albornoz, Claudio. *La España musulmana según los autores islamitas y cristianos medievales.* Second edition, revised. 2 vols. Barcelona: El Ateneo, 1960.

———— "The Frontier and Castilian Liberties," *New World Looks at its History (q.v.)*, pp. 27–46.

Sánchez Gozalbo, Ángel. "Bojar, Fredes y Corachar," *Boletín de la sociedad castellonense de cultura*, XXXVIII (1962), 349–376.

———— "Borriol y sus cartas pueblas," *Boletín de la sociedad castellonense de cultura*, XXII (1946), 17–20.

———— "Cálig y Ali del castillo de Cervera," *Boletín de la sociedad castellonense de cultura*, XX (1944), 105–107.

———— "Castillo de Cuevas de Avinromá," *Boletín de la sociedad castellonense de cultura*, XIV (1933), 288–299.

———— "Castillo de Culla," *Boletín de la sociedad castellonense de cultura*, XXV (1949), 304–325.

———— "El castillo de Polpis," *Boletín de la sociedad castellonense de cultura*, XIV (1933), 457–460.

———— "La población del termino de Cervera," *Boletín de la sociedad castellonense de cultura*, XXIII (1947), 391–393.

Sánchez Narbón, Carmen A. *La corona de Aragón y Segorbe, durante la dinastía catalana.* Castellón de la Plana: Diputación provincial, 1949. Also *Efemérides (q.v.).*

Sanchís Guarner, Manuel. *Introducción a la historia lingüistica de Valencia.* Preface, Ramón Menéndez Pidal. Biblioteca de filología, instituto de literatura y estudios filológicos, no. 1. Valencia: Institución Alfonso el Magnánimo, [1950].

—— *Els parlers romànics de València i Mallorca anteriors a la reconquista.* Second edition, revised. Biblioteca de filología, instituto de literatura y estudios filológicos, no. 6. Valencia: Diputación provincial, 1961.

Sanchís y Sivera, José. *La catedral de Valencia. Guía histórica y artística.* Valencia: F. Vives Mora, 1909.

—— *La diócesis valentina. Estudios históricos.* Anales del instituto general y técnico de Valencia. Valencia: La Voz valenciana, 1920.

—— *La diócesis valentina. Nuevos estudios históricos.* Anales del instituto general y técnico de Valencia. Valencia: La Voz valenciana, 1921.

—— "La enseñanza en Valencia en la época foral," *Boletín de la real academia de la historia,* CVIII (1936), 147–179; CIX (1937), 19–20.

—— *La iglesia parroquial de Santo Tomás de Valencia. Monografía histórico-descriptiva.* Valencia: Hijos de F. Vives Mora, 1913.

—— *Nomenclátor geográfico-eclesiástico de los pueblos de la diócesis de Valencia con los nombres antiguos y modernos de los que existen o han existido, notas históricas y estadisticas. . . .* Valencia: Casa de beneficencia, 1922.

—— "El obispo de Valencia Arnaldo de Peralta," *Boletín de la real academia de la historia,* LXXXII (1923), 40–64, 104–121.

—— "Vida íntima de los valencianos en la época foral," *Anales del centro de cultura valenciana,* VI (1933), 36–43, 109–120, 149–162; VII (1934), 41–53, 69–82; VIII (1935), 1–13.

—— See under primary sources, *Ordinatio;* "Para la historia."

Sancho Blanco, Amerio. "San Pedro Nolasco y sus primeros compañeros y la confirmación y constitución apostólica de la orden," *Estudios* [mercedarios], XII (1956), 233–264.

Sanz de Bremond, Manuel. "La iglesia arciprestal de Santa María de Castellón," *Boletín de la sociedad castellonense de cultura,* XXII (1946), 429–431; XXIII (1947), 301–313.

Sarthou Carreres, Carlos. *Datos para la historia de Játiva.* 4 vols. Játiva: Imp. Sucesora de Bellver, 1933–1935.

—— *Monasterios valencianos (su historia y su arte).* Valencia: Diputación provincial de Valencia, 1943.

—— *Provincia de Castellón.* In *Geografía general del reino de Valencia (q.v.).*

Sá Vall. See Vall.

Schlumberger, Gustave. "Le tombeau d'une imperatrice byzantine a Valence en Espagne." In his *Byzance et croisades, pages médiévales.* Paris: Paul Geuthner, 1927.

Schmitz, Philibert. *Histoire de l'ordre de Saint Benoît.* 7 vols. Maredsous: Editions de Maredsous, 1942–1956.

Schramm, Percy Ernst. "Der König von Aragon, seine Stellung im Staatsrecht (1276–1410)," *Historisches Jahrbuch,* LXXIV (1955), 99–123.

Segarra y Roca, Miguel. *Historia eclesiástica de Chert.* Sociedad castellonense de cultura, Obras de investigación histórica, no. 24. Tortosa: Algueró y Baíges, 1949.

Segura y Barreda, José. *Morella y sus aldeas.* 3 vols. Morella: F. Javier Soto, 1868.

Selgas, Fortunato de. "San Félix de Játiva y las iglesias valencianas del siglo xiii," *Boletín de la sociedad española de excursiones,* XI (1903), 50–59, 70–88.

Sevillano Colom, Francisco. "Bosquejo histórico de Oropesa," *Boletín de la sociedad castellonense de cultura,* XXVII (1951), 64–83, 89–109, 217–229, 343–352.

—— "De la institución del mustaçaf de Barcelona, de Mallorca y de Valencia," *Anuario de historia del derecho español,* XXIII (1953), 525–538; alternate title, *Estudios en homenaje a Don Eduardo de Hinojosa,* Publicaciones del instituto nacional de estudios jurídicos, series 1, no. 1, Madrid: Consejo superior de investigaciones científicas, 1953.

—— "El libro del mustaçaf de Catí," *Boletin de la sociedad castellonense de cultura,* XXX (1954), 220–228.

Shneidman, J. Lee. "Government in the Thirteenth Century Christian Kingdom of Valencia," *Hispania* [Paris], XVIII (1958), 181–189.

Smith, Robert S. "Fourteenth-Century Population Records of Catalonia," *Speculum,* XIX (1944), 495–501.

Sobrequés Vidal, Santiago. "Patriciado urbano," *Historia social y económica de España y América,* editor Jaime Vicens Vives, 4 vols. to date, Barcelona: Editorial Teide, 1957–   , II (1957), part 1.

Soldevila, Ferran. *Els grans reis del segle xiii. Jaume I. Pere el Gran.* Biografies catalanes, sèrie històrica, no. 5. Barcelona: Editorial Teide, 1955.

—— *Història de Catalunya.* 3 vols. Barcelona: Alpha, 1934–1935. Revised, augmented edition, 3 vols., 1962.

—— *Pere el Gran.* Institut d'estudis catalans, memòries de la secció històrico-arqueològica, nos. 11, 13, 16, 22. Two parts, in 4 vols., to date. Barcelona: Institut d'estudis catalans, 1950–[1962].

—— *Vida de Jaume I el Conqueridor.* Biblioteca biográfica catalana, no. 14. Barcelona: Editorial Aedos, 1958.

—— *Vida de Pere el Gran i d'Alfons el Liberal.* Biblioteca biográfica catalana, no. 35. Barcelona: Editorial Aedos, 1963.

Sorió, Baltasar. *De viris illustribus provinciae Aragoniae ordinis praedicatorum.* Editor, J. M. de Garganta Fábrega. Instituto valenciano de estudios históricos, fuentes de historia medieval, no. 1. Valencia: Consejo superior de investigaciones científicas, 1950.

Swift, E. D. *The Life and Times of James the First, the Conqueror, King of Aragon, Valencia and Majorca, Count of Barcelona and Urgel, Lord of Montpellier.* Oxford: Clarendon Press, 1894.

Teixidor, Josef. *Antigüedades de Valencia. Observaciones críticas donde con instrumentos auténticos se destruye lo fabuloso dejando en su debida estabilidad lo bien fundado* [1767]. Editor, Roque Chabás y Lloréns. Monumentos históricos de Valencia y su reino, no. 1. 2 vols. Valencia: Sociedad el archivo valentino, 1895.

—— *Capillas y sepulturas del real convento de predicadores de Valencia.* 3 vols. Valencia: Acción bibliográfica valenciana, [1755] 1949–1952.

Tejada, Francisco Elías de. *Las doctrinas políticas en la Cataluña medieval.* Barcelona: Ayma, 1950.

Tierney, Brian. *Medieval Poor Law, a Sketch of Canonical Theory and Its Application in England.* Berkeley: University of California, 1959.

Toledo Girau, José. *El castell i la vall d'Alfandech de Marinyèn des de sa reconquesta per Jaume I, fins la fundació del monestir de Valldigna per Jaume II.* Obras de investigación histórica, no. 11. Castellón de la Plana: Sociedad castellonense de cultura, 1936.

Toledo Girau, José. "Compendio histórico de Simat de Valldigna," *Anales del centro de cultura valenciana*, XXV (1957), 66–92.

—— "El monasterio de Valldigna, contribución al estudio de su historia durante el gobierno de sus abades perpetuos," *Anales del centro de cultura valenciana*, VIII (1935), 74–81 (cont.). Offprint as a book, Valencia: Hijo de F. Vives Mora, 1944.

Torelli, Luigi. *Secoli agostiniani overo historia generale del sacro ordine eremitano del gran dottore di santa chiesa S. Aurelio Agostino vescovo d'Hippona, divisa in tredeci secoli.* 7 vols. Bologna: G. B. Vaglierini, 1659–1682.

Tormo y Monzó, Elías. "La catedral gótica de Valencia," *III Congrés (q.v.)*, I, 1–36.

Torquebiau, P. "Chapitres de chanoines," *Dictionnaire de droit canonique (q.v.)*, III, cols. 530–595.

—— "Chanoines," *Dictionnaire de droit canonique (q.v.)*, III, cols. 471–488.

—— "Curie diocésaine," *Dictionnaire de droit canonique (q.v.)*, III, cols. 961-971.

Torres Balbás, Leopoldo. "Los adarves de las ciudades hispano-musulmanas," *Al-Andalus*, XII (1947), 164–193.

—— "Alcaicerías," *Al-Andalus*, XIV (1949), 431–455.

—— "Algunos aspectos de la casa hispano-musulmana: almacerías, algorfas y salezidos," *Al-Andalus*, XV (1950), 179–191.

—— "Atarazanas hispano-musulmanas," *Al-Andalus*, XI (1946), 175–209.

—— "El baño de Torres Torres (Valencia) y otras levantinas," *Al-Andalus*, XVII (1952), 176–186.

—— "Los baños públicos en los fueros municipales españoles," *Al-Andalus*, XI (1946), 443–445.

—— "Barbicanas," *Al-Andalus*, XVI (1951), 454–480.

—— "Cementerios hispano-musulmanas," *Al-Andalus*, XXII (1957), 131–191.

—— "Los contornos de las ciudades hispano-musulmanas," *Al-Andalus*, XV (1950), 437–486.

—— "Estructura de las ciudades hispano-musulmanas: la medina, los arrabales y los barrios," *Al-Andalus*, XVIII (1953), 149–177.

—— "Extensión y demografía de las ciudades hispano-musulmanas," *Studia islamica* [Paris], III (1955), 35–39.

—— "Mozarabías y juderías de las ciudades hispano-musulmanas," *Al-Andalus*, XIX (1954), 172–199.

—— "Plazas, zocos y tiendas de las ciudades hispano-musulmanas," *Al-Andalus*, XII (1947), 437–476.

—— "La población musulmana de Valencia en 1238," *Al-Andalus*, XVI (1951), 167–168.

—— "Rábitas hispano-musulmanas," *Al-Andalus*, XIII (1948), 475–491.

Torres López, Manuel. "La doctrina de las 'iglesias propias' en los autores españoles," *Anuario de historia del derecho español*, II (1925), 402–461.

Tourtoulon, Charles de. *Don Jaime I el Conquistador, rey de Aragón, conde de Barcelona, señor de Montpeller, segun las crónicas y documentos inéditos.* Second edition, revised in translation. Translator, Teodoro Llorente y Olivares. 2 vols. Valencia: José Doménech, 1874.

Tramoyeres Blasco, Luis. *Instituciones gremiales, su origen y organización en Valencia.* Valencia: Imprenta Doménech, 1889.

Traver García, Benito. *Historia de Villarreal.* Villarreal: Juan Botella, 1909.

Traver Tomás, Vicente. *Antigüedades de Castellón de la Plana, estudios histórico-monográficos de la villa y su vecindario riqueza y monumentos.* Castellón de la Plana: Ayuntamiento, 1958.

Vall, G. de Sá. "Rendición del castillo de Xivert," *Boletín de la sociedad castellonense de cultura*, XXIV (1948), 231–233.

Valls-Taberner, Ferran. "Los abogados en Cataluña durante la edad media," *Estudios histórico-jurídicos*. In his *Obras selectas* (*q.v.*), II, 281–318.

—— "Les doctrines politiques de la Catalunya medieval," *Estudios histórico-jurídicos*. In his *Obras selectas* (*q.v.*), II, 210–216.

—— *Obras selectas de Fernando Valls-Taberner*. Editors, Ramón d'Abadal y de Vinyals and J. E. Martínez Ferrando. Escuela de estudios medievales. 3 vols. Barcelona: Consejo superior de investigaciones científicas, 1952–1957.

—— *San Ramón de Penyafort*. Barcelona: Editorial Labor, 1936. Second edition. In his *Obras selectas* (*q.v.*), I, 209–380.

—— and F. Soldevila. *Historia de Cataluña*. Translator, Nuria Sales. In his *Obras selectas* (*q.v.*), III (double volume).

Vázquez Núñez, Guillermo. *Manual de historia de la orden de Nuestra Señora de la Merced (1218–1574)*. Toledo: Editorial Católica toledana, 1931.

—— See primary sources, *Actas*.

Vázquez de Parga, Luis. *La división de Wamba, contribución al estudio de la historia y geografía eclesiásticas de la edad media española*. Madrid: Consejo superior de investigaciones científicas, 1943.

Velasco y Santos, Miguel. *Reseña histórica de la universidad de Valencia. Su origen y fundación. Sus progresos y vicisitudes. Influjo que ha ejercido en el movimiento general científico y literario de España hasta el año de 1845*. Valencia: José Doménech, 1868.

Verlinden, Charles. "L'esclavage dans le monde ibérique medieval," *Anuario de historia del derecho español*, XI (1934), 283–448; XIII (1935), 361–424.

—— *L'esclavage dans l'Europe médiévale*. Publications of the Faculty of Letters, no. 19. One vol. to date. (I: *Péninsule iberique, France*). Bruges: University of Ghent, 1955– .

Véronne, Chantal de la. "Recherches sur le chiffre de la population musulmane de Valence en 1238 d'après le 'Repartimiento,'" *Bulletin hispanique*, LI (1949), 423–426.

Viard, Paul. *Histoire de la dîme ecclésiastique dans le royaume de France au xiie et xiiie siècles (1150–1313)*. Paris: A. Picard, 1912.

Vic, Claude de and Joseph Vaissète. *Histoire générale de Languedoc, avec des notes et les pièces justificatives*. Revised edition. Editors, J. Molinier *et al.* 18 vols. Toulouse: Éd. Privat, 1872–1904.

Viciana, [Rafael] Martín de. *Segunda parte de la crónica de Valencia*. Valencia: La sociedad valenciana de bibliófilos, [1564] 1881.

—— *Tercera parte de la crónica de Valencia*. Valencia: La sociedad valenciana de bibliófilos, 1882.

Vidal Tur, Gonzalo. *Un obispado español, el de Orihuela-Alicante*. Second edition. 2 vols. Alicante: Diputación provincial, 1961.

Vilaplana Gisbert, José. *Historia religiosa de Alcoy desde su fundación hasta nuestros días*. Alcoy: F. Botella Silvestre, 1892.

Villanueva, Jaime. *Viage literario a las iglesias de España*. 17 vols. in 22. Madrid: Imprenta Real, 1803–1852 [first five vols. published under pseudo-authorship of brother, Joaquín Lorenzo].

Villey, Michel. *La croisade, essai sur la formation d'une théorie juridique*. L'église et l'état au moyen age, no. 6. Paris: J. Vrin, 1942.

Vincke, Johannes. "Estado e iglesia en la historia de la corona de Aragón de los siglos xii, xiii y xiv," *VII Congrés d'història de la corona d'Aragó*, 3 vols., Barcelona: Viuda de Fidel Rodríguez Ferrán, 1962–1964, I, 267–285.

Vincke Johannes. "Die Hochschulpolitik der spanischen Domkapitel im Mittelalter," *Gesammelte Aufsätze zur Kulturgeschichte Spaniens* [Münster], IX (1954), 144–163.
—— "Kloster und Grenzpolitik in Katalonien–Aragon während des Mittelalters," *Gesammelte Aufsätze zur Kulturgeschichte Spaniens*, III (1931), 141–164.
—— "Das Patronatsrecht der aragonischen Krone," *Gesammelte Aufsätze zur Kulturgeschichte Spaniens*, X (1955), 55–95.
—— *Staat und Kirche in Katalonien und Aragon während des Mittelalters.* Spanische Forschungen der Görresgesellschaft, series 2, no. 1. Münster, Aschendorff, 1931.
—— *Zur Vorgeschichte der spanischen Inquisition. Die Inquisition in Aragon, Katalonien, Mallorca und Valencia während des 13 und 14 Jahrhunderts.* Beiträge zur Kirchen- und Rechtsgeschichte, no. 2. Bonn: P. Hanstein, 1941.
—— See primary sources, *Documenta selecta.*
Vives, Sebastián. "Memoria sobre la isla de Menorca durante el siglo décimo tercero," *Congrés I (q.v.)*, pp. 427–443.
Wadding, Luke. *Annales minorum seu trium ordinum a S. Francisco institutorum.* Third edition, revised. 31 vols. to date. Quaracchi: Tip. Barberá, 1931– .
Waley, Daniel. *The Papal State in the Thirteenth Century.* London: Macmillan, 1961.
Weckmann, Luis. *Las bulas alejandrinas de 1493 y la teoría política del papado medieval. Estudio de la supremacía papal sobre islas 1091–1493.* Publicaciones del Instituto de historia, no. 11. Mexico City: University of Mexico, 1949.
Wood, Susan. *English Monasteries and their Patrons in the Thirteenth Century.* Oxford Historical Series. London: Oxford University Press, 1955.
Ximeno, Vicente. *Escritores del reyno de Valencia chronológicamente ordenados desde el año MCCXXXVIII de la cristiana conquista de la misma ciudad, hasta el MDCCXLVII.* 2 vols. Valencia: J. Estevan Dolz, 1747–1749.
Zapater y López, Miguel Ramón. *Cister militante en la campaña de la iglesia contra la sarracena furia. Historia general de las ilustrísimas, ínclitas y nobilísimas cauallerías del templo de Salomón, Calatrava, Alcántara, Avies, Montesa y Christo.* 2 vols. Zaragoza: Agostín Verges, 1662.
Zaragoza Rubira, J. R. "Breve historia de los hospitales valencianos," *Medicina española*, XLVII (1962), 152–160.
Zunzunegui, José. "Concilios y sínodos medievales españoles," *Hispania sacra*, I (1948), 127–132.
Zurita y Castro, Jerónimo de. *Anales de la corona de Aragón.* 7 vols. Zaragoza: Colegio de S. Vicente Ferrer (vol. VII: University of Zaragoza), 1610–1621.
—— *Indices rerum ab Aragoniae regibus gestarum ab initiis regni ad annum mcdx.* Zaragoza: Dominicus a Portonariis de Ursinis, 1578.

NOTES

ABBREVIATIONS

ುುು

At first encounter, each item is usually given in full. Thereafter, most are cited by author, with short title. Exceptions to the latter rule are easily found from cross references in the bibliography. Frequent or difficult abbreviations of this latter class include:

ACCV: Anales del centro de cultura valenciana.
AHDE: Anuario de historia del derecho español.
Antigüedades de Valencia: Josef Teixidor, *Antigüedades de Valencia.*
Arch. Cath.: Archivo de la catedral de Valencia.
Arch. Cath. Huesca: Archivo de la catedral de Huesca.
Arch. Cath. Tortosa: Archivo de la catedral de Tortosa.
Arch. Cath. Zaragoza: Archivo de la catedral de Zaragoza.
Arch. Crown: Archivo de la corona de Aragón.
Arch. Munic. Val.: Archivo municipal, Ayuntamiento de Valencia.
Arch. Nac. Madrid: Archivo histórico nacional.
Arch. Nat. Paris: Archives nationales.
Arch. Vat.: Archivio segreto vaticano.
AST: Analecta sacra tarraconensia.
Aureum opus: L. de Alanya ed., *Aureum opus regalium priuilegiorum ciuitatis et regni Valentie.*
BH: Bulletin hispanique.
Bibl. Nac. Madrid: Biblioteca nacional (MSS).
Bibl. Nat. Paris: Bibliothèque nationale (MSS).
Bibl. Univ. Barcelona: Biblioteca universitaria, Universidad de Barcelona (MSS).
Bibl. Univ. Val.: Biblioteca universitaria, Universidad de Valencia (MSS).
BRABLB: Boletín de la real academia de buenas letras de Barcelona.
BRAH: Boletín de la real academia de la historia.
BSCC: Boletín de la sociedad castellonense de cultura.
Colección de cánones: J. Tejada y Ramiro ed., *Colección de cánones y de todos los concilios de la iglesia de España y de América.*
"Colección de cartas pueblas": settlement charters irregularly edited in *BSCC.*
Colección diplomática: A. Huici ed., *Colección diplomática de Jaime I.*
Collectio conciliorum: J. Sáenz de Aguirre ed., *Collectio maxima conciliorum omnis Hispaniae et novi orbis.*
Congrés I: Congrés d'història de la corona d'Aragó, dedicat al rey En Jaume I y a la seua época.
Congrés III: III Congrés d'història de la corona d'Aragó, dedicat al període compres entre la mort de Jaume I. . . .
Constitutiones sive ordinationes: M. Pérez de Miedes ed., *Constitutiones sive ordinationes insignis metropolitanae ecclesiae valentinae.*
"Constitutiones synodales": "Constitutiones synodales valentinae diocesis," in *Collectio maxima conciliorum,* V.
DDC: Dictionnaire de droit canonique.
DHGE: Dictionnaire d'histoire et de géographie ecclésiastiques.
Diócesis valentina: J. Sanchís Sivera, *La diócesis valentina* (I: *Estudios;* II: *Nuevos estudios*).
Documenta selecta: J. Vincke ed., *Documenta selecta mutuas civitatis arago-cathalaunicae et ecclesiae relationes illustrantia.*
EEMCA: Estudios de la edad media de la corona de Aragón.

Episcopologio valentino: R. Chabás, *Episcopologio valentino. Investigaciones históricas sobre el cristianismo en Valencia y su archidiócesis, siglos i á xiii.*

EUC: Estudis universitaris catalans.

Furs: Fori regni Valentiae [*Furs e ordinacions fetes per los gloriosos reys de Aragò als regnícols del regne de València*].

HS: Hispania sacra.

Itinerari: J. Miret y Sans, *Itinerari de Jaume I.*

JEH: Journal of Ecclesiastical History.

Llibre dels feyts: James I, *Crònica.*

Nomenclátor de Valencia: J. Sanchís Sivera, *Nomenclátor geográfico-eclesiástico de todos los pueblos de la diócesis de Valencia.*

Ordinatio ecclesiae valentinae: Trial records, ed. in *Diócesis valentina,* II.

Rationes decimarum: J. Rius Serra ed., *Rationes decimarum Hispaniae (1279–1280).*

Real Acad. Hist.: Biblioteca, Real academia de la historia, Madrid (MSS).

REDC: Revista española del derecho canónico.

"Repartiment" de Burriana: Ramón de María ed., *El "Repartiment" de Burriana y Villarreal.*

Repartimiento [*de Valencia*]: J. P. de Bofarull y Mascaró ed., *Repartimiento de Valencia;* also J. Ribera y Tarragó ed., *Repartimiento, edición fotocópica.*

Repartimiento de Sevilla: J. González ed., *Repartimiento de Sevilla. Estudio y edición.*

Viage literario: J. Villanueva ed., *Viage literario a las iglesias de España.*

NOTES

ﾒﾑﾐ

NOTES TO PREFACE

1. "The Closing of the Mediaeval Frontier, 1250-1350," *Speculum*, XXXIII (1958), 475.

2. C. Sánchez Albornoz, "The Frontier and Castilian Liberties," *The New World Looks at its History*, Second International Congress of Historians of the United States and Mexico, *Proceedings*, ed. A. R. Lewis and T. F. McGann, p. 30; previous quotation in editorial introduction, p. 26.

3. What Christian contemporaries of King James called the kingdom of Valencia comprises today substantially the three provinces of Valencia, Castellón, and much of Alicante. Some towns in these provinces did not belong to the kingdom, however, and conversely some kingdom towns later became geographically alienated. More important, the southern border of the kingdom under James I advanced a considerable distance to the south many years later under James II. In general this book treats of the Valencia kingdom of James I, thereby excluding consideration of towns like Alicante or Orihuela. But this policy will not be followed ungenerously; examples or discussions may occasionally incorporate fringe areas not really part of James's own Valencia.

4. Tentative studies have been made on the several frontiers in the Hispanic kingdoms. But little has yet been accomplished on this most striking period, the thirteenth century. The nearest approach to a really satisfactory study has been the volume of essays on aspects of the conquest and settlement of Seville, by Julio González, comprising volume one in his edition of the *Repartimiento* for that city. However, scholars like Miguel Gual Camarena, F. A. Roca Traver, Santiago Sobrequés Vidal, Leopoldo Torres Balbás, Julián Ribera Tarragó, Ramón de María, and others have been exploring facets of the subject as they relate to the Valencian scene (see bibliography). Studies on the Spanish frontier theme in other centuries, in connection with the church, include C. J. Bishko, "Salvus of Albelda and Frontier Monasticism in Tenth-Century Navarre," *Speculum*, XXIII (1948), 559-590; J. M. Lacarra, "La restauración eclesiástica en las tierras conquistadas por Alfonso el Batallador (1118-1134)," *Revista portuguesa de historia*, IV (1948-1949), 263-286; the brief pamphlet of A. C. Floriano, *Restauración del culto cristiano en Asturias en la iniciación de la reconquista* (Oviedo, 1949); scattered materials in Julio González' fine *El reino de Castilla en la época de Alfonso VIII*, 3 vols. (Madrid, 1960); Antonio Durán Gudiol, *La iglesia de Aragón durante los reinados de Sancho Ramírez y Pedro I (1062?-1104)* (Rome, 1962); and Ramón d'Abadal, "Origen y proceso de consolidación de la sede ribagorzana de Roda," *Estudios de edad media de la corona de Aragón*, V (1952), 7-82; see also the latter's *Els primers comtes catalans* (Barcelona, 1958), ch. 5. On current frontier studies for the realms of Aragon, see J. E. Martínez Ferrando's recent survey, "Estado actual de los estudios sobre la repoblación en los territorios de la corona de Aragón (siglos xii al xiv)," *VII Congrés d'història de la corona d'Aragó* (Barcelona, 1962-1964).

5. See especially my "Journey from Islam, Incipient Cultural Transition in the Conquered Kingdom of Valencia (1240-1280)," *Speculum*, XXXV (1960), 337-356; and my "Social Riots on the Christian-Moslem Frontier, Thirteenth-Century Valencia," *American Historical Review*, LXVI (1961), 378-400. On the Nolasco source see the qualification (which does not affect the truth of the point made here) in Chapter XIII, note 84 and text.

NOTES TO CHAPTER I. THE CHURCH AND THE
VALENCIAN FRONTIER

1. "Magna Valentia" was a contemporary term. One finds it in sources as different as Matthew Paris and the statutes of the Cistercian Order. See Matthew Paris, *Historia anglorum sive ut vulgo dicitur historia minor*, ed. F. Madden, Rerum brittanicarum medii aevi scriptores, 3 vols. (London, 1866–1869), II, 428, *an.* 1239, and II, 280, 317. See also his *Chronica maiora*, ed. H. R. Luard, same series, 7 vols. (London, 1872–1883), III, 517, 639, and V, 277. *Statuta capitulorum generalium ordinis cisterciensis ab anno 1116 ad annum 1786*, ed. J. M. Canivez, 8 vols. (Louvain, 1933–1941), III, 65, *an.* 1268, no. 44.

2. Arch. Nat. Paris, J: 589, Aragon II, no. 4 (April 23, 1241): "tota terra Regis Aragonum et suorum a Rodano usque Valenciam, et totum regnum Valencie et totum regnum Maioricarum." So writes the king in signing an alliance with the count of Toulouse, giving prominence to the conquest then going forward. The same set contains another copy (no. 3) on display in the archival museum. See, too, the *Layettes du trésor des chartes, séries inventaires et documents*, ed. A. Teulet, 5 vols. (Paris, 1863–1909), II, 445–446. King James himself describes a similar triumphal entry which he made into the fallen city of Murcia, from his camp to the main mosque, in his memoirs or *Llibre dels feyts*, ch. 450 (see below, bibliographical essay, for editions and validity; the Casacuberta edition is used here). King James's words on the Valencian entry are in ch. 284. The Catalan historian Desclot who wrote at the end of the thirteenth century says simply that the king entered Valencia with all his host. That the Valencian streets were narrow and tortuous is known from municipal legislation of the fourteenth century ("aquesta ciutat fo edificada per mòros a lur costum, estreta e meçquina"). The dates of conquest and of formal entry were recorded in the *Repartimiento de Valencia*, ed. P. de Bofarull y Mascaró, in *Colección de documentos inéditos del archivo general de la corona de Aragón*, 41 vols. (Barcelona, 1847–1910), XI, 221–222. A precious addition to help reconstruct these times is the recently published account by a Moslem eyewitness of the formal surrender ceremony; see "Un traité inédit d'Ibn al-Abbār à tendance chiite," ed. A. Ghedira, *Al-Andalus*, XXII (1957), 33n. The capitulation of Valencia may conveniently be found in the *Colección de documentos inéditos para la historia de España*, ed. Martín Fernández Navarrete, M. Salvá, *et alii*, 112 vols. (Madrid, 1842–1896), XVIII, 84–86, doc. 26. It is just possible that the city was already partly filled with Christians by the time of the formal entry. There is a dubious but colorful account of the entry in the early historian of Valencia, Gaspar Escolano, *Décadas de la historia de la insigne y coronada ciudad y reino de Valencia*, ed. J. B. Perales, 3 vols. (Valencia: [1610–1611] 1878–1880), II, *lib.* VII, ch. 261; and another in Pedro Antonio Beuter, *Primera parte de la coronica general de toda España y especialmente del reyno de Valencia* (Valencia, 1604), pp. 215–216.

3. "Lamentons-nous sur ce malheur immense," the words of an eyewitness to the subjugation of Valencia, Abu al-Muṭarrif Ibn 'Amīra; see in al-Ḥimyarī, *La péninsule ibérique au moyen-âge d'après le Kitāb ar-Rawḍ al-mi'ṭār . . .*, ed.-tr. E. Lévi-Provençal (Leiden, 1938), p. 64. "Divulgata est per universum orbem tante acquisicio civitatis," says the Latin adaptation of King James's autobiography rendered by Peter (Pere) Marsili in 1313 (MSS Bibl. Univ. Barcelona, *lib.* III, *c.* 42).

4. Arch. Vat., Reg. Vat. 19 (Gregory IX), fol. 68r, ep. 363 (Jan. 8, 1239). An original is also in Arch. Crown, Bulas, legajo VI (Gregory IX), no. 19 (same date). Only a notice of this document is given in *Les registres de Grégoire IX, recueil des bulles de ce pape, publiées ou analysées d'après les manuscrits originaux du Vatican*, ed. Lucien Auvray, 3 vols. (Paris, 1896–1955), II, no. 4,703.

5. Jerónimo Zurita, *Anales de la corona de Aragón*, 7 vols. (Zaragoza, 1610–1621), I, *lib.* III, *c.* 32. Envoys from Italy arrived in June of 1238, during the siege of Valencia, and signed a treaty with King James; see Charles de Tourtoulon, *Don Jaime I el Conquistador, rey de Aragón, conde de Barcelona, señor de Montpeller, según las crónicas y documentos inéditos,* 2nd ed., revised in translation, tr. Teodoro Llorente, 2 vols. (Valencia, 1874), I, 310.

6. Lluís Nicolau y d'Olwer, "Jaume I y los trovadors provensals," *Congrés d'història de la corona d'Aragó, dedicat al rey En Jaume I y a la seua época,* 2 vols. but consecutive pagination to form one vol. (Barcelona, 1909–1913), pp. 389–390, 392, 395. Bertran de Born the younger wrote his "Guerr' e pantais vei et afan" as Valencia was about to fall, urging James to abandon Valencia and march to southern France. Bernat de Rovenhach rebuked James in 1241. The troubadours painted James as a traitor and a laggard knight who left his father unavenged and allowed his rich heritage in Languedoc to slip from him. Their outcry was renewed at the time of the treaty of Corbeil.

7. *Chronica maiora,* III, 517: "rex Christianissimus, magnificus et in armis strenuissimus, dominus rex Arragonum, cum suis amicis adeo urbem magnam Valentiam guerra cruentissima aggravavit ut undique arctata . . . est compulsa."

8. José Sanchís y Sivera, *La catedral de Valencia, guía histórica y artística* (Valencia, 1909), p. 372, with document given in note; "ecclesiam vestram sacro volentes exenio decorare vobis unam de spinis sacrosancte corone domini nostri Christi per datores presentium in signum dilectionis transmittimus specialis." The date is March 1256, an understandable procrastination of congratulations, given the previous tensions between Aragon and France; the thorn is still at the cathedral. The putative crown came into Louis' hands, from Constantinople via the Venetians, only in 1239; he built for it that gem of Gothic architecture, the Sainte Chapelle.

9. Francisco Carreras y Candi, "La creuada a terra santa," *Congrés I,* p. 106.

10. *Llibre dels feyts,* ch. 457. King James's envoys to the khan returned to Valencia with two influential Tartars and an offer of alliance against the Moors *(ibid.,* chs. 457, 475, 481). Cf. Zurita, *Anales,* I, *lib.* III, *c.* 71.

11. According to the junior contemporary Raymond Muntaner (*Crònica catalana,* ed. Antonio de Bofarull y Brocá [Barcelona, 1860], ch. 13).

12. Arch. Nat. Paris, J: 587, Aragon I, no. 11 (July 6, 1262); *Layettes,* IV, 42–43.

13. Arch. Vat., Reg. Vat. 21 (Innocent IV), fol. 213v (July 10, 1245): "grandi gaudio exultavit ecclesia cum Regnum Valentie de sarracenorum manibus fuit ereptum." Also published in *Les registres d'Innocent IV publiées ou analysées d'après les manuscrits originaux du Vatican,* ed. Élie Berger, 4 vols. (Paris, 1884–1921), I, no. 1,375.

14. *Llibre dels feyts,* ch. 129; Sancho of Orta (Duerta) is speaking to James.

15. *Ibid.,* ch. 127; Blasco (Blaise) of Alagón is speaking to the king. The early ambitions and campaigns by the Aragonese kings in Valencia have been carefully studied by Miguel Gual Camarena, "Precedentes de la reconquista valenciana," *Estudios medievales,* I (1952), 167–246; a register of the pertinent documents has been drafted and appended (pp. 213–246).

16. *Kitāb ar-Rawḍ,* pp. 59–69.

17. The Moslem background is delineated by Isidro de las Cagigas in his *Los mudéjares,* 2 vols. (Madrid, 1948–1949), II, 331–370. A brief historical background is furnished by E. Lévi-Provençal in his "Valencia," in the *Encyclopaedia of Islam,* 4 vols. and supplement (Leiden, 1913–1938), IV, 1,070–1,071. See too the biography of the Moslem ruler of Valencia, Sīd Abū Saʿīd, by Roque Chabás y Lloréns, "Çeid Abu Çeid," *El archivo,* V (1891), 143–166, 288–304, 362–376.

18. Brief accounts of the crusade may be found in Ferran Soldevila, *Història de Catalunya*, 3 vols. (Barcelona, 1934–1935), I, 225 ff.; in the revised edition (3 vols., 1962), I, 279 ff., 290 ff.; F. Valls-Taberner and F. Soldevila, *Historia de Cataluña,* tr. Nuria Sales, 3 vols. (Barcelona, 1955–1957), in *Obras selectas de Fernando Valls-Taberner*, ed. R. d'Abadal and J. E. Martínez Ferrando, 3 vols. (Barcelona, 1952–1957), III (double volume), I, 159–160. R. B. Merriman, *The Rise of the Spanish Empire in the Old World and in the New*, 4 vols. (New York, 1918–1936), I, 293 ff.; H. J. Chaytor, *A History of Aragon and Catalonia (London*, 1933), ch. 6; Ferdinand Lot, *L'art militaire et les armées au moyen âge en Europe et dans le proche orient*, 2 vols. (Paris, 1946), II, 302–307; Teodoro Llorente, *Valencia*, España, sus monumentos y artes, naturaleza y historia, nos. 24 and 25, 2 vols. (Barcelona, 1887–1889), I, chs. 3 and 4; Vicente Boix, *Historia de la ciudad y reino de Valencia*, 3 vols. (Valencia, 1845–1847), I, 118 ff. and 505 ff. *passim*; F. Moscardó Cervera, *Breu compendi de la història del regne de València* (Valencia, 1953), ch. 3. See too the biographies of the king (below, note 21). Useful for this place and time is the essay by José M. Font y Rius, "La reconquista y repoblación de Levante y Murcia," in J. M. Font y Rius *et alii*, *La reconquista española y la repoblación del país* (Zaragoza, 1951), pp. 85–126; and Santiago Sobrequés Vidal, "Patriciado urbano," part 1 of Vol. II in *Historia social y económica de España y América* (4 vols. to date, Barcelona, 1957–   ), ch. 1, with a full account of the repopulating.

19. Percy Schramm draws a parallel between modern Belgium and the two peoples combining in conquered Valencia: "so stösst man auf das moderne Belgien, dieses halb französisch-wallonische, halb flämisch-niederländische Land, dessen Bevölkerung heute unzweifelhaft zu einer Nation zusammengewachsen ist" ("Der König von Aragon, seine Stellung im Staatsrecht (1276–1410)," *Historisches Jahrbuch*, LXXIV [1955], 106). See too J. Lee Shneidman, "Government in the Thirteenth Century Christian Kingdom of Valencia," *Hispania*, XVIII (1958), 181–189. The "Cazorla" treaty was signed not at Cazorla but at an insignificant frontier post Gazala, Cacala, or Cazolo (González, *Alfonso VIII*, I, 814n.).

20. *Crónica de San Juan de la Peña*; in the edition by Tomás Ximénez de Embún, *Historia de la corona de Aragón (la más antigua de que se tiene noticia) conocida generalmente con el nombre de crónica de San Juan de la Peña* (Zaragoza, 1876), p. 159. See too the edition of the Latin document only, by Antonio Ubieto Arteta (Valencia, 1961).

21. Standard biographies include Tourtoulon's *Jaime el Conquistador*; E. D. Swift, *The Life and Times of James the First, the Conqueror, King of Aragon, Valencia and Majorca, Count of Barcelona and Urgel, Lord of Montpellier* (Oxford, 1894); C. R. Beazley, *James the First of Aragon* (Oxford, 1890); Ferran Soldevila, *Els grans reis del segle xiii, Jaume I, Pere el Gran* (Barcelona, 1955); and the latter's *Vida de Jaume I el Conqueridor* (Barcelona, 1958). Soldevila has an ampler life of Peter in progress, *Pere el Gran*, Institut d'estudis catalans, memòries de la secció històrico-arqueològica, nos. 11, 13, 16, 22, two parts in 4 vols. to date (Barcelona, 1950–[1962]).

22. This is quoted from the French text attached to his map; the map in my possession has been detached from the book, and bibliographical detail is lacking except for date. Willem Janszoon Blaeu lived from 1571 to 1638. The kingdom of Valencia was not yet at its full extent in King James's day; these figures take it at its fullest. Sobrequés Vidal has reckoned the Valencian and Balearic conquests as increasing James's realms from 85,000 to 196,000 square kilometers, Majorca accounting for 3,600 of these; the Alicantine lands acquired by James II in 1304 added some 6,500 square kilometers more ("Patriciado urbano," pp. 8–12).

23. The frontier kingdom represented an opportunity for the king and a counter-

weight to reactionary feudal forces. As Schramm cogently remarks, "Jaime I hatte gewusst was er tat; denn im Neuland war seine Stellung wesentlich stärker als in dem traditionsgesättigten Aragon" ("Der König von Aragon," p. 106).

24. *Gesta comitum barcinonensium* (written ca. 1290); in the *Marca hispanica sive limes hispanicus, hoc est, geographica et historica descriptio Cataloniae, Ruscinonis et circumiacentium populorum*, ed. Pierre de Marca and E. Baluze (Paris, 1688), col. 555; and in a modern edition, eds. L. Barrau Dihigo and J. Massó y Torrents, Cròniques catalanes, no. 2 (Barcelona, 1925), p. 58: "omnes nationes barbaras dicti regni."

25. This indivisible union of church and society, and its exclusiveness, is the theme of Clement IV in his letter of 1266 to King James urging that he drive the Moors from his realms like poison from one's body. Arch. Vat., Reg. Vat. 29a (Clement IV), vols. 10r-11v, ep. 18 (n.d., *an.* 1266); only a notice is supplied in *Les registres de Clement IV (1265-1268), recueil des bulles de ce pape*, ed. E. Jordan (Paris, 1893-1945), no. 848. A version is given by Jerónimo Zurita, *Indices rerum ab Aragoniae regibus gestarum ab initiis regni ad annum MCDX* (Zaragoza, 1578), *lib.* II, pp. 145-146.

26. *Colección diplomática de Jaime I, el Conquistador*, ed. A. Huici, 3 vols. (Valencia, 1916-1922), doc. 1,341 (Nov. 26, 1270): "e no trobarem que en tot lo regne de Valencia age poblat de Christians oltra XXX milia homens e per zo quar nos havem vist qu'el regne no ha son compliment d'omens ni de gent, volemlo y fer; car segons semblanza nostra ben deuria aver cen millia Christians en el regne de Valencia." These are probably family heads or males—the total population would be higher (see Chapter V, notes 54, 55, 165-168, with text). Numbers of documents in the royal archives complain about non-possession of grants, and of nonresidence. The *Repartimiento* has any number of revocations of grant "quia ad diem non fuit assignatam"—even for monasteries (pp. 270, 274). Not including obvious repetitions, and counting as single units whole groups, there still were fifty revocations due to failure to claim for the year 1240 alone; this is a third of all the grants recorded for that year. Similar difficulties in populating recovered lands may be seen in the case of a frontier bishop in Portugal at this time, who feared a return of Moorish power because no one could be induced to settle the newly taken land or to man its castles (Arch. Vat., Reg. Vat. 18, Gregory IX, fol. 305r, ep. 154, July 5, 1237; only a notice of this document is given in Auvray, *Registres*, II, no. 3,730).

27. James gave this counsel to the king of Castile, that if he could not keep the favor of all parties he should choose to have on his side "the church and the people of the cities" as being both more loyal and more powerful than the knights; "for with these two he would destroy the others" (*Llibre dels feyts*, ch. 498).

28. *Fori regni Valentiae* (Monzón, 1548), *lib.* II, *rub.* VI, *c.* 23; this is the Romanized law code given by James I to Valencia and hereafter cited under its Catalan title *Furs*. Here the resistance was from towns and nobles who disliked the influence of Roman law, as we see in the *Llibre dels feyts*. Even Latin was forbidden in courts, as well as canon and civil lawyers; see the code of municipal privileges *Aureum opus regalium priuilegiorum ciuitatis et regni Valentie cum historia cristianissimi regis Jacobi ipsius primi conquistatoris*, ed. Luis de Alanya (Valencia, 1515), doc. 65, fol. 19r,v, and doc. 62, fol. 13r,v.

29. *Furs, lib.* IX, *rub.* XIX, *c.* 7. Custom law kept at least some pastors as notaries; see Chapter V, note 8. Also an exception might be made, thus underlining the general prohibition; in 1261 the Valencian monastery of Benifasá was given a privilege by which the abbot could appoint a monk as notary for wills and for monastery business "qui faciat . . . sua propria manu omnia instrumenta"

(Arch. Nac. Madrid, Clero: Castellón: Benifasá, carp. 423, June 9, 1261). Cf. the source cited in Joaquín Miret y Sans, *Itinerari de Jaume I "el Conqueridor"* (Barcelona, 1918), p. 559n.

30. *Colección diplomática*, doc. 1,038 *bis* (Aug. 28, 1238): "cognoscentes quod ad exheredacionem nostram et nostrorum evidentissime . . . vertitur, quando nostri subditi hereditates . . . ad milites transferunt vel ad loca religiosa." See also *Furs* (*lib.* IV, *rub.* XIX, *c.* 8), forbidding alienation to clerics. The *Repartimiento* has a place and contract ("locum et vocem") given to another, because the owner had sold them to clerics ("eo quia vendidit eas clericis," p. 483). In the contemporary reorganizing of Seville, the cathedral was exempted from a similar prohibition against alienation to the church (*Repartimiento de Sevilla, estudio y edición*, ed. Julio González, 2 vols. [Madrid, 1951], I, 328). The loss of taxes and feudal services alone in such cases could be substantial.

31. *Aureum opus*, doc. 38, fol. 12v (June 19, 1251).

32. *Furs, lib.* III, *rub.* V. *c.* 8.

33. The figure "bismille ecclesias in terris quas abstulit sarracenis" is found for instance in the mid-fourteenth-century *Crónica de San Juan de la Peña* (Ximénez ed., p. 155; Ubieto ed., p. 152); of the churches in the Valencian kingdom it says: "et ilico hedificavit ecclesiam cathedralem et alias multas ecclesias in dictis civitate et regno," plus the monasteries and friaries. Sanchís Sivera repeats the 2,000 number, and tries to reduce its improbability somewhat by speaking of it as implying also monasteries and hospitals (*La diócesis valentina, estudios históricos* [Valencia, 1920], and *La diócesis valentina, nuevos estudios históricos* [Valencia, 1921], cited in this book as a single work, II, 137). Even allowing half of this number to the Balearics and fringe conquests, this would mean an average of one church—counting all religious establishments—for every thirty souls or seven households in the realm, by the end of his life, though of course he was also building for the future. The figure, which is often cited today, must be taken as quite exaggerated though with a good core of truth: while James was king, churches multiplied over the conquered area in bewildering number. At any rate, royal foundations seem to have consisted largely in assigning to Christians the Moslem mosque of a locality and its supporting properties. It is interesting to note that the mere hasty redecorating of a captured mosque leads King James to speak proudly of "l'esglesia que haviem hedificada" (*Llibre dels feyts*, ch. 451). Still, even a sketchy founding was expensive, involving the gift of furnishings and regular revenues. Shortly after Valencia's conquest a legal document uses the same terminology: "contulit ecclesias in diocesi Valentie constructas Archiepiscopo Terraconensi" (*Ordinatio ecclesiae valentinae*, p. 232; on this citation see Chapter XIV, note 1).

34. "Jacobus fortunatus," his contemporaries called him (*Crónica de San Juan de la Peña*, Ximénez ed., p. 145; Ubieto ed., p. 143; Martín de Viciana, *Tercera parte de la crónica de Valencia* [Valencia, 1882], p. 66); they applied it in a military and more passive sense.

35. The history of the medieval church of Valencia has yet to be written. Studies have appeared on isolated aspects—the labors of Teixidor, Chabás, Sanchís Sivera, and Olmos Canalda have been noted in the preface. Only two general histories of the church in Spain have been published, both of them necessarily brief for this period and region, and both now badly dated: Pius Bonifacius Gams, *Die Kirchengeschichte von Spanien*, 3 vols. in 5 (Graz, [1863–1879] 1956), and Vicente de la Fuente, *Historia eclesiástica de España*, 2nd ed. revised, 6 vols. (Madrid, 1873–1875). The general relations between church and state in this part of Spain, and incidental background, are in Johannes Vincke, *Staat und Kirche in*

Katalonien und Aragon während des Mittelalters, Spanische Forschungen der Görresgesellschaft, series 2, no. 1 (Münster, 1931).

36. César Tomás Laguía, "La erección de la diócesis de Albarracín," *Teruel,* X (1953), 217: "ex hoc non solum fidelibus poterant spiritualia commoda provenire sed etiam paganorum incursibus facilius obviari."

37. Eventually eight dioceses would be represented by at least a foothold, especially as the kingdom's limits were altered (Valencia, Cartagena, Orihuela, Zaragoza, Tortosa, Teruel, Segorbe, Cuenca); but the bulk of the realm would remain the diocese of Valencia. See the map in F. Carreras y Candi, *Geografía general del reino de Valencia,* 5 vols. (Barcelona, 1920–1927), general volume on realm, facing p. 120. The diocese of Valencia later became an archdiocese. At least three of its bishops are not likely to be forgotten: the Borgia pope, Alexander VI; the "good" Borgia pope, Callistus III; and the rascally Cesare Borgia himself; Borgias occupied the episcopal throne here without a break from 1429 to 1512.

38. *Crónica de San Juan de la Peña* (Ximénez ed., p. 157; Ubieto ed., p. 154): "beatus Georgius cum magno exercitu militiae coelestis apparuit, cuius auxilio Christiani nullo eorum in bello mortuo obtinere triumphum." See Zurita, *Anales,* I, *lib.* III, *c.* 27. See too the *Golden Legend of Jacobus de Voragine,* ed.-tr. Granger Ryan and Helmut Ripperger, 2 vols. (London, 1941), I, 237–238.

39. The oldest account of the miracle of the corporals, taken in 1340 from elders under oath, is transcribed by Rafael Esteban Abad, together with commentary and bibliography in his *Estudio histórico-político sobre la ciudad y comunidad de Daroca* (Teruel, 1959), pp. 74–77. Sanchís Sivera has a long discussion in his *Diócesis valentina,* II, 171–189, with bibliographical notes.

40. *Aureum opus,* doc. 23, fols. 10v–11r (May 8, 1247): "in statum debitum iuxta Christianorum morem in melius reformare, ut abiectis vetustatibus et moribus perfidorum . . . monetam cudi fecimus." It is to bear the sign "salutifere crucis." James had other motives, also, and he would mint Arabic coins to promote trade here; the document is nevertheless instructive.

41. Document cited in note 4.

42. Bernat Desclot, *Crònica,* ed. M. Coll y Alentorn, 4 vols. (Barcelona, 1949–1950); my translations are from F. L. Critchlow's *Chronicle of the Reign of King Pedro III of Aragon,* 2 vols. (Princeton, N.J., 1928–1934); I, ch. 28 on the archdeacon. *Llibre dels feyts* of King James, chs. 53, 62, 207 for the others. William of Aguiló offers the same sort of argument as the king's in Desclot, ch. 49.

43. *Llibre dels feyts,* chs. 47 (first quote, Majorca crusade), 57, 273. In ch. 430, before a battle in the kingdom of Valencia, James tells his barons that "battles are won quickly, and God gives them to those to whom He wants to give them." But one notes that the king in his campaign leaves no detail of supply, plan, or reconnaissance to chance. Américo Castro has some interesting comments on this mentality and its Moslem coloring (*The Structure of Spanish History,* tr. E. L. King [Princeton, N.J., 1954]; e.g. p. 219). One fears, however, that he is to some extent a victim of the fallacy of the single source: cf. the review of Kurt Georg Cram's *Judicium belli,* in the *American Historical Review,* LXI (1956), 1,005. To James, "faith without works is worth nothing" (*Llibre dels feyts,* ch. 1); he harps upon this Pauline idea of good works here and elsewhere (e.g. again in ch. 48), making it clear from the context that warfare against the enemies of the people of God is what he has in mind. The wider background to this providentialist spirit here is studied by Francisco Elías de Tejada in his *Las doctrinas políticas en la Cataluña medieval* (Barcelona, 1950), e.g. pp. 48–51.

44. *Llibre dels feyts,* chs. 282, 443, 219, 84. James says St. George commonly appeared on such occasions. To the Castilians, who saw a similar knight on a

white horse at the battle of Jérez against Ibn Hūd, the figure was St. James (see Lot, *L'art militaire*, II, 294n.). On St. George as patron of Catalonia see the small book of Ramón d'Alós-Moner, *Sant Jordi, patró de Catalunya*, in Colecció Sant Jordi, series 3, no. 1 (Barcelona, 1922).

45. *Llibre dels feyts*, chs. 63, 69, 81, 83–84; Desclot, *Crònica*, ch. 36 (Moncada).

46. *Llibre dels feyts*, chs. 194, 389–390. The friar was a Navarrese and told James it had "weighed heavily" upon him that God should choose a foreign king, i.e. an Aragonese. Unimpressed by supernal evidences, the knights quarreled with the king and rode out of town in a body to form a league against him.

47. *Ibid.*, chs. 388, 460.

48. *Ibid.*, ch. 224 (at Almenara in Valencia). James takes chaplains with him on his campaigns. His field chapel appears at the conquest of Murcia, for instance, where he uses the furnishings in the mosque of the conquered city (ch. 450). He speaks of "all the clergy" attached to the army (ch. 450). His men commonly confess and receive Communion before battle, e.g. at the siege of Majorca, the battle of Puig in Valencia, at Almenara, etc.; see also Desclot, *Crònica*, chs. 5, 36, 49, etc. This argues a good supply of priests, as distinguished from other clergy, with the armies. James's chaplains Peter and Matthew received land grants in the *Repartimiento*, p. 152.

49. These were not the only failings which raised the popes' ire; see José M. Pou y Martí, "Conflictos entre el pontificado y los reyes de Aragón en el siglo xiii," in the symposium *Sacerdozio e regno da Gregorio VII a Bonifacio VIII*, Miscellanea historiae pontificiae, vol. 18 (Rome, 1954), pp. 139–160.

50. Appended by Pascual de Gayangos to the English translation by John Forster of the *Llibre dels feyts* (*The Chronicle of James I, King of Aragon, Surnamed the Conqueror . . .*, 2 vols. [London: 1883], I, 150n.). (On Nolasco and his documentation cf. below, Chapter XIII, note 84 and text.) *Llibre*, ch. 237 (vow); Desclot, *Crònica*, ch. 30 (vigil, before Majorca crusade).

51. Josef Teixidor, *Antigüedades de Valencia, observaciones críticas donde con instrumentos auténticos se destruye lo fabuloso dejando en su debida estabilidad lo bien fundado* [1767], ed. Roque Chabás, 2 vols. (Valencia, 1895), II, 10, doc. of April 11, 1239 with special reference to the Dominicans.

52. *El "Repartiment" de Burriana y Villarreal*, ed. Ramón de María (Valencia, 1935), p. 41, *carta puebla* of Burriana (Jan. 1, 1235): "qui intendunt quotidie ad exaltacionem nominis Christiani."

53. Document cited in note 13 (July 10, 1245).

54. Arch. Vat., Reg. Vat. 15 (Gregory IX), fol. 43v (Dec. 23, 1230): the same "veniam peccatorum quam haberent si proficiscerentur in subsidium terre sancte." Auvray, *Registres*, I, no. 524.

55. Arch. Vat., Reg. Vat. 17 (Gregory IX), fol. 56r,v (June 11, 1233). Auvray, *Registres*, I, no. 1,401. The concept of colonization as a species of crusade seems not to have been studied, even in the otherwise complete monograph of Michel Villey, *La croisade, essai sur la formation d'une théorie juridique* (L'église et l'état au moyen âge, no. 6 [Paris, 1942]).

56. Arch. Nac. Madrid, Ords. Milits., Montesa, R18 (Sept. 6, 1210): "multa loca a Sarracenis possessa et idolis dicata, Dei sacrificiis et christiano cultui refferantur et reformentur." The father of King James is giving to the Hospitallers, for this purpose, a Burriana grant to encourage its conquest and settlement. The crusade spirit in its wider Spanish setting is a principal theme of J. Goñi Gaztambide's *Historia de la bula de la cruzada en España*, Victoriensia no. 4 (Vitoria, 1958), esp. chs. 2, 3; see too on this period chs. 6, 7.

NOTES TO CHAPTER II. CATHEDRAL, BISHOP, AND CHAPTER

1. *Summa ad manuscriptorum fidem recognita et emendata sacrorum canonum . . .* (Verona, 1744), *lib.* III, *tit.* XXVII, no. 4, p. 331 : "multa enim alia, quae difficile esset enumerare, quum ipse sit preordinator in cunctis." Though they are not cited in this chapter, there are a large number of copies of Valencia cathedral documents concerning administration, finances, and privileges in Bibl. Univ. Val., MS codex 145, e.g. docs. 17, 20, 22; cf. also codex 799. On dioceses at this period see W. M. Plöchl, *Geschichte des Kirchenrechts*, 3 vols. (Vienna, 1959–1960), II, 155 ff. and 141 ff.; more briefly H. E. Feine, *Kirchenliche Rechtsgeschichte* (Weimar, 1955), pp. 321 ff.

2. E. Mayer, *Historia de las instituciones sociales y políticas de España y Portugal durante los siglos v a xiv*, 2 vols. (Madrid, 1925–1926), II, 288–289.

3. They were all called to the Valencian parliament of 1301, for example, as was the cathedral chapter (*Documenta selecta mutuas civitatis arago-cathalaunicae et ecclesiae relationes illustrantia*, ed. Johannes Vincke [Barcelona, 1936], doc. 94, Nov. 18, 1301).

4. See the sympathetic survey of the problem by Isacio Rodríguez, "Los orígines históricos de la exención de los regulares," *Revista española de derecho canónico*, X (1955), 583–608, and XI (1956), 243–271. The Valencian phases of the struggle are considered below in the chapters on the Orders.

5. Ramón Menéndez Pidal, *La España del Cid*, 4th ed. revised, 2 vols. (Madrid, 1947), p. 807. Quote from *Llibre dels feyts*, ch. 365. "In all the towns which were big, which God granted us to win from the Saracens, we built a church of Our Lady St. Mary" (ch. 450). There was no further title for the cathedral like the Assumption as some later writers imagined (*Viage literario a las iglesias de España*, ed. J. Villanueva, 17 vols. in 22 [Madrid, 1803–1852], I, 30–31). See also Ramón de María, "Jaime I dedica Peñíscola a Santa María y dota su culto," *BSCC*, XXI (1945), 233–235.

6. Sanchís Sivera, *Catedral de Valencia*, p. 14.

7. *Aureum opus*, doc. 28 of series for Peter III (1283).

8. *Ibid.*, doc. 35, fol. 11Cr,v (*an.* 1250); Mass was to be stopped before the Gospel, while they swore an oath before the bailiff and by this act assumed office.

9. *Llibre dels feyts*, ch. 365.

10. *Colección diplomática*, doc. 1,353 (July 28, 1271): "ad plateam Sancte Marie maiorem ad ecclesiam eiusdem."

11. "Anno Domini M/CCLXII—X kalend. Ju / lii fuit positus primarius lapis / in Ecclesia Beate Marie / sedis Valentine per / venerabilem patrem / fratrem Andream / tertium Va / lentine Civitatis Episcopum" (inscription on the cornerstone, which disappeared in the eighteenth century; see *Antigüedades de Valencia*, I, 222, where Teixidor has copied it, and the slightly different version in Sanchís Sivera, *Catedral de Valencia*, p. 5). The cathedral, like the previous mosque, was on the site of the Roman forum.

12. Elías Tormo y Monzó has published a long study of this first stage of the construction, drawing upon archeological and artistic analogies ("La catedral gótica de Valencia," *III Congrés d'història de la corona d'Aragó, dedicat al període compres entre la mort de Jaume I i la proclamació del rey Don Ferrán d'Antequera*, 2 vols. [Valencia, 1923], I, 1–36). Some conclusions of Sanchís Sivera (*Catedral de Valencia*, e.g. p. 8) modify those of Tormo; he believes the building was begun in Romanesque-Byzantine style. On the Valencia cathedral see also J. H. Harvey, *The Cathedrals of Spain* (London, 1957), esp. p. 173; and the useful but very small volume by F. Almela y Vives, *La catedral de Valencia*, in the series

Colecció Sant Jordi, series 2, no. 5 (Barcelona, 1927). There is a stimulating comparative study by Pierre Lavedan in his *L'architecture gothique religieuse en Catalogne, Valence et Baléares* (Paris, 1935), ch. 2.

13. Arch. Cath., perg. 2,366 (Mar. 25, 1249): "porticum, archus, portalia, anuanum, bescalinum, pontem nec alium quodlibet cohopertum." See also *Aureum opus*, doc. 27, fol. 11A (*an.* 1249): "sit semper undique libera et discohoperta omnino," without narrowing the streets, "in tota via et in toto circuitu vel orbicularitate ecclesie beate Marie sedis Valentie." The position of the cathedral on a height of ground, and the open plazas around, are spoken of by José Rodrigo Pertegás, "La urbe valenciana en el siglo xiv," *Congrés III*, pp. 319–322. Testaments have requests to be buried "in claustro" here (e.g. Arch. Cath. Val., perg. 5,962; Mar. 5, 1241) and a parliament is held "in claustro" in December 1283. A "master of the works" of the cathedral appears in an unrelated property transaction of 1268: "A. Vidal magistri operis ... Sancte Marie Valencie" (Arch. Crown, Reg. Canc. 15, fol. 97; April 30, 1268); in 1273 Vidal was master of works for the Alcira irrigation canal and held property nearby which "affrontat in hereditate Andree de Albalato" (not the recently deceased bishop of Valencia? *ibid.*, Reg. Canc. 19. fol. 84v, Dec. 8, 1273; see the two documents naming Vidal on fol. 105v, Feb. 24, 1273).

14. See the observations of Sanchís Sivera (*Catedral de Valencia*, pp. 56 ff., 75). Harvey believes the door to be "clearly inspired" by the main front of Tarragona "but with further reference" to the south transept of Notre Dame (*Cathedrals*, p. 174); he finds the Romanesque Puerta del Palau with its "traces of mudéjar and of the coming Gothic Transition a strange design to have been carried out" after 1262, and he remarks the "very close resemblance" to the work of the "notoriously conservative" Lérida school (p. 173).

15. Arch. Cath., perg. 1,326 (Mar. 24, 1257): "cupientes igitur ut Ecclesia Valentina que in honore beate Marie Virginis constructa esse dinoscitur congruis honoribus frequentetur, omnibus vere penitentibus et confessis qui ecclesiam ipsam in Quattuor festivitatibus ipsius Virginis et in Octavis ipsarum visitaverint annuatim de omnipotentis dei misericordia ... Quadraginta dies de iniunctis sibi penitentiis misericorditer relaxamus."

16. See, for example, the contract in Arch. Cath., perg. 1,320 (Feb. 10, 1250): "vendimus vobis Magistro Dominico precentori valentino fructus unius prebende que cotidie duodecim denarios monete Regalis valencie valere debeat, et promittimus vobis et heredibus vestris et successoribus qui ius patronatus super hoc ... fuerint consecuti, providere perpetuo sine difficultate aliqua uno sacerdoti pro anima vestra et parentum vestrorum in nostra Ecclesia in altare maiori missam ... cotidie celebranti, in portione duodecim denariorum Regalium in Civitate Valentina." Sanchís Sivera, *Catedral de Valencia*, app. B (pp. 486–507), has all the benefices culled from the documents with information on each.

17. Arch. Cath., perg. 3,104 (Aug. 8, 1267): "vendimus vobis Guillermo de areyns Canonico valentino fructus unius prebende que cotidie XII denarii ... valere debeat, et promittimus in heredibus vestris et successoribus omnibus quod" (continuation similar to document in note 16).

18. J. R. Moorman cites the example of Bishop Swinfield who moved his household of forty men 81 times in 296 days, so as to be near his food and fuel; episcopal debt in England is treated here too (*Church Life in England in the Thirteenth Century*, Cambridge, England, 1946, pp. 176, 171 ff.).

19. E. de Moreau, *Histoire de l'église en Belgique*, 6 vols. (Brussels, 1941–1952), II, 1; to appreciate the truth of this for the realms of Aragon one has only to consult the elaborate itinerary of James I (*Itinerari*, pp. 545–547).

20. Arch. Cath., perg. 2,343 (*an.* 1270): "in palacio domini episcopi Valentini"; legajo LX, fasc. I (perg., *an.* 1260): "in palacio nostro Valencie." The "palace" of the archbishop of Tarragona, when James was a child, was a building of wood (*Llibre dels feyts*, ch. 11). James speaks of "your house or houses" (Arch. Crown, James I, Reg. Canc. 21, fol. 22, April 18, 1272). The evidence as to its position is discussed both by Teixidor and Chabás in *Antigüedades de Valencia,* I, 191–193, 198–200, and II, 255. The bishop's residence was supposed to be of suitable dignity; the bishop of Toulouse from 1179 to 1200 was thought to be in straits because "vivebat in episcopali hospitio ut burgensis" upon a few rents, the knights and monasteries having all his tithes (J. H. Mundy, *Liberty and Political Power in Toulouse, 1050–1230* [New York, 1954], p. 292). The arcades acquired in Chapter VIII below, note 40 seem to have been for enlarging the bishop's palace. There is an episcopal *cellarium,* probably a part of the complex of houses, in Arch. Cath., perg. 1,229 (June 6, 1270).

21. See note 70, and Chapter VIII, note 10.

22. Arch. Cath., perg. 2,391 (Sept. 18, 1255): "in domibus Episcopi"; and perg. 4,647 (July 16, 1263): "in domo domini Episcopi valentie."

23. Arch. Cath., perg. 2,309 (June 23, 1240): Peter Salvatoris, "notarius domini episcopi." The bishop's notary appears also in perg. 2,381 (July 19, 1250) and elsewhere.

24. *Furs, lib.* III, *rub.* V, *c.* 37. A cleric answered to this court even for his land if the church owned it.

25. Litigation delayed his complete emergence and qualified his powers; see below, p. 32. Arch. Cath., perg. 2,312 (Feb. 11, 1243) is the sentence allowing one to be constituted; but the strife leading to this decision indicates a previous existence of the office. Perg. 4,647 (July 16, 1263) has: "non tenetur coram vobis Raimundo de Belester oficiali domini episcopi Valencie." See also Arch. Crown, Peter III, Reg. Canc. 56, fol. 13 (Mar. 1, 1284) where William Mollet holds the office, and Reg. 59, fol. 40v (July 23, 1282). The Official appears fully at Rheims in 1182, at Cambrai in 1194, at Thérouanne in 1196. In a single long episcopate at Tournai there were eight in succession (1215–1251). Cologne had one only from the mid-thirteenth century. His basic function was as delegate judge for the bishop in cases in the external forum, though his actual powers could proliferate in other directions. He resembles, but should not be confused with, the vicar-general or procurator whose functions were wider. See Moreau, *Église en Belgique,* III, 330 ff., and Edouard Fournier, *Les origines du vicaire général, étude d'histoire et de droit canon* (Paris, 1922), chs. 4, 5 on the Official.

26. See, for example, Arch. Cath., perg. 2,358 (July 11, 1252): "R. Belestar officialis." The crusade tithe of 1279 gives "G. de Moleto officialis domini episcopi Valentini"; see the *Rationes decimarum Hispaniae (1279–1280),* ed. José Rius Serra (Barcelona, 1946–1947), I, 260. William Mollet is Official in 1285 ("de Moleto"), and Peter Gomar later that year, in Arch. Crown, Peter III, Reg. Canc. 56, fol. 13, and Reg. Canc. 58, fol. 99. For the petition of the parent Berengar of Morena, see Arch. Crown doc., below in Chapter XI, note 45 (Dec. 9, 1284).

27. Arch. Cath., perg. 2,345 (Mar. 11, 1241); perg. 2,368 (only as "B," the "penitencialis domini Episcopi"); and in 1242, perg. 2,327 (see *Colección diplomática,* doc. 1,044). *Ordinatio ecclesiae valentinae,* p. 364 (Matthew).

28. *Ordinatio,* p. 359: "ipse iverat pro quadam causa ad Archiepiscopum Terrachonensem, et invenit ibi multos litigantes"; p. 364, other witness.

29. Arch. Cath., perg. 2,334 (Nov. 9, 1243): "P. capellanus Episcopi Valentini," but he is only among the signatories of one copy of this document; *ibid.,*

legajo LX, fasc. 1 (perg.) for the official erection and endowment (Sept. 16, 1260). *Rationes decimarum*, I, 259, 264.

30. Arch. Cath., perg. 4,657 (Dec. 20, 1273): "ego Gaston de Conyello baiulus Episcopi auctoritate domini Episcopi dono et stabilio vobis . . ."; also perg. 2,351 (*an.* 1241). Arch. Crown, Peter III, Reg. Canc. 41, fol. 98 (June 27, 1279). *Colección diplomática*, docs. 900 (*an.* 1261) and 959 (*an.* 1265). The Alcoy bailiwick is sold in Arch. Cath., perg. 707 (Feb. 12, 1259) to "Raymundo de Almenar[a] vassallo nostro." Others are noted below, in Chapter IX.

31. Arch. Crown, James I, Reg. Canc. 15, fol. 78v (Jan. 26, 1267).

32. Arch. Crown, Peter III, Reg. Canc. 44, fol. 206v (July 15, 1281): "vobis magistro Bartholomeo de Garleyno dicti Episcopi fisico."

33. Arch. Cath., perg. 4,620 (Nov. 20, 1248): "vi tabulas comedendi, inter quas est tabula rotunda, et xii banchia et iii scamna sedendi."

34. This is not surprising for the time and place. Thus, Peter of Castellnou, bishop of Gerona, enfranchised in his testament of 1278 one Matthew "baptizatum nostrum," but ordered his other slaves "ba[p]tizatos et sarracenos" to be sold. Bertrand of Berga, bishop of Elne, in Roussillon, in his testament of 1259 disposed of eight slaves, including six "pagans." See Charles Verlinden, *L'esclavage dans l'Europe médiévale*, one volume to date, *Péninsule ibérique, France* (Bruges, 1955), I, 303, 754, 254n. 257. See also J. Miret y Sans, "La esclavitud en Cataluña en los ultimos tiempos de la edad media," *Revue hispanique*, XLI (1917), 1–109. "Les esclaves sont infiniment plus nombreux aux deux derniers siècles du moyen âge qu'au xiiie," Verlinden notes (p. 427). His analogy of Valencia with Majorca on this subject (pp. 437–438) does not seem well taken, since the manner of conquest in the former involved less enslavement. The moral problem is indicated by Verlinden's examples from the next period (cf. pp. 420 ff.).

35. *Documenta selecta*, doc. 100 (Jan. 1, 1303).

36. Olmos y Canalda has a short biography of every Valencian bishop in his *Prelados valentinos* (Madrid, 1949). Statistics for each episcopate are of course listed in C. Eubel, *Hierarchia catholica medii aevi sive summorum pontificum, s.r.e. cardinalium, ecclesiarum antistitum series ab anno 1198*, 3 vols., 2nd ed. (Munich, 1913–1914), I, 512, and in P. B. Gams, *Series episcoporum ecclesiae catholicae quotquot innotuerunt a beato Petro apostolo* (Leipzig, 1931), pp. 87–88. See too the list and commentary in *Viage literario*, I, 46 ff.; and Fuente, *Historia eclesiástica*, IV, ch. 17. On the bishops of Valencia a century and a half earlier, see Menéndez Pidal, *España del Cid*, II, ch. 15. An excellent description of a contemporary diocese in action, though with obvious differences, is Pierre Andrieu-Guitrancourt, *L'archevêque Eudes Rigaud et la vie de l'église au xiiie siècle d'après le "regestrum visitationum"* (Paris, 1938); Eudes was consecrated archbishop of Rouen in 1248. For contemporary England, see Moorman's fine chapters in *Church Life*, chs. 12–17; for comparative illustrations from Belgium see Moreau, *Église en Belgique*, II, ch. 4.

37. S. Ruiz, "Bérenger de Castelbisbal," *DHGE*, VIII, col. 371. Vincke, *Staat und Kirche*, p. 269. Witness' quote is from *Ordinatio ecclesiae valentinae*, p. 364. On the effects of the tongue-cutting episode in the kingdom of Valencia see Chapter XII, note 19 and text.

38. The alternate name Ferrer of San Martín seems to be a misnomer (see *Diócesis valentina*, II, 415–416).

39. Arch. Cath., perg. 2,309 (June 23, 1240). Besides the short sketch in the *Prelados valentinos* of Olmos Canalda, see Fidel Fita, "Don Pedro de Albalat, arzobispo de Tarragona, y Don Ferrer Pallarés obispo de Valencia, cuestiones cronológicas," *BRAH*, XL (1902), 335–352. There is a longer study by José

Sanchís y Sivera, "El obispo Ferrer de Pallarés," in *Diócesis valentina*, II, 412–466. His trip to Rome, recorded in *Episcopologio valentino* (pp. 372–373), is a fable. On Ferrer see also the documents in the *Itinerari*, pp. 86–89, 94–95, 144, 152, 155, 157, 477, 551.

40. On these questions see Chapter XIV.

41. *Ibid.*

42. The *prepositus* (prior, provost, dean) at Tarragona was a prestigious figure at this time; he had choice revenues, custody of the common rents and temporalities, and the decisive vote in a deadlocked election for the metropolitanate (*Viage literario*, XIX, 85). Ferrer held the post from 1217 (*ibid.*, XIX, 184, and see p. 128).

43. *Itinerari*, pp. 86, 94; see pp. 86–89, 144, 152, 551.

44. *Llibre dels feyts*, ch. 54; but the four knights here promised became an army later.

45. Olmos Canalda, *Prelados valentinos*, p. 59.

46. Vincke, *Staat und Kirche*, p. 270. Sanchís Sivera wrongly assumes that all these rewards, including such gifts as sixty-one houses and seventy-five jovates of land, became the personal wealth of Ferrer (*Diócesis valentina*, II, 416–417); actually, he had to subdivide them among his followers. He received a good but personal gift in Valencia later (*Repartimiento*, pp. 246, 251).

47. *Colección diplomática*, doc. 989 (Feb. 26, 1274), an account by King James himself, who is aggrieved that his motives were misunderstood.

48. *Ibid.* King James says the five canons "tunc temporis de curia nostra erant."

49. *Itinerari*, p. 477 (Mar. 1, 1273).

50. The minute of the metropolitan council, the notice from Nolasco's life ("tristatus est valde"), and the cathedral necrology ("nequiter iugulatus") are all conveniently given in full in *Diócesis valentina* II, 440. On the reliability of the Nolasco source, see below, Chapter XIII, note 84 and text.

51. J. Sanchís y Sivera, "El obispo de Valencia Arnaldo de Peralta," *BRAH*, LXXXII (1923), 40–64, 104–121. The bishop of Lérida (from 1254) may have been his brother. See too A. Lambert, "Arnauld de Peralta," *DHGE*, IV, cols. 518–523; this covers the main elements of his life satisfactorily. See Olmos Canalda, *Prelados valentinos*, pp. 62–66; and Lamberto de Zaragoza and Ramón de Huesca, *Teatro histórico de las iglesias del reyno de Aragón*, 9 vols. (Pamplona, 1780–1807), II, 243–247. The cathedral documents for this reign as for the others have all been studied and are cited below where the separate subjects are given individual attention. The commission of electors in 1243 comprised the metropolitan, the bishop of Tortosa, and the canons Roderick Díaz, Matthew of Oteiza, Bertrand of Teruel, and Bartholomew Busquet, all apparently meeting at Tarragona in May.

52. There is no reason to doubt the assertions of Diago and Escolano to this effect, as does Sanchís Sivera ("Arnaldo de Peralta," p. 42). It will be precisely against his predecessor's financial surrender to James that the chapter protests (see below, Chapter VIII); and the seemingly free gifts admired by Sanchís Sivera in this episcopate are really attempts to rectify that original injustice. The case will end in the king's ungraciously yielding late in the reign (1272).

53. More closely connected with the tithes; see Chapter VIII.

54. Antonio Barberá Sentamáns, *El derecho canónico valentino comparado con el general de la iglesia* (Valencia, 1928), p. 29. The Valencian synods of the thirteenth century are carefully examined on pp. 28–42. The conciliar volumes of Aguirre and Villanuño cause confusion by attributing to Arnold synodal legislation which

belongs to his successor Andrew. Synods in Valencia usually took place in October in the cathedral.

55. Bishop Ferrer had planned the division (see note 80 and text), but Játiva had not then been conquered. The churches of Játiva itself, and their revenues with the exception of episcopal rights, were given in benefice to the new archdeaconry: "Ecclesie beate Marie Xative cum quibusdam Ecclesiis seu Capellis infra eius terminos constitutis et constituendis"; these are spelled out in detail in the document of Arnold, given by Jazpert in a subsequent confirmation (Arch. Cath., perg. 1,091, July 8, 1248). In this area around the city of Játiva, the archdeacon is to collect the first fruits and such and to provide for the resident vicars, whom he may choose and present to the bishop.

56. Papal approval of the transfer was formally given to him in a ceremony of October 24, 1248; this is copied by Sanchís Sivera in his "Arnaldo de Peralta" (pp. 117–118). But a document of August 25 from the metropolitan had previously transferred Arnold. He died about 1269. In 1259–1260 he had gone to Rome to defend the rights of Segorbe—the sees of Zaragoza and Albarracín having combined to protest Segorbe's inclusion in the province of Toledo.

57. *Llibre dels feyts*, ch. 237.

58. Arch. Cath., perg. 4,620 (Nov. 20, 1248). The list includes 3,000 "quartarios" of wine, some cloth, "unam rotam de carreta," tables and benches, "unum lectum iacendi . . . et unam cathedram, et unum foustol . . . et ii armaria que sunt in boteleria, et unam archam," "unam scalam, et unam barcelam," "i molendinum mostadie," "i quadratum fusti et xxi tabulas plumbi, et viij portas vetulas, et unam scutellam pictam, apud Moroveteri ii botas magnas et vi parvas. . . . Item apud Algesiram iiij botas et unam tinam. Item apud Xativam iiij botas. Item apud Xivam ii botas," also "unam palam ferri," "unam aliam ollam de coure," and so on. A transcription, slightly differing from my own, is also given by Sanchís Sivera ("Arnaldo de Peralta," pp. 119–120).

59. See the sketch of his life in Olmos Canalda, *Prelados valentinos*, pp. 67–72; and Vincke in *Staat und Kirche*, p. 271. A document in the cathedral archives describes the formalities attending this election. A representative of the metropolitan read the papal letter (Aug. 25, 1248) announcing the transfer of Arnold to the see of Zaragoza, and ordering a new election. Meanwhile, "dominum A[rnoldum Piquer] Valentinum sacristam unanimiter vicarium constituerunt," with spiritual jurisdiction and a partial procuration in temporals. The election took place on an assigned day, in the cathedral at the place where the chapter usually met; it was "sub forma compromissi," the choice being made by the archdeacon, the precentor, and the metropolitan. See perg. 1,318 (Oct. 24, 1248).

60. See Chapter III, note 8. Speaking of the Tarragona lord Benedict of Albalat, on the crusade with his brother the archbishop, the *Trobes* of Jaume Febrèr say: "Son germá menor Bisbe es de Valencia / E alli se ha restat ab gran convenencia" ([Valencia, 1796–1797], p. 24, *troba* 23).

61. This activity on the part of all four bishops is documented as part of the section on the economic organization of the diocese, in Chapters VIII and IX. On Andrew's synods see Barberá Sentamáns, *Derecho canónico valentino*, pp. 29 ff.

62. These *prepositurae* were lucrative for the holders but were not accounted among the dignities of the cathedral (see the *Regestum Clementis Papae V*, ed. Benedictine monks, 12 vols. [Paris, 1885–1957], III, no. 2,514, Feb. 12, 1308). "Multa litigia" were to result from this remedy (*Lettres communes de Jean XXII, 1316–1334*, ed. G. Mollat, 16 vols. [Paris, 1921–1946], III, 288, no. 13, May 23, 1321 but referring back to this period at Valencia).

63. His career as plenipotentiary of the pope is touched on by M. H. Laurent in *Le bienheureux Innocent V (Pierre de Tarentaise) et son temps*, Studi e testi, no. 129 (Rome, 1947), pp. 184-185.

64. Olmos Canalda, *Prelados valentinos*, pp. 73-75. His epitaph supplies the portrait: "presul. Jazpertus. jacet. hic. jurista. disertus," continuing later: "Pulcher. formosus. largus. letus. generosus" (copied by Villanueva, *Viage literario*, I, 48-49.)

65. See Ángel Fábrega Grau, "Actitud de Pedro III el Grande de Aragón ante la propia deposición fulminada por Martín IV," *Sacerdozio e regno*, pp. 176 ff. On the Desclot chronicle (Desclot a pseudonym or a scribe) see Manuel de Montoliu, *Les quatre grans cròniques* (Barcelona, 1959), p. 56. On Arnold of Vilanova's "Epistola ad episcopum valentinum" see *Revue d'histoire ecclésiastique*, LV (1960), 733. Quote is from Desclot, *Crònica*, ch. 96.

66. Shneidman, "Government in Thirteenth Century Valencia," p. 187.

67. Arch. Cath., perg. 4,647 (July 16, 1263): "capitulum est in Episcopo et Episcopus in capitulo." For a historical survey of chapters, their evolution, powers, internal organization, and relations to the bishop, see P. Torquebiau, "Chapitres de chanoines", *DDC*, III, cols. 530-595; also his articles "Chanoines" (cols. 471-488), "Curie diocésaine" (IV, cols. 961-971); and G. Mollat, "Bénéfices ecclésiastiques en occident," (I, cols. 406-448). See too my "The Organization of a Mediaeval Cathedral Community: the Chapter of Valencia (1238-1280)," *Church History*, XXXI (1962), 14-23; and Plöchl, *Kirchenrechts*, I, 155-163 with bibliography.

68. Arch. Cath., perg. 2,309 (June 23, 1240). Only in 1282 was the honorary silk cape made obligatory (each medieval chapter evolved its own type and colors).

69. *Aureum opus*, doc. 12, fol. 4r,v (November 1241).

70. See document in Chapter VIII, note 10. The purchase permit for fourteen houses owned by the crown (1241) was reissued again in 1265 ("domos seu hospicia . . . ad habitaciones vestras proprias," Arch. Cath., perg. 1,339; *Colección diplomática*, doc. 918, Dec. 19, 1265).

71. Arch. Cath., perg. 2,862 (Oct. 22, 1246). "Innocentius episcopus servus servorum dei, Dilectis filiis Capitulo Ecclesie Valentine, Salutem et apostolicam benedictionem. Vestris devotis precibus inclinati auctoritate vobis presentium indulgemus ut nullus sedis apostolice delegatus vel delegati subdelegatus eiusdem executor seu eciam conservator a sede deputatus eadem in vos suspensionis aut interdicti seu excomunicationis sententiam valeat promulgare sine ipsius sedis speciali mandato faciente de indulgentia huiusmodi mentionem. Nullo ergo hominum liceat hanc paginam nostre concessionis infringere vel ei ausu temerario contraire. Si quis autem hoc attemptare presumpserit indignationem omnipotentis dei et beatorum Petri et Pauli apostolorum eius se noverit incursurum. Presentibus post triennium minime valituris. Datum Lugdun., xi kalendas Novembri, Pontificatus nostri anno tertio."

72. *Documenta selecta*, doc. 94 (1301).

73. *Colección diplomática*, doc. 989 (Feb. 26, 1274).

74. *Ordinatio ecclesiae valentinae*, p. 320: "creavit ad vii vel octo canones."

75. *Ibid.*, p. 233. Chosen and installed by the metropolitan, their names were given for this trial record by his procurator. The solemn document issued by the chapter in 1247 (see below, document in Chapter VIII, note 135) has ten canons signing, with the information that "non erant alii canonici tunc presentes"; the missing canons were probably few in number, since the business on hand was a constitution on the future division of canonical income.

76. Arch. Cath., perg. 1,325 (Jan. 29, 1257).

77. Arch. Cath., perg. 1,356 (Feb. 22, 1279). And see the constitutions of Bishop Jazpert in perg. 289 (Aug. 13, 1277).

78. At the beginning of the Valencia crusade (1230), Barcelona had thirty-seven canons. Vich in Catalonia could support just twenty canons (1246); the papal legate had demanded thirty, but an appeal to Rome led to a commission of inquiry into revenues, and the first number was approved. Majorca in circumstances similar to those of Valencia had its number of canons set at twelve, of which four were priests (1244-1247); there were only three dignitaries (sacristan, precentor, and archdeacon); there was a master of grammar, a subsacristan, two ministers to chant the epistle and gospel on feasts, etc. In the reform drawn by Vidal de Cañellas for the cathedral of Barbastro there were to be twenty clerics: ten priests, six deacons, and four subdeacons; these were to be supported by the episcopal third of the tithes and by a half of the rentals (Ricardo del Arco, "El famoso jurisperito del siglo xiii, Vidal de Cañellas, obispo de Huesca, noticias y documentos inéditos," *BRABLB*, VIII, 1916, 468-469). The primate of Toledo in our period would seek to outshine the other churches; a decree of 1238 called for forty canons and an even larger number of assistants; see Javier Gorosterratzu, *Don Rodrigo Jiménez de Rada, gran estadista, escritor y prelado, estudio documentado de su vida . . .* (Pamplona, 1925), pp. 271-273. The statutes worked out for Seville (1261), a city which had been conquered at about the same time as Valencia, projected an ambitious program of forty canons too, including of course the dignitaries; this, like the unusual number of parishes (see below Chapter V, note 168 and text), probably represented an unrealistic appraisal of needs and capacity (*Repartimiento de Sevilla,* I, 354).

79. Arch. Cath., perg. 4,614 (Feb. 19, 1248): "Dominicus Mathei clericus nobis exposuit conquerendo, et cum olim per capcionem Civitatis Valencie in ordinacione ipsius Ecclesie inter ceteros canonicos ipsum creavimus in canonicum ecclesie antedicte, et ipsa canonia optinenda ad Episcopum et Capitulum valentinum multocies institisse placuit Episcopo et Capitulo quod res in iudicium duceretur et per negacionem re in dubium revocata . . ."; "per nos fuisse receptum in canonicum Ecclesie valentine in prima creatione canonicorum quam fecimus in eadem." We find Dominic functioning as a canon in cathedral documents of 1273.

80. Arch. Cath., perg. 2,309 (June 23, 1240).

81. *Lib.* III, *tit.* XXVII, no. 5, p. 332: "non prosequor quia circa eorum officia et potestates fere quot sunt Ecclesiae, tot sunt consuetudinum varietates."

82. *Ordinatio ecclesiae valentinae,* p. 250. Each of these offices in the dioceses of Spain during the early thirteenth century is analyzed from contemporary documents by Demetrio Mansilla Reoyo, *Iglesia castellano-leonesa y curia romana en los tiempos del rey San Fernando, estudio documental sacado de los registros vaticanos* (Madrid, 1945); on the sacristan or treasurer see pp. 203-204. More useful here but more elaborate is the monograph by D. E. Heintschel, *The Mediaeval Concept of an Ecclesiastical Office, an Analytical Study of the Concept of an Ecclesiastical Office in the Major Sources and Printed Commentaries from 1140-1300,* (Washington, D.C., 1956). Some would refuse the name "dignitary" to capitular officials who lacked an administrative (especially a jurisdictional) function; a further distinction of "personage" and "office" is provided for the latter.

83. Arch. Cath., perg. 2,309 (June 23, 1240); and perg. 2,310 (June 14, 1242).

84. Arch. Cath., perg. 4,616 (June 4, 1247): "notum sit cunctis quod nos Arnaldus dei gratia Episcopus Valentinus assignamus vobis Arnaldo sacriste Sedis Valencie in tota vita vestra Quatrocentos bisancios boni Argenti rectique pensi racione sacristie Valentine . . . annuatim super omnibus oblacionibus et defunccionibus Ecclesie Sedis Valencie, et super totam primiciam de Rucafa et de Melilla

et de Benimaçot . . . et super omnibus denariis Censualibus nostris quos hodie percipimus in Valencia." On Melilla, see p. 163, with note 94.

85. *Rationes decimarum*, I, 259, 264.

86. Arch. Cath., perg. 2,310 (June 14, 1242). Actually one may distinguish two offices here. At Valencia their functions seem to have been combined at first, though later in the century separate offices may have been emerging. The chanter or *capiscol* was concerned with the organization and discipline of the choir and choir services; the chancellor or precentor (*maestrescuela, magister scholarum*) provided teachers and despatched documents bearing the capitular seal. See the descriptions in Mansilla Reoyo, *Iglesia castellano-leonesa*, pp. 203-204 and nn. Even within the office of precentor, one may distinguish the earlier, separate, and noncapitular function of master of the schools; by our time he had long been brought into the capitular body in most places, either by creating the office of *scholasticus* (*magister scholarum*, even *capischola*); or by annexing the function to that of the capitular chancellor (usual in northern Europe) or precentor (*magiscola, primicerius*, etc.; often in the south). The precentor or chancellor was superintendent of schooling but sometimes he also taught the higher subjects, especially theology. See H. Rashdall, *The Universities of Europe in the Middle Ages*, ed. M. Powicke and A. B. Emden, 3 vols. (New York, 1936), I, 279-282 and nn.

87. *Rationes decimarum*, I, 259, 263; this was from his office and did not include, for example, his "portion" from the canons' income. The schools as such were unprofitable, but the Master Vincent who taught there paid 18 and 16 solidi, probably from supporting-rents for the cathedral instruction (*ibid.*, pp. 258, 264).

88. Arch. Cath., perg. 2,408 (June 23, 1260). On the dean see Mansilla Reoyo, *Iglesia castellano-leonesa*, pp. 202-203. Moreau, *Église en Belgique*, III, 338-340.

89. Peregrín L. Lloréns y Raga, "El deanato de la catedral de Valencia," *ACCV*, XXII (1954), 9-11 and 16-17, transcribing the documents from the Valencia cathedral archives.

90. *Colección diplomática*, doc. 918 (Dec. 19, 1265): "dechano, canonicis et capitulo."

91. Arch. Cath., perg. 2,418.

92. *Rationes decimarum*, I, 255, 262. Apparently his duty was recompensed by an exemption; see p. 19 where the dean of Barcelona is assessed: "quia collector est exemptorum—nichil." On p. 32 reasons are given for exempting a collector from the large sum of 300 solidi on account of his duties and modest income.

93. *Ordinatio ecclesiae valentinae*, pp. 233 and 319-320; the sacristan was also instituted (see above p. 57), but is not mentioned in these passages and seems to be a bit later. Quotation from Moorman, *Church Life*, p. 209. See Mansilla Reoyo, *Iglesia castellano-leonesa*, pp. 204-205; A. Amanieu, "Archidiacre", *DDC*, I, cols. 948-1,004; Heintschel, *Mediaeval Office*, pp. 62-64.

94. Heintschel, *Mediaeval Office*, p. 62.

95. Arch. Cath., perg. 2,310 (June 14, 1242).

96. *Ibid.*

97. Arch. Cath., perg. 2,312 (Feb. 11, 1243 or 1244): "finem litibus et discordie imponere cupientes."

98. *Rationes decimarum*, I, 258, 264. On p. 267 we find him adding 269 solidi to make good his default in the year 1277-1278; 40 more to supply for what was lacking from a *prepositura* (see above, note 62) of 1276-1277; and 200 more, apparently also for default in 1276-1277. The archdeacon of Játiva, with the Valencia dean, had charge of collecting the tax and so does not appear on the lists

himself except in an appendix for all six years where he pays a past default of 62 solidi (I, 267).

99. For example, the chapter sold the bishop their share of a Roteros (Moslem?) cemetery in Arch. Cath., perg. 1,209 (Mar. 15, 1244): "noverint universi quod nos . . . non decepti neque seducti, nec coacti nec iuris nostri ignari, libera voluntate concedimus vobis dompno Arnaldo Valentino Episcopo et successoribus vestris totum ius et partem nostram quod nos habemus et habere debemus in illo cimiterio quod dicitur de Roteros."

100. See the agreement of 1241 (note 69) and also the *guiatge* of King James to the canons and their households, under a penalty of a thousand morabatins for transgressors in Arch. Cath., perg 2,394 (codex, Liber constitutionum, fols. 61v–62r). In the first visitation and organization of the diocese by the metropolitan, the members of the canons' households were declared above the jurisdiction of the archdeacon (perg. 2,310, June 14, 1242). The houses of the canons, numbering eighteen by 1462, kept the same locations as late as 1854; Sanchís Sivera traces each for us in his *Catedral de Valencia*, pp. 15–16nn. Illuminating comparisons and sidelights on the workings of Aragonese chapters may be found in the article of Antonio Durán Gudiol, "El derecho capitular de la catedral de Huesca desde el siglo xii al xvi," *REDC*, VII (1952), 447–515. In 1238 there were both canons living in common and prebendary canons with no common life at all (pp. 452–453). In 1254 the bishop with most of the chapter decreed secularization of the canons' life; but other canons, wishing to retain the rule of St. Augustine, appealed to Rome; litigation was still going forward in 1296. The article also edits the regulations of the chapter (pp. 505–515), ten of the documents being from the thirteenth century. The life and rule of the Tarragona canons, as lived in common ca. 1154, may be seen in the document in *Viage literario*, XIX, 214–216.

101. Durán, "Derecho capitular," pp. 483, 486. On the various kinds of non-canon personnel see the *DDC* articles cited above, note 67. The *portionarii*, for example, had a share of prebendial revenue, assisted at the daily office and conventual Mass, but were not canons, and usually had no voice in chapter.

102. See document cited in Chapter VIII, note 135.

103. Arch. Cath., leg. XXXV, no. 9 (Oct. 1, 1255). Public notaries, like William of Jaca, compose many of the capitular documents; and the revenue document of 1247, cited several times, includes provision for paying a fairly large bill to the scribe Guillonus.

104. *Rationes decimarum*, I, 263–265.

105. The names are variously spelled, and variously transcribed by authors. Díaz is also Díez, Didacus etc.; Piquer is Pichet; the Bernard, Bertrand, and Berengars are sometimes confused. Oteiza (in the diocese of Pamplona) appears as Ateya, Hoteyça, d'Oteyça, Boteyça, Eteyça, and in similar forms. Targanova (a form of *Tarrega nova?*) is sometimes given as Tarazona or Tarragona; Teixidor has him as Carganova once, and Olmos y Canalda as Fayguona. Peter Pérez of Tarazona may have been a canon already at this early date; this would eliminate a "Bernard of Tarazona," who seems to have slipped in because of malpunctuation in editing the *Ordinatio*. Ralph is of course Radulphus, but sometimes Rodolphus or Roydulfus, etc. Benedict is Benedict Na Reina. Piquer acted as vicar for the diocese in 1248, between the incumbencies of bishops Arnold and Andrew.

106. Martin, Arnold, Peter Dominic, J. Vives, Vidal, Vilar, Targanova, Teruel, "et quosdam alios" (*Ordinatio ecclesiae valentinae*, p. 233). In 1247 Dominic Matthew succeeded in establishing his claim that he too had been among these (see note 79).

107. *Antigüedades de Valencia*, I, 214 (1245). Sanchís Sivera, "Arnaldo de Peralta," pp. 47-48, document of July 22, 1247.

108. *Rationes decimarum*, I, 255-267.

109. The family is from Montpellier, and the name may also be written Za Rocha, La Rocha etc. Documentation on his activities and holdings is abundant both in the cathedral and crown archives. See Miret y Sans's estimate of his importance in national affairs (*Itinerari*, p. 437) and Ricardo del Arco, "El obispo Don Jaime Sarroca, consejero y gran privado del rey Don Jaime el Conquistador (noticias y documentos inéditos)," *BRABLB*, VIII (1916), 463-480, 508-521, and IX (1917), 65-91.

110. Arch. Crown, James I, Reg. Canc. 16, fol. 237v (Oct. 25, 1270) for Benedict. On Giles see *Itinerari*, pp. 270, 299, 410, 437, 485-487.

111. Arch. Crown, Peter III, Reg. Canc. 40, fol. 5 (Aug. 2, 1277); bishop in 1306, in *Regestum Clementis Papae V*, I, 93, no. 499 (Feb. 17, 1306). And see Chapter V, note 13. Was he any relation to the William Rexach who seized the bishop's castle of Chulilla? The name may also be written as "de Richaco"; see his lawsuit in Reg. Canc. 40, fol. 5.

112. Arch. Crown, James I, Reg. Canc. 28, fol. 32 (May 31, 1271). Also Peter III, Reg. Canc. 46, fol. 47 (Aug. 16, 1280). On the embassy see *Llibre dels feyts*, ch. 475.

113. See Chapter XV, notes 145 ff. and text.

114. Arch. Crown, James I, Reg. Canc. 28, fol. 47v (Mar. 19, 1272-1273). Romaní was in the Jaca mountains; its lord fought in the Valencia crusade and was rewarded (1259) with the castle and town of Villalonga.

115. Arch. Crown, James I, perg. 1,952 (Sept. 15, 1268): "castrum meum de Alventosa situm in Regno Valencie." On his career see also the documents in *Itinerari*, pp. 205-206, 209-210, 213-214, 240, 251-252, 257, 271, 276, 373, 390, 443 (*an.* 1250-1276). See also Arch. Crown, Reg. Canc. 14, fol. 5 (Jan. 7, 1262), and Reg. Canc. 15, fol. 13v (Oct. 3, 1266). Pope Honorius recalls in 1286: "bone memorie Gundisalvim tunc Archidiaconum Valentinum in Saguntinum Ep[iscopu]m . . . unanimiter elegerunt," in Arch. Vat., Reg. Vat. 43 (Honorius IV), fol. 176r,v, ep. 173; published in *Les registres d'Honorius IV, publiées d'après le manuscrit des archives du vatican*, ed. M. Prou (Paris, 1886-1888), cols. 478-479, no. 173. His appetite for plural benefices caused him embarrassment at the time of his election to episcopal office; in Reg. Vat. 37 (Gregory X), fol. 145v, ep. 46, with list; unpublished but a notice is given in *Les registres de Gregoire X (1272-1276), recueil des bulles de ce pape publiées ou analysées d'après les manuscrits originaux du vatican*, ed. Jean Guiraud (Paris, 1892-1906), p. 164, no. 416 (Sept. 27, 1274).

116. Arch. Crown, James I, perg. 1,267 (Nov. 21, 1251). Reg. Canc. 10, fol. 17v (Sept. 1, 1257) speaks of the "hereditatis fratris Martini quondam Archidiaconi Valentie" worth 2,000 solidi of Jaca. On Martin see, for example, *Itinerari*, pp. 167, 218, 233, 239-241, 243; and see Sanchís Sivera, *Catedral de Valencia*, app. B. He received six jovates at Ladea (Feb. 13, 1239). See also the king's memoirs, on the "archdeacon of Valencia" at Huesca (*Llibre dels feyts*, ch. 380). Should he be identified with Valencian Archdeacon Martin López, holding the office in late 1259 (*Itinerari*, p. 294)? Archdeacon Martin appears also in a civil document at Valencia in 1240 (Arch. Crown, James I, perg. 821).

117. Arch. Crown, James I, Reg. Canc. 19, fol. 122v (April 9, 1274); in this kind of routine grant the term "dilecti nostri" can be ambiguous.

118. Several times he signs with a mark; an accompanying notation in one document remarks his ignorance of writing (1242): "ea qua [*sic*] non consuevit firmare

propria manu." There are knightly men of his name in our records; but it is too common a name from which to surmise relationships.

119. Arch. Crown, James I, Reg. Canc. 10, fol. 98 (June 29, 1258); Reg. 16, fol. 277v (Dec. 31, 1270). Arch. Cath., perg. 4,652 (Mar. 5, 1272), and perg. 1,343 (Feb. 5, 1270).

120. See too the selection in *Diócesis valentina*, II, 116n. and 442–443.

121. On Michael see *Itinerari*, pp. 175, 246, 249, 251–252, 254–264, 266, 269, 277, and 556.

122. Arch. Cath., perg. 5,012 (Nov. 4, 1256): "Castrum meum de Spioca"; "omnes alias vero domos meas et corrallia et casallia et etiam illas domos quos emi . . . et cellarium meum . . . et omnia utensilia et hostilia dicti celarii et mille solidos . . . et roncinum meum virmillum et omnia arma mea ferri et fusti"; "omnes vineas meas . . . in melilla et terminis suis"; "de regali meo de rozafa quod pro me tenet Bernardus de rossillione"; "baptizatus meus." Espioca was near modern Benifayó de Espioca (or "de Falco").

123. Is John of Monzón any relation, for example, to the important knight who was bailiff of Valencia for the region below the Júcar? What is the relation, if any, between Roderick Díaz and the baron of the same name? Both Busquet and Boxadós, as well as Boxadors, suggest eminent families in James's kingdoms. Peter of Portugal, who appears only fleetingly, must have been the celebrated prince of that name, so involved then in affairs of Aragon and its frontier, who was son of the king of Portugal, and commander of Alcañiz of the Order of Calatrava (see, for example, the documents of the *Itinerari*, pp. 78, 79, 96, 99, 103, 104, 117, 123, 124, 137, 160, 164, 169, 172, 178, 194, 195, 205).

124. Arch. Cath., perg. 1,362 (Nov. 21, 1279). Arch. Crown, Peter III, Reg. Canc. 38, fol. 42v (Sept. 30, 1276); see also Reg. Canc. 44, fol. 157v (Oct. 12, 1279). Was he the son of the justiciar Martin or of the earlier justiciar Peter? Martin had among his sons a Roderick; as justiciar of Aragon in 1257 he appears with Roderick, for example, both being associated on crown business concerning Castile. He also had a "P. Martineç, clergue" who may have been our Peter Pérez. But "the son of the justiciar of Aragon" named as Valencian canon in the early *Ordinatio ecclesiae valentinae* may have been the son of the earlier justiciar Peter Pérez. Nor is it impossible that sons of both justiciars held canonries here. (On the justiciar Peter Pérez see *Llibre dels feyts*, ch. 168; on Martin and Peter Martin see ch. 402.)

125. Geoffrey Barraclough, *Papal Provisions, Aspects of Church History Constitutional, Legal and Administrative in the Later Middle Ages* (Oxford, 1935), p. 54.

126. Arch. Cath., perg. 1,318 (Oct. 24, 1248).

127. Arch. Cath., perg. 5,982 (Nov. 26, 1259). This same line of inquiry into aristocratic origins might be carried into the ranks of the parish rectors. Thus, Raymond of Montañans is rector of Alcira, canon of Lérida, archdeacon of Tarragona, counselor to the king, and eventually chancellor of the queen (see Chapter V, note 15). The name is also given as Montanyana, Montanya, and Montaynans.

128. *Llibre dels feyts*, ch. 515. A baron here contemptuously refuses to receive a charge of treason sent by Prince Peter through Thomas of La Junquera, who was "learned in law" (ch. 511).

NOTES TO CHAPTER III. NEIGHBORS, AND INTRUDERS

1. *Aureum opus*, doc. 3, fol. lv (Nov. 13, 1236). See Arch. Cath., perg. 2,354 (*id.*). On the 1228 episode see below, notes 11 ff. and text.

2. *Viage literario*, XIX, 89–90.

3. This was to be the third Sunday after Easter, according to the statutes of the Lérida council of 1229; but the crowds congregating then for the fairs made it difficult to lodge the bishops and their retinues, so the time was changed in 1247 to the fourth Sunday of Lent ("Concilios tarraconenses en 1248, 1249 y 1250", ed. Fidel Fita, *BRAC*, XL [1902], 444). See too José Zunzunegui, "Concilios y sínodos medievales españoles," on the Tarragona provincial councils, in *HS*, I (1948), 127–132. Including the council at which Valencia was not yet represented, there were twenty-two provincial meetings in the thirteenth century: in 1211, 1229, 1230, 1239, 1240 (at Valencia), 1242, 1243, 1244, 1246, 1247, 1248, 1249, 1250, 1257, 1261, 1266, 1273, 1277, 1282, 1284, 1293, 1294.

4. Penyafort, *Summa, lib.* III, *tit.* XXVII, no. 3, p. 329.

5. Arch. Cath., perg. 2,310 (June 14, 1242).

6. On Barca see J. Blanch, *Arxiepiscopologi de la santa església metropolitana i primada de Tarragona*, ed. J. Icart, 2 vols. (Tarragona, 1951), I, 133–141; Emilio Morera y Llauradó, *Tarragona cristiana, historia del arzobispado de Tarragona y del territorio de su provincia (Cataluña La Nueva)*, 2 vols. (Tarragona, 1888–1889), II, app., doc. 6 (Jan. 29, 1233); *Llibre dels feyts*, chs. 11, 91, 107, 109.

7. On Montgrí, see Blanch, *Arxiepiscopologi*, I, 143–148.

8. J. Capeille, "Albalat (Pierre de)," *DHGE*, I, col. 1,364; "Don Pedro de Albalat" in Chapter II, note 39; Morera, *Tarragona cristiana*, II, 274–289; Blanch, *Arxiepiscopologi*, I, 149–158. He was awarded the important Valencian town of Alcira; when the knight García Romeu claimed it, Albalat had to be satisfied with an indemnity of 12,000 besants (1241).

9. Morera, *Tarragona*, II, 75–87; cf. 289–296. Another of the family was metropolitan in 1199–1214, and yet another in 1309–1315.

10. Blanch, *Arxiepiscopologi*, I, 159–167 and 169–172; Morera, *Tarragona*, II, 296–304.

11. Roque Chabás, "Obispo de Denia en el siglo xii," *El archivo*, VII (1893), 140. Toledo seems to have established a bishop of Denia *in partibus infidelium* as the conquest of the southern regions became imminent; one is found in a document given at the siege of Cordova. Cf. *Diócesis valentina*, II, 144–145. For the early Valencia bishop see Olmos Canalda, *Prelados valentinos*, pp. 55–56. Oddly enough a bishop Paternus de Tortosa is in evidence too in 1058.

12. *Ordinatio ecclesiae valentinae*, p. 322. As early as the treaty of Cazorla with Castile (1179), it is interesting to note that Aragon reserved, as part of her secular conquest of Valencia: Játiva, Biar, "et totum regnum Denie."

13. *Ibid.*, p. 322: "qui tunc temporibus tenebat vicem Tarrachone ecclesie hereme et desolate."

14. See José de Peray y March, "Un documento inédito de D. Jaime el Conquistador, la concesión á la sede barcelonesa de las iglesias de Mallorca, Menorca, Ibiza, Denia y Orihuela," *Congrés I*, pp. 444–456; Josep Mas, *Antigüetat d'algunes esglésies del bisbat de Barcelona*, in the Notes històriques del bisbat de Barcelona, no. 13 (Barcelona, 1921), apps. 10, 11. In the *Ordinatio ecclesiae valentinae* (p. 233) the Tarragona metropolitan was to include an argument from immemorial assumption that Valencia was in his province, a reflection of these documents; later he emphasized the point explicitly (p. 323). For prescriptive rights see pp. 322–323, where the court is told that Barcelona had been "in pacifica possessione" from the

time of the Moslem grant. Puig y Puig and others accept the Moslem document as authentic; Lambert scornfully rejects it (see his arguments in A. Lambert, "Baléares," *DHGE*, VI, cols. 374–375).

15. *Ordinatio*, p. 369; see p. 359; "alta voce" (p. 366); the benedictions described seem to have been part of the ceremony of consecration, but probably done in haste. "Quis precepit ei, maledicatur, quid habebat hic ad faciendum ipse" (p. 366). "Et extraxerat inde clericum violenter," according to the witness (p. 358). "De altari librum missalem rapuerat" (p. 320).

16. "In ecclesiam et extra ecclesiam in temporalibus et spiritualibus et in clericis et laycis" (*ibid.*, cf. pp. 358, 368). "Non stat hic bene, faciatis illud in illo alio loco" (p. 366). There were compensations; the carpenter recalls the king exclaiming: "ecce melior magister regni mei ad faciendum altare." A picture of the Virgin and Child, provided by the king, seems to have decorated the altar (see the picture and the account of this tradition in *Diócesis valentina*, II, 117–118).

17. *Ordinatio*, p. 319: "antequam civitas esset capta"; at the trial the procurator was to say "capta civitate" (p. 233). On the election see above, Chapter II, p. 22. Some have thought the election must have taken place on September 28, assuming that the bishop-elect would have been among the signers of the capitulation, had the election been held before that (*Diócesis valentina*, II, 413); this is possible, but the phrase quoted, and the foresighted policies followed by the metropolitan, suggest that some other explanation should be sought for the missing signature.

18. *Ordinatio*, p. 369; see pp. 233, 250, 319, 358.

19. Document published by Chabás, *El archivo*, IV (1890), 224 (June 22, 1246): "priusquam ad pontificale assumptus esset officium ex regiae familiaritatis gratia tantum in tua curia obtinuisse favorem, ut inter maiores ibidem quasi honorabilior haberetur."

20. *Repartimiento de Sevilla*, I, 350. Mansilla Reoyo, *Iglesia castellano-leonesa*, pp. 187–188. He became bishop-elect, but abandoned the office a decade later and married the daughter of Haakon IV of Norway.

21. *Ordinatio*, pp. 233, 319, 356, 357. Sanchís Sivera, in an interpretation slightly different, has the ceremonies of purification all on October 10 (*Diócesis valentina*, II, 116).

22. See Pascual Esclapés de Guilló, *Resumen historial, de la fundación, i antigüedad de la ciudad de Valencia de los Edetanos, vulgò del Cid, sus progressos, ampliación, i fábricas insignes, con notables particularidades* (Valencia, 1738), pp. 45–46. Beuter's *Coronica de Valencia* has the scene not at the consecration but on a subsequent day when the bishop lays a cornerstone for a new cathedral (part 1, p. 229).

23. Voragine, *Golden Legend*, II, 769–779. A similar purification of the great mosque of Cordova at this time is described by the contemporary primate of Toledo. The bishops enter; "eliminata spurcitia Machometi, et aqua lustrationis perfusa, in Ecclesiam commutavit, et in honore beatae Mariae erexit altare, et missam solemniter celebravit, et sermonem exhortationis divinae proponens . . ." See Roderick Simon of Rada, *De rebus Hispaniae* (in the *SS. Patrum toletanorum quotquot extant opera*, ed. F. de Lorenzana, 3 vols. [Madrid, 1782–1793], III), *lib.* IX, *c.* 17, 206; see too the similar description for Toledo, *lib.* VI, *c.* 24, 137. For the Valencian witnesses see Chapter XIV. Tradition also has a preliminary Mass at the city wall as part of the ceremonies, but our documentation is silent on this.

24. *Ordinatio*, pp. 356, 358; this witness saw two of the canons formally installed. See also Chapter II, notes 73–74, 76.

25. *Ibid.*, p. 233, but cf. the transcription in Roque Chabás, *Episcopologio valentino, investigaciones históricas sobre el cristianismo en Valencia y su archi-*

diócesis, siglos i á xiii (Valencia, 1909), p. 380. Sanchís Sivera has rectors in the churches "quarum tenent christiani," but Chabás has the more probably original reading "quantum tenent."

26. *Ordinatio*, p. 363: "vidit eundem Archiepiscopum de quibusdam meçquitis facientem ecclesias, ac audivit a multis quod limitaverat eas"; see pp. 233, 250, 319, 357. "Ibat cum eo ostendendo ei loca et consulendo ei" (p. 364).

27. *Ibid.*, pp. 234, 250, 319, 358–359, 347.

28. *Ibid.*: "inde clerici recipiebant de manu eius ecclesias," "fecerat sibi inde instrumentum" (p. 364); a witness recalls seeing him confer the church of St. Bartholomew on some cleric (p. 362); another reports on the tithe being formally assigned to St. Bartholomew's (p. 367). Cf. p. 234. Quotes from p. 363: "dixit quod tanta erat pressura quod non poterat accedere illuc," though he saw it from some distance; and, "osculando manus eius et petendo mercedem ab eo et petendo benefficia ab eo et servando precepta eius."

29. Morera, *Tarragona cristiana*, II, 269.

30. *Ordinatio*, p. 320. Chabás believes he is the bishop-elect of a document of July 7, 1239; he contends Castellbisbal was not elected but merely proposed.

31. *Ibid.*, p. 196: "per vacationem diutinam novella . . . plantatio, exquisitis colenda studiis . . ."

32. R. Menéndez Pidal, "Sobre los limites del valenciano," *Primer congrés internacional de la llengua catalana* (Barcelona, 1908), p. 342: "por coincidencia inexplicable, es la jurisdicción eclesiástica la que en esta región conviene con los limites lingüísticos." See also M. Sanchís Guarner, *Els parlers románics de València i Mallorca anteriors a la reconquista*, 2nd ed. revised (Valencia, 1961), pp. 107–108.

33. E. Bayerri, *Historia de Tortosa y su comarca*, 8 vols. to date (Tortosa, 1933–1960), VII, 452.

34. "Colección de cartas pueblas," no. LVII, *BSCC*, XVI (1935), 385–388. See also no. LXII, *ibid.*, XVIII (1943), 32 (April 27, 1225); no. LXI, *ibid.*, 30–31 (same date). Ramón de María, "Fadrell, Almazora, y Castellón, para la catedral de Tortosa," *BSCC*, XVI (1935), 390–397; and *idem*, "Un regalo que en realidad es una restitución," *ibid.*, XVIII (1943), 33–36. Arch. Cath. Tortosa, cartulary III, fols. 6–12. Cf. *Itinerari*, p. 53. On the Tortosa diocese, see especially the comprehensive documentation in the manuscripts of the Bibl. Nac. Madrid, no. 13079, Dd-98; it includes an index of the royal gifts to the diocese, and materials on the limits of the dioceses in the new kingdom.

35. *Itinerari*, p. 546 (Aug. 13, 1229). See also p. 53 (grant of April 27, 1225); and doc. no. LVII in note 34, above. Arch. Cath. Tortosa, cajón Donaciones y Privilegios, docs. 1, 23. *Itinerari*, p. 56 (Sept. 3, 1225).

36. *Itinerari*, pp. 105–106, 134 (docs. of 1233); p. 173 (June 13, 1245) where James gives the diocese Almazora castle and town plus Benimocar hamlet, in exchange for the claims to Castellón and Hadrel. See also Arch. Cath. Tortosa cartularies; the pergs. here note some gifts (e.g. Donaciones, doc. 27, May 1240: "illud alfondicum quod dicitur açichaf quod est in Valencia"; and doc. 38 on a Burriana estate).

37. "Quia magis quam alii regni nostri, pro republica labores subeunt corporales" (James I, 1228, in Bayerri, *Tortosa*, VII, 129).

38. Sobrequés Vidal has recently insisted on emigration in his "Patriciado urbano" (pp. 30–31); cf. Bayerri, *Tortosa*, VII, 202, 205.

39. See the sustained analysis by Sobrequés (esp. pp. 30–42). A prizewinning dissertation (Valencia, 1965) has been prepared, but not yet published, by Juan R. Torres Morera, on the repopulation of the kingdom of Valencia.

40. See Chapter XII, notes 70 ff. and text.

41. On these bishops see the *Viage literario*, V, 86–92; Bayerri, *Tortosa*, VI, 394–397, 403.

42. Arch. Cath. Tortosa, cajón Común de Cabildo, doc. 18 (1250), where the chapter gets all the tithes of places like Morella and Corbera; the document covers non-Valencian places too. The cajón Obispo y Cabildo has a 1287 exchange (doc. 35) by which the bishop gives half the tithes of Carrascal, Chivert, Pulpis, and Villafamés, gaining the tithes of Barig and Benlloc. Claims to press included compensatory holding for the loss of Burriana (Obispo-Cabildo, doc. 9; 1245). The parish and castle of Rossell were given to the dean by the bishop and chapter in 1273 (cajón del Deán, doc. 5). In 1266 the bishop took Cabanes, Almazora, and other properties, the chapter getting an equivalent set of properties elsewhere in the diocese. In 1270 Bishop Arnold gave the parish of Bechí with its tithe to the bishop of Zaragoza.

43. Bayerri, *Tortosa*, VII, 457.

44. Laguía, "Erección de Albarracín," pp. 201–230, and for this whole history his catalogue for the Albarracín cathedral archives (*Catálogo de la sección de pergaminos del archivo de la s. i. catedral de Albarracín*, Instituto de estudios turolenses, Colección catálogos documentales, no. 2, Teruel, 1955) with its introductory essay and documentary appendix. *Viage literario*, III *passim*; Morera, *Tarragona cristiana*, II, 279. In "Arnaldo de Peralta," Sanchís Sivera touches upon our story, but from a chauvinistic Valencian point of view. There is a general summary with a list of the bishops by M. Legendre, "Albarrazin," *DHGE*, I, cols. 1,383–1,386. An excellent account of both Albarracín itself and of its episcopate is given by Martín Almagro Basch *et alii*, *Historia de Albarracín y su sierra* (3 vols. to date; Teruel, 1959), esp. III. Cf. also J. F. Rivera Recio, "La provincia eclesiástica de Toledo en el siglo xii," *Anthologica annua*, VII (1959), 95–145. To replace the J. B. Pérez *Episcopologium segobricense*, reworked and published by F. de Asís Aguilar y Serrat (Segorbe, 1883), the present cathedral archivist of Segorbe, Peregrín Lloréns y Raga, has prepared his own *Episcopologio*; until its publication see the summary of the medieval chapters in his *Presencia histórica de la sede de Segorbe en el reino de Valencia* (Segorbe, 1960), esp. chs. 2–4. Useful background may be found too in C. A. Sánchez Narbón, *La corona de Aragón y Segorbe, durante la dinastía catalana* (Castellón, 1949), ch. 1.

45. "La dita esglesia de Sogob e de Xericha," a phrase from the king's letter cited in note 70.

46. See Chapter V on diocesan boundaries.

47. Almagro, *Albarracín*, III, 232.

48. F. de Asís Aguilar y Serrat, *Noticias de Segorbe y de su obispado*, 2 vols. (Segorbe, 1890), I, 144: "cum favore dicti regis occupavit locum de Muroveteri et multa alia, et tenuit occupata, de dioecesi Segobricen. et applicavit ea diocesi Valentino"; this is a fourteenth-century witness repeating what he has heard from elders of his locality.

49. *Itinerari*, pp. 104–105 (doc. of July 9, 1233); cf. *Viage literario*, III, 39–41.

50. Gorosterratzu, *Rada*, p. 57.

51. Aguilar, *Noticias de Segorbe*, I, 78n.: "nequeat commode sustentari . . . tale auxilium [des, ut] non cogatur in opprobrium pontificalis officii mendicare."

52. *Viage literario*, III, 11; see too pp. 42–43. Almagro also gives the document (*Historia de Albarracín*, III, 296–297, doc. 41 and p. 298, doc. 42 confirming it to Bishop Simon in 1238). Chabás, "Çeit Abu Çeit," p. 164.

53. See note 15 and text; and Chapter XIV.

54. Aguilar, *Segorbe*, I, 81–82 citing from Segorbe archives. Lloréns gives the document establishing a papal commission (*Sede de Segorbe en Valencia*, p. 39).

55. Arch. Cath., perg. 2,310 (June 14, 1242): "sicut alie ecclesie sui diocesis pertinent pleno iure."

56. King James gave Prince Peter of Portugal, in return for his fief of Majorca and Minorca, a great barony comprising Segorbe, Almenara, Castellón de Burriana, Murviedro, and Morella; this was in mid-August 1244, three months after the Almizra treaty (cf. *Itinerari*, p. 169). Between then and spring of 1248 the crown intruded settlements in the area; Peter complained of this, but condoned it in 1248 (Arch. Crown, James I, perg. 1,146).

57. Aguilar, *Noticias de Segorbe*, pp. 83-84. *Viage literario*, III, 45 and n. Pérez, Almagro, and others date this incident 1237 as representing the earliest opportunity for its occurrence; but Lloréns convincingly argues that the documentary evidence favors 1245 (*Sede de Segorbe*, p. 16n.).

58. James may have had to reconquer the region just before 1245. Saʿīd gave to the bishop of Zaragoza in 1246 Mula, Arenoso, Montán, Tormo de Cirat, Cortes, Villamalefa, Villahermosa, Villamalur, Ibi, Tibi, Castalla, and so on.

59. Sometimes two men are suggested as filling part of this reign: Peter Argidi to 1259, Martin Alvarez to 1265, and then Peter Garcés succeeding to 1271. But Almagro and Villanueva consider them all one man, Peter Garcés or García a Cistercian of Piedra monastery and a native of Teruel (*Viage literario*, III, 46 ff.; *Historia de Albarracín*, III, 238, 273 ff.). Almagro also inclines to putting a Bishop Giles briefly between Simon and Peter; possibly Giles was the bishop involved in the bell-ringing episode.

60. Aguilar, *Noticias de Segorbe*, I, 85-86. Lloréns contests Aguilar's date for the letter to James, changing it from March 18, 1246 to April 16, 1247 (*Sede de Segorbe en Valencia*, p. 17 and n.).

61. Laguía transcribes the first bull in his documentary appendix (*Catálogo*, pp. 228-229) as does Lloréns (*Sede de Segorbe*, pp. 40-41). Almagro gives the bull to determine boundaries (*Albarracín*, III, 127-128, doc. 20) and the first bull (pp. 129-130, doc. 22). See too Aguilar, *Segorbe*, I, 86. Some of Segorbe's canons and dignitaries, apparently appointed in 1239, appear in the *Ordinatio ecclesiae valentinae*; Simon Peter is archdeacon of Segorbe, Diego (*Didacus*) is sacristan, Roderick is archdeacon of Alpuente (pp. 353, 376).

62. The wry characterization is Fuente's (*Historia eclesiástica*, IV, 261).

63. Innocent's bull of 1248 describing the ensuing tumult is in Aguilar, *Noticias de Segorbe*, I, 86-87. See also Sanchís Sivera, "Arnaldo de Peralta," pp. 106-107, and accounts in Lloréns and Almagro.

64. Morera, *Tarragona cristiana*, II, 79.

65. Aguilar, *Segorbe*, I, 86-87: "nolentes igitur tantum facinus relinquere impunitum, ne transeat aliis in exemplum."

66. Arch. Cath., perg. 4,615 (Feb. 24, 1248): "constituimus procuratorem nostrum vos P. Guillelmum Rectorem ecclesie de Carayana." Is this a cleric of the Valencia diocese despatched to Rome? Or one already there, from somewhere in James's realms, now delegated? The name is close to any number of towns: Cayrent, "Xericha" (Jérica), Gayaran, Carabaña, and so on. Sanchís Sivera makes him rector of Cariñena ("Arnaldo de Peralta," p. 109).

67. Aguilar, *Noticias de Segorbe*, I, doc. on p. 88.

68. *Ibid.*, p. 89: "defendens, sibi restitui facias . . . universa quibus per praedictos Episcopum et Archidiaconum se quaeritur expoliatum."

69. *Ibid.*, docs. on pp. 89-90. Almagro and Villanueva date it 1258, Laguía and Aguilar 1259. Laguía gives a fresh transcription in the appendix to his *Catálogo*, pp. 230-231.

70. Arch. Crown, James I, Reg. Canc. 10, fol. 98 (June 28, 1258). Sanchís

Sivera transcribes it in his "Arnaldo de Peralta" (p. 108) and Almagro in his *Albarracín* (III, 353-354, doc. 71). The pope had asked that Valencia's legitimate interests not be harmed, so James argued that "las cartas del apostoli eran contrarios la una de la otra." Almagro discusses the Toledo influence.

71. Aguilar, *Noticias*, I, 93 (May 7, 1274).

72. *Ibid.*, p. 94 (Nov. 15, 1275 and July 13, 1277). Tortosa seems to have got a share by unfair means (see p. 145); on her role see also Bayerri, *Tortosa*, VII, 151, 448.

73. There is a whole series of documents in the cathedral archives of Valencia on the towns lost in 1275-1277. Separately treated, for example, are Algar, Algimia, Almedíjar, Alpuente, Andilla, Aras de Alpuente, Benaxebe, Chelva, Domeño, Matet, Soneja, Sot, Toro, Tuéjar, Valle de Almonacid, and others.

74. *Rationes decimarum*, I, 271-272. Excommunication in Arch. Crown doc., Chapter V, note 48.

75. *Viage literario*, III, 60; Morera, *Tarragona cristiana*, II, 300. There are documents in the royal archives on Peter Costa or Zacosta for 1278-1279 and later. See, for example, Arch. Crown, Peter III, Reg. Canc. 40, fol. 83v, three documents of April 3, 1278, ordering the officials to surrender revenues and goods belonging to the Segorbe diocese; fol. 84, a document of the same date and tenor to the "Christianis et Sarracenis de termino de Altura et de Castellnova," and one ordering that the widow of a lay lord restore the "instrumenta, privilegia, et alia bona Episcopalia"; Reg. Canc. 41, fol. 88v, on the opposition of four townships to the first fruits "et alia iura" of Segorbe in their parishes (June 3, 1279); see too the documents given in Chapter IX, note 29.

76. *Viage literario*, III, 58-59.

NOTES TO CHAPTER IV. THE PARISH AS A FRONTIER INSTITUTION

1. *Repartimiento de Sevilla*, I, 354-355. See my "The Parish as a Frontier Institution in Thirteenth-Century Valencia," *Speculum*, XXXVII (1962), 244-251.

2. See the strong letter to the pope by James II of Aragon in 1311, complaining of this fact in the kingdom of Granada (Manuel Mariano Ribera, *Centuria primera del real y militar instituto de la inclita religión de Nuestra Señora de la Merced redempción de cautivos cristianos* [Barcelona, 1726], p. 3).

3. Antonio Ubieto Arteta, "La introducción del rito romano en Aragón y Navarra," *HS*, I (1948), 299-324.

4. Arch. Crown, James I, Reg. Canc. 19, fol. 162 (Aug. 20, 1274): "non solum Christiani set iudei etiam et sarraceni quilibet."

5. Document quoted in Chapter V, note 1.

6. Al-Ḥimyarī, *Kitāb ar-Rawḍ*, pp. 64, 66.

7. Aguilar, *Noticias de Segorbe*, I, 84; the details emerge in a trial of 1323, where the witnesses recalled hearing this local history from their fathers. See above, Chapter III, note 57 and text.

8. John Langdon-Davies, *Gatherings from Catalonia* (London, 1953), pp. 111-112; an Englishman is describing the impression made today by parish bells of the Catalan village where he is resident. The primate of Toledo at the period of the Valencia crusade, Roderick Simon of Rada, speaks fondly of the introduction of the bells, "bene sonantibus," into conquered Cordova (*De rebus Hispaniae*, p. 206, and see p. 137).

9. R. B. Donovan in his *The Liturgical Drama in Medieval Spain* (Toronto, 1958) is a victim of these arguments in the case of Valencia, a minor flaw in an

excellent monograph. For the quotes above, and background, see especially pp. 29, 74, 98, 120, 139, and 168–169. Chabás and Sanchís Sivera regrettably contributed to the Mozarabic thesis the support of their authority and ingenuity.

10. Arch. Cath., James I, perg. 1,316 (Nov. 17, 1243): "propter terre novitatem et sacerdotum raritatem."

11. Arch. Cath., perg. 1,320 (Feb. 10, 1250): "cupientes circa ministros Christi cultum divini nominis ampliare, Ecclesie nostre utilitate et necessitate et servitorum raritate pensatis."

12. Arch. Cath., perg. 3,104 (Aug. 8, 1267).

13. Arch. Cath., perg. 1,325 (Jan. 29, 1257), a confirmation by the pope: "cum itaque sicut ex parte vestra fuit propositum coram nobis in Ecclesia vestra pensatis ipsius facultatibus diligenter Quindenarium Canonicorum numerum dixeritis statuendum, Nos . . . confirmamus." Also perg. 1,356 (Feb. 22, 1279) raising the number to twenty. Both documents show that the number is equated to the revenues; one must remember that the canons had numerous assistants also at the services. In 1259 the bishop was planning to increase the liturgical splendor, the daily payment to the canons, the number of canons, or the number of the "ecclesie servitorium," as revenues grow (legajo 661, fasc. 1, fol. 3r).

14. Moorman, *Church Life*, pp. 52–53, 55–56, 67, 69, 198.

15. Johannes Vincke, "Das Patronatsrecht der aragonischen Krone," *Gesammelte Aufsätze zur Kulturgeschichte Spaniens*, Spanische Forschungen der Görresgesellschaft, vol. X (Münster, 1955), pp. 57–58, 69 ff. "Die Krone nahm nur ihre eigenen Interessen wahr, wenn sie diese Entwicklung tatkräftig förderte" (p. 57); examples follow from the reign of James I. In Valencia the royal generosity in this respect will be noted for St. Vincent's (below, Chapter XV); James I also had chaplaincies at the Valencia cathedral, at his Valencia palace or residence, at the castle chapel of Játiva, and so on. Somewhat over a hundred years later, the total of crown chantries in the kingdom of Valencia would be considerable; besides those at St. Vincent's and the half dozen or so at the palace, there was one each at Játiva, Liria, and Segorbe; and one each in the capital at St. John of Jerusalem, St. Clare's, the Zaidia, St. Stephen's, St. John of Boatella, and the cathedral. In the royal chapel at Valencia by 1346 there were "sechs Kaplaneien und zwei Sängerstellen" (p. 66); at the Perpignan chapel, about this time, there were twenty priests, twelve canons, and eight clerics.

16. Arch. Cath., perg. 2,374 (Nov. 11, 1277): "ut sic servitores condecentem remunerationem maiorem habeant vel minorem."

17. *Constitutiones sive ordinationes insignis metropolitanae ecclesiae valentinae ab eius primaeva fundatione et origine*, ed. Miguel Pérez de Miedes (Valencia, 1546), fols. 50v–51. There would sometimes be a kind of religious congregation also to support at a parish church, pious men and women who took vows and dedicated themselves to the parish church in residence there. We have no documentation on this for Valencia, but a contemporary example at Vich may be seen in the *Diplomatari de Sant Bernat Calvó, abat de Santes Creus, bisbe de Vich*, ed. E. Junyent (Reus, 1956), doc. 93 (Aug. 20, 1236).

18. *Viage literario*, III, 57–58n.; these were ejected in that year by the claimant of Segorbe.

19. *Ibid.*, IV, doc. on pp. 265–266. The vicar was Ferrer Dareys; there was a priest, Berengar Ferrer, and apparently two lesser clerics. At St. Felix's in the Játiva castle, Raymond of Montblanch is chaplain.

20. Arch. Crown, James I, perg. 1,556 (1258).

21. "Constitutiones synodales valentinae diocesis," *Collectio maxima conciliorum omnis Hispaniae et novi orbis*, ed. José Sáenz de Aguirre and Giuseppe

4—II

Catalani, 6 vols. (Rome, 1753–1755), V, 197, 209. It is interesting to note that, within the restricted limits of what has become modern Belgium, there were some ninety fully organized chapters around 1125; only five were cathedral and fifteen religious, the others being secular. Every town of importance had one and sometimes two chapters; they could be found in lesser places too. (Cf. Moreau, *Église en Belgique*, III, 346.) Daily Mass in all churches and chapels, with matins beforehand, seems to have been the usual thing in England; parishioners attended the office frequently (Moorman, *Church Life*, pp. 69, 73, 74n.); one English decree even had to remind priests that absence of a congregation did not excuse them from recitation of the office for that day (p. 229).

22. *Colección diplomática*, doc. 1,051 (Jan. 28, 1246): "hi qui sua largiuntur ecclesiis non videntur suum patrimonium diminuere sed augere."

23. Arch. Crown, James I, Reg. Canc. 22, fol. 43 (June 15, 1276). "Noverint universi cum nos Jacobus . . . a manibus infidelium eripuerimus castrum Xative in Regno Valencie . . . in eo debeant divina semper officia celebrari. Idcirco . . . instituimus unam cappellaniam pro capella beate Marie castri Xative memorati. In quo unus presbyter semper celebret divina officia tam de die quam de nocte." See also *Viage literario*, IV, 265–267.

24. *Colección diplomática*, doc. 1,033 (Dec. 11, 1234): "loca religiosa," "divinum officium ibi semper indessinenter celebretur."

25. See the emphasis on the parish along these lines in J. M. Font y Rius, "Orígenes del régimen municipal de Cataluña," *AHDE*, XVII (1946), 284 ff., and cf. pp. 291, 239.

26. Luigi Nanni carefully traces the development of the sub-parish in his *La parrocchia studiata nei documenti lucchesi dei secoli viii–xiii*, Analecta gregoriana, no. 47 (Rome, 1948); see esp. pp. 56–59, 145 ff., 188–190. One can distinguish from the strict sub-parish the situation where one priest served or held two parishes. The "substantial transformation" from chapel to semi-parochial status began from the end of the twelfth century (p. 182); the process was faster in the city than in the country (pp. 157–158); the Lucca diocese had 59 original parishes in the country areas, but 611 churches parochial or quasi-parochial in 1260 (p. 188). C. Boyd, *Tithes and Parishes in Medieval Italy, the Historical Roots of a Modern Problem* (Ithaca, N.Y., 1952), gives details of the parish in the twelfth and thirteenth century, illustrating with examples from northern Italy; she sees all this as a part of the general movement to local autonomy (p. 158). On the evolution of Belgian parishes see Moreau, *Église en Belgique*, II, 1–22. Moorman has synthesized a large amount of information available on English parishes, especially in his first chapter. There is nothing comparable for the parishes of thirteenth-century Aragon. Some peculiarities of the Spanish Visigothic background are detailed in G. Martínez Díez, *El patrimonio eclesiástico en la España visigoda, estudio histórico-jurídico*, (Miscelánea Comillas, no. 32 [Palencia, 1959]); the author's theses are still being discussed, but deepen understanding of the later, thirteenth-century situation.

27. *Diplomatari de Sant Bernat Calvó*, doc. 226 (Dec. 17, 1241). Another case at Vich (1239) seems to have involved a parish and its emancipated chapel. The "parishioners" of St. Julian's and the "parishioners" of St. Felix's conducted an extensive dispute over their common "cleric," a priest named William. William was vicar for a cathedral dignitary; he celebrated daily and Sunday Mass at St. Julian's and would conduct all parochial duties there; but at the St. Felix's subchurch he would offer no more than the Sunday Mass and a Mass on each of three weekdays. The bishop presided over an arbitration, by which each church received a permanent "chaplain" in residence; each was to be a curate, sharing

William's cure of souls under his jurisdiction and giving him two-thirds of the revenues (doc. 142, June 20, 1239).

28. Document cited in Chapter XI, note 98. See note 38 for Murviedro.

29. "Colección de cartas pueblas," no. XV (Villahermosa, Mar. 9, 1243), *BSCC*, IX (1928), 166–168: "concedimus quod filii vestri sint semper rectores in ecclesiis dictorum locorum dum sint tamen sufficientes in predictis."

30. This is called a *patronato colletivo* by Nanni, who says that many Italian churches at this time were thus controlled, having been rebuilt or enlarged by them (*Parrocchia*, p. 190). Possibly this was not uncommon in the rural hinterland of Valencia. The community would name and present the candidate; and diocesan authorities then confirmed, invested, and led him into possession (*ibid.*).

31. The document expresses uncertainty whether the land can hold 150 families.

32. Manuel Betí, "Primeros señores de Castellón," *BSCC*, VII (1926), appendix of documents, doc. 7 (Feb. 22, 1252), pp. 187–188, where James calls the director of the monastery church of St. Vincent's "priori vel Rectori eiusdem ecclesie." Resident clerics in charge of outlying churches were "often styled rector" in thirteenth-century England (Moorman, *Church Life*, p. 14). About half of the English parishes had rectors, the others being vicarages (p. 24). Vicarages spread rapidly in England from the year 1200 (pp. 44–45, with figures); the Lateran council drew the "Magna Carta of the parish priest," by insisting upon a proper salary and perpetual incumbency for vicars. Moorman offers some interesting conjecture on the word "chaplain" (p. 35). Nanni views the sub-parishes as "vere e proprie parrocchie," even though he underscores their dependence (*Parrocchia*, p. 188).

33. See Chapter V, note 35 (no parishioners). The Tortosa document is in Hipólito Samper, *Montesa ilustrada*, 2 vols. (Valencia, 1669), part 4, art. 4. In a corresponding settlement of 1243 with the Hospitallers the Valencia bishop refers to the "capellani parochiales." In the feudal vocabulary, a *capellania* was a church, church revenue, or church appointment (especially a pastorate) belonging to a lord.

34. Nanni, *Parrocchia*, p. 57. After the conquest of Majorca, there were rectors at Pollensa from 1252 to 1257, vicars from then on.

35. "Colección de cartas pueblas," no. III (Aras, Jan. 23, 1243), *BSCC*, I (1920), 187–188; and no. XV, *ibid.* Aras had already had one priest for many years. One document tells us that "rectors" were shortly to be put in charge in the churches "de Domenyo, de Andilla, de Canalibus, de Altoponte, de Ariis et de Arcubus" (Lloréns, "Deanato de Valencia," pp. 16–17, doc. of Sept. 22, 1277).

36. Arch. Cath., perg. 1,316 (Nov. 17, 1243). Cf. Chapter XIII, note 31.

37. Arch. Cath., perg. 4,639 (Dec. 23, 1256): "rectorem ecclesie ville et termini de cuyllera."

38. J. Toledo Girau, *El castell i la vall d'Alfandech de Marinyèn des de sa reconquesta per Jaume I, fins la fundació del monestir de Valldigna per Jaume II* (Castellón de la Plana, 1936), pp. 56, 63. Would contributory sub-churches help explain the surprisingly large income of "the major church" at Murviedro, which paid a crusade assessment of 1,200 solidi (600 each year)? Even in the unlikely event of the sum's covering all five years of crusade tax, this would be the wealthiest pastorate in all Valencia, unless part of the income is nonparochial (*Rationes decimarum*, I, 256, 263; the rector of St. John's in Murviedro gives 76 plus 131 in 1279, and 155 in 1280—both goodly sums also).

39. *Repartimiento* p. 325: "omnes ecclesias de Roteros," "omnes ecclesias de Boatella" (*an.* 1242); *Rationes decimarum*, I, 262–263. A crusade tax for the six years 1275–1280 was paid "a Petro Lupi, rectore ecclesiarum Rivi de Milariis," in 1280. The holdings on the upper Mijares at this time must have been poor enough,

yet a tax of over 150 solidi per annum was returned, much more than the average pastor in the kingdom gave. How many were these plural "churches," under the one rector, is unknown. (*Rationes*, I, 266). But allowance was earlier made for future expansion and for the provision then of rectors in this area (1260): see document in note 131.

40. *Nomenclátor geográfico-eclesiástico de los pueblos de la diócesis de Valencia con los nombres antiguos y modernos de los que existen o han existido*, comp. J. Sanchís Sivera (Valencia, 1922), pp. 174, 192, 399. An interesting Valencian illustration of the system may be drawn from the sixteenth century. The parish of Beniardá was separated from Guadalest and made independent in 1535; the rector was to say a Mass on feast days both here and at Benifato. To these places were joined the populations of Adzaneta, Benihalet, Benichays, Maurar, Benimuça, Benicácin, and Morescas—yet the total census of the parish amounts to only eighty-three households. Morescas had fifteen households, so the average village here averaged ten or less. By this date of course Morisco villages are probably in question (*ibid.*, p. 105).

41. *Ibid.*, pp. 250 (Guadalest), 211 (Chiva), 14 (Adzaneta), 249 (Gandía), 23 (Albalat), 196 (Confrides), 219 (Madrona). Mateo Rotger y Capllonch, *Historia de Pollensa*, 3 vols. (Palma de Mallorca, 1897–1906), I, 26.

42. See notes 94 ff., 123 ff., and in Chapter VIII, notes 145 ff., with text.

43. Arch. Cath., perg. 2,301 (Oct. 28, 1236): "primo et ante omnia dotemus ibi cathedralem Ecclesiam et alias Suffraganeas." See also *Aureum opus*, doc. 1, fol. 1; *Collectio conciliorum Hispaniae*, V, 188; *Itinerari*, p. 125; and the king's agreement with Bishop-elect Ferrer in Arch. Cath., perg. 1,304, *an.* 1240. The manner of endowment was to be decided by five arbiters: the archbishop of Tarragona, the masters of the Hospital and Temple, Prince Ferdinand, and the viscount of Cardona.

44. Arch. Cath., perg. 2,302 (Oct. 18, 1238); *Colección diplomática*, doc. 184; *Aureum opus*, doc. 3, fol. lv, cf. doc. 12, fol. 4r,v (1241). A *Repartimiento* note sums this: "ecclesia Cathedralis Valencie: omnes mezquitas sive ecclesias infra et extra muros Valencie constitutas et constituendas et omnes domos et hereditates supradictis ecclesiis pertinentes" (p. 291). The 1236 and 1238 documents are also in Vicente Branchát, *Tratado de los derechos y regalías que corresponden al real patrimonio en el reyno de Valencia . . .*, 3 vols. (Valencia, 1784–1786), II, ch. 1, doc. 1; III, ch. 10, doc. 1. The gift gave "ciminteria ultra duodecim vasa continentia." González perhaps unwisely concludes that in Seville the supporting properties of the mosques were not given to the church at the conquest of that city (*Repartimiento de Sevilla*, I, 351).

45. See, for example, Chapter X, note 158; and Chapter XV, note 164.

46. *Aureum opus*, doc. 2, fol. lv; *Colección diplomática*, doc. 185 (Oct. 22, 1238).

47. *Llibre dels feyts*, chs. 445, 448–449. Valencia city mosque below, in Chapter VIII, note 92.

48. Vicente Pelufo, "Topografía de Alcira árabe," *ACCV*, VII (1934), 26.

49. *Nomenclátor de Valencia*, pp. 122 (Benigánim), 213 (Chiva), 178 (Carpesa), 177 (Carlet; it is not known whether this is the thirteenth-century church or a subsequent one), 273 (Calpe), 295 (Mirambell).

50. *Ibid.*, p. 285: "cum mali exemplum sit, et preteriti sceleris recordationem habeat, videtur averti prorsus debere, ut nullum eius supersit vestigium."

51. *Ibid.*, pp. 312 (Navarrés), 341 (Petrés), 334 (Pardines). A Morisco parish was added at Pardines in the fourteenth century, served by this ex-mosque; however, Mass was rarely said here, and it remained a Moslem symbol, so that it was ordered destroyed and the Moriscos sent to the original parish.

52. *Ibid.*, p. 568.

53. *Aureum opus*, doc. 12, fol. 4r,v (*an.* 1261): "excepto ciminterio in quo assignavimus generale forum Valencie fieri," apparently a building, in which eminent men may have been interred.

54. *Repartimiento*, pp. 530 (stable), 24 ("Guido").

55. Arch. Cath., perg. 1,820 (Dec. 18, 1260): "stabilimus vobis Boneto Fusterio et vestris imperpetuum ad censum et ameliorandum quandam mezquitam sive oratorium quam habemus [*the bishop and chapter*] in civitate valencie in parrochia sancti bartholomei." His alodial property fronts it on three sides; a neighbor's inn closes the fourth side.

56. See perg. of 1256 transcribed in Chapter VIII, note 123.

57. Arch. Cath., perg. 4,653 (Mar. 28, 1270): "quoddam spacium terre in quo fuit mesquita tempore sarracenorum quod debet continere in se octo braxias regales in longitudine et duas et dimidium in latitudine." We do not know if this was a usual size, or just what kind of building stood here; perhaps it was a single-room oratory. For the oratory see document in Chapter VIII, note 86.

58. Arch. Cath., perg. 1,308 (Oct. 21, 1240); published in Chabás, *Episcopologio valentino*, pp. 69-70.

59. Arch. Cath., perg. 2,912 (May 5, 1265) as transcribed in Chapter VIII, note 93.

60. See Chapter VIII, e.g., in notes 95, 104, 109.

61. Arco, "Vidal de Cañellas obispo de Huesca," pp. 516-517, doc. 8 (July 15, 1250).

62. *Repartimiento*, p. 516: "mezquita domini regis." See pp. 536-537, 606. "G. de Seger miles et homines de archiepiscopo: de X meçquitis ad opus domorum illam . . . et statice cum illa domo sive domibus quae pertinebant ad illam meçquitam" (p. 299). In 1244 four men acquire as many mosques, which have names: "Metalponti," "Magi Celili," "Dalabidi," and in the Jewish sector "Xopelela" (pp. 300-301). "Dalabidi" may be the "Dalgalcha" of p. 240. There is a Moslem monastic stronghold near the sea: "turrim sive rapitam sitam iuxta mare et Guadalaviar et dicitur Rapita orationis" (pp. 195, 203).

63. See, for example, the analogous situations at Huesca and at Zaragoza in Zurita, *Anales*, I, *lib.* I, *c.* 44.

64. *Repartimiento de Sevilla*, I, 534-542. Mosques were fairly numerous in these Moslem cities of Spain, there being a central one in the medina and others in each suburb and section of the city. See Leopoldo Torres Balbás, "Estructura de las ciudades hispano-musulmanas: la medina, los arrabales y los barrios," *Al-Andalus*, XVIII (1953), 149-177.

65. Arch. Cath., perg. 2,327, and *Colección diplomática*, doc. 1,044 (May 15, 1242): "quoddam fosarium sarracenicum et Mezquitam que cum ipso continetur . . . in civitate Valencie"; "mezchita simili"; "in alio fossario."

66. But see Chapter V, notes 31, 167 with text; the English urban parishes were tiny and numerous.

67. The 1241 confirmation and interpretation shows that this is to be understood of the whole diocese (Arch. Cath., perg. 2,303; *Colección diplomática*, doc. 224).

68. "Colleción de cartas pueblas," no. LVII, *BSCC*, XVI (1935), 386: "meschidam maiorem cum omnibus alodiis et possessionibus suis, necnon et meschidas exteriores tocius episcopatus, tam edificatas quam desertas, cum omnibus alodiis et possessionibus suis," as well as "omnia cimiteria." Cf. documents above, note 44, and Chapter III, notes 34, 35 with text.

69. Samper, *Montesa ilustrada*, part 4, art. 4, Hospitaller agreement.

70. Arch. Cath., perg. 2,331, quoted in Chapter VIII, note 67.

71. See document cited in note 86.

72. *Repartimiento*, for example pp. 601 (St. Bartholomew's), 524 (St. Andrew's), 598 (St. Lawrence's), 543 (St. Thecla's). See pp. 577, 536, 547.

73. Julián Ribera Tarragó, "Enterramientos moros en Valencia," *El archivo*, I (1886), 209-212. Cf. also F. A. Roca Traver, "Un siglo de vida mudéjar en la Valencia medieval (1238-1338)," *EEMCA*, V (1952), 134-135.

74. Arch. Cath., perg. 2,341 (Feb. 7, 1241). Is Peter the brother of the bishop of Zaragoza (see *Itinerari*, p. 70)?

75. Arch. Cath., perg. 2,368 (Dec. 5, 1241): "pro omnibus possessionibus quondam ad mezchitas pertinentibus unam iovatam . . . francham et liberam in predicto Castro in secano."

76. Arch. Cath., legajo LX, fasc. 1: "attendentes quod periculosum sit altaria erigi nisi ministros habeant."

77. Arch. Cath., perg. 1,304, where the bishop-elect lays down the principle that no church of the diocese is to be without an endowment (June 1240). Ferrer was bishop-elect also in the May 1240 provincial council at Valencia.

78. Arch. Cath., pergs. 2,341 (Feb. 7, 1241); 2,368 (Dec. 5, 1241); unnumbered, following perg. 2,368 (same date). Is "Toris" Torás near Segorbe, or perhaps Torres, or Turís?

79. Arch. Cath., perg. 2,431, for example (Jan. 19, 1263).

80. Arch. Crown, Peter III, Reg. Canc. 41, fol. 98 (June 29, 1279). "Intelleximus per venerabilem electum Segorbicensem quod aliqui homines de Segorbio detinent occupata aliqua loca in quibus ipso tempore Sarracenorum fuerunt mezquite et cimiteria. Quare mandamus vobis quatenus dicta loca faciatis restitui visis presentibus dicto electo vel inde sibi respondere ut de iure . . . fuerit faciendum."

81. *Ordinatio ecclesiae valentinae*, p. 233: "omnes parrochiales meçquitas episcopatus Valentie."

82. Arch. Cath., perg. 5,960 (July 1240): "ad opus Capellanorum ibidem." Again in perg. 2,351 (April 1242), with house and garden.

83. Arch. Crown, James I, Reg. Canc. 22, fol. 50v: "illud podium quod est ante castrum de corbaria ad construendum ibi ecclesiam, et domos . . . et unum ortum quattuor fanecatarum contiguum domibus predictis et duas iovatas terre contiguas dicto podio, cum introitibus et . . . suis pertinenciis . . ." The document is a renewal of his grant to the present pastor's predecessors, and this is the original document incorporated in it; hence the late date, July 12, 1276.

84. Arch. Crown, Peter III, Canc. 44, fol. 180v (May 10, 1280): "mandamus vobis quatenus assignetis ferrando de orto rectori ecclesie de pego domos et ortum in valle de pego ad opus eiusdem ecclesie prout in aliis plantationibus Regni Valencie est sic consuetum." Moorman says that the English pastor got a similar land grant; ancient law called for twice as much as a villein's holdings; in some places in thirteenth-century England a pastor (though hardly a vicar) would have as much as forty-nine or a hundred acres in land of all kinds, such as arable, meadow, waste, forest, etc. (*Church Life*, pp. 112-115).

85. Arch. Cath., perg. 2,341 (Feb. 7, 1241): "et ad opus capellani ibidem pro tempore servientis donum [*for* domum] et ortum competens."

86. *Collectio conciliorum Hispaniae*, V, 189-190. Arch. Cath., legajo XXII, no. 3 (perg.), (Nov. 9, 1241): "donamus et promittimus assignare singulis cappellanis in singulis ecclesiis paroquialibus, in quibus ordinati fuerint deservientibus, singulas domos et singulos hortos competentes."

87. *Colección diplomática*, doc. 1,017 (Sept. 10, 1225): "tradimus domino Deo et ecclesie beate Marie de Peniscola que adhuc, auxiliante Domino, est edificanda et construenda, et . . . dertusensi episcopo, et capellano prefate ecclesie de Penis-

cola, domos et possessiones quas Zuleima Bolahan sarracenus [habet] in Peniscola et in terminis ejus."

88. Samper, *Montesa ilustrada*, pt. 4, art. 4, p. 17: "mansum, et hortum, et domos, et cimiterium."

89. *Colección diplomática*, doc. 942 (May 7, 1268): "indulgemus ecclesiis parochialibus civitatis et diocesis Valencie, quas vos . . . episcopus et successores vestri simul vel successive duxeritis erigendas, quod possint adquirere et habere per empcionem, legatum, donacionem, vel alium quencumque titulum sive modum a quibuscunque personis, parrochianis suis vel aliis centum viginti jovatas terre franchas et liberas . . ."

90. Thus the first fruits at Tales, paid by the Moors to the church of Onda, were a fraction less: "primiciam videlicet de XXX barchillas unam et sic de universis rebus quod consuetum est dare primiciam" ("Colección de cartas pueblas," no. LXXXIV, *BSCC*, XXVIII, 1952, 137–138). See the *Aureum opus*, fol. 14r,v, *an.* 1261; and *Furs, lib.* IV, *rub.* XXIV *c.* 1. See tithe and first-fruits settlement, below, in Chapter IX.

91. Arch. Cath., doc. cited in note 86.

92. Arch. Cath., perg. 2,310 (June 14, 1242): "ut rectores earundem inde valeant comode sustentari."

93. Arch. Cath., perg. 2,418 (Mar. 16, 1279), for example. The first fruits of the cathedral parish and of other parishes helped support the sacristan of the chapter (e.g. perg. 4,616, June 4, 1271). Even in the constitution cited, some first fruits were reserved to the precentor by way of a vicarship. The Játiva churches would similarly lose their first fruits to a dignitary. After a prolonged struggle, the people of Morella lost two-thirds of their first fruits to the bishop and chapter of Tortosa (*Colección diplomática*, doc. 1,173; June 16, 1263). The Valencia dean took the first fruits, tithe, and patronage of two churches in 1260, but six of the churches later assigned him kept the first fruits (Lloréns, "Deanato de Valencia," pp. 16–17).

94. Arch. Cath., perg. 2,432 (June 14, 1257). Artal of Luna finally yielded the first fruits of Paterna and Manises; past nonpayment was indulgently remitted. A compromise over the ecclesiastical revenues on the domains of Maria Ferrandis (February 1263) retained the first fruits for the rector there, but allowed that lady to keep those on flocks wintering or transient (perg. 2,431). First fruits were also retained, by an arbitration, in the wide domains of Simon Pérez of Arenós for the rectors (perg. 2,413; cf. the case in perg. 2,418); and indeed this is the universal rule.

95. Arch. Crown, Peter III, Reg. Canc. 59, fol. 100 (Aug. 25, 1282). Peter insists on collecting them in one set of places as James had also done ("exceptis tamen locis in quibus dictus dominus Rex pater noster ipsas primicias recipit [*sic*] et recipere debet"). And see Peter III, Reg. Canc. 40, fol. 155 (Sept. 1, 1278). Cf. Chapter IX, notes 66–68.

96. "Colección de cartas pueblas," no. III (of Ares, above): "et supradictam primiciam concedo vobis concilio ego Dompnus latrone quod mittatis ad oppus de illas ecclesias [*sic*]" (*an.* 1243). Is this the Latron near Morella, or a form of Ladrón? *Opus* here is construction or, more properly, upkeep and improvement (see p. 190).

97. *Ibid.*, no. XXXI (Vistabella, April 1251), *BSCC*, XIII (1932), 132–134.

98. *Ibid.*, no. XVIII (Catí, Jan. 25, 1239), *BSCC*, X (1929), 85–87: "dando scilicet decimam fideliter Sancte ecclesie et primiciam vestro concilio." And see the phrase nearly identical in his charter to Villafranca (no. XXXVIII; Villafranca, Feb. 7, 1239, *BSCC*, XIII [1932], 190–192). Blaise has the same phrase in his charter for Corachar and Peña de Aronoal (*ibid.*, XXXVII [1961], 268–269).

99. E.g. no. XV (of Villahermosa) March 9, 1253, *BSCC*, IX (1928), 166–168; and no. XLVII (Villanueva, area of Castell de Cabres), February 1237, *BSCC*, XIV (1933), 200–201.

100. Arch. Cath., perg. 2,351 (April 1, 1242): "recipiat Capellanus parochialis a nobis instituendus primicias et alia sicut in Episcopatu Valentie recipient ceteri capellani."

101. Anastasio López, "Confesores de la familia real de Aragón," *Archivo ibero-americano*, XVI (1929), 152–153.

102. Juan Puig, "Senyors de Morella durant el segle xiiiè," *BSCC*, XXXI (1955), pp. 100–101. See *Colección diplomática*, doc. 1,173 (June 16, 1263).

103. But at Ballestar we find "primiciam rectori ecclesie loci predicti"; this is because the diocese of Tortosa means to insist that the monastery of Benifasá is not to have it ("Collección de cartas pueblas," no. L, Mar. 9, 1278, *BSCC*, XIV [1933], 433–436). At Calatayud in 1315 in Aragon proper, the "usum antiquum," which the town "ab antiquo consueverunt," and which previous bishops had always respected, was that the people sent out their own collectors without reference to the bishop. The funds "consueverunt converti in ornamentis, luminariis, hedificacionibus et aliis apparatibus ecclesiarum ipsarum" (*Documenta selecta*, doc. 262, Nov. 16, 1315). This has some application to Valencia, not only by analogy and because settlers came also from the Tarazona diocese bringing their local customs for private law, but also because in the tithe controversy the customs of Tarazona and other dioceses would be used to stabilize those of Valencia (see below, Chapter IX).

104. *Rationes decimarum* I, 177–178: "ab hominibus de Burriana," etc. Cf. p. 174. The same pattern is seen in the 1279 lists, p. 170.

105. A. Sánchez Gozalbo, "El castillo de Polpis," *BSCC*, XIV (1933), 459: "et vos populatores teneamini facere in dicto loco ecclesiam."

106. Arch. Cath. Tortosa, cajón Donaciones y Privilegios, doc. 5: "pro operibus ecclesie vel aliis necessariis hominum de Morella."

107. "Colección de cartas pueblas," no. XX (Culla, Mar. 23, 1244), *BSCC*, XI (1930), 36–38: "etiam volumus et concedimus vobis . . . quod habeatis et percipiatis semper et in secula seculorum primiciam dicti loci et terminorum suorum ad reparacionem eclesiam [*for* ecclesiarum?] et murorum dicti loci." The repair of walls was an object of the first fruits elsewhere in James's kingdoms too (see Vincke, preface to *Documenta selecta*, p. xvii).

108. Arch. Cath., perg. 2,341 (Feb. 7, 1241); but the sentence is not altogether free of ambiguity.

109. *Servicia* seems to be a generic name for many of these (Arch. Cath., perg. 2,413); *defunciones* and *oblaciones* seem to be equally wide (e.g. perg. 1,317). The latter two revenues along with candles are surrendered to the religious Knights of Mercy, to be collected from the resident parishioners ("abitancium ibidem," "hominum ibi comarancium") in perg. 2,363 and perg. 2,364. "Luminaria cotidiana" are an expected free-will offering (perg. 1,317), also oil for the church lamps; a distinction is made between different offerings of oil and candles, depending upon the intention of the donor (perg. 1,216). See too a typical enumeration in perg. 2,391. Ramón Bidagor discusses offerings in his *La "iglesia propia" en España, estudio histórico-canónico* (Analecta gregoriana, no. 4 [Rome, 1933], pp. 131–132). English fees as described by Moorman (*Church Life*, pp. 127–130) are similar, allowing for local differences; there was a Martinmas tax on grain, a mortuary of the second best piece of property from deceased parishioners owning three or more animals, bread for the altar (not for Mass, but to be blessed and dis-

tributed after Mass as a symbol; the cleric kept the surplus for domestic use), offerings when the ill were visited, etc.

110. Arch. Cath., perg. 2,391 (Sept. 18, 1255).

111. Arch. Cath., perg. 2,310 (June 14, 1242); the bishop's wishes were to be respected in the spending of this.

112. Moorman, *Church Life*, p. 137.

113. *Repartimiento de Sevilla*, I, 360. On the tithe see below, Chapters VIII and IX.

114. Arch. Cath., perg. 2,309 (June 23, 1240).

115. Arch. Cath., perg. 2,311 (Oct. 21, 1245), where this information is summed up.

116. Arch. Cath., perg. 2,413 (Aug. 29, 1260). The division of the tithes between bishop and chapter of the Segorbe diocese is described in a document of late 1232 (*Viage literario*, III, 225-226); this would surely have applied to the Valencian regions then being added.

117. Arch. Cath., perg. 2,432 (June 14, 1257). After a careful consideration of necessary expenditures as balanced against known income, in the plentiful English records, Moorman concludes that an ordinary vicar or pastor was just making ends meet and had "little more than the average wage of a working man"—yet the English clergy had the tithe for themselves (*Church Life*, pp. 137-138).

118. Arch. Cath., perg. 2,374 (Nov. 11, 1277); the last are goods given "intuitu sue parrochie."

119. The case in note 29 may amount to this.

120. Arch. Crown, James I, Reg. Canc. 19, fol. 106v (Feb. 22, 1273). "Damus et concedimus tibi Johanni Gutierres consanguineo fidelis scriptoris nostri porcionis [?] bartholomei thome diebus omnibus vite tue ecclesiam de villa regali prope burrianam. Ita quod tu habeas dictam ecclesiam cum omnibus iuribus, et deservias eam die ac nocte in omnibus horis prout capellanus vel Rector ecclesie facere tenetur. Mandantes baiulis . . ."

121. Arch. Cath., perg. 4,639 (Dec. 23, 1256): "sit notum cunctis quod nos Frater Geraldus Amici castellanus emposte . . . elegimus et instituimus te Iohannem Capellanum et rectorem ecclesie ville et termini de cuyllera, dando . . . te dictam ecclesiam cum omnibus rebus et iuribus suis habitis et habendis." William Thomas was his successor, sometime before 1279 (see Chapter V, note 16).

122. Arch. Cath., perg. 2,381 (July 19, 1250). "Et quidquid beneficii redditus et proventus sollicitudine tua studio vel labore aut pia devocione fidelium ibidem advenerit seu accreverit, in usus tuos cedat et convertatur. Ita quod non tenearis nobis vel successoribus nostris aliquam reddere rationem. Salvo hoc nobis tantummodo et retento quod racione predicte comande tibi vel Ecclesie [priori] . . . ius aliquod vel dominium in predictam Ecclesiam nullatenus acquiratur. Et quod in festo Nativitatis domini nobis unum par caponum propter dominii recognicionem nomine census annuatim persolvas." A promise was given by the new chaplain (*ibid.*): "iuxta possibilitatem meam fideliter deservire et meliorare sine preiudicio tamen prefate Ecclesie [priori] . . ." St. Julian's was not parochial.

123. Arch. Crown, Peter III, Reg. Canc. 49, fol. 48v (Mar. 3, 1280): "visis presentibus inquiratis numerum et nomina Ecclesiarum parochialium omnium villarum et locorum tam nostrorum quam Ecclesiarum Religiosorum, nobilium militum . . ." The document is of the year 1280, but is making inquiry into charters published in Valencian parishes "ab antiquo."

124. Arch. Crown, Bulas, legajo I (Gregory VII), no. 3 and (Urban II), nos. 5-6. Sanchís Sivera defends the authenticity of the bulls (*Diócesis valentina*, II, 113). See especially Bidagor's *Iglesia propia* (e.g. p. 144); in ch. 8 he traces the evolution

of the feudal proprietary rights over the *iglesia propia* into personal patronage over the material aspects, half tolerated and half conceded to founders by our period. Bidagor challenges a number of Stutz's conclusions (cf. the latter's "Eigen-kirche, Eigenkloster," *Realencyklopädie für protestantische Theologie und Kirche,* 3rd ed., XXIII, 371). Vincke has pertinent general remarks in his "Patronatsrecht der aragonischen Krone," though he is specifically concerned with chantry bene-fices. See too Manuel Torres López, largely on the subsequent period, "La doctrina de las 'iglesias propias' en los autores españoles," *AHDE,* II (1925), 402–461. Mansilla Reoyo, *Iglesia castellano-leonesa,* p. 88.

125. See Chapter XIV.

126. Arch. Cath., perg. 2,310 (June 14, 1242).

127. Arch. Cath., perg. 5,960, for example (June 28, 1240).

128. Arch. Cath., perg. 787 (Feb. 1, 1246).

129. Arch. Cath., perg. 2,432 (June 14, 1257); and the sweeping claim in the "Colección de cartas pueblas," no. LVII (cited in note 68).

130. Vincke, "Patronatsrecht," p. 57.

131. Arch. Cath., perg. 2,413 (Aug. 29, 1260): "tamquam vero loci domino et fundatori ecclesiarum ius patronatus in omnibus ecclesiis terre rivi de Millares factis et in posterum faciendis in ecclesia ville de Andilla ut cum ipsas vel aliquam de predictis vacare rectore contigerit." See Aguilar, *Noticias de Segorbe,* I, 147–148, similar document in Segorbe capitular archives.

132. Chabás, "Çeid Abu Çeid," p. 164.

133. Arch. Cath., perg. 1,317: "in omnibus istis ecclesiis et aliis aliorum locorum quas dicti fratres dante domino per se adquirent eripient et liberabunt de mani-bus Sarracenorum vel et aliunde cum armis vel sine armis . . ."

134. Arch. Cath., perg. 3,104 (Aug. 8, 1267) where a cathedral chantry is in question. "Ydoneitatem quidem vel suficienciam intelligimus si sit honestus et noverit officium Ecclesiasticum, si sacerdos sit vel talis qui possit infra tempus modicum vel ad minus infra annum ad sacerdotalem ordinem promoveri. Nolu-mus eciam nec intendimus quod potest [habere] ignoranciam artis gramatice . . ." In the interval between presentation and appointment, the bishop promises to pay the candidate every day: "interim quidem videlicet dum presentatus in promo-vendo fuerit promitimus dare cotidie duodecim denarios sicut superius est expres-sum scilicet sex denarios presentato . . ."

135. The situation in England shortly before this time may persuade one that clerics who were priests would not be common on the Valencian frontier either. The bishop of Lincoln instituted (1209–1325) in the archdeaconry of Oxford one hundred and four rectors of whom one was definitely a priest, nineteen may very well have been, ten are undesignated, but five were deacons, forty-five were sub-deacons, five acolytes, and fifteen "clerics" (Moorman, *Church Life,* p. 34); such incumbents could chant the office but of course not say Mass nor hear confessions. Even if "chaplain" always means a priest, Hugh of Wells would have installed as rectors in three Lincoln archdeaconries only sixty-one priests out of two hundred and forty-eight chosen (i.e., less than a fourth) and his successor Grosseteste only one in five, out of two hundred and twenty-nine in the archdeaconry of Northamp-ton (p. 36). Some would probably be ordained later in their careers.

136. *Diócesis valentina,* II, 419–420n. This practice was perhaps connected, at least for some of its clerics, with the attempt by Toledo to establish jurisdiction here, a point suggested by the context of this legislation but overlooked by Sanchís Sivera.

137. See below, Chapter IX. See also Vincke, "Patronatsrecht," p. 55; the chantries founded by James and his successors, eighteen at Valencia city alone by the early fifteenth century, are listed and discussed there.

138. *Documenta selecta*, doc. 6 (Jan. 9, 1239): "quibuslibet . . . ecclesiis et monasteriis regni Valencie."

NOTES TO CHAPTER V. THE PARISH IN ACTION

1. Arch. Cath., perg. 1,316 (Nov. 17, 1243): "ex tunc tanquam veri rectores"; "in divinis ministrent officiis, parrochianos suos baptizent, et in foro penitenciali solvant, eligent [*sic*], nupcias eciam celebrent et cum iure funerandi omnia conferant ecclesiastica sacramenta quae per sacerdotes alios rite in Episcopatu valencie conferuntur." In a Vich document of 1234 the new rector is seen swearing fidelity and canonical obedience to his bishop (*Diplomatari de Sant Bernat Calvó*, doc. 44, Dec. 13, 1234). Cf. F. Claeys-Bouuaert, "Cure" and "Curé," *DDC*, IV, cols. 889–900 and 900–942; X. A. Baraniak, "Curé religieux," *ibid.*, cols. 941–959.

2. Juan Puig, "Capbreu d'algunes persones distingides d'Ares del Maestre," *BSCC*, XIII (1932), 432: "causa celebrandi . . . cum divinis quoque rebus, ac eciam schibis pulsandis nocte diebus."

3. Document in note 1: "ad Episcopalem Sinodum et Capitula conveniant temporibus consuetis."

4. Arch. Cath., perg. 2,364. See in the 1258 synod the instruction: "et ab ipsis Sacerdotibus populo praedicetur" (*Collectio conciliorum Hispaniae*, V, 197). The metropolitan council of 1229 at Lérida noted the lack of qualified men for parish preaching and ordered the bishops to provide special auxiliary clergy for this function where needed, especially in the bigger churches (*Colección de cánones y de todos los concilios de la iglesia de España y de América*, ed. J. Tejada y Ramiro, 7 vols., Madrid, 1859–1863, III, 331, no. 5). See too the sensible comments of D. W. Robertson, Jr. in his "Frequency of Preaching in Thirteenth-Century England" (*Speculum*, XXIV [1949], 376–388); though the point is still under discussion, parish preaching seems to have been more common than was previously thought.

5. Cf., for example, Chapter IV, note 106 (1263, Morella). Part of the service fee the appointee to the church of Cullera had to pay to his patrons the Hospitallers, 60 solidi every Christmas, was to be spent on the poor under their care (Arch. Cath., perg. 4,639; Dec. 23, 1256).

6. See note 1. This cherished privilege led to argument with the religious Orders (see Chapters X–XIII). The cemeteries appear in wills for example in 1271: "eligo namque sepulturam meam in ciminterio Sancti Stephani valencie" (Arch. Cath., perg. 1,105).

7. "Constitutiones synodales," p. 201: "caute et diligenter." The rector of a parish could even excommunicate according to Penyafort (though he cites as well the opinion of Hostiensis against this).

8. This is a neglected aspect of the history of notaries in James's realms. In 1282 a crown inquiry was being made, with documents to the justiciars of Valencia, Játiva and Morella as well as elsewhere in the kingdom of Aragon, as to all the parish churches both under diocesan and other jurisdiction where the notarial office has been filled "ex antiquo" by parish rectors (F. Carreras y Candi, *Miscelánea histórica catalana*, 2 vols. [Barcelona, 1905–1918], II, 350, doc.). See above, Chapter I, note 29.

9. Sanchís Sivera discusses the Valencian cemeteries of the time from the documents in "Vida íntima de los valencianos en la época foral" (*ACCV*, VI [1933], 40 ff.); the bishop's complaint was made in 1316. A synodal decree of 1262 forbade "ne aliquis sepelliatur intra principales parietes ecclesie" ("Para la historia del

derecho eclesiástico valenciano," ed. J. Sanchís Sivera, *AST*, IX [1933], *sub an*. 1262).

10. *Furs, lib.* I, *rub.* IX ("daquells qui fugiran a las iglesies"). In *c.* 4 James grants the right "a la iglesia de sancta Maria, e de sent Vicent; e a la huna major iglesia de cascun loch del regne de Valencia." The barons also claimed this right, but King James refused to acknowledge it (*Llibre dels feyts*, ch. 324). See also the contemporary Catalan, Raymond of Penyafort, "De immunitate ecclesiae," in his *Summa, lib.* I, *tit.* XIII, 113 ff. For the general legal background see G. Le Bras, "Asile," *DHGE*, IV, cols. 1,035–1,047. In Valencia this privilege was formally spelled out, with treason an exception, in a letter to the chapter in 1265 (Arch. Cath., perg. 2,379, Dec. 11, 1265): "quod si aliquis vel aliqui intraverint et receperint se in ecclesia valentina racione alicuius maleficii ab ipso vel ipsis perpetrati quod non expellantur vel extrahantur de ipsa ecclesia per iustitiam Valencie vel aliquem alium nisi illud maleficium prodiciose [?] fuerit perpetratum ut in foro Valencie continetur."

11. Arch. Cath., perg. 2,391 (Sept. 18, 1255), rectors "et vicariis civitatis et suburbii Valencie." The obligation of personal residence found in an occasional document suggests that absenteeism was a problem in the early church of Valencia, though on what scale we cannot say (see, e.g., perg. 2,432). In contemporary Vich, one canon had at least seven parishes (1250); as rector he appointed a procurator to designate vicars and to collect revenues (F. Carreras y Candi, "Notes dotze-centistes d'Ausona," *BRABLB*, VI [1911], 10). At Vich in 1256 a rector farmed the revenues of two of his churches to a group headed by two priests, for 700 Barce-lonan solidi (*ibid.*, doc. on pp. 10–11). In contemporary Huesca a statute was promulgated urging that the clerics in possession of parish churches be ordained priests.

12. Document of 1294 in J. Sanchís Sivera, *La iglesia parroquial de Santo Tomás de Valencia, monografía histórico-descriptiva* (Valencia, 1913), pp. 15–16.

13. Arch. Cath., perg. 1,091 (July 8, 1248): "vicarios" in a document of Bishop Arnold, given in a document by his successor Jazpert who is renewing the privilege. In practice perhaps the seizure was not so universal, since Jazpert in his introduction prefers to say "some" churches; but the word is ambiguous: "noverint quod vir discretus Arnaldo de Rezacho Archidiaconis Xative coram nobis Jaçperto postulavit ut donatione . . . Ecclesie beate Marie Xative cum quibusdam Ecclesiis seu Capellis infra eius terminos constitutis et constituendis ac unionem sanctam ipsi Archdiaconatui de predictis per Venerabilem in Christo patrem bone memorie dominum Arnaldum Episcopum Valentinum sicut in eius ordinatione cuius forma subiungitur plenius continetur, dignaremur liberaliter confirmare." The resident vicar of St. Mary's of Játiva appears in a document of 1272: "Berengarium Martinum vicarium Xative" (perg. 2,389, June 6, 1272); he was being appointed to a perpetual chaplaincy here as well, according to the last testament of Mary Núñez, the wife of a Játiva resident, Simon Zapater.

14. Lloréns, "Deanato de Valencia," pp. 9–11, doc. pp. 16–17.

15. *Regestum Clementis V*, II, 128–129, no. 2,119 (June 22, 1307). It is hard to say in what order he held offices; by 1307 his Alcira pastorate was somewhere in his past; he appears as Lérida canon in the *Rationes decimarum* for 1280 (I, 135).

16. *Rationes*, I, 255, 261. Cullera was a Hospitaller church but conducted by secular priests for the knights. William had the important job of collecting the crusade tithe of exempt groups in 1279 and 1280, a task not entrusted to obscure village pastors.

17. Arch. Cath., perg. 2,381 (July 19, 1250). "Pateat universis quod nos Frater Andreas miseracione divina Valentinus Episcopus commendamus tibi Arnaldo

Capellano Ecclesie Sancti Salvatoris Valencie in vita tua Capellam sive Ecclesiam sancti Juliani que est iuxta viam que itur apud Murum veterem. Ita ut eam teneas habeas et possideas ac fideliter deservias omnibus diebus vite tue libere et pacifice ac quiete." The two churches were to be kept in every way independent of each other.

18. James II to the Knights Hospitallers who had the patronage here (mid-1301), published in *BSCC* (II [1921], 106n.): "regie benevolentie convenit domesticos et familiares suos iuxta merita beneficiis decorare." The parishes of the Valencia crusade-lists in 1279 include a rector for Pina who is absent on crusade (*Rationes decimarum*, I, 256). It is just possible that a rector was assigned to the poor village of that name north of Jérica; if so, his crusading might suggest knightly status. But this Pina should probably be identified with an alien barony; its owner Simon Pérez, who also held Benimaclet in Valencia, put his brother into this parish of Pina. Even so, the pastorate underscores the general thesis. (The *Nomenclator* omits Pina; its rector apparently held some Valencian benefice.) See Arch. Crown, James I, perg. 1,234 (Mar. 21, 1250): "concedimus et ad feudum tradimus vobis Eximino Petro de Pina et Guillelmo rectori ecclesie de Pina fratri tuo et vestris successoribus imperpetuum Castrum nostrum de Pina cum valle eidem contigua." On Simon Pérez, see *Itinerari*, pp. 132, 211, 273, 340, 347. Other knightly rectors who probably did not attend the round of liturgical duties may include William of Coll rector at Benifayó de Espioca (*Nomenclátor*, pp. 404, 119) and Peter of Albalat vicar at Alpuente. The former is apparently the landowner who appears in the crown registers, and the latter bears a prominent family name; but this is conjecture.

19. *Viage literario*, V, 283-284, synod of 1274.

20. Arch. Crown, James I, perg. 2,176 (Jan. 11, 1273).

21. *Itinerari*, pp. 539-541 with Miret y Sans's consideration as redactor. Albert appears in the *Llibre dels feyts* as Micer Umbert (ch. 466). The recommendation to Peter by King James's will is in perg. 2,287. Soldevila, *Pere el Gran*, II, 196, 199-202.

22. Pascualino de Montbrun or Montbrú leased the ship for 36,000 solidi in 1269, his brother Simon appearing as witness (*Itinerari*, p. 424).

23. See later in this chapter, the discussion of Valencia city parishes in the tithe lists. On St. Stephen's in general, see Teixidor's chapter in *Antigüedades de Valencia*, I, 339-340. In late 1239 the pastor here received a house, noted in the *Repartimiento*. In 1245 the pastor was William of Pelagals.

24. This rare and valuable document demands full transcription. "Sit omnibus notum: quod Ego Jacobinus de Solario Procurator Alberti de Lavania Patris legitimi Hugueti de Lavania Rectore Ecclesie Sancti Stephani Valencie auctoritate procuracionis predicte qua fungor vendo vobis Guillermo de Trencard Presbitero et vestris a primo venturo festo Sancte Marie Candelarie usque ad tres annos primos venturos et continue completos omnes redditus exitus et proventus taxia et defunciones et omnia alia que ex devocione fidelium pervenerint per dictos annos ad Ecclesiam Sancti Stephani predictam vel eidem Ecclesie aliquo modo pertinent vel pertinere possunt ac debent et etiam statica Domorum dicte Ecclesie cum uno cubo et una bota predicta omnia vobis vendo, precio nongentorum solidorum regalium Valencie pro precio uniuscuiusque anni dictorum trium annorum quos in primo anno in hunc modum solvatis videlicet DC solidos in presenti; et residuos CCC solidos in festo proximo omnium sanctorum. Et in secundo anno persolvatis dictos DCCCC solidos in hunc modum scilicet CCCCL solidos in introitu ipsius anni scilicet in festo Sancte Marie Candelarie et residuos CCCCL solidos in festo tunc venturo omnium Sanctorum. Et Soluciones tercii anni pro-

regnantur ut in secundo anno. Et teneor vobis quod dictus Albertus de Lavania et filius suus dictus solverint per dictos annos cenas Domini Episcopi Valentini et etiam Decimam subsidii terre Sancte, et etiam omnia alia subsidia Domini Pape seu alterius persone, que infra dictos tres annos facere ac dare opportuerint pro ecclᵃ dicta. Et si vos et vestri habeatis et percipiatis per dictos annos, dictos redditus exitus et proventus taxia defunciones et omnia alia que dicte Ecclesie pervenerint et ex ipsis faciatis voluntates vestras et etiam habeatis per dictos omnes statica Domorum dicte Ecclesie cum cubo et bota predictis vos vero teneamini servire per dictos annos dictam Ecclesiam et facere et complere in ea omnia que rector facere tenetur. Et si dicti redditus in anno valuerint ultra dictum precium illud vobis et vestris dono et relinquo auctoritate procurationis predicte. Et sic promito dictos redditus vobis et vestris servare, et facere habere tenere possidere et expletare per dictos annos in forma supradicta. Obliganda ad hoc vobis et vestris auctoritate procurationis predicte bona dicti Alberti de Lavania ubique sint et Ego certificatus de iure meo obligo vobis et vestris pro predictis complendis bona mea ubique sint habita et habenda. Et ad maiorem firmitatem dono vobis et vestris fidanciam salvitatis Micer Simonem de Montebruno civem Valencie qui de predictis omnibus vobis et vestris teneatur ad forum Valencie quam fiduciam Ego Micer Simon de Montebruno predictus facio et concedo vobis dicto G. de Trencard super bonis meis que ad hec vobis et vestris ubique obligo. Ad hec ego G. de Trencard predictus recipio a vobis Jacobino de Solario procuratore predicto empcionem dictorum reddituum per dictos annos sub dicto precio in forma supradicta. Promittentes servare per dictos annos dictam Ecclesiam ut moris est et facere, et complere, omnia in ea que rectos facere tenetur, et dictum precium quolibet anno dictorum trium annorum persolvere dicto Alberto de Lavania vel cui ipse mandaverit terminis predictis: obliganda ad hec me et bona mea dicto Alberto de Lavania et suis ubique. Quod est actum Valencie. III. idus Ianuarii anno Domini M.CC.LXX. tercio. Signum Iacobini de Solario = Signum Ser Simonis de Montebruno = Signum G de Trencard: predictorum qui hec firmamus = Ego P. Michaelis Precentor Valencie gerens vices Domini Episcopi Valencie qui hec laudo et firmo. Testes sunt inde Magister R. Nepotis Capellanus, G. de Picco. Bg. de Na Johanna, et G. Gaucerandi Nobilis Valencie. Signum Bernardi Gaucerandi Publici notarii Valencie qui hec scripsit."

25. Arch. Cath., perg. 4,639 (Dec. 23, 1256).

26. *"Repartiment" de Burriana*, p. 50.

27. Arch. Cath., perg. 24 (Oct. 28, 1236).

28. *Repartimiento de Valencia*, pp. 258, 267, 506.

29. Arch. Crown, Peter III, Reg. Canc. 46, fol. 221 (July 8, 1284). Family chapels began to become common in England in the thirteenth century, especially appearing in the records after 1277 (Moorman, *Church Life*, with examples, pp. 15–17).

30. Arch. Crown, Peter III, Reg. Canc. 49, fol. 48v (Mar. 3, 1280).

31. Arch. Crown, Peter III, Reg. Canc. 56, fols. 108–110; assessments for military expenses. The other dioceses offer more detail. Secondary works touching individual Valencian churches are generally quite disappointing for these early years since so little material exists. Contemporary England had some 9,500 parishes, most of them manor churches in origin; the overwhelming majority (9,000) were rural. In such a long-settled area, twenty parishes per city was not uncommon, with London boasting one hundred, and Norwich, Lincoln, and York about fifty. The average population of these parishes would be three hundred (two hundred for a city parish). It would comprise some 4,000 acres, including the outlying churches; the Winchester statutes wanted such an outlying church, with

cemetery, for every hamlet situated more than two miles from the main church. (Moorman, *Church Life*, pp. 4-5, 12.)

32. Arch. Cath., codex 98, Constituciones synodales ecclesiae valentinae, fol. 1.

33. *Diócesis valentina*, II, 129.

34. For example, Arch. Cath., perg. 2,341 (Feb. 7, 1241), a settlement of ecclesiastical affairs including the tithe with a feudal lord, looks forward to "parishioners" and their "chaplain" here, when settlement is made; but this simply safeguards ecclesiastical revenue, without telling us what present or future plans for a resident cleric or for a parish had been intended. Some churches probably had a brief life, soon disappearing; an example is the parish at Mas de Xirosa in 1267 in the Hospitaller *encomienda* of Cervera, where Berengar Puig is "rector ecclesie Xerer" (Manuel Betí, *Ro[s]sell, pleito que por su dominio sostuvieron en el siglo xiii la orden de San Juan de Jerusalén y el real monasterio de Benifazá* [Castellón de la Plana, 1920], p. 15, doc. of Feb. 24, 1267).

35. Honorio García, "La parroquial del Santo Ángel de la Vall de Uxó," *BSCC*, XXII (1946), 320: "quaedam capella intus castrum . . . cum non habitent ibi nisi sarraceni, nec sint ibi christiani nisi alcaydus et aliqui tabernarii vina vendentes." No church appears for Eslida in the *Rationes decimarum* either.

36. Arch. Cath., perg. 2,450 (*an.* 1340): "in quo loco dei servicia cessantur fieri"; "ad completum numerum centum presentibus et recipientibus." See too the *Rationes decimarum*, I, 263. The rector of Chulilla will also appear, in the early fourteenth century, on the list of pastors who had attended the synods for some time past.

37. *Aureum opus*, doc. 12, fol. 4v (Nov. 2, 1241): "a finibus termini castri de Almenara quod dividit terminum cum murvedre usque ad Biar vel ultra." See also *Collectio conciliorum Hispaniae*, V, 189-190. The Visigothic diocese had penetrated inland as far as Alpuente and had run from Silla to Murviedro, at least if one is to believe the division of King Wamba (*Ordinatio ecclesiae valentinae*, pp. 204-205).

38. Almizra evolved from the previous agreements of Tudilén (1151) and Cazorla (1179). Castile got most of modern Alicante province, Murcia, and Granada. In 1304 the treaty of Agreda was to put within the kingdom (but not the diocese) of Valencia the territory down to Orihuela.

39. Arch. Cath., perg. 2,309 (June 23, 1240): "usque ad Alchala sub Yorca et usque ad portum de Biar et usque ad Alachant et usque in mari."

40. *Ibid.* The document speaks of the territory rather than of the diocese of Valencia, a term moreover not applicable in context to the countryside or municipal environs alone; so it is possible that certain tithe rights had been gained by royal gift until such time as the rest of the diocese to the south could be conquered.

41. Gonzalo Vidal Tur, *Un obispado español, el de Orihuela-Alicante*, 2nd ed., 2 vols. (Alicante, 1961), I, 29-30. See also Pedro Díaz Cassou, *Serie de los obispos de Cartagena, sus hechos y su tiempo* (Madrid, 1895), ch. 2.

42. There have been important changes recently in the diocesan map of the area formerly comprising the Valencian kingdom. Castellón and Segorbe now form one diocese with two centers; a map of the present archdiocese of Valencia, prepared with great care, was published in the 1963 *Guía de iglesia en la diócesis de Valencia* (see my bibliographical essay). Some idea of the ancient Valencia diocese may perhaps be had from the rare official map of 1761 above in vol. I, following p. 82.

43. *Documenta selecta*, doc. 318 (Nov. 22, 1317): "magna valde est et diffusa."

44. Arch. Cath., perg. 1,091 (July 8, 1248).

45. Arch. Cath., perg. 289 (Aug. 13, 1277): "quod sit unus novus Archidiachonus qui . . . Archidiaconus Muriveteris appeletur"; and another "qui scilicet

Archidiaconus de Algezira vocetur"; the former is to receive 200 "aureos" yearly
from the rector of Murviedro. Neither new archdeacon appears in the *Rationes
decimarum*, either because of poverty owing to initial expenses or because effective
organization was not yet accomplished.

46. *Rationes decimarum*, I, 255–260 and 261–267.

47. Though information of value may be found in the prefatory pages of each
volume of Rius Serra's edition of the Spanish tax lists (the *Rationes decimarum*
cited throughout this book), a far longer and fuller disquisition on the *decimae* is
supplied by Pietro Guidi as an introduction to his *Rationes decimarum Italiae nei
secoli xiii e xiv* (in the volume *Tuscia, la decima degli anni 1274–1280*, no. 58 in the
series Studi e testi [Rome, 1932]). The quotation is on p. xiii. The payments were
due on December 25 and June 4, so that a list for 1279 represents the two lists of the
fifth year, i.e. late 1278 and early 1279. See also the remarks of W. E. Lunt in his
Papal Revenues in the Middle Ages (New York, 1934), I, 40 ff., 51, 71–75, etc. By
the thirteenth century ecclesiastical temporalities, as well as spiritualities, were
assessed (p. 73). See too the general treatment by Adolf Gottlob, *Die päpstlichen
Kreuzzugs-Steuern des 13 Jahrhunderts* (Heiligenstadt, 1892), with appendix of
Clement IV and Gregory IX on exemptions and problems of collecting.

48. A severe example of this in the kingdom of Valencia occurred at this time.
The king writes of the collector: "intelleximus . . . vos . . . excomunicasse omnes
canones dicte Ecclesie Segorbicensis . . . qui decimam . . . solvere recusabant,"
and have absolved only two (Arch. Crown, Peter III, Reg. Canc. 40, fol. 97, April
22, 1278). At the time, the Segorbe church was upset and angry over its great loss of
territory (cf. Chapter III, note 74 and text).

49. Rius Serra thought rather the opposite since a few places which did not pay
were listed along with their excuses (*Rationes decimarum*, I, x–xi).

50. This is the conclusion of Guidi (*Tuscia, la decima*, p. xxxvi) concerning the
Lucca diocese for which he has independent, complete listings to serve as checks;
his experience with *decima* lists leads him to conclude that the two-thirds percentage
is probably valid for other diocesan lists also (p. 245). Of the parish churches of
Valencia city, all are in evidence in our own lists (St. Michael's having just been
suppressed, and Peter Martyr's apparently being the former St. Nicholas'); but
the sub-church of St. Julian's is not here nor the sub-churches like that of the
port (Grao). Income from a church in the Valencia diocese seems not to have been
taxed unless about 20 solidi could be realized. There is a scattering of tithes of only
18 or 19 solidi and one of 17; lesser amounts belong to chantry or similar incomes
or to what appear to be rare cases of partial default (e.g. St. Andrew's pays 10
solidi on p. 262 but supplements this with 96 on p. 267 for the same year).

51. *Rationes decimarum*, I, 175–177. Since the assessment itself was nominal
"and usually much below the gross income actually received" (Lunt, *Papal
Revenues*, I, 74), deductions and interpretations will always be on the safe side.

52. This is not true of the ordinary diocesan tithe assessed on the resident lord's
income, including his rents from Moslems. But the tithe in Valencia was not part of
the parochial revenue, and therefore did not affect the crusade tithe required from
the local rector.

53. Sanchís Sivera has extracted a great deal of pertinent data from the older
local histories for his *Nomenclátor de Valencia*. The results, though meager for
this earlier period, are sometimes quite valuable. On the local histories see bibliographical essay.

54. The king's own figure (in *Colección diplomática*, doc. 1,341, Nov. 1270) is
given in a context of formal recrimination and, if it had been too inexact, would
have invited retort from the knightly families whose land grants had been revoked.

J. C. Russell, authority on medieval population, arrived at a population of little more than quarter of a million in the fourteenth century, using the *monedatge* tax records ("The Medieval Monedatge of Aragon and Valencia," *Proceedings of the American Philosophical Society*, CVI [1962], 497). The vastly different internal organization of the modern diocese is not helpful to us; Sanchís Sivera, writing several decades ago, puts it at three hundred and forty parishes, containing a million and a half people.

55. The total number of taxpayers in the twelve parishes of the city in 1355 was 4,729 which gives a city population of almost 30,000 by that time (Russell, "Monedatge," p. 495 with tables).

56. Arch. Crown, James I, Reg. Canc. 16, fol. 192 (June 7, 1270).

57. Almiserá, to judge from its place in the list, refers to this rural borderland, apparently taking its name from an extinct Moslem village. It is not impossible that Almiserat in the Gandía region is meant or even Almizra which stood just north of Biar at modern Campo de Mirra. In all these cases nearby parishes can be found in the tax list.

58. Miguel Gual Camarena, "Contribución al estudio de la territorialidad de los fueros de Valencia," *EEMCA*, III (1947-1948), esp. the systematic chart on p. 272 and the map on p. 280. Should one be prepared to admit also the possibility of specimens of the old-type *iglesia propia*, surviving and unrevealed by records? It seems unlikely that many would escape both the tax and synodal listings.

59. See, for example, the patterns worked out by Sobrequés Vidal ("Patriciado urbano," pp. 28-40).

60. In both lists, working from the transcriptions of Rius Serra and Sanchís Sivera, allowance must be made for their occasional lapses. There are curious forms in our several lists: "Nonarres" (Navarrés), "Ans" (Aras), "Albaxeraie" (Alboraya), "Garti" (Gorga; not Garg), "Feta" and "Sera" (Seta), "Oraful" (Jarafuel).

61. Not the Alfafara above Alcoy, but the place near Torrente given to Michael and García Lodréu in 1238.

62. "Archubiis"; perhaps not a satisfactory identification, though in the context it is impossible to suggest a more probable one. It lies just over the modern border, north of Aras de Alpuente.

63. Torre de Espioca itself no longer exists; nor does Rebollet, for which Fuente Encarroz is substituted here; however, there was later a church at the latter place as well, erected in 1329.

64. The jurisdiction would seem to include Cirat, Ayódar, Ribesalbes, Cortes de Arenoso (which appears in the later, synodal list), Puebla de Arenoso, Espadilla, and so on.

65. A problem in identification: "Parcaciis" near Jalón, served by a vicar from Játiva. There is also a "Morariis," perhaps Moraria near Alcira, or Mora just outside the diocese to the west of the churches of the Mijares River. Another problem is "de Senentries de Parataciis," which may represent Senija and Parcent together; if Senentries is Sinarcas, this parish may be deleted from the synodal list which follows ("Senargues").

66. A dubious identification: "Centya," "den Sentiu."

67. Simply Alcalá in the synodal list, Alfandech in the tax list; the identification is probable.

68. Serrella, to the east of Bañeres, is a logical but not necessary identification; context excludes Albalat dels Sorells, while Soria and Soraya are dubious.

69. The knight de Lizana held this from 1238; other owners followed and it reverted to the crown in the early fourteenth century. The rector received a licence

in 1334 to absent himself for studies. James I gave a legal decision for Buñol that the Moslems were to pay first fruits to the church here. It was under Siete Aguas later, and not a parish until the sixteenth century.

70. Sanchís Sivera believes this to be Agres, but this may well have been served from Bocairente; the two places had a total of three hundred and twenty settlers by 1255 (*Nomenclátor de Valencia*, p. 16).

71. Cf. Chapter IV, note 84.

72. *Nomenclátor*, p. 272; on Canales and Cullera cf. Chapter IV, notes 35, 37.

73. *Ibid.*, p. 224.

74. Except where otherwise noted, the following information has been gleaned from the geographical *Nomenclátor* of Sanchís Sivera; items may be traced alphabetically. The author drew his information both from documents and local histories; he is a good authority, but not all his evidence has equal value. A dubious methodological principle he resorted to was assuming that churches founded by James I could be discerned from their later titles (see his principle on p. 453); he also speaks loosely of "ancient" or "conquest period" churches, when the evidence does not really carry back into the thirteenth century. Again, the juridical title to a church one hopes will appear is not the same as an actual church in an area already settled; so that one cannot really say of the transfer of title from Segorbe to Tarragona in 1247, for example: "nos prueba su existencia en aquella época" (p. 85). Some of the findings may now be corrected too by such recently uncovered documents as the *Rationes decimarum*.

75. Arch. Crown, James I, Reg. Canc. 10, fol. 62 (April 28, 1268): "operatorium in A[l]gezira in placia Sancte Katarine que est in carraria maiori eiusdem ville."

76. Aguilar, *Noticias de Segorbe*, I, 104.

77. The *Rationes decimarum* for 1275 and 1280 give only the "ecclesia maior de Muro veteri" or "rector de Muro veteri" (at 600 solidi tithe each time), with a benefice in the church too; and the rector of St. John's of Murviedro, at 155 and 76 solidi, plus a supplementary 131 solidi (see pp. 256, 263, 267). The *Nomenclátor* gives Holy Savior's; it may be St. John's or it may be a third church (p. 378). The Trinitarian church was St. Michael's.

78. *Nomenclátor de Valencia*, p. 452.

79. Arch. Crown, James I, perg. 1,874 (Jan. 21, 1266): "capellani Ecclesie de Colera." The Lucena rector is in Bibl. Univ. Val., codex 145, charter of Alcora; the Morella quote is from Arch. Cath. Tortosa, cajón Diezmos, doc. 25.

80. The original list (see Chapter VIII, note 136) should be examined. It is not difficult to trace "Nichera" to Náquera and "Baleta" to Valle de Segó, or to correct such forms as "Pictacen," "Amacasta," "Alhala," and "Benalcuacir"; but can one be sure that "Captuli" is correctly related to Catadau, "Terris" to Turís, and "Tubar" to Tuéjar? The transcription is not satisfactory, and the document itself needs restudy.

81. Through Almenara, Uxó, Nules, Onda, Bounegre, Alcalatén, Mora, Culla, Ares, Morella, Matarrania, Peñarroya, Flix, Garchia, Marzá, Cabaces, Tivisa, Pratdip, to Coll de Balaguer and the sea.

82. *Rationes decimarum*, I, 165-178. The tax here was collected, or at least reckoned, in Valencian money; elsewhere in the diocese of Tortosa the solidus of Jaca prevailed. To reconstruct the diocese the only help in the Tortosa cathedral archives, at least in their present half-organized condition, is an 1818 index culling manuscript references to all rectories medieval and modern in the diocese. Of twenty-six entries over half coincide with churches in our own listing.

83. Some modern equivalents for the names in the original lists are suggested in the index to volume one of the *Rationes*, and by F. Mateu y Llopis in his "La

circulación monetaria en las diócesis de Tortosa y Segorbe-Albarracín en el reino de Valencia, según la décima de 1279–1280," *BSCC*, XXII (1946), 497 ff. There are a few remarks on the thirteenth-century parish at Chert, especially on the raising of a new church, in Miguel Segarra y Roca, *Historia eclesiástica de Chert* (Tortosa, 1949), pp. 11–13. There was apparently no parish or church at Vall de Uxó (Xon or Son to the Moors); see García, "La parroquial de Uxó," p. 319, and his *Notas para la historia de Vall de Uxó* (Vall de Uxó, 1962), pp. 44 ff., 75 ff., 80–81.

84. Manuel Betí, *Ro[s]sell, pleito que por su dominio sostuvieron en el siglo xiii la orden de San Juan de Jerusalén y el real monasterio de Benifazá* (Castellón de la Plana, 1920), p. 15, document of February 24, 1267.

85. See Chapter X, note 133.

86. Cf. A. Amanieu, "Archiprêtre," *DDC*, I, cols. 1,004–1,026. Even an established diocese like Dax in southwestern France seems to have had no archpresbyteries at all until the second half of the thirteenth century, when they were constituted along ancient geographical divisions (C. Higounet, "Dax," *DHGE*, XIV, col. 133).

87. Document cited in note 31; "aliis rectoribus Episcopatus et diocesis."

88. Juan Puig, "Iglesia arciprestal de San Mateo, su construcción, modificaciones impertinentes, su restauración," *BSCC*, XXX (1954), 72 and n., 73, plates II and VIII; documented from the municipal archives. *Monumentos españoles, catálogo de los declarados histórico-artísticos*, ed. J. M. de Azcárate, 3 vols. (Madrid, 1953–1954), I, 339, with plan, interior photograph, and bibliography.

89. Bernard's will is in Arch. Nac. Madrid, codex of Poblet (B-1220), pp. 28–34, doc. 12: "Lucas rector ecclesie Castilionis." See also on this church Manuel Sanz de Bremond, "La iglesia arciprestal de Sta. María de Castellón," *BSCC*, XXIII (1947), 302, 305. V. Traver Tomás, *Antigüedades de Castellón de la Plana, estudios histórico-monográficos de la villa y su vecindario riqueza y monumentos* (Castellón de la Plana, 1958), pp. 164–165, 223–228 (for the considerable endowment by 1341).

90. *Llibre dels feyts*, ch. 564.

91. *Monumentos españoles*, III, 305–306 with plan, interior photograph, and bibliography. Lavedan, *L'architecture gothique en Valence*, pp. 68–69 and plate 11.

92. Lavedan, *Architecture*, p. 69. The other or cathedral mosque replaced at Segorbe seems ironically to have been itself a reconverted Visigothic church (J. Carot y García, *Origen y vicisitudes del templo catedral de Segorbe a través de los tiempos* [Castellón de la Plana, 1949], pp. 5–6).

93. Lavedan, *Architecture*, pp. 69–70, with plate 12.

94. Bibl. Univ. Val., codex 145, doc. 39: "en la porche de Santa Maria de la Iglesia de Morvedre."

95. *Monumentos españoles*, I, 336 with plan, interior photograph, and bibliography. Lavedan, *Architecture*, pp. 192–196 with comparisons to the Valencia cathedral and St. Catherine's parish church of Valencia city.

96. *Nomenclátor de Valencia*, under Puzol.

97. *Ibid.*, p. 399, perhaps an early fourteenth-century structure.

98. Segarra y Roca, *Historia eclesiástica de Chert*, p. 12.

99. José Vilaplana Gisbert, *Historia religiosa de Alcoy desde su fundación hasta nuestros días* (Alcoy, 1892), pp. 18–19, 22, 27.

100. *Provincia de Castellón* (in the *Geografía general del reino de Valencia*), pp. 501, 360, 461n.; see also pp. 639, 646, and *passim*. Benito Traver, *Historia de Villarreal* (Villarreal, 1909), p. 258.

101. Fortunato de Selgas, "San Félix de Játiva y las iglesias valencianas del siglo xiii," *Boletín de la sociedad española de excursiones*, XI (1903), 50; and cf. its

plates and plans. See also C. Sarthou Carreres, *Datos para la historia de Játiva*, 4 vols. (Játiva, 1933–1935), I, 81–86.

102. Quotes from Selgas, *ibid.* See also *Monumentos españoles*, III, 303–305 with bibliography.

103. Lavedan, *Architecture en Valence*, pp. 68, 81–82.

104. So Mateo Rotger y Capllonch believes, in his monograph on Pollensa, one of the eight divisions of Majorca after its conquest (the situation here was analogous to that in Valencia); thus "ecclesia de Ginyent" meant there was a parish and a municipality (ca. 1250), the two being also conterminous. One is reluctant to accept transference of the three words in places thinly settled; besides, "ecclesia" is used several times in Valencian records for semi-public chapels. But the relation, if not the universal identity, between the words is significant. (See Rotger's *Historia de Pollensa*, I, 126).

105. Arch. Crown, James I, Reg. Canc. 9, fol. 25 (Mar. 7, 1257): "placet nobis quatenus de unaquaque parochia civitatis unus probus homo super predictis officiis . . . et casis infra civitatem, et super aliis negociis principalibus communitatis qui donent consilium et auxilium . . ." These men are also to oversee the roads, watercourses, and the like. See *Aureum opus*, doc. 55, fols. 17r–18v (Mar. 7, 1257). In thirteenth-century Barcelona the seven parishes of the city were its only interior administrative divisions (Font y Rius, "Regimen municipal," XVII [1946], 242–243). In Toulouse at this time all but the most recent of the six divisions of the *cité* "coincided with [the ancient] parishes or parts of parishes"; the bourg divisions were mostly by gates, but this too may reflect parochial divisions (Mundy, *Toulouse*, p. 371). The "universitas parrochianorum" in the thirteenth century here even sued in court (p. 372).

106. *Aureum opus, ibid.*

107. *Ibid.*, doc. 53, fol. 13v (*an.* 1251).

108. *Furs, lib.* I, *rub.* III, *c.* 30: "sex probi homines sint electi uniuscuiusque parrochiae . . ."; "iurati cum quattuor hominibus de unaquaque parrochia eligant unum probum hominem et nominent pro Iustitia . . ." See the *Aureum opus*, doc. 55, fols. 17r–18v (Mar. 7, 1257).

109. "In parroquia Beati Martini" (*Repartimiento*, p. 656; "in parrochia Sancti Thome," p. 223). Elsewhere in his realms, James sometimes specified a place by its parish: e.g. an alod in the parish of St. Marcellus (*Colección diplomática*, doc. 791), a castle to be built in the parish of St. Felix (doc. 379).

110. Arch. Crown, James I, Reg. Canc. 10, fol. 69 (July 3, 1258): "illis quattuor operatoriis . . . in partida Sancti Salvatoris." Two similar examples are given in notes 126 and 132.

111. José Sánchez Adell, "Las murallas medievales de Castellón," *BSCC*, XXVIII (1952), documentary appendix, doc. 10 (Dec. 26, 1385): "en temps passat" (for the use as administrative units) and "en temps antichs" (for the origin of the divisions). This may not refer back a full hundred years, but it should go back far enough to confirm this point. There was at first only a single parish when James moved the town to its present site, and some time must be allowed therefore for growth. A municipal salary was paid to the layman who headed the parish council here, and taxation for public works was made by parishes, all according to this old pattern (*ibid.*). The early fourteenth-century parishes and their growth are displayed on maps in Traver Tomás, *Antigüedades de Castellón*, pp. 162, 171. Cf. Mundy, *Toulouse*, pp. 155, 371–372.

112. Sanz de Bremond, "Iglesia de Castellón" [XXII (1946)], p. 430.

113. *Crònica*, ch. 296.

114. *Repartimiento de Sevilla*, I, 354.

115. Sanchís Sivera, whose *Santo Tomás* has furnished this information on the Valencian parish structure, is probably using early fourteenth-century documents; but one has no hesitation in subscribing to his conclusions, both because he knew so well the ecclesiastical archives of Valencia and because it is antecedently improbable that such an organism, which appears full-blown and in possession in the early fourteenth century, did not also exist in the later thirteenth. There are besides hints of it above in the *cartas pueblas*.

116. Traver Tomás, *Antigüedades de Castellón*, p. 225. On thirteenth-century power of the purse by laymen in parochial affairs, see treatment of the first fruits on pages 91 ff.

117. "Era pues una institución completamente laica, entre cuyos fines ocupaba el primer lugar el religioso"; this lay domination survived here until the sixteenth century (Sanchís Sivera, *Santo Tomás*, pp. 31, 33).

118. Arch. Crown, James I, Reg. Canc. 20, fol. 322v (Feb. 14, 1275): "civis Valencie parrochie Sancte Katerine." See also Arch. Cath., perg. 1,351 (June 24, 1274) and perg. 5,975 (April 24, 1251).

119. Their choice was one of the very first activities upon the capture of the capital; the metropolitan "fecit X ecclesias parrochiales in civitate Valentie de decem locis que fuerunt meçquite sarracenorum" (*Ordinatio ecclesiae valentinae*, p. 233). Whether the choice was influenced by surviving memories of the mosques converted here by the Cid in 1096 is not known; St. Catherine's had become the major mosque at that time (Menéndez Pidal, *España del Cid*, pp. 522, 807).

120. It is to these that the *Ordinatio* seems to refer, when it speaks in general terms: "instituit rectores in ecclesiis que sunt extra Valentiam de eiusdem diocesi quarum tenent Christiani" (pp. 233–234). The reference is to hurried acts of diocesan jurisdiction to establish precedent, and it therefore seems unlikely to relate to the business of establishing the more distant network of parishes; besides, the Christians resident in the diocese in these first days were largely congregated near the capital. Escolano has a chapter of dubious value on the Valencia parishes (*Décadas de Valencia*, lib. V, chs. 4–5). Mentioned in the *Repartimiento* are: the cathedral (pp. 223, 244, 264, 271, 286, 289, 298, 301, 308, 557, 578, 617, 633, 635, 636), St. Andrew's (pp. 245, 252, 267, 268, 272, 316, 325, 383, 524, 616), St. Bartholomew's (pp. 230, 548, 601), St. Catherine's (pp. 256, 311), Holy Cross (pp. 325, 534, 591, 645), St. Stephen's (p. 225), St. Lawrence's (pp. 598, 641), St. Martin's (pp. 231, 268, 281, 304, 313, 318, 656), St. Michael's (p. 604), St. Nicholas' (pp. 384, 647), Holy Savior's (pp. 583, 639), St. Thomas' (pp. 223, 324, 382, 579), the Boatella churches (p. 325), and those of Roteros (pp. 325, 534, 591, 645). Cf. the Chabás index in *Episcopologio valentino*, p. 364.

121. It would be possible, with a late nineteenth-century map of Valencia and much patience, to delineate the boundaries of each city parish much as they were from 1238 to 1896, from the streets listed for each of them in *Antigüedades de Valencia* (II, 410–425).

122. It is not in the *Rationes decimarum* for 1279 or 1280; nor is Holy Cross, exempt perhaps because owned by the order of Roncesvalles. St. Michael's had been suppressed before the time of this tax list. St. Andrew's crusader-rector was dead in 1279, but the church appears in two entries for 1280.

123. *Diócesis valentina*, II, 119.

124. *Antigüedades de Valencia*, I, 221.

125. Arch. Cath., perg. 2,309 (June 23, 1240): "in tota parochia assignata Ecclesie maiori sancte Marie." In a 1245 document he signed before all the other rectors but as "Clericus Altaris Sancti Petri Ecclesie Maioris"; the prologue of

the document shows that *clericus* and *rector* are here equivalent terms (*Antigüedades de Valencia*, I, 212–214). Under the Cid the cathedral parish (at St. Catherine's: see above, note 119) was also St. Peter's altar, named for St. Peter of Cardeña according to Menéndez Pidal (*España del Cid*, pp. 549–550n.; see also *Diócesis valentina*, pp. 36–37n., 46).

126. Arch. Cath., perg. 1,229 (June 6, 1270): "in civitate valencie in parrochia sancte Marie sedis."

127. *Rationes decimarum*, I, 258, 263; possibly he had thirty solidi more from this office; on this, and allied ambiguous evidence, see below, note 130.

128. Arch. Cath., perg. 1,354 (Sept. 30, 1276).

129. See especially *Antigüedades de Valencia*, I, 353–355; and Chabás, *Episcopologio valentino*, p. 358.

130. The *Rationes decimarum*, like some other documents on this parish, are not free from ambiguity. The abbreviation "m̄rs" (as in the García Pérez will, below) is a normal shorthand for "martyris" in this century. But it just possibly could sustain the reading "maioris [ecclesie]" and so refer to St. Peter's altar at the cathedral; a scribe's error here would also be understandable, and serious in its consequences for the historian. The transcription of the *Rationes* may also be faulty. The 1280 list supplies a "rector of St. Peter Martyr," a cathedral "chaplain of St. Peter"; and a cathedral chaplain of St. Peter "Maioricarum"; the 1279 list has a "church" of St. Peter "Maioricarum," a "chaplain of St. Peter of the see," and a "chaplaincy" of St. Peter "Mayoricarum." If the "Mayoricarum" entries are misreadings or scribal errors, this third item may be additional revenues held by either the cleric at the cathedral parish or the cleric at St. Peter Martyr. Both listings of a church ("ecclesia de sancto Petro Maioricarum" and "rector sancti Petri martiris") give a substantial sum, 112 and 140 solidi; the chaplaincy of St. Peter of the see brings 54 and 52 solidi, that of St. Peter "Mayoricarum" 31 and 31.

131. Arch. Cath., perg. 1,357 (Mar. 4, 1279): "in cimiterio ecclesie sancti Petri martyris Valencie."

132. Arch. Cath., perg. 1,817 (Aug. 4, 1258): "in Civitate Valencie in parrochia Sancti Petri martyris."

133. Arch. Nac. Madrid, Clero: Valencia, Santo Domingo, leg. 2,107, arm. 45, fab. 1 (Alexander IV to Valencia Dominicans).

134. Document in notes 144 and 146.

135. Arch. Crown, James I, Reg. Canc. 16, fol. 224 (Jan. 23, 1270): a transfer of the lands of "Bartholomeus presbyter qui fuit capellanus ecclesie sancti Nicolai Valencie," consequent upon their confiscation "ratione vitii sodomie de quo exstitit in culpam et propter quod etiam factus est fugitivus." See the *Furs*, *lib.* IX, *rub.* VII, chs. 63, 70; also the *Aureum opus*, doc. 35, fol. 14r,v (*an.* 1250); "heretges, e sodomites sien cremats."

136. Teixidor would put it just beyond the walls at the southwest angle in the suburb of Villanueva. Chabás and Sanchís Sivera though speaking of Villanueva place it within the walls near St. Bartholomew's, suggesting as a site the modern Plaza del Ángel (*Episcopologio valentino*, pp. 358, 362; *Diócesis valentina*, II, 123–124; *Nomenclátor de Valencia*, p. 450). This other Villanueva would parallel Roteros, running up from the river at the extreme northwest of the city. Considering the evidence at the trial between Toledo and Tarragona concerning metropolitan jurisdiction over Valencia—which seems to assume that St. Michael's is within the walls, so that jurisdictional acts could be performed within the city as legal precedents—there is something to be said for Plaza del Ángel (*Ordinatio ecclesiae valentinae*, p. 401); besides, St. Michael's owned a building here. But none of it fits the traditional story of St. Michael's disappearance when King

James angrily moved the city's Moslems out into a suburb; perhaps the real explanation of its suppression is related to the fight over metropolitan jurisdiction. St. Michael's later (1521) was resuscitated in the Moslem quarter (see the text and map of Roca Traver, "Vida mudéjar," and the map and article of J. Rodrigo y Pertegás, "La morería de Valencia, ensayo de descripción topográfico-histórica de la misma," *BRAH*, LXXXVI [1925], 229-251). Justus was rector in 1238, and Peter in 1242 and 1245. The *Rationes decimarum* have a "chaplain" for St. Michael's under the clergy of the "see"; is this simply a cathedral benefice? Our St. Michael's may have disappeared or been incorporated into St. Bartholomew's by then, or have survived as an oratory church.

137. Arch. Crown, James I, Reg. Canc. 21, fol. 46 (July 6, 1272). A "capellanus de regali" was tithed twenty solidi in the *Rationes decimarum* of 1280 (I, 267).

138. *Antigüedades de Valencia*, II, 209-221; *Diócesis valentina*, I, 281-283, II, 127-128.

139. *Nomenclátor de Valencia*, p. 453; the wills are cited below, in Chapter VII, notes 53, 56 and Chapter XI, note 13.

140. *Nomenclátor*, pp. 128, 295, 336, 166. (The latter seems to be the "ecclesiam que est in Alcafiphi" in the *Repartimiento*.)

141. Arch. Cath., perg. 2,310 (June 14, 1242).

142. *Repartimiento de Sevilla*, I, 358, large map and overlay. The author remarks on some ingenious mathematical conjectures as to the plan on which the area was first divided (p. 355); he suggests also that the initial division was plotted from the high tops of the converted mosques.

143. It is assumed here that the four collections represented in the lists of 1279 and 1280 bear a realistic relation to income for at least the majority of churches given. The difference of income for the individual parish of Valencia city (except in the case of St. Bartholomew's) is probably not substantial enough, between the two lists, to disturb the calculations. But this difference is sufficient to suggest that the Moslem revolt in Valencia upset somewhat the collections of the fifth year (1278-1279). The higher sums listed for 1280 probably do not reflect an increase of income but rather a more realistic or more rigorous assessment (see Guidi, *Tuscia, la decima*, pp. xxxi-xxxii). In round numbers, the 1280 parishes of Valencia city were thus assessed: St. Stephen's 173 solidi, St. Catherine's 141, St. Lawrence's 132, St. Martin's 126, St. John's 117, St. Andrew's 10+96, Holy Savior's 93, St. Thomas' 59, St. Peter's 54, St. Bartholomew's 46 (but 110 the year before). St. Andrew's also paid in 1280 a lump sum of 500 solidi for the deceased rector's previously exempt years; this comes to at least 100 per annum, if he were away on crusade all five years. Cf. note 130, for income of the parishes of St. Peter of the see and St. Peter Martyr.

144. *Antigüedades de Valencia*, I, 212-214; also published in Esclapés, *Resumen historial*, pp. 58-60, and elsewhere.

145. Arch. Cath., perg. 4,638 (given in Chapter VIII, note 131). Also perg. 5,011 (Mar. 16, 1256): "Bernardus Ferarii, presbyter altaris sancte Marie sedis Valencie." In perg. 2,368 (Dec. 5, 1241) "B" is chaplain of St. Peter's and penitentiary of the bishop.

146. Arch. Cath., perg. 2,391 (Sept. 18, 1255).

147. *Antigüedades de Valencia*, I, 308, docs. of 1244 to 1266.

148. Arch. Cath., perg. 1,343 (Feb. 5, 1270); perg. 2,358 (July 11, 1272): "G. F. rector ecclesie sancti Martini"; this is William Ferrer, pastor for thirty years at least.

149. Arch. Cath., perg. 1,214 (April 18, 1252): "Johanni de Campolo Sacerdoti ecclesie Sancti Andree."

150. *Rationes decimarum*, I, 262.

151. Arch. Cath., perg. 2,381 (July 19, 1250).

152. Chabás, *Episcopologio valentino*, p. 363 (from Albocácer *carta puebla*) and document above in note 144.

153. Arch. Cath., perg. 2,382 (Sept. 4, 1280); see Chapter IX, note 31.

154. Arch. Cath., perg. 2,355 (Aug. 29, 1252) and document in note 146. He appears again in perg. 1,221 (Jan. 21,¶1261): "rectorem ecclesie Sancte Katerine."

155. Document in note 146: "Bartholomeum Rectorem Ecclesie Sancti Nicholaij."

156. *Repartimiento de Sevilla*, I, 359.

157. "Adhuc ipsa est sicut erat, meçquita, et omnes aliae civitatis factae sunt de novo," reports the chapter (Sanchís Sivera, *Santo Tomás*, p. 21). The phrase "modum ecclesiarum more christiano constructarum" appears in a letter of James in 1274 encouraging Huesca to replace its mosque with a proper (*honestum*) cathedral. A hundred years after our time, in the late fourteenth century, nearly all the parish churches of Valencia city had to be expanded or rebuilt again (*Antigüedades de Valencia*, I, 368).

158. Sanchís Sivera, *Santo Tomás*, p. 32.

159. St. Thomas' parish is seen doing this in the document cited *ibid.*, pp. 22–23.

160. *Aureum opus*, doc. 28, fol. 11Ar (*an.* 1249): "in omnibus . . . universis et singulis ecclesiis . . . civitatis Valencie."

161. Arch. Crown, Peter III, perg. 495.

162. *Antigüedades de Valencia*, I, 212 (on dogbite see p. 335). *Repartimiento*, pp. 223, 324, 382, 579, 637. On this parish, besides the monograph of Sanchís Sivera just cited see Pertegás, "Urbe valenciana," pp. 247 ff.

163. Sanchís Sivera in his *Santo Tomás* reproduces an eighteenth-century map of the parish (from Tosca's map of the city) facing p. 162, and the extramural area facing page 169.

164. I am taking the population figures arrived at by Chantal de la Véronne and dividing it by parishes, including the cathedral parish. See her "Recherches sur le chiffre de la population musulmane de Valence en 1238 d'après le 'Repartimiento,'" *BH*, LI (1949), 423–426. See too the comments above on p. 81.

165. Leopoldo Torres Balbás, "La población musulmana de Valencia en 1238," *Al-Andalus*, XVI (1951), 167–168. The author measures the walled city then at forty-five hectares; from his previous studies he postulates a population of 333 persons in each hectare, in a Hispano-Moslem city of that time. We may divide this interior population by ten parishes, to arrive at an average. The figure conjectured by González for Valencia, only eight thousand souls for the entire city, seems unjustified (*Repartimiento de Sevilla*, I, 316). One must of course allow for a sizable Jewish quarter and, in the first few years, for a large Moslem population within the city, adjusting the real parochial figures accordingly.

166. Russell, "Monedatge," p. 495 with tables.

167. *Repartimiento de Valencia*, p. 656. Pertegás says the parish was not a large one but he refers of course to its area ("Urbe valenciana," pp. 325–327). In 1550 when Valencia had become a more populous city St. Michael's parish held 1390 parishioners in 364 buildings (*Antigüedades de Valencia*, I, 388).

168. *Repartimiento de Sevilla*, I, 359.

169. The last testament of William of Jaca in 1263 left 20 solidi to the *opus* (building or upkeep) of St. Thomas' (Arch. Nac. Madrid, Poblet cartulary, pp. 19 ff., doc. 9).

170. "Item quod ecclesia Sancti Thome incorporetur sacristie cum multoties

tractatum fuit" (Sanchís Sivera, *Santo Tomás*, p. 15; there is also a good account of the fight here).

171. *Ibid.*, p. 15; but see the list on pp. 215–217 (corrected date).

172. See note 159. Though some have cited this as the beginning of construction, Sanchís Sivera argues from the archaeological evidences that it is only the continuation of work begun long before (*Santo Tomás*, p. 23).

173. *Ibid.*, p. 37.

174. *Ibid.*, p. 219, no. 17 on the list; and no. 2 (June 27, 1291). A future chantry priest in this church would be the famous Valencian St. Vincent Ferrer.

175. *Ibid.*, p. 18.

NOTES TO CHAPTER VI. THE SCHOOL SYSTEM IN VALENCIA

1. "Contra impugnantes Dei cultum," IV, 12, quoted in Rodríguez, "Exención" (see above, Chapter II, note 4). "Nunquam fuit tanta apparentia scientiae nec tantum exercitium studii in tot facultatibus, in tot regionibus, sicut a quadraginta annis. Ubique enim sunt doctores dispersi et maxime in theologia in omni civitate et in omni castro et in omni burgo, praecipue per duos ordinis studentes; quod non accidit nisi a quadraginta annis circiter." Vicente de la Fuente has only the briefest reference to the primitive Valencian university in his *Historia de las universidades, colegios, y demás establecimientos en España*, 4 vols. (Madrid, 1884–1889), I, 229. There is a short account in C. Ajo G. y Sáinz de Zúñiga, *Historia de las universidades hispánicas*, 3 vols. to date (Madrid, 1957–1959), I, 286–288. The period just subsequent to our own, and shedding some light perhaps by implication, is covered well by Antonio de la Torre y del Cerro, "Precedentes de la universidad de Valencia," *Anales de la universidad de Valencia*, V (1924–1925), 175–301.

2. Montpellier had a widespread reputation in medicine by 1160; the schools were licenced and organized later (1180–1220) under ecclesiastical auspices. Formal pontifical erection was accorded by Nicholas IV only in 1289. Its evolution, unlike that of Paris, was sure and peaceful. The development of the law faculty in the thirteenth-century period was favored by troubles at Bologna. The three "nations" in this faculty were Provence, Burgundy, and Catalonia. In 1293 Philip of France got suzerainty over Montpellier but only as vassal to the king of Majorca; in 1349 direct overlordship passed to France. See Stephen D'Irsay, *Histoire des universités françaises et étrangères des origines à nos jours*, 2 vols. (Paris, 1933–1935), I, 116–120; and Rashdall, *Universities of Europe*, II, 116–139.

3. Besides the well-known interjection of the royal authority into purely university affairs by James I at Montpellier in his law of 1272 (D'Irsay, *Universités*, I, 164, and cf. Rashdall, *Universities*, II, 122n., 126–127), and his founding of a theological *studium* for the Carthusians at nearby Valmagne in 1263 (*Universities*, II, 133), see the fight between James and the bishop over jurisdiction and the right of the king to grant degrees at Montpellier, settled by Pope Clement IV in 1268 (I, 22–23).

4. *Repartimiento de Valencia*, p. 544, "Suma Montispesulani: LXXV [domus]". Also grants on pp. 180–181, 215, 282, 331, 374, 467, 480, 539, 622. Cf. pp. 531–532 for Barcelona and Lérida.

5. Sanchís Sivera, "La enseñanza en Valencia en la época foral," *BRAH*, CVIII (1936), 157–158. Paris, Bologna, and Montpellier (the last being favored) were the universities most frequented by James's subjects (pp. 158–159).

6. J. Miret y Sans, "Escolars catalans al estudi de Bolonia en la xiiia centuria," *BRABLB*, VIII (1915), 137–155. Tourtoulon, *Jaime I*, II, 34–35. J. Ochoa Sanz,

Vincentius Hispanus, canonista boloñés del siglo xiii (Rome, 1960), pp. 100, 102 ff., 111. Cf. below, Chapter XIV, note 31 and text.

7. Palencia still existed in 1243 but seems dead by 1263. Salamanca was refounded by Ferdinand III in 1243 and received a royal charter in 1254 and a papal confirmation of its statutes in 1255. Valladolid was a *studium generale ex consuetudine*; its serious development came only in the fourteenth century. D'Irsay calls the *Siete partidas* "la première législation universitaire d'un État," which opens "une ère nouvelle dans l'histoire de l'enseignement," a peaceful *reconquista* during which more responsibility is assumed by the state in close collaboration with the church (*Universités*, I, 143). The Castilian school and university movement is described by González (*Reino de Castilla*, I, 626–635).

8. With the partial exception of Palencia; there are analogies in the voluntary migrations of academic bodies in the past (Rashdall, *Universities*, II, 161).

9. Arch. Vat., Reg. Vat. 21 (Innocent IV), fol. 213v (July 10, 1245); in Berger, *Registres*, I, no. 1,375.

10. D'Irsay, *Universités*, I, 142 where a passing reference is made incorrectly to "un petit *studium* local." Rashdall notes the charter (*Universities*, II, 107); but "nothing further appears to have been done." Formal treatment of this early period by historians of the medieval universities was lacking until the recent short account by Ajo G. y Sáinz de Zúñiga (see note 1). Some accounts mislead the reader; see, for example, the fables concerning the scholarly circle of Mozarabic Basilians teaching, at what became St. Bartholomew's parish, in the early thirteenth century, in Miguel Velasco y Santos, *Reseña histórica de la universidad de Valencia, su origen y fundación, sus progresos y vicisitudes, influjo que ha ejercido en el movimiento general científico y literario de España hasta el año de 1845* (Valencia, 1868).

11. Rashdall (*Universities*, II, app. 1) treats the subject of paper universities. Dublin (1312) eventually proved abortive; Gray (1291) was got by Count Otto IV of Burgundy from Pope Nicholas IV but was stifled by disastrous fires, wars, and temporary French annexation. There are similar examples at Alcalá (1293), Verona (1339), and Pamiers (1295). On the concrete protection and encouragement to learning which a university charter offered see Pearl Kibre, "Scholarly Privileges: their Roman Origins and Mediaeval Expression," *AHR*, LIX (1954), 543–567.

12. Rashdall, *Universities*, III, 457; II, 80, 209.

13. See in the *Repartimiento*: Almeric Petragaricensis (p. 216), the canon Bernard Soler (pp. 180, 381, 459), Berengar of Villabertran (p. 218), Berengar of Graseca (pp. 238, 268, 433), Evi (p. 605), the physician G. Anglés (p. 217), G. of Teruel (pp. 214, 280), the king's physician Guido (pp. 157, 161, 229, 241, 481, 619, 667), Elias (p. 455), the physician James (p. 399), John of Tarragona (pp. 460, 575, 635), J. Nuño (p. 293), the physician Lobo (p. 630), Martin (pp. 176, 238), Michael (p. 540), Paris (p. 591), Ponce of Sumidria (pp. 304, 537, 625), Richard of Barcelona (pp. 182, 287, 526), Vincent (p. 574), and William (pp. 548, 569, 625). Of these and similar names, some of course would be Jews. On the cathedral canons see note 41. On the general educational climate of the Spanish churchmen see V. Beltrán de Heredia, "La formación intelectual del clero en España durante los siglos xii, xiii, y xiv," *Revista española de teología*, VI (1946), 313–357.

14. Document in note 9. Berger's transcription in the *Registres d'Innocent IV* (I, no. 1,375) mal-copies the phrase "nimis erit utile," putting "vicinis erit utile" and thus obscuring the idea of a *studium generale*. On the other hand, he puts "exceptis" in the phrase "distributionibus cotidianis dumtaxat acceptis," thus erroneously supplying the Valencian scholars with this added support. August Potthast's *Regesta pontificum romanorum*, 2 vols. (Berlin, 1874–1875) dates the

letter incorrectly as of July 15. The privilege of drawing scholars from all over Christendom would alone demonstrate a *studium generale*; the great canonist Hostiensis explained that with this concession "de studio generali intelligendum est, non de studio speciali alicuius castri vel ville, cum hoc in fraude fiat"; see reference to his *Summa* in H. Denifle, *Die Entstehung der Universitäten des Mittelalters bis 1400* (Berlin, 1885), I (*unicus*), 19n. Denifle's short treatment of the Valencia university concerns almost exclusively the much later history (pp. 643–646).

15. Arch. Vat., Reg. Vat. 21, fols. 213v–214r, also July 10, 1245 but a separate document from that in note 9; "ut scolares Regnorum tuorum et totius alterius terre tuo subjecte dominio qui in predicta Civitate studuerint beneficiorum . . . proventus in huiusmodi studio percipere valeant sicut alii scolares yspanie alibi studio insistentes percipere dinoscuntur." The preface to this document also repeats the note of "great joy" in Christendom.

16. Arch. Vat., *ibid.*, fol. 214 (same date); not published in *Registres*.

17. *Furs, lib.* IX, *rub.* XXXII, *c.* 17: "atorgam que tot clergue o altre hom pusque francament, e sens tot servi, e tribut tener studi de grammatica, e de totes altres artes, e de fisica, e de dret civil, e canonich en tot loch per toda la ciutat."

18. *Viage literario*, II, 96.

19. Rashdall, *Universities*, II, 92.

20. *Ibid.* p. 107, Besides Lérida, Aragon was to have universities at Perpignan (1350, 1375) and Huesca (1354); others came in the following century.

21. Arch. Cath., perg. 2,309 (June 23, 1240): "item assignamus ei scholam civitatis." Also in *Constitutiones sive ordinationes*, fol. 42 (a misprint for 47), and in *Viage literario*, doc. in II, 94.

22. Rashdall, *Universities*, I, 279. See Chapter II, note 86 and text.

23. Arch. Cath., perg. 2,310 (June 14, 1242): "quicunque docere voluerit pueros in psalmis et cantu et gramatica possit hoc facere sine licentia precentoris; sed examinatio magistrorum pertineat ad episcopum sicut in quibusdam ecclesiis de consuetudine est obtentum." Master Peter Dominic was *capiscol* (*chantre, precentor*) at this time. Soon Gonzalvo Pérez and others will succeed him.

24. "Constitutiones synodales" (Oct. 22, 1258): "utrum cantent vel legant, vel loqui sciant latinis verbis, et qualiter in domo domini debeant conversari"; "ad quartum gradum nisi loqui sciat latinis verbis." Sanchís Sivera, "Enseñanza en Valencia," p. 156: "muy completa."

25. *Summa, lib.* I, *tit.* III, under simony: "tenerent singulos magistros liberalium artium, ad minus grammaticae quae earumdem Ecclesiarum clericos et alios scholares pauperes gratis instituerent"; "scientia donum Dei est, unde vendi non potest." In the previous century, already "la plupart des chapitres ont une école" (Philippe Delhaye, "L'organisation scolaire au xiie siècle," *Traditio*, V [1947], 240).

26. *Constitutiones sive ordinationes*, fol. 57, *an.* 1259, has: "statuimus quod unus magister qui regat scholas grammaticas in Ecclesia recipiat sex denarios." See also "Constitutiones synodales," p. 180; and J. M. Madurell y Marimón, "Las escuelas de la seo de Barcelona," *HS*, I (1948), 389–401. The council of Lérida in 1219 had ordered a school of grammar also in each archdeaconry. Excellent background, though Valencia is touched only lightly, is Johannes Vincke's "Die Hochschulpolitik der spanischen Domkapitel im Mittelalter," *Gesammelte Aufsätze zur Kulturgeschichte Spaniens*, IX (1954), 144–163; cf. pp. 152, 157.

27. *Rationes decimarum*, I, 258, 264: "item pro censuali scolarium magistri Vincentii," and "item a redditibus scolarium magistri Vincencii" at 18 and 16 solidi. See the similar situation in parts of France (Delhaye, "Organisation scolaire," pp. 247–248).

28. Carreras Candi, "Notes dotzecentistes" [1911], pp. 9–10, document of 1257 organizing the existing academic situation. The school's object is "nepotes canonicorum"—probably the households or boy servitors at the cathedral, with the extern poor students understood as included. At Mayence in 1190 intern students boarded with the canons (Delhaye, "Organisation scolaire," p. 250).

29. Sanchís Sivera, "Enseñanza en Valencia," p. 167. The author sees him as coordinator of schools, though the form "scolarum" does not necessarily indicate this. The term *doctor* rather than *magister* may suggest a legal training (see Rashdall, *Universities*, I, 19–20).

30. Sanchís Sivera, "Enseñanza," p. 160; *Viage literario*, doc. in II, 98–99.

31. Sanchís Sivera, "Enseñanza," p. 162 (*an.* 1336); doc. 6, in appendix of the series of articles *ibid.*, CIX (1937), 23.

32. *Ibid.*, doc. 2, pp. 20–21: "scolares aliqui, tam clerici quam layci." Also doc. 3, p. 21.

33. *Ibid.*, doc. 5, p. 22. The reorganization of pre-existent elementary schools in the early fourteenth century was not a local phenomenon. Thus, at Brussels there was a small school for boys, another for girls, and a third larger school; in 1320 these expanded to comprise ten in this one city, including four for girls (Moreau, *Église en Belgique*, III, 626–627). There seems to have been a school under the local pastor's jurisdiction in every town (p. 626).

34. *Universities*, II, 107n.

35. Sanchís Sivera, "Enseñanza en Valencia," pp. 169–170. See *Viage literario*, II, 99 though the objection here seems groundless. Medicine was always a favored subject in King James's realms; even Barcelona was to organize into a medical *studium* at the end of the next century, acquiring thereby royal patronage and a guarantee of public corpses for dissection (Rashdall, *Universities*, II, 101).

36. *A Life of Ramón Lull Written by an Unknown Hand About 1311*, ed.-tr. E. A. Peers (London, 1927), p. 4; yet he could both "write and compose" his poems (p. 2). In his novel *Blanquerna*, Lull's nun "learned perfectly to read" in a short time.

37. *Itinerari*, p. 518 (April 19, 1275): "quod possis tenere sub te discipulum et quos volueris qui pro te conficiant et scribant a memoriis testamentorum." At this time (1230) Toulouse had at least thirty-two public scribes (Mundy, *Toulouse*, p. 327).

38. Silversmiths (two do not take up their claim) appear in the *Repartimiento de Valencia* (pp. 211, 276, 279–280, 311, 528, 560); painters (516, 533); troubadours (213, 336, 362, 499, 528, 553, 565, 631); and so on.

39. *Constitutiones sive ordinationes*, fols. 12v–13r (July 1, 1254).

40. *Ibid.*, fol. 13r (*an.* 1279).

41. In the early chapter, besides Soler, the archdeacon Martin and the precentor (Peter) Dominic were masters; others soon follow. The *Repartimiento* has "Magister P. portugalensis canonicus valentinus" (p. 274). Theological masters were rare, the course being a postgraduate one usually for men planning an academic career, and it increased one's university time to sixteen or seventeen years; only Oxford, Cambridge, and Paris then had theological faculties; many of the clerics sent by bishops to study theology or scripture did not mean to return with formal degrees (Moorman, *Church Life*, p. 95). The number of masters in a diocese with good bishops and a convenient university is given by Moorman: the deaconry of Stowe, in the diocese of Lincoln, had eight incumbents with masters' degrees out of eighty-six (1205–1235), then thirteen out of eighty-five (1235–1253), then sixteen out of seventy-six (1258–1279), i.e. a percentage of nine, then sixteen, then twenty-one.

42. *Viage literario*, II, 100, document.

43. Rashdall, *Universities*, I, 347.

44. See Chapter XI, note 44 and text.

45. For a general treatment of this subject, with some reference to Valencia, see José M. Coll, "Escuelas de lenguas orientales en los siglos xiii–xiv," *AST*, XVII (1944), 115–138, XVIII (1945), 59–90, XIX (1946), 217–240. The date 1281 is sometimes incorrectly cited for the foundation of the Valencian *studium*. Rashdall and others do not mention the Valencian school, though it existed earlier than its famous counterpart at Seville. Further treatment of this fascinating subject falls outside the scope of the present book.

46. Sanchís Sivera, "Enseñanza en Valencia," pp. 158, 173.

47. Thus the will of one Berengar of 1279 at Valencia provides for the support of "unum scolarium," apparently in connection with the Templars' residence (Arch. Nac. Madrid, Ords. Milits., Montesa, R134). There is a "scolaris" at St. Vincent's from 1266; the holder of this benefice in 1269 is William Bernard (see the documents cited in Chapter XV, note 58, and comments). A "scolaris" named John Peter is among those exempt from the 1280 crusade tithe in Valencia (*Rationes decimarum*, I, 261, cf. 255).

NOTES TO CHAPTER VII. FRONTIER PASTOR AND PEOPLE

1. "Constitutiones synodales," p. 197: "ingrediuntur civitatem frequentius quam expediebat . . . illicitis et inhonestis se actibus immiscendo." La Fuente considers these early synods of Peralta and Albalat "curiosísimos para el estudio de la disciplina y liturgia del siglo xiii en España" (*Historia eclesiástica*, IV, 260).

2. "Constitutiones," p. 201. "Spectaculis vel choreis mulierum" may have been the work of wandering entertainers. See R. S. Loomis and G. Cohen, "Were There Theatres in the Twelfth and Thirteenth Centuries?," *Speculum*, XX (1945), 92–95. More to the point, the great metropolitan council for the realms of King James, held at Lérida scarcely a decade before the fall of Valencia, warned the clergy: "ioculatoribus, mimis, et histrionibus non intendant" (*Colección de cánones*, III, 333, no. 9).

3. "Constitutiones," p. 198: "in spiritu lenitatis eis compatiendo"; "nec admirentur de commissis quantumcumque turpibus." In the *Summa* of Penyafort there is an instruction on hearing confession (*lib*. III, *tit*. XXXIV).

4. "Constitutiones synodales," p. 197 (*an*. 1255); also p. 201 (*an*. 1258): "clerici pannos listatos non portent, nec manicas sutitias, nec sotulares rostratos, et maxime Presbyteri."

5. *Ibid*., p. 208: "pannis rubeis, viridibus et croceis in chlamydibus Chori longis, et colorum similium."

6. *Ibid*.: "non omnes" (*an*. 1273); *ibid*., for synod of 1269.

7. *Ibid*.: "arma portant diversorum generum, et signanter costalarios, et gladios maiores quam laici"; "portent ensem pennatum vel Segovianum publice." They are to put this aside after arrival in a town (*an*. 1269).

8. *Ibid*., pp. 201, 208; "ita quod probari potest," the latter decree prudently adds. Penyafort has a long treatise on clerical dicing in his *Summa* (*lib*. II, *tit*. VII).

9. "Constitutiones," *ibid*.: "nonulli se inebrient impudenter, et eorum ebrietas cedat in grave scandalum plurimorum." There is to be "nullam super hoc misericordiam habiturus."

10. *Ibid*., p. 199: "ne Sacerdotes habeant secum prolem ad servitium altaris propter scandalum."

11. *Ibid*., p. 207: "quod plures Clerici nostrae Civitatis, et Dioecesis de bonis

424   NOTES TO CHAPTER SEVEN

Ecclesiae, cui praesunt, emunt possessiones, et immobilia ad opus filiorum suorum, quos debent prorsus a se abiicere, si Ordinis honestatem attenderent."

12. *Repartimiento*, p. 493: "Geraldus de Massoteriis sacerdos cum filia sua Berga." See cases below, in note 28 and text.

13. "Constitutiones synodales," p. 208: "item cum multoties, tam in Synodis quam in visitationibus Ecclesiarum, Clericos duxerimus commonendos, ut abiectis a se penitus concubinis, honeste viverent, ut deceret; nec propter hoc multi ex ipsis se curaverint emendare; statuimus, quod quicumque fuerunt inventi publici concubinarii a tempore obsidionis Murciae, vel de caetero poterint inveniri; ipso facto triginta morabetinorum poenam incurrant . . ."; "qui de caetero de tam damnato coitu generabunter, distrahendos esse censemus." Cf. Penyafort in his *Summa, lib.* III, *tit.* XIX, "de filiis presbyterorum et caeteris non legitime natis."

14. "Constitutiones synodales," p. 208.

15. *Furs, lib.* III, *rub.* V, *c.* 8: "enadi lo Senyor Rey que clergue que port corona, a haje muller, sie tengut de respondre en poder de la cort del loch de tot pleyt."

16. Sanchís Sivera, "Derecho valenciano," p. 145: "prohibemus ne quisquam diaconus, subdiaconus vel sacerdos civitatis vel diocesis Valentine, prolem suam illegitimam in domibus quas habitant tenere presumant."

17. *Viage literario*, V, 284–287, 311 (Tortosa synods). See also "Barraganía" in the *Enciclopedia jurídica española*, 30 vols. (Barcelona, 1910), IV, cols. 277–282, and the shorter article in the *Enciclopedia universal ilustrada* [Espasa], VII, cols. 894–896; E. Jombert, "Concubinage," *DDC*, III, cols. 1,513–1,524; A. Aunós Pérez, *El derecho catalán en el siglo xiii* (Barcelona, 1926), pp. 68–70; Bienvenido Oliver, *Historia del derecho en Cataluña, Mallorca y Valencia, código de las costumbres de Tortosa*, 4 vols. (Madrid, 1876–1881), II, 349–353. For the Tarragona metropolitanate area see the laws of the provincial council in 1229 against clerical concubinage and lay "contubernia" in *Colección de cánones*, III, 332–333, 335.

18. Documents in Chapter V, note 135.

19. Arch. Crown, James I, Reg. Canc. 12, fol. 62 (June 1, 1262). "Per nos et nostros remitimus, absolvimus et diffinimus vobis dilecto nostro Guillermo de Alarico [Alarch?] Sacristano Valencie et familie vestre et vestris imperpetuum omnem petitionem, questionem et demandam et omnem penam . . . quam contra vos et dictam familiam vestram et bona vestra possemus facere movere infligere vel imponere ratione sive occasione querimonie quam A. March contra vos opponebat coram nobis pro facto uxoris sue quam ut ipse asserebat vos cum dicta familia vestra in Gerunda abstuleratis et eam carnaliter cognoveratis. Ita quod ratione predicta non teneamini nobis nec dicto A. March nec alicui alie persone unquam aliquo tempore in aliquo respondere." Since Bishop Andrew wished the office of sacristan to be held only by a priest (*Constitutiones sive ordinationes*, fols. 57v–58r, *an.* 1255), William of Alaric may well have been one. In 1271 William appears in a document loaning the prince a thousand solidi of Jaca (Reg. Canc. 28, fol. 32, May 31, 1271).

20. The trial record of this Blaise (Blasco) Pérez is preserved at Zaragoza, dated 1267 (MSS, Diputación del Reino de Aragón). King James tells the story in his *Llibre dels feyts*, chs. 465–470. Was it in order to pass his coins freely that he and a pensioner of the diocese obtained from the crown a license for treasure hunting ("liberam potestatem querendi thesaurum subtus terram in termino Tirassone")? See *Itinerari*, p. 366.

21. "Constitutiones synodales," pp. 205–207: "item, quia cum avaritia, quae est idolorum servitus, nonnullos Clericos adeo excaecet, quod non solum non contenti terminis, et stipendiis suis, aliena qualitercumque habere satagunt, sed

ipsos etiam exponendo venales . . ."; "illud modicum, quod ipsi defuncti pro suis restituendis iniuriis, vel ob modum, et remedium animarum suarum, ad pias caussas reliquerunt, aliquando subticent, et occultant, et in proprias bursas convertunt." The legacies are to be placed "in Aede sacra." The sin was "quaedam turpis impietas et peccatum horribile" which "quasi in consuetudinem fit redacta."

22. *Ibid.*, p. 201. Bishop Jazpert will later rebuke this at some length as an ingrained evil ("huic morbo letali . . . in nostra diocessi dampnabiliter inolevit") of "some"—whether cleric or lay is not specified. All sorts of church goods are thus sold, "maxime calices ubi Corporis et Sanguinis Domini beatissimum conficitur sacramentum." (Sanchís Sivera, "Derecho valenciano," p. 146.)

23. Sanchís Sivera, *ibid.*; this too may apply to the laity.

24. "Constitutiones synodales," p. 207: "plures Cappellanias" (*an.* 1263).

25. *Ibid.* (*an.* 1263).

26. Treated in Chapters VIII and IX.

27. *Constitutiones sive ordinationes*, fols. 70r-71 : "quod multae dissensiones et scandala in nostra ecclesia multoties sunt exorta."

28. *Ibid.*, fol. 26v (*an.* 1286).

29. *Ibid.*, fol. 28v (*an.* 1286).

30. Arch. Cath., perg. 6,082 (April 27, 1268); *Aureum opus*, doc. 22, fol. 11r,v (May 8, 1247); *Colección diplomática*, doc. 941. Cf. also the opinions of Penyafort in his *Summa, lib.* I, *tit.* XVI.

31. Faustino Gazulla, "El puig de Santa María," doc. 2 (Dec. 9, 1256), *Congrés III*, II, 649-650. Arch. Vat., Reg. Vat. 17 (Gregory IX), fol. 206v (Sept. 5, 1234); cf. *Registres*, I, no. 2,083: "ius humani federis litigatorum abusus extingueret et . . . concordiam extra mundi terminos exularet."

32. See Chapter XV, note 129 and text.

33. "Constitutiones synodales," p. 200: "item mandamus, quod Fratres Praedicatores et Minores honorifice a Clericis recipiantur."

34. Sanchís Sivera, "Derecho valenciano," pp. 143-144; "in nostra diocesi Valentina"; for three months' absence excommunication is decreed. Cf. pp. 142-143 (*an.* 1258). "Citamus talem et talem," says another decree, "qui sine licentia nostra se illicite se [*sic*] absentant, ut infra duos menses, et alii absentes infra sex menses" ("Constitutiones synodales," p. 202, *an.* 1258).

35. Sanchís Sivera, "Derecho valenciano," pp. 144-145.

36. *Ibid.;* "propter multa scandala et frequentes quaerelas quae ex ista causa coram nobis multoties perveni[u]nt."

37. See Chapter IV, note 136 and text.

38. Arch. Crown, Peter III, Reg. Canc. 60, fols. 68-69r and 88v; Reg. Canc. 61, fol. 120 (March-April 1283), four documents. "Guillem de Caceria presbiterem et familiarem dilecti nostri Raimundi de Muntanyana consiliarii dicti domini Regis" is the victim. Caceria may be Cáceres, or perhaps Cárcer. On William see Chapter II, note 127 and Chapter V, notes 15, 29 and text.

39. Arch. Crown, Peter III, Reg. Canc. 76, fol. 221 (July 8, 1284). The king tells the justiciar of Morella "quod custodiat bene et diligenter los [*sic*] de Vilarnau quos captos tenet racione mortis fratris G. de Talamacha de qua fuerunt predicti inculpati, et quod capiat quoscumque invenerit culpabiles in dicta morte." The king gives his attention to this business from his camp "in obsidione de Albarrazino."

40. Moorman, *Church Life*, p. 267n.

41. See Appendix II, "Saints on the Valencian Frontier."

42. Antonio Michavila y Vila, "Apuntes para el estudio de la vida social del

reino de Valencia en la época de los reyes de la casa de Aragón," *Congrés III*, II, 144–145.

43. "Orgoglio e cupidigia," a phrase used to characterize Assisi by a contemporary chronicler (*St. Francis of Assisi, the Legends and Lauds*, ed. Otto Karrer [London, 1947], p. ix).

44. See in this connection the chapter on the *corpus mysticum* by Ernst Kantorowicz (*The King's Two Bodies, a Study in Mediaeval Political Theology* [Princeton, N.J., 1957], ch. 5) and the works of Mersch, Ladner, de Lubac, and others whom he cites; though the theological foundations are slighted in favor of the external juristic and institutional aspects, one can see how popular at this period was the concept of the *corpus mysticum*, even to its being applied in a sort of secular analogy to the very different idea of corporate personality, thus becoming significant in the origins of modern patriotism and nationalism.

45. See Chapter XI, note 53 (Dominican church) and the indulgence in the *Ordinatio* given at St. Vincent's for a bridge.

46. Desclot, *Crònica*, I, ch. 47.

47. The subject will be dealt with more fully in my work, now in progress, on the Moslem problem in the kingdom of Valencia.

48. *Furs, lib.* IX, *rub.* XIX, *c.* 7.

49. *Colección diplomática*, doc. 1,069 (June 13, 1251): "attendentes quod redempcio captivorum inter ceteras virtutes obtineat principatum."

50. *Itinerari*, p. 537, doc. of July 23, 1276.

51. *Repartimiento*, pp. 460–461: "Raymunde uxori Dominici Cospin: domos in Xativa franchas et liberas ita quod incontinenti possit eas vendere prae redemptione sue corporis."

52. *Llibre dels feyts*, ch. 229.

53. Arch. Cath., perg. 5,975 (April 24, 1251) will of Peter Armer: "gravi egritudine dete[n]tus de qua mori timeo"—one of several formulae; and "quinquaginta solidos in redempcione unius captivi." One bequest is for the port (Grao) church: "item operi sancte Marie maris, ii sol." There are two documents on a property of Armer in the cathedral archives; his wife was Mary; his son, daughter, and son-in-law appear by name in the document quoted in ,Chapter XI, note 87.

54. Arch. Cath., perg. 1,351 (June 24, 1274) will of Peter Abrafim: "vicinus et habitator Valencie."

55. Arch Cath., perg. 2,917 (June 4, 1275); of Petrus Marchesii (March, or Marqués) whose brother was already buried at the cathedral: "duo clerici qui celebrent missa[m] de requie pro anima [*sic*] parentum meorum"; "ita quod dantur cuilibet captivo ii solidi." On Marqués see Chapter XV, note 153.

56. F. Gazulla, "Los mercedarios en Arguines y Algar (siglo xiii)," *BSCC*, VI (1925), 69.

57. Arch. Cath., perg. 5,011 (Mar. 16, 1256) will of Jordana, wife of the knight John Garcés of Mazón: "item dimito omnibus et singulis operibus Ecclesiarum parochialium Valencie infra muros eiusdem unicuique earum quinque solidi."

58. Arch. Cath., perg. 1,105 (Nov. 13, 1271) will of Barberan Oller: "honorifice."

59. Arch. Cath., perg. 1,098 (May 22, 1268) will of Jazpert, viscount of Castellnou: "inter Templarios et alios religiosos et captivos redimendos et ad virgines maritandas et reservandos [?] pauperes maxime verecundos."

60. Arch. Cath., pergs. 3,910 and 3,507 (Oct. 16, 1272): "in tumulum de petra"; "pro virginibus maritandis" and "pauperibus induendis." She is Guillelma (Willelma), daughter of William of Soler and wife of Peter Gilabert. Twenty

solidi seem to be given to a confraternity at the cathedral, "et quod detur eis victus una die"; a similar bequest to the "fratribus Sancte Marie" is in the will of Peter Marqués (document in note 55).

61. Arch. Cath., perg. 1,330 (May 11, 1259). Perg. 5,980 (Dec. 30, 1257) is a similar will, rather too dim for comfortable detailed analysis.

62. Arch. Nac. Madrid, Clero: Valencia, Franciscanas, Concepción, leg. 2125, arm. 45, fab. 2 (Jan. 15, 1255): "ad opus unius biblie." The name may also be spelled Alamany or Alemany.

63. Arch. Cath., perg. 1,216 (July 25, 1257). See J. Bonduelle, "Convers," DDC, IV, cols. 562-588; Moorman, Church Life, p. 300 for the infirmary service.

64. Colección diplomática, doc. 1,009 (July 21, 1276): "noveritis quod nos, volentes ex nunc Dei servicio totaliter intendere, ut Paradisi gloriam facilius consequi mereamur, suscepimus modo habitum ordinis cisterciensis et destituimus ac relinquimus carissimo filio nostro infanti Jacob, regnum et terras . . ." And in his Llibre dels feyts, the writer of the last chapters says for James: "I became a monk of that Order" (ch. 565).

65. Furs, lib. I, preface.

66. Ibid., lib. III, rub. XXII, c. 8: "si alcun jurara en joch dient mal de Deu, e de sancta Maria, pach X solidos o nuu sossira X açots . . . si alcun dira mal de deus: o de sancta Maria pach C solidos et si dira mal dels Apostols pach L solidos, e si dels Martirs sancts XX solidos." The whipping, "nuu," as we learn from a later (1342) addition, applies to men and women ("nudi . . . tectis dumtaxat verendis") but is commuted to a money payment at least from the latter date, for those whose status is above that of manual laborer.

67. Arch. Cath., perg. 2,310 (June 14, 1242), with perg. 2,312 (Feb. 11, 1243).

68. Furs, lib. II, rub. XVII, c. 13: "assat es que nostre Senyor ne sie venjador. Car abaste la pena del perjuri la qual spera de nostre Senyor." The prospective grantees of the Peñíscola territory were to swear upon the four Gospels that they would reside upon the properties received, residence being a sore point with the authorities at that time (Arch. Nac. Madrid, Montesa, R95; Jan. 28, 1250).

69. Furs, lib. I, rub. XV, c. 1: "les vults ne les ymatges de deus ne dels sancts no sien entallats publicament ne feyts ne pintats en les places, ne sien posats, ni portats a vendre per les places, e qui ho fara pach vint sous per pena." Light may perhaps be thrown on this prohibition from a similar later law (1375) designed to control the unseemly multiplications of images on clothing and the like (cf. Escolano, Décadas, I, 527).

70. Furs, lib. IX, rub. XXIII, c. 10: "sia celebrat de tots Chrestians, e de juheus, e de sarrahins: car nostre senyor Iesu Christ volch que hom se abstengues . . ."

71. Ibid., lib. I, rub. VIII, c. 2. A law passed at this time in Lérida reminded barbers that "neither they nor a substitute may presume to cut hair or shave anyone from the evening before a Sunday or feast . . . after the time arrives in which one cannot shave without a light," until the dawn of the day after the feast; nor may they lend the equipment to a client to serve himself (Colección diplomática, doc. 587, Sept. 17, 1257).

72. Furs, lib. IX, rub. XXXII, c. 1: "si doncs primerament lo malalt no haura presa penitencia" (apparently referring to impenitent public sinners).

73. "Colección de cartas pueblas," no. XV, pp. 166-168: "si obierit [in] sua egritudine sine confessione et receptione corporis Christi sua negligentia quintetur suum haver."

74. Furs, lib. IX, rub. VII, c. 63: "sien cremats"; confiscation in c. 70; outlawing in lib. I, rub. VII, c. 1.

75. "Constitutiones synodales," p. 208: "multi sunt in nostra civitate, et

5—II

Dioecesi, qui ignorant Orationem Dominicam, scilicet, *Pater Noster*; seu ipsam perfecte non sciunt; et sunt paucissimi qui sciunt *Credo in Deum.*"

76. See Chapter I, note 29 and Chapter V, note 8 on the prohibition of clerics drawing wills.

77. Sanchís Sivera, "Vida íntima," pp. 114–115. Later problems were caused by the loafers who, for lack of a convenient public shelter from sun or rain, stepped into the cathedral to continue their dice or cards, and also people who carried along lunch to devotions (*ibid.*, pp. 112–113, citing *Aureum opus* for 1314; this is a relatively late legislation). The cemetery was a favorite gaming place too, according to this law. Packing a bit of lunch to long devotions is an eccentricity not unobserved in the churches of some lands in our own day; as for getting out of the sun, an English tourist of a generation past reported a horse stepping into the cathedral of Pisa for this purpose and remaining there unremarked and undisturbed by the devout.

78. "Constitutiones synodales," p. 208.

79. *Viage literario*, I, 183–188, doc. 3, a codification of funeral customs by Bishop Deçpont near the end of the century; "illi qui in torneamentis moriuntur."

80. "Constitutiones synodales," pp. 198, 200: "et caveat Sacerdos, ne de aqua baptismali sortilegia fiant"; "ne sortilegia fiant, nec maleficia nec ligationes, quae fiunt per malificas mulieres"—at marriages; under pain of excommunication. Cf. also above, Chapter II, note 65 and text on Arnold of Vilanova's dedication to the bishop of Valencia of his work on witchcraft.

81. F. A. Roca Traver, citing his unpublished book "El justicia de Valencia," in his "Vida mudéjar," p. 147 and n.

82. St. Martin also recalls the Carolingian antecedents of the Catalans; Holy Savior was a devotion widespread in early thirteenth-century Catalonia.

83. F. Mateu y Llopis, "Lérida y sus relaciones con Valencia" (running title for "Datos y documentos para la historia monetaria de Lérida, siglos xiii a xviii"), *Ilerda*, V (1945), 41–43; there is much supporting argumentation in this article for the similarity of the two populations.

84. The twenty-four parishes of Seville also recently conquered by the Christians included most of these titles, with understandable local deviations. These invocations were also found in the dioceses of origin of many of the Valencian settlers, whose tastes had been formed in those places previously. To some extent therefore the choice must have been conventional and reflexive. But, since it was a free choice, designed to please the people and conform to their devotion, it is not without significance. See *Repartimiento de Sevilla*, I, 356, and chart on 357 for variant patterns of the Castilians.

85. Arch. Crown, James I, Reg. Canc. 15, fol. 80v (Feb. 23, 1268); cf. *Furs, lib.* I, *rub.* VIII, *c.* 2. On feast days and fast days, what to do and what to avoid, the contemporary Catalan spirit is reflected in Penyafort's moral *Summa, lib.* I, *tit.* XII, esp. no. 2.

86. *Viage literario*, I, 183–188, doc. 3: "saepe atque saepissime."

87. "Constitutiones synodales," p. 199; "debent enim iniungere [confessores] ieiunium, eleemonsynas, venias, orationes, peregrinationes et huiusmodi."

88. *Ibid.*, p. 198: "peccata enormia . . . publica."

89. For evidence for early existence of trade brotherhoods in Valencia and some discussion of their nature see Luis Tramoyeres Blasco, *Instituciones gremiales, su origen y organización en Valencia* (Valencia, 1889), pp. 41–51; Leopoldo Piles Ros, *Estudio sobre el gremio de zapateros* (Valencia, 1959), pp. 15–19 and ch. 6; the Marqués de Cruilles, *Los gremios de Valencia, memoria sobre su origen, vicisitudes y organización* (Valencia, 1883) under individual trades (e.g. pp. 62, 65, 79,

94, 136, 143, 148, 152); Francisco A. Roca Traver, "El gremio de curtidores de Castellón: unas ordenanzas desconocidas del siglo xiv," *BSCC*, XXVI (1950), 195–215 with the thirteenth-century documentation cited; Roca Traver's more general article, summing much of our present knowledge on the thirteenth-century brotherhoods, is cited below in note 97. José Ibarra y Folgado, *Los gremios del metal en Valencia . . . en los siglos xiii al xviii* (Valencia, 1911) has little for this period. In a more general way, see the survey of Antonio Rumeu de Armas, *Historia de la previsión social en España, cofradías, gremios, hermandades, montepíos* (Madrid, 1944), esp. ch. 5 on medieval background, and appendix of documents and lists of brotherhoods. H. Durand has an article "Confrérie" in the *DDC*, IV, cols. 128–176.

90. The brotherhoods may be found in *Gremios y cofradías de la antigua corona de Aragón*, ed. Manuel de Bofarull y de Sartorio, 2 vols., *Colección de documentos inéditos del archivo general de la corona de Aragón*, XL–XLI (Barcelona, 1876), I, docs. 4 ff. On these brotherhoods see too below, chapters on the Orders.

91. Arch. Crown, James I, Reg. Canc. 15, fol. 98 (May 3, 1268): "nos Jacobus . . . ad honorem Sancti Dominici domus fratrum predicatorum Valencie, concedimus ut pelliparii civitatis Valentie quod faciatis et facere possitis . . . licite et sine aliquo impedimento confratriam."

92. Arch. Nac. Madrid, Clero: Val., Franciscanas, leg. 2,124, arm. 45, fab. 2 (Mar. 3, 1252): "et dimit[t]o confraternitati pellipariorum valencie v sols et quod solvatur xii d. eidem." Is this the Dominic pelliparius of *Itinerari* (p. 197, June 21, 1249)? The *pelliparius* was processer of furs and skins after the tanning. On Pelliparius (Pellicer) as a family name see Chapter VIII, note 82. Teixidor considers the Peter Martyr brotherhood in his *Capillas y sepulturas del real convento de predicadores de Valencia*, 3 vols. (Valencia, [1755] 1949–1952), III *ad initium*; for the furriers he could push the date back only as far as 1290.

93. Arch. Cath., perg. 1,334 (Aug. 4, 1261).

94. Arch. Crown, Peter III, perg. 166 (Oct. 24, 1279): "dimitto confratrie Sancti Bartholomei cuius sum confrater quinque solidos." Chicot (Xicot in the document) was a "vicinus et habitator Parrochie Sancti Bartholomei Valencie" in whose cemetery he was to be buried; he left five solidi to the rector and five to the "opus" (building, or perhaps furnishing and upkeep) of the parish church. At Toulouse, confraternities were "among the earliest associational forms known," and "were known all over the Midi at this period" (for their activities see Mundy, *Toulouse*, pp. 55, 64, 267–268, 276).

95. *Colección diplomática*, doc. 1,051 (Jan. 28, 1246). King James was not the founder of the group, though King Peter IV in 1371 was later to make that claim; it was a spontaneous association of local origin. King James I appointed as lifetime chaplain to the altar of St. James the priest James of Brull (*ibid.*); this priest later also received the secretariate of the town of Elbayo (*Itinerari*, p. 460, Mar. 23, 1272).

96. Arch. Crown, James I, perg. 1,556 (Jan. 29, 1258).

97. Arch. Crown, James I, Reg. Canc. 12, fol. 23 (April 29, 1263): "attendentes caritates et helemosinas ac sacrificia quas et quae vos canonici et clerici . . . cum suis confratribus facitis in confratria quam nunc fecistis et vocatur Sanctus Jacobus, per nos et nostros concedimus vobis predictis canonicis et clericis quod possitis recipere in dicta confratria centum laicos . . . [et] concedimus in hunc modum quod vos simul cum centum laicis predictis construatis et hedifficetis et construere et hedifficare teneamini altare Sancti Jacobi in Sede Valencie ex quo dicta confratria ut dictum est Sancti Jacobi nuncupatur." Cf. the *Antigüedades de Valencia*, II, 339–342, and the thorough discussion with documents and maps by

F. A. Roca Traver, "Interpretación de la 'cofradía' valenciana: la real cofradía de San Jaime," *Estudios medievales* [Valencia], II (1957), 37–83.

98. Arch. Crown, James I, perg. 2,289: "faticam et laudimium censuales ipsius capellanie et operatorium pro quibus ipsum fit censuale." See the two bequests to this confraternity (1272, 1275) in note 60.

99. *Antigüedades de Valencia*, I, 299–300: "recognosco et confiteor quod sum Confrater Domus Hospitalis Sancti Ioannis Hierosolymitani, et in Cimiterio eorum Valentiae eligo et statuo sepulturam meam." On Dalmau see *Itinerari*, p. 287. On brotherhoods under the guidance of Orders see the individual Orders below, Chapters X to XII.

100. *Itinerari*, p. 140 (Mar. 17, 1268): "extrahendo sibi dentes . . . et dando ei salmorrada bibere et aliis modis pluribus quod dictus Hugo in dicta capcione diem clausit extremum."

101. *Ibid.*, p. 486 (Sept. 7, 1273): "invenisti Tholosam uxorem tuam quondam et A. Sarcadel quondam simul fornicacionem sive adulterium comitentes [et] ipsos ambos interfecisti." The penalties for both fornication and adultery are given in Furs, *lib.* IX, *rub.* II.

102. Manuel Carboneres has gathered all the materials on prostitution in medieval Valencia into his study *Picaronas y alcahuetes ó la mancebía de Valencia, apuntes para la historia de la prostitución* (Valencia, 1876). *Repartimiento*, pp. 534, 621: "[Maria] Portogalesa meretrix." Vincke, *EUC*, IV, 71; cf. R. Chabás, "Glosario de algunas voces oscuras usadas en el derecho foral valenciano," *ACCV*, XII (1944), 12. See Vicente Boix, *Apuntes históricos sobre los fueros del antiguo reino de Valencia* (Valencia, 1855), p. 137.

103. There is nothing satisfactory on slavery in Valencia in the thirteenth century; but a useful introduction is the monumental work of Verlinden, *L'esclavage*, with the articles by Miret y Sans and others cited there.

104. *Llibre dels feyts*, chs. 36–37, and my article "Journey From Islam" cited above in the preface.

105. *Colección diplomática*, doc. 452 (Dec. 3, 1221), about the attacks on Poblet.

106. *Ibid.*, doc. 590 (Sept. 18, 1257) where James speaks of it as a problem throughout his realms; "simus multipliciter obligati ut omnes domos religionis et cetera sua loca nostri dominii ab incursibus et infestacionibus malorum hominum viriliter deffendamus." For Valencia one might cite here the damage done by men of Tortosa to the Benifasá properties (Arch. Crown, James I, Reg. Canc. 10, fol. 7v, Aug. 10, 1257), though the townsmen were involved in this; and a similar case in Peter III, Reg. Canc. 49, fol. 67 (April 1, 1281). See too the severe letter of Pope Innocent IV against the "malefactors" who harm Benifasá by seizure of properties (Arch. Nac. Madrid, Clero: Castellón, Benifasá, carp. 421, Sept. 30, 1245).

107. *Llibre dels feyts*, ch. 237.

108. *Furs, lib.* IX, *rub.* XX: "de guiatge e de treues." An instance of such retaliation is given in the *Llibre dels feyts* after a knight had plundered another knight traveling under protection.

109. Arch. Cath., Liber constitutionum, fols. 61v–62r. Again in perg. 2,395 (July 17, 1263); *Colección diplomática*, doc. 1,178. One to the bishop is in Arch. Crown, James I, Reg. Canc. 37, fol. 66 (July 30, 1273); one for a holding of the Escarp monks in the Valencia kingdom *ibid.*, Peter III, Reg. Canc. 60, fol. 48 (Feb. 11, 1282). There are many for Valencian ecclesiastical properties in the archives.

110. *Colección diplomática*, doc. 264 (Mar. 15, 1243): "specialiter contra Guillelmum d'entenza et suos."

NOTES TO CHAPTER VIII. ECONOMIC FOUNDATIONS OF THE DIOCESE OF VALENCIA

1. *Viage literario*, III, 63 quoting witnesses; and see documents 6 and 7 from Gregory IX in the appendix.

2. Claude de Vic and Joseph Vaissète, *Histoire générale de Languedoc*, 18 vols. (Toulouse, 1872-1893), VI, 712; V, 1,789, no. 416, Dec. 19, 1239. Chabás, *Episcopologio valentino*, pp. 368-369; Sanchís Sivera, *Diócesis valentina*, II, 86.

3. Documents in Chapter IV, notes 43, 44.

4. Arch. Vat., Reg. Vat. 19 (Gregory IX), fols. 102v-103. The Latin text is easily available in Auvray, *Registres*, III, no. 4,815; and in *Diócesis valentina*, II, 195-197.

5. Arch. Cath., leg. 32, no. 3, perg. 2,303 (Nov. 9, 1241). See too *Aureum opus*, doc. 12, fol. 4r,v; *Collectio conciliorum Hispaniae*, V, 189-190. There is another original of the endowment in Arch. Cath. Huesca (9-12-209, perg.); probably the canonist bishop there, Vidal, was adviser to the crown on this business.

6. Sanchís Sivera thinks the arrangement had been informally agreed upon as early as sometime before October 1241 (*Diócesis valentina*, II, 434); but his only reason for this is an undated minute of the agreement giving Ferrer as "elect," a circumstance useless in assigning a date here (see discussion of the latter point below, in Chapter XIV).

7. Arch. Cath., perg. 589 (Nov. 2, 1241): "damus licentiam vobis F[errer] . . . et tuo capitulo quod ex illis decem mil[l]ibus besanciorum argenti quos vobis damus pro dotacione ecclesie valentine possitis emere domos ortos possessiones hereditates Castra villas seu alcherias in toto termino civitatis et Regni valencie a Richis hominibus militibus personis Religiosis et secularibus, non obstante constitucione civitatis que prohibet possessiones vel alique de supradictis ad ecclesiam non transferre."

8. Arch. Crown, James I, perg. 896 (Dec. 20, 1242). Was this given in properties, and expressed in money of account? See the houses and shops given (or perhaps bought and here confirmed?) to the bishop in 1241 ("pretio V millium bisantiorum" [*Repartimiento*, p. 286]).

9. Arch. Cath., perg. 2,308 (Dec. 23, 1242); cf. *Itinerari*, p. 155.

10. Arch. Cath., perg. 1,312 (Nov. 2, 1241). After repeating the general privilege of perg. 589 it includes a further document allowing purchase of fourteen "domos sive hospicia que sunt de realencho ad habitaciones vestras proprias non obstante quia in foro valentino continetur quod nulli liceat vendere domos vel aliquas possessiones clericis vel personis religiosis." Cf. notes 38, 44; also Chapter II, notes 70, 100.

11. See Chapter II, note 69 and text; and below, pp. 302-303.

12. Arch. Crown, James I, perg. 2,144. *Colección diplomática*, doc. 999 (Mar. 1, 1273 or 1274).

13. "Quasdam domos in Muroveteri" frank and free, bordering on the town wall, in Arch. Cath., perg. 2,443 (May 1, 1256); "quoddam farraginale ante Realum nostrum" in Valencia frank and free, in perg. 2,304 (Sept. 29, 1242); a park in Játiva where a treaty had been signed between the king and the Moors, in perg. 5,973 (Mar. 30, 1249) and perg. 2,305 (same date).

14. Document cited in note 12.

15. See Chapter IX, section 3, "The King's Share."

16. Arch. Crown, Peter III, Reg. Canc. 56, fols. 108-110, esp. 108r,v (May 22, 1285): "aliis rectoribus Episcopatus et diocesis, ii millia," "universis Canonicis Ecclesie valencie quilibet, ii millia." There are two individual assessments of 5,000

and 2,000 each. The bishop of Lérida is to pay 40,000; the bishop of Vich 10,000; the Tarragona metropolitan 100,000; his prior (dean, provost) 50,000; three of his archdeacons respectively 2,000, 4,000, and 8,000; his Official 6,000; the abbots of Holy Crosses and Poblet 20,000 and 40,000. Some dioceses have long lists; the Lérida church has many individuals with high assessments. There is of course the difficulty of deciding how much revenue a given individual received from extra-diocesan sources, such as plural benefices elsewhere.

17. *Documenta selecta*, doc. 318 (Nov. 22, 1317): "opulenta," "manebit opulenta." Allowance must be made for the king's optimism since he is pleading for an extra diocese; besides, the plea was not granted. It seems safe to conclude that substantial prosperity and stability had been achieved. Still, by 1257 great expenditures had put the diocese deeply in debt (cf. below, Chapter XIV, note 30).

18. *Cortes de los antiguos reinos de Aragón y de Valencia y principado de Cataluña*, 26 vols. in 27 (Madrid, 1896–1922), I, 126, no. 18.

19. Arch. Cath., perg. 2,309 (June 23, 1240).

20. Arch. Cath., perg. 2,379 (Dec. 11, 1266). The privilege carried with it a statement of exemption of such properties from services and regalian taxes. Cf. Chapter I, note 30 with citations to *Furs* and *Aureum opus*. Branchát, *Derechos y regalías de Valencia* (III, 427 ff., docs. 1–5, 8), reproduces some of the legal property restrictions of James I, including taxation of land left to the church, compulsory sale of such land within a month, use of rents for anniversary Masses if property remains in secular hands, and so on.

21. See Rosalind Hill, "Bishop Sutton [of Lincoln] and His Archives: A Study in the Keeping of Records in the Thirteenth Century," *JEH*, II (1951), 45; this was safer than the parish chest.

22. *Documenta selecta*, doc. 118 (Mar. 4, 1306). The document is a late one but is used here to illustrate a pitfall; the revenues it refers to are those given by James I "pro dote et sustentatione." The *Repartimiento* offers a few notes, but nothing solid; thus in 1240 (p. 318) a man has bought a shop from Master Martin the archdeacon. These Alcira nuns are discussed below in Chapter XII, section 7, "Other Nuns."

23. Arch. Cath., codex 162, Liber instrumentorum. It opens with a colorful miniature of James in full armor, kneeling before the Virgin and offering her a small church, representing the church of Valencia.

24. Document cited in note 5.

25. Arch. Cath., perg. 4,609 (Jan. 4, 1241); perg. 2,902 (Dec. 26, 1242); perg. 4,613 (June 7, 1245); perg. 5,970 (June 29, 1246); other examples are preserved here.

26. Arch. Cath., perg. 4,601 (April 26, 1238); perg. 5,956 (April 28, 1238); perg. 4,602 (June 11, 1238); perg. 2,329 (July 23, 1238); perg. 1,305 (Aug. 20, 1238); perg. 1,202 (Sept. 30, 1238); perg. 1,803 (Nov. 18, 1238); perg. 2,326 (same date); perg. 1,824 (Jan. 27, 1239); perg. 4,606 (Oct. 6, 1240); perg. 4,607 (same date); perg. 1,805 (Nov. 13, 1240); perg. 1,522 (June 22, 1243); perg. 1,211 (Dec. 15, 1245); perg. 1,810 (Mar. 26, 1249); perg. 5,976 (Aug. 1, 1252); etc.

27. Arch. Cath., pergs. 5,957 and 5,958 (April 13, 1239); perg. 1,083 (July 5, 1240); perg. 1,804 (July 18, 1240); perg. 4,808 (Sept. 18, 1241); perg. 5,561 (Sept. 13, 1242); perg. 1,807 (Dec. 19, 1244); perg. 4,618 (Feb. 26, 1248); perg. 1,813 (Aug. 9, 1250); perg. 4,621 (Oct. 8, 1250); perg. 4,623 (April 22, 1251); perg. 4,626 (Nov. 10, 1252); perg. 4,627 (June 13, 1253); etc.

28. Arch. Cath., perg. 4,604 (July 2, 1240); perg. 1,203 (Dec. 13, 1239); perg. 5,561 (Sept. 13, 1242); perg. 4,611 (Oct. 13, 1242); and other instances here.

29. Arch. Cath., perg. 2,903 (June 16, 1244).

30. Arch. Cath., perg. 2,371 (Jan. 24, 1238), with perg. 2,333 (Aug. 18, 1242); perg. 653 (July 1, 1238).

31. Arch. Cath., pergs. 5,957 and 5,958 (April 13, 1239); this is a pleasure garden in Beniferri near Valencia city, "et fuit de Mudef patre de Çahen."

32. Arch. Cath., perg. 5,956 (April 28, 1238): two parks (*raal*).

33. Arch. Cath., perg. 4,626 (Nov. 10, 1252): "quendam corrallum nostrum in valencia in parochia sancti bartholomei."

34. Arch. Cath., perg. 1,803 (Nov. 18, 1238); perg. 5,957 (April 13, 1239); perg. 1,804 (July 18, 1240); perg. 1,813 (Aug. 9, 1250).

35. Arch. Cath., perg. 1,203 (Dec. 13, 1239).

36. Arch. Cath., perg. 653 (July 1, 1238), Benimaclet; perg. 2,371 (Jan. 24, 1238), Puzol.

37. Arch. Cath., perg. 5,976 (Aug. 1, 1252). Anglés means "English(man)," though the word here may have some other derivation such as a connection with the town of La Cellera de Anglés near Gerona; see C. Pujol y Camps and P. Alsius y Torrent, *Nomenclátor geográfico-histórico de la provincia de Gerona desde la más remota antigüedad hasta el siglo xv* (Gerona, 1883), p. 12.

38. Arch. Cath., pergs., 2,306 and 2,307 (Aug. 18, 1242); are these part of, or supplementary to, the houses bought from the king before (see note 10 and text)?

39. These were next to the cemetery of the cathedral (Arch. Cath., perg. 5,962 [Mar. 5, 1240]). "Sit notum cunctis quod Ego Egidius d'Ungaria et Milia uxor mea consulte . . . vendimus . . . irrevocabiliter vobis Magistro Dominico precentori sedis valencie et A. Picherio sacriste eiusdem sedis et Bertrando de Turolio et Iohanni de Montisono canonicis eiusdem sedis et toto capitulo dicte sedis . . . illas domos nostras . . . iuxta ecclesiam maiorem sedis valencie ante Cimiterium eiusdem sedis."

40. Arch. Cath., perg. 1,340 (Dec. 19, 1266): "ad augmentationem domorum vestrarum videlicet quandam partem illarum domorum nostrarum scilicet duas archatas"—from a local couple.

41. Arch. Cath., perg. 1,573 (Mar. 28, 1258): "de domibus que sunt in Civitate valencie in parrochia sancte Marie Sedis valencie."

42. See notes 64–65.

43. Arch. Cath., perg. 5,012 (Nov. 4, 1256): houses willed by a deceased canon, Bertrand of Teruel, which face the cathedral.

44. Arch. Cath., perg. 1,089 (Aug. 18, 1242): "concedimus, tradimus et vendimus vobis Venerabili et dilecto nostro [episcopo] F[errer] . . . imperpetuum per proprium liberum et franchum alodium omnia statica atque domos nostras sitas in civitate Valencie ante sedem Sancte Marie."

45. *Repartimiento*, p. 284: "F. episcopus Valentie: ferraginale ante reallum suum et affrontat partim in suo reallo"; a *ferraginale* seems to have been a field or farm with soil suitable only to certain crops. Items such as these may be personal grants; the distinction could be made, as one sees in the dispute between James and the see of Barcelona over a Valencian estate, which the king insisted had been only a personal gift to the deceased bishop.

46. Arch. Cath., perg. 2,305 (Mar. 30, 1249); perg. 5,973 (same). *Repartimiento*, pp. 463–464: "Fr. A. episcopo Valentie et . . . successoribus . . . per hereditatem propriam francham et liberam illum reallum in termino Xative . . . in quo primam composicionem fecimus cum alcaydo et sarracenis Xative de castro et villa de Xativa."

47. *Repartimiento*, p. 418: "Fr. A. episcopo Valentie: domos in Liria que fuerunt de Aceyt Abalfachin . . . franche."

48. Documents cited in notes 37–38: "statica atque domos nostras sitas in

civitate Valencie ante sedem sancte Marie." *Repartimiento*, p. 286: "F. episcopus Valentie: Statica ante sedem Sancte Marie que confrontantur in via et domibus Sancii . . . et includit domunculas secundum clausuram ibi factam muri nostri . . ." See also Arch. Cath., perg. 1,089 (Oct. 18, 1242) and perg. 2,308 (Dec. 23, 1242).

49. Arch. Cath., Liber instrumentorum, fol. 37, given at the siege (Mislata, Valencia properties).

50. Arch. Cath., perg. 1,809 (Feb. 21, 1248): "noverint universi quod nos Jacobus . . . damus vobis venerabili et dilecto nostro A. dei gratia Episcopo Valencie . . . imperpetuum domos in Xativa ante Ecclesiam maiorem sancte Marie sicut circumdantur viis publicis."

51. Arch. Cath., perg. 1,090 (Nov. 15, 1243); and see note 36.

52. *Nomenclátor de Valencia*, p. 154; it is near Callosa de Ensarriá, and is not the Bufila (or Boylla or Bulla) near Bétera which was held by Calatrava from 1237.

53. Arch. Cath., Liber instrumentorum, fol. 139 (*an.* 1262); also perg. 2,443 (May 1, 1256).

54. *Nomenclátor de Valencia*, p. 274 (1271).

55. *Colección diplomática*, doc. 989 (Feb. 26, 1274). Carrícola had belonged to the king's mistress, the Lady Berenguela. Chulilla had been attached to the office of dean at the cathedral; when transferred to the bishop by James II, the knight William of Rexach claimed and seized it; James I forced him to restore it to the diocese in 1294. Is the gift of Bolulla a variant of Chulilla? Did James give a separate castle of Garig, or is Carrícola somehow identified with it? The Arch. Crown codex, Liber patrimonii regni Valentiae (fol. 84v), speaks simply of Chulilla and Gargio. It is variously given also as Girig, Garg, Garchi, and Garxio. One must distinguish it from both Gorga and Gorgo (*Nomenclátor de Valencia*, pp. 242, 248–249). Perhaps it should be identified with Gata de Gorgos; the Garg of several crown documents is located near there, on the river, near Jalón. Cf. also below, Chapter IX, note 62.

56. Arch. Cath., perg. 1,314 (Aug. 24, 1242), a royal permit to buy properties for this purpose: "noverint universi quod nos Jacobus . . . damus licentiam et plenum posse ac etiam concedimus . . . quod possitis emere et sine alicuius impedimento domos in Candia Algezira Ontanye et Cocentania ad opus granariorum vestrorum et Cellariorum." The chapter is to hold them, frank and free.

57. *Nomenclátor de Valencia*, pp. 44 (Albal), 30 (Albuixech).

58. *Ibid.*, p. 95.

59. A case of this kind seems to be the cathedral benefice founded by James I in 1246 (see Chapter VII, note 95); the rents of eighteen shops are to be collected directly for life by the chaplain and his successors, not even the lieutenant or bailiffs of the king intervening.

60. Such a fund is studied carefully in K. Major, "The Finances of the Dean and Chapter of Lincoln from the Twelfth to the Fourteenth Century: A Preliminary Survey," *JEH*, V (1954), 149–167. Some useful remarks on the properties and financial problems of the contemporary bishops of Vich in Catalonia may be found in the *Diplomatari de Sant Bernat Calvó*, pp. xl–xli.

61. Arch. Cath., perg. 2,413 (Aug. 29, 1260). The procuration substitute is to be deducted from the cathedral's share of the tithe as set by this agreement, before that share is divided between bishop and chapter.

62. Arch. Cath., perg. 2,330 (Mar. 4, 1240). He was a member of the queen's household and had received the houses in 1238 along with a farm here and two jovates of land in Mislata; cf. perg. 2,329 (July 23, 1238). "Sit notum cunctis quod nos F. dei gracia Episcopus Valencie . . . excambiamus vobis predicto Ray-

mundo Seguino et vestris in perpetuum illam Mezchitam quam habemus in civitate Valentie in partita hominum Barchinonensium iuxta portam Boatelle Civitatis."

63. Arch. Cath., perg. 1083 (July 5, 1240): "tradimus et transferimus irrevocabiliter sine retentu quem ibi non facimus," in free alod.

64. Arch. Cath., perg. 2,326 (Nov. 18, 1238). See *Itinerari*, p. 136 and n., and also p. 112 where he appears with relatives. The name is also written *de les Celles*, and in the document *de ciliis* (lit., eyebrows).

65. Arch. Cath., pergs. 2,327 and 2,328 (May 15, 1242), both in *Colección diplomática*, docs. 1,044-1,045.

66. Arch. Cath., perg. 2,337 (Mar. 15, 1244). The original is misdated as the ides of March "MCC Quarto"; Bishop Ferrer was involved in the first transaction, Bishop Arnold in this one. The exchange involved "totum ius . . . quod nos habemus et habere debemus in illo cimiterio quod dicitur de Roteros[?]."

67. Arch. Cath., perg. 2,331 (April 5, 1241): "per liberum et franchum alodium il[l]am mezchitam quam habemus in civitate Valencie in Carraria pontis et domos dicte mezquite." An *alfondicum* or inn on Lérida square in the city was taken in exchange. The family of Orta or Huerta or Duerta were of knightly rank; but similar names were not uncommon here and perhaps his name was simply Bernard of Orts.

68. Arch. Cath., perg. 2,371 (Jan. 24, 1238).

69. Arch. Cath., perg. 2,333 (Aug. 18, 1242).

70. Arch. Cath., perg. 2,334 (Nov. 9, 1243).

71. Arch. Cath., perg. 1,090 (Nov. 15, 1243); see perg. 2,336 (Oct. 16, 1243). This included all residents and revenues, woods, vines, countryside, etc., "cum fortitudine et domibus."

72. Arch. Cath., legajo XXXV, no. 9 (Oct. 1, 1255): "attendentes quod id quod communiter possidetur a pluribus negligi consuevit." See also perg. 1,323 (July 21, 1252).

73. Arch. Cath., perg. 1,804 (July 18, 1240).

74. Arch. Cath., perg. 1,807 (Dec. 19, 1244).

75. Major, "Finances of Lincoln," p. 151.

76. *Ibid.*, pp. 161-162.

77. Arch. Cath., perg. 1,526 (May 3, 1256): "faciatis ibidem opus et melioramentum quod valeat et costet decem solidi regalium." Some of the mosques in the diocese, though originally used as revenue properties, were to be available to later generations for use as churches. One sees such a mosque at Huesca in Aragon in 1250; it had been leased but was now being converted into a church; the priest had to renovate and adapt it at his own expense (Arco, "Famoso jurisperito," pp. 516-517, doc. 8).

78. Arch. Cath., perg. 4,713 (April 13, 1275): "in melioramento dicte Meschite et non liceat vobis concedere alicui dictam meschitam sub maiori censu quam dictum est." Cf. Mundy, *Toulouse*, pp. 61, 272.

79. Document given in note 89 (1249): "teneatis eum bene cultum et populatum" (Andarella); document in note 93 (1265) for the second mosque.

80. Arch. Cath., perg. 4,624 (Dec. 31, 1251): "sit omnibus notum quod ego Bernardus de Vilario canonicus valentinus nomine Capituli valentini et Raymundus de belestar clericus nomine domini valentini episcopi . . . stabilimus ad censum sive damus vobis Raymundo de Savasona . . . et vestris imperpetuum quamdam mezquitam maiorem quam sedes valentina habet . . . in alcaria de Lomber in termino de calp"; "opera et melioramenta."

81. Arch. Cath., perg. 4,567 (Dec. 20, 1273): "construatis ibi unam domum cohopertam"; also given as a "solarem."

82. Arch. Cath., e.g. perg. 4,652 (Mar. 5, 1270): "ego Petrus Michael precentor stabilio ... ad operatorium construendum et edificandum vobis Arnaldo Pellipario capellano et vestris imperpetuum quoddam pati [sic] terre prout vobis assignatum est ... extra portam boatelle civitatis Valencie." This cleric's name may be Pellicer, Latinized. Rather than being indicative of a family trade, it suggests that he was a member of the knightly Catalan family of that name. He also rented a shop in Alcira from the crown (1258).

83. Settlement charter cited in note 69: "septimam mensuram et numerum," "paria gallinarum," etc.

84. Arch. Cath., perg. 4,605 (Sept. 9, 1240): "quandam Mezquitam quam habemus in vico Sancti Iohannis de Bouatella"; "singulis annis in festo sancte Marie Septembris pro censu sex denarios Iaccensium et preter istum censum nullum alium censum vel usaticum inde faciatis."

85. Arch. Cath., perg. 4,653 (Mar. 28, 1270). Given in Chapter IV, note 57.

86. Arch. Cath., perg. 4,610 (Oct. 1, 1242): "tibi Arnaldo bertrandi ... quoddam oratorium in suburbio civitatis Valencie"; "de cera bona"; "dominos vel seniores."

87. Arch. Cath., perg. 1,521 (June 21, 1243): "sit omnibus notum quod nos frater Arnaldus mis[eraci]one divina Episcopus ... et Totum valentinum capitulum ... stabilimus ad censum sive damus vobis Guillelmo ... et uxori vestre ... et vestris imperpetuum quoddam fosarium quod habemus in Andarialla." (See note 79 and text.)

88. *Ibid.*: "ita quod vos et successores vestri teneatis eum bene cultum et populatum, et melioretis et non peioretis."

89. Arch. Cath., perg. 1,811 (Aug. 27, 1249): "quoddam fosarium quod habemus in Andariella ... et cum arboribus cuiuslibet generis que ibi sunt aut erunt, aquis cequiis adrigendum." He was a notary public of Valencia in 1245, and bailiff of the mountains of Prades and Ciurana for Prince Peter and (from 1263) for King James; in 1266 he bought the castle and town of Montornés (*Itinerari*, pp. 171, 340, 389). The rent was one Josephine mazmodin.

90. Arch. Cath., perg. 2,863 (Mar. 1, 1250).

91. Arch. Cath., perg. 1,308 (Oct. 21, 1240): "attendentes devotionem et legalitatem" she displayed toward the church of Valencia; it includes "Mesquitam cum cimiterio eidem pertinenti cum casalibus sibi contiguis."

92. Arch. Cath., perg. 2,872 (June 1, 1277): "sit omnibus notum quod ego Bernardus de Vilario ... nomine ecclesie valentine dono et stabilio ... quandam mesquitam in moreria Valencie quam Sarraceni eiusdem morerie tenere solebant." The rent was a Josephine mazmodin.

93. Arch. Cath., perg. 2,912 (May 5, 1265): "quedam corrallia [que] in tempore Sarracenorum consueverunt esse mezquita que est in Civitate Valencie in parrochia sancti Laurentii."

94. Arch. Cath., perg. 5,969 (Jan. 2, 1244); one Josephine gold piece was to go to each of three canons named.

95. Arch. Cath. Val., perg. 6,946 (Aug. 12, 1244): "de quadam Mezquita cum domibus que se tenent [sic] cum ea domo quam dominus Episcopus et capitulum habeant in Valencia in porcione barchinonensi." The original document follows: "sit notum omnibus quod Ego Bertrandus de Turolio canonicus sedis valencie per me et meos dono et stabilio vobis Iohanni de Gerunda et uxori vestre Astruge perpetuo quandam meschitam cum domibus que se tenent que omnia tenentur per dominum Episcopum valencie et capitulum eiusdem loci in Valencia in porcione barchinonensi."

96. The document is given no date in its published form except that it belongs

to the reign of James I (Roca Traver, "Vida mudéjar," p. 134 and n.); it may therefore be the previous mosque, resold.

97. Arch. Cath., perg. 1,210 (April 30, 1244): "sit notum cunctis quod nos Magister Martinus archidiachonus . . . et totum capitulum valentine Sedis . . . stabilimus ad censum vobis Guillelmo Ferrarii Capellano ecclesie sancti Martini et vestris . . . imperpetuum totum illud fossarium nostrum Sarracenicum quod valli Civitatis valencie ante fontem superioris pontis porte Civitatis Valencie contiguatur."

98. Arch. Cath., perg. 1,343 (Feb. 5, 1270): "ego Guillelmus Ferrarii rector ecclesie Sancti Martini Valencie . . . trado titulo pure et perfecte vendicionis vobis Petro Michaelis precentori valentino . . . quoddam fossarium antiquum Sarracenorum quod habeo et teneo in bouatella valencie sub dominio capituli valentini ad censum unius bisancii fini argenti." It was twenty-three "bracias regales" in length.

99. Arch. Cath., perg. 1,348 (May 5, 1271). The cemetery would also seem to be distinct (cf. the dates) from the Moslem property below in note 101.

100. Arch. Cath., perg. 1,324 (Feb. 25, 1245); at this date the king had it; "que loca tenebas ad censum pro Episcopo Valencie"; "in qua platea et domibus et orto fuit quondam fossarium Sarracenicum."

101. Arch. Cath., perg. 4,617 (Feb. 9, 1248); "unum fossarium extra porta[m] de buatella."

102. Arch. Cath., perg. 1,808 (May 18, 1248). This might be the Cistercian monk of Santes Creus (see doc. of 1252, Itinerari, p. 218n.); there are others of this name, however, including a P. Copons in the Repartimiento.

103. Arch. Cath., perg. 1,523 (Feb. 11, 1250) and perg. 2,864 (Sept. 22, 1250): "stabilimus tibi Arnaldo de Sancto Celidonio . . . quandam mesquitam intus villam Xative" for two Josephine mazmodins. He is in the Repartimiento.

104. Arch. Cath., perg. 4,622 (Mar. 18, 1251): "unam meschitam in exerea Valencie" to William and his wife.

105. Arch. Cath., perg. 2,865 (Nov. 12, 1251).

106. Arch. Cath., perg. 2,356 (Sept. 20, 1252).

107. Arch. Cath., perg. 2,355 (Aug. 29, 1252).

108. Arch. Cath., perg. 4,625 (April 16, 1252): "stabilimus vobis Bernardo Alamayn et vestris imperpetuum ad meliorandum et in aliquo non deteriorandum quandam Meschitam in Muro veteri que confrontatur cum muro ville et in via publica . . .," with all appurtenances.

109. Arch. Cath., perg. 4,713 (April 13, 1252): "stabilio vobis Arnaldo Guillermo de Morlans . . . quandam meschitam in Xativa quam tenent fratres minores que afrontatur cum alfundico Regis . . . et in Carraria stricta et in tendis vestris."

110. Arch. Cath., perg. 1,214 (April 18, 1252).

111. Arch. Cath., perg. 1,524 (April 7, 1254): "nomine Ecclesie valentine dono vobis Raymundo Dolmalla[?] . . . quoddam fossarium usque ad fanecatum et plus et unam mezquitam destructam contiguam eo dicto fossario in alcaria de Poligna que est in termino de Corbera." This may have been a ruined or partly dismantled mosque, but it was more probably a site where a mosque once stood.

112. Arch. Cath., perg. 4,710 (Mar. 20, 1254): "unum fossarium quod est in Ravallo de benicabra de Xativa."

113. Arch. Cath., perg. 4,628 (April 22, 1254): "stabilio vobis Berengario darbeta comoranti in castello . . . unum fossarium in termino de Castello in alcaria que vocatur Ereco [Creco?] . . . ita quod laboretis et custodiatis eum bene ad consuetudinem boni laboratoris . . . et detis mihi annuatim . . . pro censu Duos solidos regalium Valencie et post obitum meum capitulo Valencie."

114. Arch. Cath., perg. 4,713 (April 13, 1252).

115. This is the same property seen in note 100, its revenues having been transferred to Constantine by the king.

116. Arch. Cath., perg. 2,338 (June 17, 1242).

117. Arch. Cath., perg. 4,635 (Dec. 13, 1255): "stabilimus vobis Bernardo reg et vestris imperpetuum ad censum et meliorandum quamdam mezquitam que est intus villam Muriveteris et affrontatur in muro," and adjoining the houses of Na Catalina.

118. Arch. Cath., perg. 2,357 (Aug. 20, 1255): "in illa Mezchita quam vos consuevistis tenere in Xativa pro nobis et capitulo valentino," bordering on the renter's houses. Does the wording imply that unrented mosques were cared for by local agents; or is this simply a new lease, showing that undocumented leases for such mosques may have been numerous in the previous decades? Only the bishop signs here, and the phrasing suggests that only his share is being alienated.

119. Arch. Cath., perg. 4,364 (Dec. 4, 1255): "stabilimus vobis Egidio de Fraga et vestris imperpetuum ad censum et meliorandum quamdam mezquitam que est in ravallo de Liria"; "aliam mezquitam parvulam in qua est ficulnea et est in ralaya [?] Lirie et affrontatur ex una parte . . ."; the latter rented at only a hundred pence yearly.

120. Arch. Cath., perg. 1,525 (Feb. 18, 1255): "illam mezquitam quam habemus et habere debemus in muroveteri et eam tenere consuevit pro nobis Iohannes de palacio . . . cum parietibus, ianuis, fenestris, suppositis introitibus et exitibus et omnibus iuribus et pertinenciis suis a celo in abissum vobis et vestris perpetuo damus et stabilimus ad censum." In case of nonpayment (at each Christmas) it could be recovered.

121. Arch. Cath., perg. 4,636 (April 9, 1256); perg. 2,912 (May 5, 1265); perg. 4,653 (Mar. 28, 1270).

122. Document in Chapter IV, note 55; see this chapter for more Valencia city mosques.

123. Arch. Cath., perg. 4,636 (April 9, 1256): "quemdam locum sive solum terre que tempore Sarracenorum consuevit esse mesquita quod est in parrochia Sancti Bartholomei prope domos vestras." See also Chapter IV, note 56 and text.

124. Arch. Cath., perg. 1,526 (May 3, 1256): "stabilio ad censum vobis Petro de rovax . . . unam mezquitam que est in Alcaria de Fortaleney cum turre que in dicta mezquita est . . . cum parietibus, ianuis, fenestris, tectis . . ."

125. Arch. Cath., perg. 4,643 (Nov. 17, 1258): "nos Frater Andreas dei gratia valentinus episcopus et Bernardus de Vilario canonicus eiusdem sedis nomine capituli valentini per nos et successores nostros damus et stabilimus vobis Raimundo Mata et . . . uxori vestre et vestris imperpetuum quandam mesquitam nostram quam habemus et habere debemus in alcharia de carpesa termino civitatis valentie."

126. Arch. Cath., perg. 1,527 (April 9, 1260): to one Martin, "unum fossarium sarracenicum in alqueria de Nacla termini de Corbera quod esse arbitror unius fanachate terre."

127. Arch. Cath., perg. 4,638 (Sept. 18, 1256); perg. 4,657 (Dec. 20, 1273 or 1274).

128. Arch. Cath., perg. 1,595 (June 16, 1279): "concedo ad censum perpetuo et meliorandum vobis Guillelmo de Colle presbitero rectori ecclesie de Spiocha, tres petias terre in dicto loco de Spiocha in quibus fuerunt fossaria tempore Sarracenorum quas extimo [aestimo] tenere in sum[m]a usque ad novem fanechatas terre." The name may be written Coll or Descol; there were several knightly families of the name.

129. For example, in the Valencian part of the Tortosa diocese: "Colección de cartas pueblas," no. V (for Cabanes, *an.* 1243), *BSCC*, II (1921), 183-185; and *ibid.*, VI (Benlloch, *an.* 1250), pp. 297-300, where the land "vadit ad mesquitas dominicature nostre." Arch. Crown, James I, perg. 2,077 (mid-1277) mentions a property near the Templars' gate of the city, "sicut affrontat in mezquita que ibi est et in via publica."

130. *Llibre dels feyts*, ch. 246. For Moslems, certain open places could also be considered mosques.

131. Arch. Cath., perg. 4,638 (Sept. 18, 1256): "sit omnibus notum, Quod Ego Bernardus Ferrer capellanus altaris sancte Marie sedis valentine et procurator Bernardi de Vilario canonici Valencie cum carta ad utilitatem et commodum domini Episcopi et capituli Valencie stabilio ad censum et ad bene meliorandum vobis Raymundo dalmenar et vestris imperpetuum unum fossarium quod est in Alcoy . . ."

132. *Rationes decimarum*, I, 259 and 264: "item pro portione Vilarii et censu fossariorum."

133. Arch. Cath., perg. 2,652 (April 13, 1341): "noverint universi quod ego Raimundus ferrarii Canonicus Valencie administrator et gubernator censualium meçquitarum et fossariorum que olim fuerunt Sarracenorum totius diocesis valentine et iurium pervenientium ex eisdem per reverendum patrem et dompnum . . . Episcopum et Ecclesie honorabile capitulum specialiter deputatus prout patet per quoddam publicum instrumentum confectum in Idus Aprilis . . ."

134. *Repartimiento de Sevilla*, I, 532.

135. Sanchís Sivera publishes the document in his "Arnaldo de Peralta," pp. 47-48 (July 22, 1247).

136. *Ibid.* Retaining the forms as read by Sanchís Sivera, these are: Albalat, Baleta, Sagart, Torres, Tovares, Serra, Nichera, Maruride, Puçol, Lullen, Podium Sancte Marie cum parochia sua, Paterna, Maniçes, Benalcuacir, Liria, Cullela, Rocharoya, Villamerchant, Chest, Curia Terris, Toux, Entramnes, Agues, Terrabona, Madçona, Pedralia, Monserat, Vallis de Alhala, alcherye omnes P. de Montagut, alcherye omnes de Galaubia, alcherye omnes de S. Ferrandi, Buynol, Amacasta, Cataroya, Albaida, Captuli, Torrent, Montroy, Alcacer, spreta, pictacen, alcherye omnes de Almuçafres, Sallaria, Parilmas, Tubar, Cullera. "Galaubia," who also appears as a landowner ("un tal Galaubia") in the *Nomenclátor de Valencia* (p. 279), is really Guillem Olabia, holder of Llombay, Catadau[ro], and other lands in the Valle de Alcalá. This is the "Galabia" of Huici and Miret y Sans (*Itinerari*, p. 197) and of Tourtoulon (*Jaime I*, II, 493). Peter of Montagut held the regions of Alfarp and Carlet there. "Baleta" seems to be Valletes—i.e. Valle de Segó; and so on.

137. Arch. Cath., leg. 661, fasc. 1, fol. 1.

138. *Ibid.*, fols. 1, 2.

139. *Ibid.*, fol. 1: "redditibus, exitibus, proventibus, et obventionibus, ac aliis omnibus." All Santiago and Calatrava income was included in the 2400 solidi total collected by the three final priorates for the non-huerta area above the Júcar.

140. *Rationes decimarum*, I, 265.

141. One of these may have had all three priorates below the Júcar with Bertrand as vicar. This would account for the total of thirteen in the 1280 list; or is Pontilianus, with a mere seven solidi, an addition north of the Júcar? Other fragments of information on these priorates turn up in the records. For example, in 1284 those of February, June, September, and December were surrendered and then reassigned; in 1285 Arnold of Riusech received the February priorate formerly held by the archdeacon of Valencia William of Alaric.

142. See Chapter IX, pp. 160, 171.

143. Thus Mansilla believes that the daily distributions, a considerable sum when considered in total, were exempted (*Iglesia castellano-leonesa*, p. 209).

144. Ferran Soldevila, *Pere el Gran*, III, 460–461, doc. 36, Dec. 10, 1273; cf. p. 333.

145. Cf. Chapter IV, *ad finem*. There is a most useful collection of late copies of documents dealing with the Valencia kingdom tithes and first fruits in the Bibl. Univ. Val. manuscript collection: codex 145, Bulas, reales ordenes, y concordias sobre diezmos. The early development of the tithe is covered by Paul Viard, *Histoire de la dîme ecclésiastique principalement en France jusqu'au décret de Gratien* (Dijon, 1909); more pertinent to our own era is his *Histoire de la dîme ecclésiastique dans le royaume de France au xiie et xiiie siècles, 1150–1313* (Paris, 1912). Giles Constable furnishes much background information and bibliography on tithes in general, up through the twelfth century, while pursuing his special theme in *Monastic Tithes from their Origins to the Twelfth Century* (Cambridge, 1964), especially ch. 1. An excellent introduction to the tithe in the Spanish kingdoms is the small but well documented study by Jesús San Martín, *El diezmo eclesiástico en España hasta el siglo xii* (Palencia [for Gregorian University, Rome], 1940). See also G. Lepointe, "Dîme," "Dîmier," "Décimateur," *DDC*, IV, cols. 1,231–1,244, 1,059. Moorman has an instructive chapter on the contemporary English situation (*Church Life*, ch. 9); see also Boyd, *Tithes and Parishes in Medieval Italy, passim*. On the Valencian tithe see my "A Mediaeval Income Tax: the Tithe in the Thirteenth-Century Kingdom of Valencia," *Speculum*, XLI (1966), 438–452.

146. Arch. Cath., perg. 2,430 (Sept. 12, 1268): "animalium extraneorum."

147. Arch. Cath., perg. 2,431 (Jan. 19, 1263): "extraneorum," "cabañarum." They go to the local rector.

148. *Summa, lib.* I, *tit.* XV, no. 4. Some medieval pirates are said to have tithed to available hermits, to appease their consciences.

149. *Ibid.*, discussion "de decimis, primitiis et oblationibus"; the tithe is taken from "balneis, fullonicis, argentariis, metallariis, lapidicinis; item de negotiis, et artificiis, et ceteris bonis."

150. Arch. Crown, Peter III, Reg. Canc. 48, fol. 176 (Nov. 8, 1280): "sicut tempore fratris Andree quondam episcopi Valentini . . . dari fuerat consuetum episcopo et capitulo"; an order by the king to his collectors to pay this to bishop and chapter.

151. Arch. Cath., perg. 2,341 (Feb. 7, 1241): "et sciendum est quod decima predicta debet deduci non tantum de decima [*i.e. the secular tribute*] set de omnibus quae vos haberetis a Sarracenis illius castri aliquo iusto vel consueto modo."

152. Endowment of diocese, "Colección de cartas pueblas," no. LVII, p. 387. Cf. Moorman, *Church Life*, p. 119.

153. Other divisions included personal and property; the latter were "old" or, if from lands uncultivated from time immemorial but recently put into cultivation, "new." Is there a reflection of greater and lesser tithes in contemporary Vich, where the income from the "decima que dicitur usualiter terra[e] minor" was to be applied to church furnishings; or was this an idiomatic name for first fruits? (See *Diplomatari de Sant Bernat Calvó*, doc. 37, June 5, 1234).

154. Arch. Cath., perg. 1,304 (June 1, 1240).

155. Clerical benefices and personal properties were tithable, though the pastor's primitive glebe was exempt; other exemptions included the bishop, leper hospitals, and some monastic groups (on distinctions in the clerical and monastic exemptions, see Penyafort, *Summa, lib.* I, *tit.* XV, no. 1).

156. *Collectio conciliorum Hispaniae*, V, 199 (*an.* 1258), Valencia diocese.

157. *Aureum opus*, doc. 12, fol. 4r,v (Nov. 2, 1241).

158. Arch. Crown, Peter III, Reg. Canc. 48, fol. 20v (May 13, 1280).

159. Arch. Crown, Peter III, Reg. Canc. 41, fol. 98 (June 27, 1279).

160. See Chapter IV, note 115. In 1142 the tithes in frontier Daroca ("in estremo Sarracenorum") were assigned by the king's settlement charter, half to the bishop and chapter (but only "de pane, et vino, et agnis, et non de aliis"), the rest to the local clergy (T. Muñoz y Romero, *Colección de fueros municipales y cartas pueblas de los reinos de Castilla, León, corona de Aragón y Navarra coordinada y anotada* [Madrid, 1847], pp. 534-543).

161. Arch. Cath., perg. 2,309 (June 23, 1240): "de toto vero alio episcopatu habeat Capitulum terciam partem omnium decimarum . . . et Episcopus duas partes." This document is published in full by Sanchís Sivera but incorrectly analyzed (*Diócesis valentina*, II, 421-422). Expenses of the bishop would include the support of the archdeacons of Valencia and Játiva in their functions: respectively a tenth and an eleventh of the bishop's share of the tithe in the archdeaconry (*ibid.*).

162. Arch. Cath., perg. 2,360 (April 27, 1268); also see *Furs, lib.* IV, *rub.* XXIV, *c.* 1; *Colección diplomática*, doc. 941; and *Aureum opus*, doc. 22 (*an.* 1268).

163. Arch. Cath., perg. 2,341 (Feb. 7, 1241): "fraude et dolo." Doc. of 1247 cited in note 135: "violenter aut quocunque modo redditus . . . aufferrentur seu denegarentur."

164. In England too contemporaries struggled for a prededuction of wages and expenses (Moorman, *Church Life*, p. 124).

165. See the evidence and interpretation of Giles Constable, suggesting the rarity of opposition at least for the eleventh and twelfth centuries: "Resistance to Tithes in the Middle Ages," *JEH*, XIII (1962), 172-185. On resistance in France see Viard, *Dîme au xiie et xiiie siècles*, pp. 72 ff.

166. *Furs, lib.* IV, *rub.* XXIV, *c.* 1: "els rich homens, cavallers, ciutadans, e altres habitadors."

167. Arch. Cath., perg. 2,360; also *Colección diplomática*, doc. 941 (April 27 1268).

168. Arch. Cath., perg. 2,320 (Mar. 28, 1254); at least for such important crops as grapes or grain.

169. Arch. Crown, Peter III, Reg. Canc. 40, fol. 155 (Sept. 1, 1278), an instruction by the king on tithe gathering for the Valencia kingdom; "super mandatum quod vobis fecimus super decimis et primiciis dandis nobis et Ecclesie . . . quod deinceps [etc.]." Arch. Cath., perg. 2,321 (same date). See also *Furs, lib.* IV, *rub.* XXIV, *c.* 8: "statuimus quod non obstante poene lx solidorum quod nullus posset decimare vel primitiare absque delmario nostro, et episcopi Valentie."

170. Arch. Crown, *ibid.*: "decimarius . . . primiciarius."

171. Arch. Cath., perg. 2,341 (Feb. 7, 1241) where it is stipulated that the bishop's bailiff will transfer the lord's third of the tithe to him, after the collection.

172. This may have been a late development. It can be seen in a 1364 document about collecting the tithe in the "rectoria loci Castilionis termini Xative," and in a 1357 collection of the Alboraya-Almácera regions commonly called the "decimarium de Alboraya," bordered by the respective *decimaria* of Rambla, Carpesa and Foyos (Arch. Crown, Liber patrimonii regni Valentiae, fols. 31v, 102v).

173. The names of these men can be found in the lists of the *Rationes decimarum* for 1279 and 1280, in Appendix III, below. A number of documents showing them at work may be seen in the cathedral archives (e.g., the settlement of some revenues in perg. 1,106 [Sept. 15, 1272]).

174. *Constitutiones sive ordinationes*, fols. 69-70: nothing had been built at

Valencia, Albal, Gandía, or Játiva. See also fol. 67v, and Arch. Cath., perg. 1,314.

175. Arch. Crown, James I, perg. 2,289 (July 23, 1276): "item mandamus restitui Episcopo et Ecclesie Valencie bladum totum et vinum et alia victualia que accepimus nobis ab eis."

NOTES TO CHAPTER IX. ENDING THE TITHE WAR

1. Arch. Cath., leg. 35, no. 4 (Mar. 28, 1254); copy in Bibl. Univ. Val., codex 145, doc. 25; published in *Colección diplomática*, doc. 492. The people "novas questiones et illicitas contra ecclesiam conantur indebite suscitare"; "faciatis integre . . . decimas de omnibus fructibus olivarum, bladi, vindemie, lini, canabi, et ortalicie, animalium, et aliarum omnium."

2. *Colección diplomática*, doc. 839 (May 15, 1260): "de ovis, gallinis, pullis et olivis et uvis parralorum et porcellis et ficubus" (cf. *Itinerari*, p. 301; and *Aureum opus*, doc. 59, fol. 18r).

3. *Ibid.:* "et eciam purpuram et candelas, quas mortuis duci feceritis, violenter auferunt vobis."

4. *Ibid.*, doc. 762 (Feb. 15, 1258): "possitis auctoritate propria compellere et pignorare . . . omnes homines regni Valencie diocesis dertusensis ad dandum vobis decimas de omnibus sicut debent." Arch. Cath. Tortosa, cajón Obispo, doc. 11 (possibly 1257).

5. *Colección diplomática*, doc. 839.

6. *Ibid.*

7. Arch. Cath., perg. 4,645 (Aug. 11, 1260). "Quia fidelis homo de omnibus fructibus solvere Decimas deo tenetur. Ideo volumus et mandamus firmiter et districte quatenus de ficubus et amigdalis quas ad vendendum desicatis seu facitis desicari decimas sine difficultate qualibet persolvatis."

8. *Itinerari*, p. 558n., and *Colección diplomática*, doc. 1,125 (Nov. 5, 1260).

9. Arch. Crown, James I, Reg. Canc. 9, fol. 20v (Feb. 15, 1258): "donamus vobis venerabili et dilecto nostro Bernardo dei gratia Episcopo Dertusensi et vestris successoribus ecclesie Dertusensi imperpetuum quod omnes homines Morelle et omnium aliarum villarum et locorum Regni Valencie diocesis Dertusensis donent primicias vobis et vestris successoribus et ecclesie Dertusensi de omnibus, sicut alii homines eiusdem Regni Valencie diocesis donant Episcopo et Ecclesie Valencie, exceptis tamen hominibus burriane qui faciant vobis in Ecclesia Dertusensi super premissis in posse nostro justicie complementum."

10. *Colección diplomática*, doc. 1,173 (June 16, 1263), an arbitration.

11. *Ibid.*, doc. 900 (July 24, 1261).

12. *Ibid.:* "volumus quod omnia supradicta in statum pristinum reducantur, donec nos in eisdem videamus; quare . . . donetis decimam primiciamque, prout hactenus eam dare consuevistis, et si quod statutum in preiudicium earum Valencie fecistis, illud statim revocetis."

13. Arch. Cath., perg. 2,360; in *Colección diplomática*, doc. 941 (April 27, 1268). Some fragments of the settlement of April 1268 are also preserved among the papers of the military Orders at Madrid (Arch. Nac. Madrid, Ords. Milits., Montesa, R122–123). The document entered into public law and as late as 1797 was reprinted in booklet form with alternate columns of Catalan and Castilian: *Versión literal del fuero I, lib. IV, rub. 24, de los del reyno de Valencia sobre diezmos, primicias, y derechos parroquiales, que es la sentencia arbitral del señor rey Don Jayme I de Aragón . . .* (Valencia, 1797).

14. *Ibid.:* "fortiter requirentibus . . . clericis et probis hominibus, . . . quod

antequam nos recederemus de partibus Valencie, per nos illa dissensio et discordia determinaretur."

15. *Ibid.*: "tractando et loquendo cum una parte et altera et laborando super premissis ac coequando et dirigendo ea quae . . . videbantur male facta"; "quia honestius et melius est componere . . . quam sequi rigorem iuris."

16. *Gremios y cofradías*, I, 86–88, doc. 21.

17. *Aureum opus*, doc. 36, fols. 11Cv–12 (*an.* 1250).

18. The argument is from figures available a century after the conquest (*Censo de Catalunya ordenada en tiempo del rey Don Pedro el Ceremonioso*, ed. P. de Bofarull y Mascaró, *Colección de documentos inéditos, corona de Aragón*, vol. XII [Barcelona, 1856], p. 262).

19. Bibl. Univ. Val., ms. codex 145, doc. 34 (July 22, 1271); also in *Aureum opus*, doc. 90, fol. 28r.

20. Codex, *ibid.*, doc. 35; Arch. Cath., perg. 2,396 (Feb. 26, 1273).

21. Arch. Crown, Peter III, Reg. Canc. 40, fol. 125v (June 15, 1278): "noveritis nos vidisse nuncios vestros"; "cum super facto decime que nobis et Episcopo Valencie competit in terra Valencie, cum dicto Episcopo incedere proponamus et procedere exigere iustitia[m]."

22. *Aureum opus*, doc. 1, fol. 29r.

23. Arch. Crown, Peter III, Reg. Canc. 40, fol. 155 (Sept. 1, 1278): "super mandatum quod vobis fecimus super decimis et primiciis dandis nobis et Ecclesie temperavimus de consensu venerabilis Jazperti Dei gratia Episcopi Valentini et nuntiorum civitatis et aliquorum locorum Regni predicti [*sic*] quod deinceps dicta decima . . . et primicia dentur in area in garba fideliter . . . "Also Arch. Cath., perg. 2,361 (Sept. 1, 1278); in Bibl. Univ. Val., codex 145, doc. 38; and cf. Arch. Crown, Liber patrimonii regni Valentiae, fol. 288r.

24. Arch. Crown, Peter III, Reg. Canc. 42, fol. 201 (Nov. 25, 1279), and Arch. Cath., perg. 2,362. He also refers to the "composicionem . . . fecimus . . . prout in nostra litera super hec facta continetur."

25. Arch. Crown, Peter III, Reg. Canc. 50, fol. 201v (Nov. 24, 1281): "faciamus compelli omnes illos . . . racione decime vel primicie Ecclesie Valencie ad dandum et solvendum eidem prout debuerint." The controversies may be followed into the next century in the documents of codex 145 at the Bibl. Univ. Val.

26. Perg. 2,360 in note 13: "pro primicia autem detur tricesima quinta pars de omnibus supradictis, de quibus debet dari decima." And again in the solution of 1280 (perg. 2,382; see note 32): "de omnibus de quibus decima dari debet . . . dentur primicie."

27. *Ibid.*

28. Document in note 4.

29. Bayerri, *Historia de Tortosa*, VII, 150. Arch. Cath. Tortosa, cajón Donaciones y Privilegios, docs. 5 and 46 (Castellón, Morella agreements). See above, note 8 for Burriana. The tithe unrest continued here too, though in a minor way; for example in 1309 the bishop settled his dispute over certain tithes with the communes of Burriana, Onda, Nules, Villarreal, and Almenara (Bibl. Univ. Val. codex, doc. 43, cf. doc. 42).

30. Arch. Crown, Peter III, Reg. Canc. 41, fol. 98 (June 27, 1279): "intelleximus quod quidam de Segorbio . . . contradicunt dare primicias venerabili electo Segorbicensi." Cf. fol. 88v (June 3, 1279) on the same subject and area. The document is a decade later than the Valencian troubles, because the struggle just to establish a Segorbe diocese had to come first. The districts involved included most of the diocese: Castelnovo, Altura, and Begís (see Chapter III, p. 51).

31. Arch. Cath. (August–September 1280), pergs. 2,383 and 2,386 (Huesca);

pergs. 2,382 and 2,384 (Zaragoza); perg. 2,385 (Tarragona); perg. 2,387 (Tarazona). The answers are "traddendas discreto viro Dominico debiscarra Rectori Ecclesie Sancti Laurentii Valentie presencium portatori." A description of how the tithes and first fruits were given according to custom (ca. 1200) at Toulouse is furnished by the chronicler William of Puylaurens (Mundy, *Toulouse*, pp. 292–293).

32. Arch. Cath., perg. 2,382 (Sept. 4, 1280): "in numero primicie."

33. J. Martínez Aloy, *La diputación de la generalidad del reino de Valencia* (Valencia, 1930), pp. 4–10, 17–18.

34. Perg. 2,361 in note 23: "decima Deo et nobis debita." *Aureum opus*, doc. 12, fols., 4r,v (Nov. 2, 1241): "deducta parte nostra quam ibi accipere debemus." Arch. Crown, Peter III, Reg. Canc. 40, fol. 125v (June 15, 1278): "que nobis et Episcopo Valencie competit"; fol. 155 (Sept. 1, 1278): "super decimis et primiciis dandis nobis et Ecclesie."

35. Arch. Cath. Tortosa, cajón Obispo y Cabildo, doc. 36.

36. Arch. Crown, James I, perg. 2,148. Arch. Cath. Tortosa, cajón Diezmos, doc. 25 (Mar. 27, 1263); cartulary II, fols. 155–157. Copy in Bibl. Univ. Val., codex 145, doc. 33; in *Colección diplomática*, doc. 1,398.

37. *Colección diplomática*, doc. 191 (Nov. 27, 1238): "dominus rex habeat in feudum perpetuum duas partes de decimis iure divino debitis, videlicet, in pane, vino et oleo; in reliquis autem decimacionibus, tam animalium grossorum et minorum quam ovium, lane et casei ac piscium, habeat rex tantum medietatem."

38. *Ibid.:* "quod si dominus papa composicionem hic annotatam nolit habere ratam, dominus rex vel infans non teneantur ad composicionem istam aliquatenus obligati."

39. *Ibid.*, doc. 989 (Feb. 26, 1274).

40. *Ordinatio ecclesiae valentinae*, p. 368, where a witness "audivit ab Archipresbytero [*probably of Teruel; a Valencian canon*] quod hoc anno medietatem decimarum percipiebat rex, et alteram medietatem clerici" (1238).

41. Arch. Cath., perg. 1,304 (*an.* 1240): "in beneficium perpetuum et in feudum vobis domino Iacobo dei gracia Illustri Regi Aragonum . . . terciam partem fructuum omnium Decimabilium . . . totius Episcopatus Regni Valentie." And cf. *Aureum opus*, doc. 12, fol. 4r,v (1241).

42. Arch. Cath., leg. 35, fasc. 1, fols. 1–2v (Nov. 2, 1241), and perg. 2,303 (same date).

43. See Chapter VIII, note 135: "composicionem."

44. Document as cited in note 42: "illam enim cum vendicare poterimus nobis et successoribus nostris integre retinemus."

45. Arch. Crown, Peter III, Reg. Canc. 48, fol. 82v (July 14, 1280).

46. See Arch. Crown, Peter III, Reg. Canc. 41, fol. 11 (Nov. 3, 1278); also fol. 60 (April 20, 1279), where he is bent on collecting some.

47. Arch. Cath., perg. 1,304 (June 1, 1240). Martínez Aloy (*Diputación*, p. 10) and Sanchís Sivera (*Diócesis valentina*, II, 431) also see this as a victory of diocese over crown.

48. Lorenzo Matheu y Sanz, *Tractatus de regimine urbis et regni Valentiae sive selectarum interpretationum ad principaliores foros eiusdem* (Valencia, 1654), pp. 167 ff., 178 ff., 186. Sanchís Sivera, *Diócesis valentina*, II, 113.

49. Arch. Crown, Real Patrim., Real Casa, extra series, no. 47; cf. *Documenta selecta*, doc. 7 (Nov. 7, 1241): "terciam partem in decimis ville Algezire et terminorum suorum," to be held "in feudum pro nobis et Ecclesia Terrachonensi."

50. Arch. Cath., pergs. 486, 2,316, and 2,451, and Arch. Crown, James I, perg. 988 (all May 29, 1245): "imperpetuum mille solidos annuatim habendos et percipiendos in exitibus Albufere Valencie, pro illis videlicet duabus partibus sive toto

iure decime quas et quod vos debetis percipere et habere in unoquoque anno in Albufera Valencie." See also Arch. Crown, *Liber patrimonii regni Valentiae*, fol. 294v, and the *Itinerari*, pp. 172–173 and n.

51. Arch. Crown, James I, perg. 1346.

52. Arch. Cath., perg. 2,452 (July 26, 1256).

53. F. de P. Momblanch y Gonzálbez, *Historia de la Albufera de Valencia* (Valencia, 1960), p. 53.

54. Arch. Crown, James I, Reg. Canc. 15, fol. 13v (Aug. 13, 1268). "Constituimus et ordinamus . . . procuratores nostros in curia romana . . . in negotio quod habemus cum Episcopo Valentino super facta tertie partis decime."

55. Arch. Crown, James I, perg. 2,148 (Mar. 27, 1273): "volentes saluti nostre anime providere."

56. See Arch. Crown, James I, perg. 2,144; *Itinerari*, p. 477 (Mar. 1, 1273). Also *Colección diplomática*, doc. 999 (*an.* 1274): "et dixistis pluries quod nos iniuriabamus vobis et ecclesie valentine, tam super tercia parte decimarum, quam retinuimus usque modo, et modo percipimus in civitate et diocesi valentina, de castris et villis nostris . . . quam eciam super possessionibus mesquitarum, quas dedimus ipsi ecclesie." There are several similar documents of February 1273 in the cathedral archives too (e.g. perg. 2,380, or the Liber instrumentorum, fols. 78v–80).

57. Arch. Crown, *ibid.*: "contencio sive quaestio diu fuerit inter nos . . . et vos."

58. *Ibid.*: "dicta definicio non valet, pro eo videlicet quia per capitulum valentinum firmata non fuerit, sed tantum per ipsum Ferrarium . . . et quinque canonicos ipsius ecclesie, qui tunc temporis de curia nostra [regis] erant."

59. *Ibid.*: "dicta ecclesia in predicta diffinicione enormiter erat lesa."

60. *Ibid.*: "cupientes eciam ora multorum claudere, qui possent dicere quod nos iura predicta ipsius ecclesie iniuriose et voluntarie detinemus."

61. *Ibid.*: "licet secundum conscienciam nostram, nos teneri non credimus" and: "ecclesia quam nos eripuimus de manibus paganorum et proprio sanguine acquisivimus ac redegimus ad cultum fidei Christiane."

62. *Ibid.*: "castrum nostrum de Xulella et castrum nostrum et villam de Garg sita in regno Valencie et diocesi vestra cum fortitudinibus ipsorum et hominibus et feminis." On these two places see Chapter VIII, note 55.

63. Arch. Cath., perg. 2,396 (Feb. 26, 1273): including first fruits, tithes, and other church revenues throughout the diocese; crown officials are to enforce this.

64. *Censo de Catalunya*, pp. 262–263: "item lo terç del delme del pa et del vin de la orta de la ciutat de Valencia . . . 6,500 solidos," in the city revenues; and "item lo terç del delme de la ortelissa de la dita ciutat, 2,020 solidos."

65. Arch. Vat., Reg. Vat. 19 (Gregory IX), fol. 68r (Jan. 9, 1239); noted in Auvray, *Registres*, II, no. 4,705, and published by Vincke in *Documenta selecta*, no. 6: "quibuslibet aliis ecclesiis et monasteriis Regni Valentie que construxisti et dotasti de novo." Cf. below, Chapter XV.

66. Arch. Crown, Peter III, Reg. Canc. 59, fol. 100 (Aug. 25, 1282): "locis in quibus dictus dominus Rex pater noster ipsas primicias recipit et recipere debet."

67. Arch. Crown, Peter III, Reg. Canc. 40, fol. 155 (Sept. 1, 1278).

68. Arch. Crown, James I, Reg. Canc. 12, fol. 51v (May 15, 1262): "in redditibus . . . cenis et aliis iuribus nostris tam decimis, primiciis, quam quibuslibet aliis."

69. Arch. Crown, James I, Reg. Canc. 21, fol. 57 (Aug. 26, 1272): "totam ab integro partem nostram et iura omnia quam et que percipimus . . . in decima totius bladi . . . in Vall bona et Arbers, Sobirans, aldeis Morelle et in terminis suis."

70. E.g. "Colección de cartas pueblas," no. III (Ares, 1243): "et ita illud forum

[Caesaraugustae] postulat et demandem [*sic*] dando decimam et primiciam"; no. XXXVIII (Villafranca, 1249): "ita quod dando fideliter domino Deo et sancte Ecclesie"; no. XLVIII (Villanueva, 1237).

71. *Ibid.*, no. I (Adzaneta, Jan. 8, 1271), *BSCC*, I (1920), 122–124: "nobis et nostris"; similarly no. XXI (Vistabella, 1251); no. XX (Culla, 1244): "et teneamini nobis et Sancte matri ecclesie solvere atque dare decimam ut est as[s]uetum in civitate Caesarauguste."

72. Arch. Cath., leg. 35, fasc. 1, fols. lv–2v.

73. On the Zaragoza tithes see above, Aguilar, *Noticias*, I, 85. For the Huesca bishop's holdings see below, notes 80, 88, 101; for the Barcelona bishop's holdings, note 116; for the Vich bishop, note 100. See in general the lists of bishops and monasteries culled from archives and later chroniclers by Juan de Mariana, *Historia general de España*, 9 vols. (Valencia, 1783–1796), IV, appendix 2.

74. See Chapters X–XIII, *passim*. A series of interesting tithe items for the Cistercians of Benifasá may be found in their papers in Arch. Nac. Madrid (e.g. carp. 423, nos. 2 and 13, *an.* 1258 and 1261; carp. 424, nos. 7, 17, and 18, *an.* 1266 and 1269; 425, no. 4, *an.* 1272; and 421, nos. 1–5, *an.* 1245). See also the Tortosa Cathedral Archives below in Chapter XII, section 1, "The Cistercians: the Monks of Benifasá." The Corachar people are committed to paying "conventui Scarpii [*Escarp*] presenti et futuro primicias omnium rerum," in carp. 422, no. 11, *an.* 1247.

75. Arch. Cath., perg. 2,341 (Feb. 7, 1241): "ius percipiendi decimas quod in laycum cadere non potest, dare non possumus." Again in perg. 2,413 (Aug. 29, 1260) the tithe as a special favor is given in fief, but it is expressly stated that the "ius percipiendi decimas" does not go with it; this "in dominio retinemus." Similar expressions occur in other homages (e.g. perg. 2,344 [July 21, 1242]; and perg. 2,345 [Mar. 11, 1241]).

76. *Ibid.* (perg. 2,341): "concedimus vobis Petro de Monte acuto et successoribus vestris in perpetuum beneficium et feudum terciam partem fructu[u]m decime." On the schools of thought as to origins of lay possession of tithes, see San Martín, *Diezmo en España*, pp. 110 ff.; cf. 127–128, 135–136.

77. *Ibid.:* "et sitis inde nostri fideles et legales vasalli et defensores Ecclesie nostre, et teneamini facere pro hiis fidelitatem et hommagium."

78. Additional document, also on perg. 2,341.

79. Arch. Cath., perg. 2,339 (July 25, 1242), for example.

80. Arch. Cath., perg. 2,340 (Nov. 27, 1242). Cf. note 92.

81. As in the agreement of 1241 in note 75 (perg. 2,341), and perg. 2,344 (July 21, 1242).

82. Arch. Cath., perg. 2,343 (July 15, 1308): "iuravit et fecit homagium P. de Monte Acuto in palacio domini Episcopi Valentini in forma hic contenta super feudo cum pertinenciis decime castrorum . . . et aliis locis que obtinet in diocesi Valentina." This is a later copy or repetition by an heir (July 15, 1308); see the homage of 1241 in note 89. Perg. 2,344 (July 21, 1242): "si que eciam dominus Rex vobis dederit in Episcopatu nostro, sub eadem forma concedimus vobis et successoribus vestris de omnibus decimabilibus terciam partem predictam." Perg. 2,365 (but *an.* 1306, for Mogente and Llombay castles): "congregato capitulo in domo domini Episcopi."

83. Arch. Cath., perg. 1,208 (Feb. 21, 1245): "de nostris quidem duabus partibus nichil vobis intendimus concedere vel dare."

84. As in Arch. Cath., pergs. 2,431 (Jan. 19, 1263) and 2,432 (June 14, 1257).

85. As in Arch. Cath., pergs. 2,351 and 2,368 (two documents), for 1242; perg. 2,413 for 1260.

86. Arch. Cath., perg. 2,432 (June 14, 1257): "ab eo vel a Christianis sive sarracenis." He held, for example, Paterna and (1237–1273) Manises.

87. Arch. Cath., perg. 1,304 (see note 41).

88. Arch. Cath., pergs. 5,959, 5,960, and 2,325 (June 27–28, 1240): the agreement here is with the bishop "elect" Ferrer and the chapter. See also the Liber de bisbalia, fol. 25r,v (June 28, 1240): "notum sit omnibus quod cum questio verteretur inter Venerabilem patrem Vitalem dei gracia Oscensem Episcopum ex una parte [et] Ferrarium per eandem [gratiam] sedis Valentine Electum et propositum Tarrachonensis Ecclesie et Capitulum eiusdem sedis ex altera super decimis et ecclesia Alqueriarum Alborayi et de Almaçera . . . amicabili voluntate ad invicem statuerunt et ordinaverunt quod dictus Episcopus Oscensis . . . habeat ius patronatus in dictorum locorum ecclesia. Item habeat in perpetuum decimam decem iovatarum terre quascumque elegerit in predictis alchariis. . . . Et Episcopus et Ecclesia Valentina habent omnia iura specialia et ecclesiastica in predicta ecclesia."

89. Arch. Cath., perg. 2,341 (Feb. 7, 1241): "et successoribus vestris in perpetuum beneficium." In 1286 he got the castle of Ibi. He had received Carlet and Alarp on July 7, 1238. Alarp or Alfarp or Alharb was a village in the valley of Alcalá, an area then including everything from Carlet to Turís. Alcudia is discussed by Sanchís Sivera, but with the owner given incorrectly as Peregrin of Montagut, in Nomenclátor de Valencia, p. 46.

90. Arch. Cath., perg. 2,345 (Mar. 11, 1241): "concedimus vobis Lupo de Sparsa . . . in feudum terciam partem fructuum decime a nobis recipiende in omnibus honoribus et possessionibus que vos habeatis in loco qui Benazamen nuncupatur in orta Valencie et in terminis suis." This could also be Benejama near Alcoy. López held other land near Burriana (Itinerari, p. 116). See also perg. 2,421 (same date): "Luppus de Sparça."

91. Arch. Cath., perg. 2,368 (Dec. 5, 1241). This was still held by the bishops in 1306, when "nobilis Gonbaldum d'Entença" swore homage for Chiva castle (perg. 2,369). See too the clarification of 1314 in perg. 2,412. The same man held Puig and other places.

92. Arch. Cath., perg. 2,342 (Jan. 25, 1242): "Mireto de Ciutadilla"—is he, then, a Minorcan? Almácera was held by the bishop of Huesca previously, and it appears again in the bishop's hands as late as September 1242 (Arch Cath., perg. 1,206, Sep. 27, 1242).

93. Arch. Cath., perg. 2,351 (April 1, 1242). A Tarazona knight, the son of Blaise (Blasco) Simon, he had married Alda Fernández, daughter of Saʿīd the ex-king of Moslem Valencia. She brought him the castle and area. He held other important Valencian lands. For example, in 1251 King James took his stronghold of Castalla here and Torre de Onil, giving in exchange the Valencian towns of Villamarchante and Cheste. He had Ibi (1251) and Masarrojos (1246), the latter soon being exchanged for Alventosa.

94. Arch. Cath., perg. 2,346 (May 28, 1242): "subtus Ruçafam" (today the partida de Melilla).

95. Arch. Cath., perg. 2,352 (June 27, 1242). Peter "de Auro" (Liber instrumentorum, fols. 55–56); possibly this is a Doria, or from Aura? He appears as a member of the king's household in his travels from 1260 to 1269 (cf. Itinerari, pp. 302, 308, 348, 351, 414, 427, 578). He seems to have bought up the various grants, or otherwise to have acquired them, around Albalat dels Sorells (Codinats) before 1240 and may be considered the first lord here.

96. Arch. Cath., perg. 2,419 (June 29, 1242). Cf. the Liber instrumentorum, fols. 121–122v, Liber constitutionum, fols. 83v–84r (June 29, 1242). "Petrus Azlor,"

perhaps Dezláur, could belong to one of two noted families of King James's nobility; the devices of both stand upon fields of gold, and may explain the alternate form of "d'auro." Senquier, Cinquayros, or Cinqueros stood close to the sea, just north of Valencia city, near Albalat and Foyos; Peter Dezlor received his first grant here in 1238. The d'Açlors are an important noble family; figures like Sancho Peter and Blaise Peter d'Açlor appear on royal documents of our time. The village of Binahalim near Penáguila, for example, belonged partly to the latter (1250).

97. Arch. Cath., perg. 1,087; and perg. 2,428 (both July 8, 1242).

98. Arch. Cath., perg. 2,344 (July 21, 1242).

99. Arch. Cath., perg. 2,429 (July 23, 1242): "desplargues," "de Spalangues," etc. This may be one of the Espluga (Spluga, Çaspluga, etc.) who came on the crusade, whose name derived from holdings at Esplugas near Barcelona; but is more probably the knight William of Espailargas, Despaylarges or Spallargas the Perelada native (according to Febrèr) who appears in the *Repartimiento* of Valencia. He seems to have had the lordship of Campanar from 1242; later it reverted to the crown. See below, Chapter X, note 98.

100. Arch. Cath., pergs. 2,420 and 5,964 (June 17, 1242). This was for all his holdings. He received in the Valencia chapter: "a vobis promissionem manualem de indempnitate et utilitate ecclesie valentine curanda et observanda."

101. Arch. Cath., perg. 2,339 (July 25, 1242). But in September he renewed the Almácera homage; perhaps he had again taken direct ownership (pergs. 2,340 and 2,421, both of 1242). See also Arch. Cath. Huesca, 2-9-567 (perg.): "sit notum cunctis quod nos dei gratia episcopus Valencie et prepositus Tarrachone et commune Capitulum Valentinum per nos et successores nostros damus et concedimus vobis venerabili et dilecto V[itali] dei gratia episcopo oscensi in feudum et beneficium personale . . . terciam partem decime omnis . . . de honoribus et possessionibus vestris quas in Episcopatu Valencie possidetis" (8 kals. Aug.).

102. Arch. Cath., pergs. 2,425 and 2,424 (both Aug. 5, 1242).

103. Arch. Cath., pergs. 2,348 and 2,427 (both Aug. 8, 1242): "de Falcibus" and "de Salces." The first Roderick was a Navarrese, the latter apparently from Salses in Roussillon. Both knights were on the crusade; the former appears in the *Repartimiento* of Valencia.

104. Arch. Cath., perg. 2,423 (Aug. 19, 1242): "Siri Garcie"; this is more probably a foreign title (Ser or Sir) than a name (Catalan Sir, Castilian Siro).

105. Arch. Cath., perg. 2,347 (Aug. 22, 1242).

106. Arch. Cath., perg. 2,349 (Sept. 10, 1242); he is King James's "azemilario nostro" in 1274, when he is purchasing Rafalaxat near Valencia (*Itinerari*, p. 500), and remained in this office until the king's death.

107. Arch. Cath., perg. 2,350 (Sept. 12, 1242). The Rosanes were a knightly family (e.g. Berengar in *Itinerari*, p. 54, and in the *Repartimiento*); Rosans, 100 kilometers from Nîmes, may be their place of remote origin.

108. Arch. Cath., perg. 2,424 (Sept. 26, 1242). The place is left blank in the document. There is a Vernet in the French Pyrenees. An Arnold of Venice came to Valencia, according to Febrèr's dubious *Trobes*, his shield showing a Lion of St. Mark; our man is more probably the Barcelona knight who appears in three documents (1242, 1260, 1264) signed at Barcelona and who owns houses there on St. Anne street (*Itinerari*, pp. 163, 305, 362).

109. Arch. Cath., pergs. 1,208 and 2,410 (Feb. 21 and 22, 1245): if he can recover it from the king who holds it in fief from the church of Valencia. The place was an extensive area in the region of Cuart de Poblet, centering on a fort or tower called Aleis (perhaps Ladea or Aldaya). See Chapter XV, p. 289, and notes 66, 67.

110. Arch. Cath., perg. 2,415 (Aug. 6, 1248); apparently an important knight in Valencia (cf. *Itinerari*, p. 144, *an.* 1240).

111. Arch. Cath., perg. 2,432 (June 14, 1257). Artal, a loyal but violent man, was one of the most important barons in the realms of King James. He appears in the *Llibre dels feyts* prominently, in chs. 21, 25, 455, 503–504, 517, 547–548; and in over fifty documents scattered through the *Itinerari*. The lord of Paterna again signed an agreement for that place in 1262, perhaps a confirmation (perg. 1,096 [Dec. 4, 1262]).

112. Arch. Cath., perg. 2,413 (Aug. 29, 1260). This included his castle of Arenós.

113. Arch. Cath., perg. 2,431 (Jan. 19, 1263): "tam a Sarracenis quam a Christianis."

114. Arch. Cath., perg. 2,367 (Oct. 1, 1271); on the transcription and on these places, see note 158 and text.

115. See note 162.

116. Arch. Cath., perg. 2,430 (Sept. 12, 1268): "tam a Christianis quam a Sarracenis." He appears in the *Itinerari* (pp. 435, 438) and was dead by 1270. The bishop of Barcelona also claimed Almonacid. Benaguacil passed to Roderick's daughter Sancha.

117. Arch. Cath., perg. 2,358 (July 11, 1272). The Aragonese knight Maza was a close adviser of the king, appearing as signatory to important royal documents from at least 1217 to 1273. He signed the capitulation of Valencia city (1238), the treaty with the viscount of Cabrera (1223), and the privileges of Balaguer and of Collioure (1236, 1223). In 1220 he received for seven years the revenues of Roures; in 1275 he was summoned by name to help put down the revolt of the Valencian Moslems. (See *Itinerari*, pp. 21, 23, 25, 36, 37, 44–46, 48, 70, 92, 96, 101, 105, 106, 112, 123, 134, 405, 451, 458, 483–484, 526). He was also a member of Prince Peter's retinue on the latter's Castilian trip of 1269, being one of the few Aragonese rather than Catalans, and taking one of the more imposing baggage-trains (Soldevila, *Pere el Gran*, III, 248–249).

118. There are a number of important men of this name; this man would seem to be the James of Oblites who held Chella at about this time (1283).

119. See *Itinerari*, p. 129, *an.* 1237.

120. There are several knightly families or branches of a family of this name, especially one with lands at Alcira and Picasent and another at Játiva. This particular Simon may be the one who soon became lieutenant of the royal procurator of the kingdom of Valencia, for the region below the Júcar.

121. There are a number of knights with this surname, and several with the first names, but it is difficult to identify him exactly.

122. Martin may have belonged to the Roiz (or Rois) de Corella clan prominent in medieval Valencia; a Roiz de Corella was among the prominent feudatories convoked to military service in a Valencia document of 1277.

123. He had bought some three thousand solidi worth of territory near Játiva in the preceding five years, and probably held other lands of his own besides those he cared for as royal agent. He was the first administrator for that part of the Valencian conquest which fell below the Júcar River, as one of the two lieutenants of the procurator-general of the kingdom of Valencia.

124. Perhaps this is the Aragonese who appears as bailiff of Montblanch in documents of 1262 and 1267; he fought with the king in a feudal war; the king at one time owed him 3,900 solidi (*Itinerari*, pp. 328, 398).

125. Arch. Cath., perg. 2,358 (July 11, 1272). Is this the cleric Peter Martínez, who was the son of the justiciar of Aragon Martin Pérez (cf. *Llibre dels feyts*, ch. 402)?

126. Arch. Cath., Liber instrumentorum, fol. 58v: "Lupus Sancii de B."

127. *Ibid.*, *passim;* see also Peter Pons on fol. 119, R. Díaz on fols. 128v–130.

128. Arch. Cath., perg. 2,359 (July 12, 1273); "Tyvi." He also held Maçot near Torrente, and other places.

129. *Troba* 11, p. 18 has an Agramunt from Navarre who "gotja la mitad / Dels Delmes de Nules, que el Bisbe li ha dat"; *troba* 452, p. 238, tells how William Salines "gotja á Campanar / Per mercè del Rey, è per capitol / Lo ters delme te, de qui el va comprar"; *troba* 461, p. 244 is about Raymond of Seguí of the queen's household, who got "Alazadi" and two jovates "ab dècimes totes al Bisbe pagades." There are several Agramunts in the records, including one from France and one from Lérida (Acromonte). The William of Salines may be the Simon of Salinas or Salines in note 98 and text. Raymond of Seguí must be the queen's porter Seguí who got lands and houses during the siege of Valencia in Arch. Cath., perg. 2,329 (July 23, 1238). On the lay share of the tithes of Nules see note 139 and text.

130. Arch. Cath., perg. 2,335 (Sept. 10, 1243): "permutamus vobis domino Iacobo . . . Duas partes decimarum quas nos in Ecclesia de Quart iure episcopali habemus[,] pro illa parte tercia decime quam vos domine Rex habetis in Ecclesia de Puzols."

131. Arch. Cath., perg. 1,208 (Feb. 21, 1245): "hec autem vobis sub tali prestatione concedimus si dictam terciam partem a domino Rege poteritis obtinere quam scilicet ipse in feudum tenet pro episcopo et ecclesia Valentina."

132. See note 83.

133. Arch. Cath., perg. 2,448 (April 30, 1258). Cf. note 161.

134. Arch. Cath., perg. 2,413 (Aug. 29, 1260). See notes 93, 112, and, in Chapter IV, note 131 and text.

135. Arch. Cath., perg. 2,322 (Feb. 10, 1268); Valencia church authorities had protested that Blaise Simon "debebat et tenebatur sibi facere homagium pro decimis," precisely because of the admission of jurisdiction implied by his father's contract with them. The king followed the same line of argument. The document is significant as showing the juridical importance of the contracts, even though they had only seemed to consecrate the status quo.

136. Arch. Cath., perg. 2,432 (June 14, 1257).

137. Arch. Cath., perg. 1,096 (Dec. 4, 1262); these lands seem to have changed hands.

138. Arch. Cath., perg. 2,370 (Feb. 4, 1260): "retinemus tamen decimam omnium Christianorum qui ibi habitant vel decetero habitabunt." On other tithes of Peter Ferdinand, see notes 150, 176, and text.

139. Arch. Cath. Tortosa, cajón Obispo, nos. 8, 35, 39, 52 (for items of 1250, 1268, 1306); cartulary no. VIII, fols. 147–149 (1250); cajón Alcalatén, no. 11 (1282).

140. For instance, Bartholomew Matoses, who did homage for the place of Benifayó de Espioca (Oct. 25, 1304), may not have been the first to make such an agreement here; there was a well-established parish before 1340, to which also the Christians of Almusafes came. Peter Boyl received the third-tithe of Castellón de Játiva (modern Villanueva de Castellón) in 1364, again confirmed in 1375. John of Procida received the tithe of Cocentaina, as did his successors in the fifteenth century. Gilet, held by John of Zaragoza from 1249, had its third-tithe given to the lord Peter William Catalán in 1375. Jaraco, held by Arnold Busquet and his thirty settlers in 1248 and later by the lord of Gandía, gave its third to the lord, as can be seen when the third is transferred to another man in 1417. The Mislata third was given in 1392 to Anthony of Vilaragut, though the lord of the area then was Ber-

nard of Codinats. In 1393 the third-tithe of Rafalell, an Arab place settled by Christians in 1248, was held by Andrew Salvador, together with the third-tithe of Farnals and Cruz de Vistabella. Rocafort, after several masters, had been confiscated in 1349 and soon given to the Matet family; in April 28, 1354 the third-tithe went to them "ad tempus centum annorum."

141. Almagro, *Historia de Albarracín*, III, 276.

142. Arch. Cath., perg. 2,418 (Mar. 16, 1279). James and others held part of the tithes of Jérica, Toro, Chelva, Tuéjar, and Altura (Aguilar, *Noticias de Segorbe*, I, 593, and cf. the settlement on p. 94).

143. *Colección diplomática*, doc. 1,398 (Mar. 27, 1273): "terciam partem decimarum recipimus nos et milites ac religiosi in diecesi [sic] valentina."

144. Arch. Crown, James I, perg. 2,148 (Mar. 27, 1273).

145. Arch. Crown, Peter III, Reg. Canc. 41, fol. 60 (April 9, 1279).

146. Arch. Crown, Peter III, Reg. Canc. 40, fol. 29v (Oct. 21, 1277).

147. See document cited in note 146: "racione peticionis tercie partis decimarum quam petebat [rex] a militibus Burriane." The verb is here translated as "required," because the tense in the text is also ambiguous and may refer to a settled custom.

148. Arch. Crown, Peter III, Reg. Canc. 42, fol. 149 (April 13, 1280): "custodi cabanee bestiarii . . . reginae." For Burriana and Ademuz documents see Chapter X, notes 162, 163, and text.

149. Arch. Crown, Peter III, Reg. Canc. 48, fol. 82v (July 14, 1280): "et faciat sibi hostendi per venerabilem Episcopum Valencie si que iuste raciones sunt que impedire debeant dicto Regi dictam tertiam partem."

150. Arch. Crown, James I, Reg. Canc. 18, fols. 5 (April 18, 1273), 5v (*an*. 1273), and again on 5v (*an*. 1271); "de qua non solvit decimam" (Albaida, Ademuz, Luchente, Bocairente, Castielfabib, Finestrat), and "de locis de quibus tenetur dare decimam Episcopo Valencie." On Peter Ferdinand and the tithe of Buñol and Ribarroja, see notes 138 and 176 with text.

151. "Colección de cartas pueblas," no. XV (Villahermosa, Mar. 9, 1243). He lists things subject to and exempt from the tithe. James in 1242 gave Peter Sanz the grant of Montornés "cum iure decimarum parti nostre contingenti" (no. XIV of the same series, *BSCC*, IX [1928], 86-87).

152. *Pere el Gran*, IV [pt. 2, I], 90-91, doc. 68 (May 28, 1277). Were these men direct vassals of the crown, or can some be understood to be included in the tithe agreements as vassals of the greater lords? Useful for purposes of comparison perhaps is the later document listing the nobles convoked by Alphonse III at Valencia city in September 1286, thirty-one men including many family names belonging to tithe-vassals (Martínez Aloy, *Diputación*, doc. on p. 49); see also the families discussed by Viciana, *Crónica de Valencia*, part 2.

153. Arch. Cath., perg. 2,338 (June 17, 1242): "pro vestris debitis et iniuriis persolvendis," as a personal benefice until his death (when the debt, if unpaid, is canceled).

154. Arch. Crown, James I, pergs. 990 (1245) and 1,649 (1260). These are Jaca solidi, to be paid twice a year.

155. Arch. Crown, Peter III, Reg. Canc. 59, fol. 165v (Nov. 27, 1282) with a reference to previous payments (but "nomine quondam Ecclesie de A[l]barraçine").

156. Doc. edited by R. Chabás, *El archivo*, IV (1890), 310-311, no. 39 (June 3, 1273): "et tertio nostro decime." Bailiff Simon of Denia appears in a 1274 document again in the *Itinerari*, p. 492.

157. Arch. Cath., perg. 1,100 (Jan. 27, 1270): "vendimus vobis Blasco Massa

militi et vestris hinc usque ad decem annos . . . duas partes omnium fructuum terre et arborum Episcopo et capitulo valentino pertinentes in Castro vestro et termino de Villamerxat . . . precio Ducentorum solidorum regalium in quolibet anno" on the feast of St. Andrew.

158. Arch. Cath., perg. 2,367, cf. note 114 (Oct. 1, 1271): "nos Frater Andreas . . . assensu capituli Valencie vendimus et concedimus vobis Furtado de Alihori militi . . . et Egidio Roderico filio vestro tantum [,] totam decimam panis, vini, arborum et aliorum fructuum omnium quam nos habemus . . . excepta decima bestiarii, de turribus et alcheriis de Cot, de Villar, de Xera et terminorum suorum, que loca sunt vestra." The diocese would succeed the Lihori or Liori family in ownership of Villar (del Arzobispo, or de Benaduf) here at least by 1308. Was some such transfer envisaged when this agreement was signed?

159. See documents cited in notes 139 (Urrea) and 113 (Simon's wife), and text.

160. Document cited in note 116.

161. *Itinerari*, p. 462n. Cf. also Bayerri, *Historia de Tortosa*, VII, 150–151; the author does not realize this is an infeuded and farmed tithe, or perhaps better a compromise farming to end a dispute. The area was heavily Moslem, so the tithe is rather the two-thirds of Teresa's personal revenues from these places; she must have received more than 2,000 solidi here. Note that this is a different tithe lease than that gained by Teresa above in note 133.

162. Arch. Cath., perg. 2,416 (Aug. 12, 1260). Had he leased it from William? It seems so, since the latter apparently still held the seigniory.

163. Arch. Cath., perg. 6,010 (Jan. 6, 1276): "sit omnibus notum quod nos Raimundus de Belestar decanus sedis Valencie et Arnaldus de Buscheto canonicus dicte Sedis procuratores constituti pro capitulo valentino in bonis episcopatus Valencie sede vacante . . . vendimus vobis Raimundo Jalandi civi Valencie et vestris hinc ad unum annum primum venturum totam decimam piscium maris episcopatus."

164. Arch. Cath., perg. 2,918 (Jan. 6, 1276): "sede vacante . . . vendimus vobis Hugueto d'Iumanino et vestris hinc ad annum venturum totam decimam carnagii [?] episcopatus Valencie prout actenus consuetum est vendi et alienari et collegi sive percepi [*sic*] ita quod vos et quem volueritis colligatis et percipiatis dictam decimam."

165. Arch. Cath., perg. 707 (Feb. 12, 1259). "Pateat universis presentem paginam inspecturis, quod nos Frater A. divina miseratione valentinus Episcopus Damus et concedimus tibi Raymundo de Almanar vassallo nostro baiuliam Castri sive omnium terminorum de Alcoy, nostrorum reddituum . . . Ita quod laboribus tuis et expensis quos et quas facies in collectione nostrorum reddituum recipias tantum retentione decimam, decem [novem?] partibus nobis et Ecclesie Valentine fideliter reservatis. Hanc autem concessionem sive donacionem concedimus tibi sicut superius est iamdictum dum tamen nobis et Ecclesie valentine legatus fueris et devotus, et ut presens pagina maioris roboris gaudeat firmitate, eam Sigilli nostri munimine fecimus roborari. Quod est actum apud Cocentaniam pridie idus Februarii, anno domini millesimo cc quinquagesimo nono; Ego Fr. Andreas valentinus episcopus subscribo." This would seem to concern the revenues of the episcopal and capitular *mensae*, revenue-producing properties; but the tithe would probably be included. The high salary suggests that Raymond was being paid in this wise for other services as well; he appears in other cathedral documents and in the crown registers as a familiar and agent of the bishop.

166. "Colección de cartas pueblas," no. XXV (Mallo; June 18, 1289), *BSCC*, XI (1930), 354–357: "por muytos agradables servicios que a nos avedes feytos, damos a vos . . . todo el terçio dieçmo del pan del termino del Mallo, es a saber,

de trigo, de centeno, de ordio . . . de vino, de corderos o de cabritos e de otras cossas que dieçmo se deva dar."

167. *Ibid.*, no. XXXII (Mar. 27, 1303), *BSCC*, XIII (1932), 134–138: "et cum parte decimarum."

168. Arch. Crown, Liber patrimonii regni Valentiae, fols. 34v, 102v, 136.

169. López, "Confesores de la familia real," pp. 152–153.

170. Arch. Cath., perg. 3,005 (June 30, 1269). "Noverint universi quod nos Iacobus . . . concedimus imperpetuum vobis venerabili fratri A. per eandem [gratiam] Episcopo, Decano et Capitulo et Canonicis et aliis clericis Valencie et vestris successoribus imperpetuum quod decetero possitis libere et sine contradiccione alicuius . . . portare fructus omnes redituum vestrorum tantum ubicumque eos habueritis et mittere eos in Civitatem Valencie quandocumque volueritis et etiam libere . . . aportare de uno loco ad alium per totum Regnum Valencie ac vendere inde, set etiam de Regno ipso extrahere per mare et per terram et aportare ad quemcumque locum volueritis et facere inde vestras voluntates, constitutione aliqua facta vel facienda in aliquo non obstante. Mandantes firmiter baiulis curiis iusticiis et universis aliis officialibus et subditis nostris . . ."

171. Arch. Cath., perg. 1,199 (Sept. 6, 1311): a late confirmation by James II of a privilege given by James I.

172. Arch. Cath., perg. 2,392 (Jan. 2, 1267); perg. 2,393 (June 30, 1269).

173. Quoted by Moorman, *Church Life*, p. 33. See pp. 211–212, 218 and note. Lepointe blames the tithe troubles of Christendom especially upon the tithe farmers; greed and fraud apart, they received 5 percent or more of the collection ("Dîme," col. 1,240).

174. Arch. Cath., perg. 2,318 (Jan. 27, 1246): "multa possunt pericula imminere tum racione sterilitatis tum racione nebule grandinis et alterius tempestatis."

175. Arch. Cath., leg. 35, no. 1, fol. 3: "insultus populi seu propter Principis oppressionem, et generalem sterilitatem."

176. Arch. Crown, James I, Reg. Canc. 18, fol. 5r,v (two documents, 1271 and 1273): "item de locis de quibus tenetur dare decimam Episcopo valencie"; "de quibus levamus pro decima Episcopi cxxxiii solidorum, vj denariorum," etc. Cf. notes 138, 150, and text.

177. The list is in Arch. Crown, James I, Reg. Canc. 18, fol. 5v (*an.* 1271), and fol. 5 (*an.* 1273).

178. *Crònica*, ch. 36; there is probably exaggeration here, for Muntaner is irritated at papal anti-Catalan policies and is scolding Rome; but the substance of his statement is significant.

179. See note 64.

180. Statistical lists in Philip Hughes, *History of the Church*, 3 vols. (New York, 1935–1947), app. 5, pp. 539–540. King Alphonse at this time petitioned Rome to break the prosperous kingdom into two additional dioceses, Castellón and Játiva.

NOTES TO CHAPTER X. THE MILITARY ORDERS AS FRONTIER INSTITUTIONS

1. The Pedro Sucías Aparicio manuscript tomes at the municipal archives of Valencia (Los monasterios del reino de Valencia, 3 vols., 1907; and Los conventos del reino de Valencia, 3 vols., 1906) are uneven and incomplete but furnish useful data. Sucías lists and totals the houses in Monasterios, pp. 9–18. Escolano figured one hundred and fifty houses; Sarthou Carreres from the background of

his own researches is sure this is no exaggeration (*Monasterios valencianos, su historia y su arte* [Valencia, 1943], p. 14). Américo Castro has seventeenth-century quotations on this general subject which help make the figures credible (*Structure of Spanish History*, pp. 645-646). Sanchís Sivera lists the establishments by date for Valencia city from 1238 to 1800 (*Nomenclátor de Valencia*, pp. 421-423), and for the diocese (pp. 429-431). On each of the Orders about to be considered, see the encyclopedic *Dictionnaire des ordres religieux ou histoire des ordres monastiques, religieux, et militaires* by Pierre (Hippolyt) Hélyot (1660-1716), ed. M. L. Badiche, 4 vols. (1847-1859), in the massive series *Encyclopédie théologique ou série de dictionnaires*, ed. J. P. Migne, 168 vols. in 170 in 3 sets (Paris, 1844-1866), set 1, vols. XX-XXI. This may be supplemented by the *Dictionnaire historique, géographique et biographique des croisades* by M. D'Ault-Dumesnil in the same *Encyclopédie*, set 2, vol. XVIII (1852), and by such leisurely older works as Giuseppe Francesco Fontana, *Storia degli ordini monastici, religiosi e militari*, 8 vols. (Lucca, 1738-1739). An introduction to the extensive modern bibliography on each Order is supplied in Max Heimbucher's exhaustive *Die Orden und Kongregationen der katholischen Kirche*, 3rd ed. revised, 2 vols. (Paderborn, 1933-1934). The important rules, including those of the Templars, Hospitallers, Cistercians, Carthusians, Carmelites, Trinitarians, Augustinians, Dominicans, Franciscans, and Mercedarians, are conveniently available in the recent reprint of *Codex regularum monasticarum et canonicarum*, ed. Lucas Holstenius [Holstein], 6 vols. in 3 (Graz, [1759] 1957-1958).

2. Documents in Agustín Sales, *Memorias históricas del antiguo santuario del santo sepulcro de Valencia* (Valencia, 1746), pp. 88n., 89-90. On the Order in general see Heimbucher, *Orden und Kongregationen*, I, 411-412; *DHGE*, XI, cols. 345-348: N. J. Cinnamond, *Contribución al estudio de la orden del santo sepulcro* (Vich, n.d.), *passim*; and Georges Tessier, "Les débuts de l'ordre de saint sépulcre en Espagne," *Bibliotheque de l'école des chartes*, CXVI (1958), 5-28. The Villafranca *corts* put all religious under the king's protection but specified especially the Temple, Hospital, and the Holy Sepulchre (*Cortes de los antiguos reinos de Aragón y de Valencia*, I, 96).

3. *Antigüedades de Valencia*, I, 212-214.

4. Sales, *Memorias*, p. 91 (docs. of Nov. 2, 1251 and Aug. 7, 1279), p. 95.

5. Arch. Cath., perg. 1,334 (Aug. 4, 1261): "fratrum sancti sepulcri," and perg. 1,354 (Sept. 30, 1276).

6. Sebastián Puig y Puig, *Episcopologio de la sede barcinonense, apuntes para la historia de la iglesia de Barcelona y de sus prelados* (Barcelona, 1929), p. 447. On the nine bishops, see Zurita, *Anales*, I, *lib.* III, *c.* 33.

7. *Gallia christiana novissima, histoire des archevêchés, évêchés et abbayes de France d'après les documents authentiques*, ed. J. H. Albanès and U. Chevalier, 7 vols. (Montbéliard and Valence, 1899-1920), III, 510, doc. of June 18, 1277.

8. Humbert de Romans O. P. (†1272), quoted by Joaquín Miret y Sans, *Les cases de templers y hospitalers en Catalunya, aplech de noves y documents històrichs* (Barcelona, 1910), p. 365.

9. Desclot, *Crònica*, ch. 67.

10. Arch. Crown, Bulas, legajo X (Innocent IV), nos. 43, 44, 45, 50, 54 (1248-1249): "per Hispaniam et Cathaloniam constitutis."

11. The Latin text from his *De rebus Hispaniae* (VII, 26) is conveniently accessible in Castro, along with a translation of the somewhat different Spanish version of the *Crónica general* (*Structure of Spanish History*, pp. 212, 214). Translation from the Latin is my own.

12. *Llibre dels feyts*, ch. 128.

13. Francisco de Rades y Andrada, *Chrónica de las tres órdenes y cavallerías de Sanctiago, Calatraua y Alcántara* (Toledo, 1572), fol. 24v.

14. *Llibre dels feyts*, chs. 153-154, 156, 423-425; their presence at Biar is probable (see *Itinerari*, p. 170; cf. p. 112). The "Roderic Boso" in Miret y Sans's transcription of a 1235 document (p. 118) is this same commander Buesa.

15. Arch. Nac. Madrid, Ords. Milits., Santiago: Uclés, caj. 221, no. 3 (both the papal document and the earlier royal grant): "provide pensans labores multiplices gravesque sumptus quos pro tuenda fide catholica et cultu ampliando divino continue sustinetis." For the settlement see *Antigüedades de Valencia*, II, 252.

16. *Antigüedades*, II, 253 (April 9, 1239).

17. Arch. Cath., perg. 2,319 (Feb. 1, 1246) for Anna, Orcheta, and Torres. Arch. Nac. Madrid, Ords. Milits., Santiago: Uclés, caj. 115, no. 1 (Mar. 25, 1244) for Enguera "castrum et villam"; see too *Colección diplomática*, doc. 336, and *Itinerari*, pp. 167-168. Arch. Crown, James I, Reg. Canc. 16, fol. 258 (April 9, 1271) for Serra, Orcheta, and Mola. Anna ("Yanna") was given on September 24, 1244 (*Itinerari*, p. 170). Very few of their grants appear in the *Bullarium equestris ordinis S. Iacobi de Spatha* (ed. A. F. Aguado de Córdova and J. López Agurleta; Madrid, 1719); the Enguera gift is on p. 138 (1244), gifts from Saʿīd on pp. 138-139; and the pact between James and Saʿīd on p. 199 (1262). Mola may be Murla, south of Sagra, or Muela northwest of Enguerra; Torres could be any number of places, context indicating the south.

18. Arch. Nac. Madrid, Ords. Milits., Santiago: Uclés, caj. 207, no. 40 (June 5, 1260).

19. Arch. Crown, James I, Reg. Canc. 20, fol. 216 (Feb. 12, 1274): William "dedit in excambium cum carta nostra." Also in Arch. Nac. Madrid, *ibid.*, no. 1. The master of Uclés, Pelayo Pérez de Correa, appears in this transaction of 1274 as he does in earlier grants of 1244.

20. Perhaps an early gift; the document of July 7, 1270 grants to García Pérez of Loriz, "de ordine," freedom from royal and regional taxes, including host and cavalcade (Arch. Nac. Madrid, *ibid.*, caj. 208, no. 2; cf. Arch. Crown, James I, Reg. Canc. 16, fol. 199).

21. They had rights in the Carmogente area ("in quacumque parte volueritis infra terminos Castri de Carmuxen," apparently to raise rabbits, "conegrillorum"), as early as April 3, 1257; see Arch. Nac. Madrid, *ibid.*, caj. 207, no. 36. Wider interests are discerned in documents of Peter III for 1276 and 1282 (Arch. Crown, Reg. Canc. 38, fol. 95v; and Reg. Canc. 46, fol. 75). Their previous ownership of the castle is demonstrated by their having partially dismantled it on their own authority before 1301: "noveritis nos ordinare, quod si Fratres Ordinis Uclesii destruxerint seu destrui fecerint, Castrum seu opus, quod est constructum in Castro vocato Carmuxen sito in regno Valencie, quod non compellantur ad construendum seu reparandum Castrum predictum" (James II, in Arch. Nac. Madrid, *ibid.*, no. 65, Feb. 24, 1301).

22. *Nomenclátor de Valencia*, p. 383.

23. *Ibid.*, p. 376 (fourteenth century; perhaps a late acquisition).

24. Arch. Nac. Madrid, will cited in Chapter VII, note 62.

25. Arch. Cath., perg. 5,009 (Feb. 1, 1246); see also pergs. 787, 463, 2,319 (same date). Perg. 787 reads: "quod cum questio sive controversia esset diucius agitata inter venerabilem Arnaldum dei gracia Episcopum et Capitulum valencie ex una parte et dilectos in Christo fratrem Garciam Garcez comendatorem de Montem albano et fratres domus sue in Valencia et eius diocesi constitutos ex altera super ecclesiis de museros et de engera de anna de orcheta et de torres et eorum iuribus scilicet decimis et primiciis et omnibus aliis que ad episcopum et Capitulum lege

diocesana vel iurisdiccionis aut privilegiorum optentu spectare poterant, tandem pro bono pacis et concordie . . . ad composicionem amicabilem et concordiam devenitur."

26. Santiago Vidiella, "Cartulario de Monroyo (Aragón)," *Congrés I*, p. 182. On Calatrava see Francis Gutton, *L'ordre de Calatrava, la chevalerie militaire en Espagne* (Paris, 1955), e.g., appendix 1 on relations with the Cistercians and on their daily life. Cf. Hélyot, *Dictionnaire des ordres*, VI, 34–54.

27. *Itinerari*, p. 155; the mastership was in dispute at the time, 1240–1243 (see Gutton, *Calatrava*, p. 60).

28. See collection of documents in Vidiella, "Cartulario," pp. 172–189.

29. *Llibre dels feyts*, ch. 127. Cf. Gutton, *Calatrava*, p. 42.

30. *Llibre dels feyts*, chs. 153–157, 255, 315, 343. Gutton, *Calatrava*, p. 66, for their help in 1275.

31. Arch. Crown, Peter III, Reg. Canc. 61, fol. 108 (April 27, 1283); and Reg. Canc. 46, fol. 180 (April 14, 1284).

32. Arch. Crown, James I, Reg. Canc. 16, fol. 237 (Oct. 27, 1233). "Unde [concedimus] rafal Hauadaiub et rafal Arais et rafal Abinsalmo et rafal Algebeli sicut affrontat in cimiterio Maurorum. . . . Damus item vobis unum ortum ad portam Valencie . . . et damus vobis domos in villa Burriane . . . cum aliis domibus . . . [et] illud alfondicum." This is a later copy made by James more formally, and properly sealed ("redigi faceremus . . . in forma propria et bullari plumbea bulla nostra"). There is almost nothing for us in the *Bullarium ordinis militiae de Calatrava*, et. I. J. de Ortega y Cotes (Madrid, 1761) except a tithe settlement of 1242 (p. 74) and a transcription of the 1233 gift which names the estates as Huaradajub, Amiz, Algebeli, and Abinsalmo. A manuscript copy in the Arch. Nac. Madrid has "Raphal Huabadajub et Raphal Arayz et Raphal Abinsalmo et Raphal Algobali" (Ords. Milits., Calatrava, docs. reales, R265). Cf. *Itinerari*, p. 108.

33. *Antigüedades de Valencia*, II, 254–255. It was just south of St. Nicholas'. Cf. the *Repartimiento*, pp. 160, 246, 371. There would soon be a lawsuit with the Hospitallers over property lines near the Calatrava church (see below, n. 97). Pérez doc. in Escolano, *Décadas*, II, 513.

34. Lupo Martin the commander of Alcañiz received Bétera on July 13 (*Nomenclátor de Valencia*, pp. 146–147). The nearby Bufila (or Boylla, Bulla) surrendered to the king on April 10, and was also given to Lupo Martin on July 13 (p. 157); this is not the Bolulla, near Callosa de Ensarriá, owned by the diocese (p. 154; cf. above, Chapter VIII, note 52). See also Arch. Cath. perg. 2,317 (Jan. 27, 1246): "Boilla." Escolano gives them "Bosilla," explaining that only a tower remained there in his day; he puts it at a crossbow-shot from Bétera (*Décadas*, I, 513).

35. *Nomenclátor*, p. 212. The father of Na Valençona (Muntaner's future wife) must have bought the place before 1279; its church by then was diocesan (*Rationes decimarum*, I, 262).

36. Frey Matthew and the Order received the hamlet of Maçelnazar on May 15, 1238 (*ibid.*, p. 283). On Masanasa see Arch. Crown, James I, Reg. Canc. 20, fol. 286v (Sept. 11, 1275); Escolano, *Décadas*, II, 538; Arch. Cath., perg. 2,317 (Jan. 27, 1246).

37. Arch. Nac. Madrid, Ords. Milits., Calatrava, docs. partics., no. 106 (May 17, 1246), a Calatrava chaplaincy commission, where reference is made to the "comendatori Xilvela" and the "comendatori Betera." If Chilvella is really Chirivella, it can only have been a minor defensive outwork of Valencia city.

38. Arch. Nac. Madrid, *ibid.*, docs. reales, R273–274 (April 27, 1273). An earlier copy is in Arch. Crown, James I, Reg. Canc. 14, fol. 3 (Nov. 10, 1262). The town

was Begís near Jérica and Segorbe, not Bechí (Betxí) near Nules in Castellón. In 1281, Roderick Pérez Pons (again master of Alcañiz, or a successor of the same name) received permission from the king to exchange this with James of Jérica, the king's brother, for other holdings (Reg. Canc. 44, fol. 202, Oct. 17; and see Reg. Canc. 61, fol. 144 [May 25, 1283]).

39. Arch. Crown, James I, Reg. Canc. 14, fol. 3 (Nov. 10, 1262).

40. Aurea L. Javierre Mur, *Privilegios reales de la orden de Montesa en la edad media, catálogo de la serie existente en el archivo histórico nacional* (Madrid, 1956), pp. 72–73.

41. Arch. Crown, James I, Reg. Canc. 9, fol. 27 (Mar. 15, 1258): "confirmamus vobis . . . concambium quod fecit vobiscum Eximinus Petri de Pina de domibus et hereditate sua quas habebat in Valencia et suis terminis, quas dedit vobis pro castro et villa de Favara que vos dedistis." The commander appears in a general chapter at Alcañiz in 1307 (Vidiella, "Cartulario de Monroyo," pp. 185–186). See too *Itinerari*, pp. 272–273; Peter Alphonse, son of the former king of Portugal, was commander of Alcañiz in 1258. Favara was in the Cullera district and perhaps should be assimilated to modern Favareta.

42. Arch. Crown, Peter III, Reg. Canc. 40, fol. 21 (Sept. 18, 1277). Cf. the *Nomenclátor de Valencia*, p. 289. Zorita was an earlier possession; there is a commandery here in 1263 (Vidiella, "Cartulario de Monroyo," p. 181).

43. *Nomenclátor*, p. 182. Escolano, *Décadas*, I, 514.

44. Arch. Cath., pergs. 787, 5,010, 2,318, 1,317, 2,317 (Jan. 27, 1246); "quod cum quaestio sive controversia esset diutius agitata"; "aliis aliorum locorum quos dicti fratres dante domino per se adquirent, eripient et liberabunt de manibus Sarracenorum vel et aliunde cum armis vel sine armis."

45. *Ibid.* (perg. 1,317): "cum in dictis locis ecclesie fundate fuerint et clerici instituti populo Christiano . . . procurationes . . . debentur."

46. Document in Chapter VII, note 62.

47. Arch. Nac. Madrid, Poblet cartulary (B–1220), pp. 28–34, doc. 12.

48. Samper, *Montesa ilustrada*, II, docs. on pp. 825 ff. A. Sánchez Gozalbo, "Castillo de Cuevas de Avinromá," *BSCC*, XIV (1933), 294 (Dec. 6, 1248). Bayerri, *Tortosa*, VII, 457, misdates this as 1238.

49. *Colección diplomática*, doc. 111 (June 5, 1233); *Itinerari*, p. 104. "*Repartiment*" *de Burriana*, pp. 172–173 (Mar. 26, 1307), a confirmation of the grants of Carabona and Benaquite, by James II. On the "Cavalleria del Benaventurat Sent Jordi," see *Antigüedades de Valencia*, II, 100; Bayerri, *Historia de Tortosa*, VII, 521–525; Samper, *Montesa ilustrada*, I, 200 ff., II, 794 ff.; and M. R. Zapater, *Cister militante* (Zaragoza, 1662), p. 581.

50. See the principle as given by King James in Arch. Cath., perg. 1,307 (July 15, 1240).

51. *Repartimiento*, p. 206: "Fr. Geraldus de Prato commendator de Alfama." This becomes "Sancius Georgius," and the "in via de Daroca Sanctus Georgius parva" of pp. 593, 645.

52. The Murviedro properties do not appear until 1370, in an exemption from taxation; so these may have been much later acquisitions. Another document not quite so late (1303), shows them acquiring estates in Valencia, which occasions difficulties with local officials. Samper says in general only that they received "algunos lugares, alquerias, y tierras en esta ciudad y reyno" (Samper, *Montesa ilustrada*, II, 794 ff.).

53. Luis Más y Gil, "La orden de San Jorge de Alfama, sus maestres, y la cofradía de Mossén Sent Jordi," *Hidalguía*, X (1963), 247–256.

54. The confusion between the residence of the Order and the chapel of the

brotherhood is cleared up in *Antigüedades de Valencia* (I, 358–359n., and II, 96–101).

55. *Rationes decimarum*, I, 256, 263.

56. In Arch. Nac. Madrid, the Montesa documents (R13) have the Bujaraloz grant (Borialaroç) on alms of daily prayer for the king plus defense and settlement, to "Hospitali Sancti Georgii Dalfama et Fratribus eiusdem Hospitalis."

57. Miret y Sans, *Cases de templers*, pp. 365–366.

58. *Colección diplomática*, doc. 1,013 (Dec. 23, 1221): "nullam questiam vel peytam, nullam toltam vel forciam, nullam hostem vel cavalcatam, vel eorum redemptionem aliquam, nullumque malum servicium vel demandam, nullum bovaticum vel monetaticum, . . . herbaticum, . . . censum vel usaticum, nullam lezdam vel portaticum . . . nullamque aliam exaccionem regalem vel vicinalem." See also for privileges to the two Orders in Valencia the *Itinerari*, pp. 104, 105 and the Hospital cartularies cited there; also a number of specific documents of exemption for one or both Orders in Valencia during this period (e.g. pp. 104, 105, 472). A general privilege, based upon their defense and propagation of Christianity and upon their "extending of Christendom" ("ampliationem Christianitatis"), given by King James's father, is in Arch. Nac. Madrid, Ords. Milits., Montesa, R14–15 (Jan. 27, 1208). At the Burriana siege the Hospitallers and Templars elicited from King James a confirmation of all previous privileges, somewhat against his will (*Llibre dels feyts*, ch. 165).

59. Zurita, *Anales*, I, *lib.* iii, *c.* 36.

60. *Llibre dels feyts*, ch. 95.

61. These are William Hugh in 1235, Peter of Exea in 1238 (cf. *Antigüedades de Valencia*, I, 296), Peter of Alcalá in 1250 and 1252 (Sanchís Sivera has him here in 1233 in the *Nomenclátor*, p. 392), Peter of Granyen in 1253, Gerard Amich in 1257, Guy or Hugh de la Vespa in 1264, Simon of Luna in 1267 (*Itinerari*, p. 400), Berengar of Almenara in 1273 (*ibid.*, p. 489), and Raymond of Ribelles in 1283. The master "in the five realms of Spain" was Roderick Gil in 1240, receiving the Denia grants in Valencia, and Ferdinand Ruiz or Roderick in 1253 and 1265.

62. Bernard of Miravalls in 1290, and Peter of Soler in 1304 (Miret y Sans, *Cases de templers*, p. 251).

63. *Llibre dels feyts*, chs. 127–128.

64. *Ibid.*, ch. 97.

65. Escolano was much puzzled by this; unable to solve it by documentation, he suggested the untenable theory that they were a parish church in the early years (*Décadas*, I, 515). The rather discredited *Trobes* of James Febrèr speaks of a particular Hospitaller contingent when considering the Hospitaller knight Peter Matoses, "cap dels demés de sa Religió," a man who "en armes è en lletres fonch molt erudit" (*troba* 318, p. 171).

66. S. García Larragueta, in his *El gran priorado de Navarra de la orden de San Juan de Jerusalén, siglos xii–xiii*, 2 vols. (Pamplona, 1957); restated again in his "El carácter de los primeros establecimientos de la orden de San Juan en el reino de Navarra," *Annales de l'ordre souverain militaire de Malte*, XIX (1961), 18–23. On the Order at this period see also Anthony Luttrell, "The Aragonese Crown and the Knights Hospitallers of Rhodes: 1291–1310," *English Historical Review*, LXXVI (1961), 1–19.

67. Arch. Nac. Madrid, Ords. Milits., Montesa, R4 (April 1171): "castella in hyspania . . . cerveria scilicet et chulleria"; and R18 (Sept. 6, 1210) for the rights "in Villa de Burriana et infra omnes terminos suos." For Olocau see Miret y Sans, *Cases de templers*, pp. 126, 251. On Oropesa see the grant in "Colección de cartas pueblas," no. LXXI, *BSCC*, XXIII (1947), 279–280; and Ramón de María,

"Oropesa, por donación y cambio, para la orden de San Juan del Hospital," *ibid.*, pp. 283-286. See also Arch. Crown, Peter III, Reg. Canc. 40, fol. 150v (Aug. 30, 1278); and in Arch. Nac. Madrid, Montesa, R98 (Sept. 3, 1250); and notes 80, 127.

68. *Cartulaire général de l'ordre des hospitaliers de S. Jean de Jérusalem (1100–1310)*, ed. J. Delaville Le Roulx, 4 vols. (Paris, 1894-1901), II, doc. 2,201 (June 12, 1238). The estate "Damocrem" refers to the previous holder "Amocres."

69. *Colección diplomática*, doc. 105 (Jan. 15, 1233) for Torrente, Silla. Possession was taken of both, in April 1238 (Fernando Llorca, *Una fundación del siglo xiii, San Juan del Hospital de Valencia* [Valencia, 1930], p. 46; document also given on pp. 46–47n.). See *Nomenclátor de Valencia*, p. 389. Samper has the Hospital holding Sueca still at the end of the century (Samper, *Montesa ilustrada*, I, 14n.); and King James has the Amposta commander ill here in 1273: "in quodam loco ipsius ordinis nomine Zuecha qui est in Termino de Cuyllera" (*Itinerari*, p. 489).

70. Arch. Nac. Madrid, Ords. Milits., Montesa, R28, and copies on R29-30 (June 28, 1233): "que fuerunt et tenebant Abdezalem Sarracenus . . . cum tota illa hereditate her[e]ma et populata que pertinebat eidem Sarraceno." For a different version of this grant, see R39-40 (Nov. 9).

71. *Ibid.*, R33; copies in R34-36 (July 25, 1233): "et universis."

72. *"Repartiment" de Burriana*, p. 35 (June 11, 1234).

73. Arch. Nac. Madrid, Montesa, R50, copies on 51-53 (Dec. 23, 1235): an alod "per puram concessionem, donationem et confirmationem nostram." Copy in Bibl. Univ. Val., codex 145, no. 10.

74. Aguilar, *Noticias de Segorbe*, I, 77. Pope Gregory IX set up a commission of inquiry on the dispute on December 7, 1236. Cf. *Privilegios reales*, p. 79. They won the churches and church revenues of Castielfabib. The Temple too has rents here.

75. *Cartulaire de l'ordre des hospitaliers*, II, doc. 2,220, on February 5, before the city's fall. See also *Nomenclátor de Valencia*, p. 49, and Miret y Sans, *Cases de templers*, p. 251.

76. *Colección diplomática*, doc. 1,046 (*an.* 1243), for San Mateo. Arch. Crown, Peter III, Reg. Canc. 41, fol. 102 (July 5, 1279) for Cálig, a royal order to Peñíscola officials: "restituatis et tradatis Comendatori Cervarie ordinis hospitalis possessionem loci de Calix et omnibus fructibus . . ." See also the dispute involving Cálig in James I, perg. 1,451.

77. The story of the Hospitallers in Cullera is told by A. Piles Ibars, *Historia de Cullera* (Sueca, 1893), esp. ch. 12. A 1241 arbitration gave the castle and half the countryside to the Order, half to the king; Arch. Crown, James I, perg. 15; Arch. Cath., perg. 1,307; *Itinerari*, p. 143; published in Hospital *Cartulaire*, II, doc. 2,254; cf. also doc. 2,363 where the Order settles a Cullera farm on a widow. A privilege in Arch. Crown, James I, perg. 1,456, allows them to have a Cullera justiciar elected with all civil and criminal justice. On Sueca see *Privilegios reales*, p. 68.

78. Arch. Nac. Madrid, Ords. Milits., Montesa, R71 (July 18, 1240): "quasdam bonas domos in Denia et decem iovatas." *Cartulaire*, II, 2,255. See also Arch. Crown, Real Patrimonio, Real Casa, extra series (James I), doc. no. 68.

79. Arch. Nac. Madrid, *ibid.*, R100, copies on 101-102 (April 5, 1252): "quoddam Alfondicum in Xativa . . . ad opus faciendi domos."

80. "Colección de cartas pueblas," no. LXXIII, *BSCC*, XXIII (1947), 280-282. See also the *Llibre dels feyts*, ch. 230, for their holding Burriana early. At the siege of Foyos, to cite an example of small but important gifts, King James gave the provincial master of the Hospitallers the fifth-share of a Burriana mill he had

acquired (*Itinerari*, p. 118; Arch. Nac. Madrid, Ords. Milits., Montesa, R49, June 25, 1235). On the Traiguera and similar holdings in dispute, see below, p. 188.

81. *Nomenclátor de Valencia*, p. 283.

82. Its secular settlement document of 1241 which later came into Montesa hands is in Arch. Nac. Madrid, Montesa codex Poblaciones, fol. 37v. On Hospitaller possession see *Privilegios reales*, p. 81; *Nomenclátor*, p. 340.

83. Arch. Crown, Peter III, Reg. Canc. 41, fol. 91 (June 3, 1279): "dummodo domus hospitalis Burriane solvat vobis illos denarios cene . . . non petatis ab ipsis hominibus de Vilaphameç ipsam cenam, cum dictis locus sit . . . sub dicta domo . . ." There is a statement of tithe customs for Villafamés, drawn by the Hospital in 1283, close to the rules of James in 1268; cf. "Declaración de costumbres de Villafamés," *BSCC*, III (1922), 390-393; it is in the series "Colección de cartas pueblas," though the settlement charter had already been given in 1241 and may be found here on pp. 264-265. The Hospital undertook settlement projects at Villafamés in 1283 and Perpunchent in 1289; they bought the *mero et mixto imperio* jurisdiction over Villafamés from the crown in 1312 for 35,000 solidi of Barcelona.

84. Samper, *Montesa ilustrada*, I, 14n. See *Privilegios reales*, p. 79.

85. *Cartulaire*, III, doc. 3,735 (Dec. 2, 1280). Arch. Crown, Peter III, perg. 222 (*idem*). See also E. Bayerri, *Llibre de privilegis de la vila de Ulldecona, cartulario de la militar y soberana orden de San Juan de Jerusalén (ahora de Malta) en su comendadoría de Ulldecona* . . . (Tortosa, 1951), p. 13. Cf. Miret y Sans, *Cases de templers*, p. 251; *Privilegios reales*, pp. 77, 81; *Nomenclátor de Valencia*, p. 340. See too the Onda documents and settlement in Arch. Nac. Madrid, Montesa codex Poblaciones i privilegios, index ("de la vila i moreries donda"); and Ords. Milits., Montesa, R87-90 (April 28, 1248), description in non-Hospitaller license.

86. Torrente should be the key commandery for the Valencia kingdom (see note 95 with text), but Miret y Sans found no commander before the fourteenth century. Miret believes there was a residence at Morella. For Roslain (Roscelin?) see Momblanch, *Historia de la Albufera*, documentary appendix, doc. 1 (Oct. 20, 1242); for Guerard and Silla's William see *Antigüedades*, I, 296-297; for Granyen or Grañana see Llorca, *San Juan*, p. 47; for John of Paris, Arch. Cath., perg. 2,391, Sept. 18; cf. also Miret, *Cases de templers*, pp. 126, 251. Miravalls is commander "bajulie Valencie." Samper puts a commandery at Perpunchent at least at the beginning of the next century (*Montesa ilustrada*, I, 14n.). Raymond of "Ciri" commands in 1235 at Oropesa. The 1237 Rossell settlement charter gives "Valleforti" and "Bellovicino." Sanchís Sivera has Peter of Queralt at Valencia city in 1244 (*Nomenclátor*, p. 392); this seems unlikely: cf. note 121. "Valfort" is conjectural for "de Valleforti", perhaps in Languedoc.

87. Arch. Cath., pergs. 1,315, 2,313 (both Oct. 28, 1243); 2,411, 2,314, 4,104 (all Oct. 29, 1243); and 2,315 (Aug. 31, 1244). Cullera received the attention of a separate document. The day after the accord was signed, Amposta issued a settlement charter to Silla, in which the castellan noted: "decimam et primiciam quam nobis et domui Hospitalis de omnibus fructibus prebeatis" ("Colección de cartas pueblas," no. IV, *BSCC*, II [1921], 23-24). Later one finds them (1283) receiving only a third of the tithe at Castielfabib; but this may refer merely to the portion credited to the account of the non-Valencian commandery at Aliaga. Were Montroy and Macastre under direct Hospitaller control in the thirteenth century? It is likely; but perhaps only the patronage of the church was theirs. Both places were given to Roderick of Lizana in 1238, and their subsequent ownership is obscure; in 1319 Bernard of Boxadós held Macastre, and later the count of Buñol; in 1436 the order of Montesa secured the lordship of Montroy.

88. Arch. Cath., perg. 4,104 (Oct. 29, 1243); and perg. 2,391 (Sept. 28, 1255).

89. See, for example, the notice of appeal to Rome, in Arch. Cath., perg. 4,647 (July 16, 1263). This argument concerned injuries the knights claimed to have suffered from the chapter in the latter's capacity as lord of Albal. The chapter protests: "non concedimus dictas iniurias esse illatas per nos nec dicta dampna esse data. . . . Item quia ospitalarii nullum Iudicem habent supra se nisi Romanum pontificem . . . ad eundem tanquam ad specialem iudicem nostrum incontinenti nunc ut tunc appellamus." On their litigation with the Calatrava knights, see note 97.

90. *Cartulaire*, III, doc. 3,091 (April 8, 1264).

91. See Chapter XII, note 15 and text.

92. Samper, *Montesa ilustrada*, part 4, art. 4.

93. Arch. Cath. Tortosa, cartulary no. VIII, fols. 90–92 (1243). On the Hospitallers in the Tortosa diocese, especially outside the kingdom of Valencia, see Bayerri, *Historia de Tortosa*, VII, 499 ff., 513–521.

94. The conjecture of Llorca, based upon their usual custom; he also says flatly that theirs was the first church opened to worship after the cathedral (*San Juan del Hospital*, pp. 31, 22). The castellan of Amposta Peter of Egea had received a sizable pre-grant of buildings here on April 26, 1238 (*Antigüedades de Valencia*, I, 296). Teixidor offers a more solid evidence for hospital work in Valencia city, from the unusual extent of their cemetery and the supply of oils for the last sacraments.

95. Llorca, *San Juan del Hospital*, pp. 44–45; but see above, note 86. The *comensales* are beneficed chaplains who are not really brothers (p. 45); there were other beneficed "outside" priests attached to the house. On non-Hospitaller care of the church see the reference, to past custom, in *Lettres communes de Jean XXII*, VII, 118–119, no. 30,882 (Dec. 30, 1327).

96. Arch. Cath., perg. 2,391 (Sept. 28, 1255).

97. *Antigüedades de Valencia*, II, 254–255 (Jan. 20, 1241). They proceeded to carry on extensive litigation with Calatrava over the intervening space, until 1273 (*ibid.*).

98. Llorca, *San Juan del Hospital*, p. 51; *Antigüedades de Valencia*, I, 296–297. On William, see above, Chapter IX, note 99.

99. Llorca, *San Juan*, p. 52; *Antigüedades*, I, 299–300. On Dalmau, see above, p. 127 with note 99.

100. *Cartulaire*, II, doc. 3,091; Simon of Luesia is the Roderick Ximèn de Luesia below, in note 134. He was at the king's side in many important affairs between 1221 and 1237, giving James Chivert in 1237 for Foyos (*Itinerari*, pp. 38, 45, 49, 51, 56, 57, 79, 86, 89, 91, 94, 96, 105, 108, 109, 112, 114, 115, 117, 118, 122, 128).

101. I was unable to see her tomb in Valencia, but was assured by the caretaker that it had been all but destroyed during the bombings of the recent civil war. See Llorca, *San Juan del Hospital*, pp. 52 ff.; *Antigüedades de Valencia*, I, 300–301; also D. J. Geanakoplos, *Emperor Michael Palaeologus and the West, 1258–1282: A Study in Byzantine-Latin Relations* (Cambridge, Mass., 1959), pp. 48, 60, 144–145; and Gustave Schlumberger, "Le tombeau d'une imperatrice Byzantine a Valence en Espagne," *Byzance et croisades, pages médiévales* (Paris, 1927), pp. 57–86, with plates.

102. Arch. Cath., perg. 1,351 (June 24, 1274): "eligo sepulturam meam in cimiterio hospitalis sancti Iohannis Ierosolomitani"; three hundred solidi are to be used to pay his debts "et pro ornamentis sepulture mee."

103. Arch. Cath., perg. 1,354 (Sept. 30, 1276): "et dimitto hospitali sancti Iohanis decem sol."

104. Llorca, *San Juan del Hospital*, p. 32. This monograph furnishes interesting

photographs of the elements remaining from the Gothic church, as well as a map exactly situating it in the streets of modern Valencia.

105. Mundy, *Toulouse*, pp. 4–5.

106. Bayerri, *Historia de Tortosa*, VII, 143–145; e.g. Ulldecona 1222, Amposta 1226, Godall 1228, Pauls 1228 and 1239, Mas de Barberáns 1235, Carles 1237, Alfara 1237, Alcanar 1238, La Vall 1238.

107. Some of these are published in the series "Colección de cartas pueblas," in *BSCC*. No. IV is for Silla (1243; see above, note 87). No. LXXIV is for Cervera (1235; XXIII [1947], 389–390). No. LXXXVII is for Rossell (1237; XXXVII [1961], 127–129). The charter for Sueca, and other places of the Cullera district, has been edited by Roque Chabás in *El archivo* (1244; II [1888–1889], 386–390, and see 205–208). A license to settle Cullera is in Arch. Nac. Madrid (Ords. Milits., Montesa, R98; Sept. 3, 1250), by which both the king and the Amposta castellan allow John of Paris, preceptor of the Valencia house, "plenariam potestatem stabiliendi et populandi ad octavum omnes alquerias et terminum Castri de Cuylera." The Cervera, San Mateo, and Carrascal charters are in copy at Bibl. Univ. Val., codex 145. Many of the settlements are indicated in *Privilegios reales*, section III, *passim*; see too the Montesa codex in Arch. Nac. Madrid, Poblaciones (index *sub* "Cervera"), and also the *Nomenclátor de Valencia*, pp. 341, 392–394, and *passim*.

108. *Nomenclátor*, p. 406.

109. *Privilegios*, pp. 11–12. See Luttrell, "Aragonese Crown and Hospitallers," p. 6 and *passim* for background and details.

110. Soldevila, *Pere el Gran*, IV, [pt. 2, I], 100, doc. 87.

111. For example, in 1332 King Alphonse reminded Montesa and the Hospital that they were obliged to defend the Valencia frontier as long as the current war lasted, and not only for the king's lands but for those of the barons (Arch. Crown, Liber patrimonii regni Valentiae, fol. 185r).

112. Arch. Nac. Madrid, Ords. Milits., Montesa, R14–15 (Jan. 27, 1208): "attendentes quam fideliter, quam solicite, quamque devote Fratres militie templi, ubicumque christiane fidei religio viget, eius propagationi et defensioni intendunt; considerantes etiam quam utiles, quam fideles, et quam necessarii fuerunt predecessoribus nostris in omnibus, que ad ampliationem christianitatis visa sunt expedire, et quantum nos ipsos in nostris necessitatibus curaverunt adiuvare . . ." Background information and bibliography on the Order may conveniently be found in Thomas W. Parker, *The Knights Templars in England* (Tucson, Ariz., 1963); the Order's knights, of noble lineage, may not have numbered more than four or five hundred; the dark-robed sergeants, often serving as light-armed troops, and the menial brothers, were numerous (pp. 7, 135–136).

113. Arch. Nac. Madrid, *ibid.*, R70–74 (Oct. 18, 1238): "reducentes ad memoriam grata servitia que vos . . . nobis fecistis et facitis cotidie et fecistis specialiter nunc in adquisicione Civitatis et Regni Valentie."

114. *Llibre dels feyts*, ch. 559. The *Trobes*, for what it is worth, has "Donis Sent Feliu, frances de nació" as one Templar on the crusade (*troba* 465, p. 245); and a Peter Boix from Pau in Languedoc ("entre los Templaris assistí en la guerra," *troba* 202, p. 63); and the Templar John Matoses (perhaps related to the Hospitaller Peter Matoses of *troba* 318; *troba* 317, p. 170). In the *Llibre dels feyts* James several times speaks of their military service in the war, as in ch. 235 where the contingents of the Hospital, Temple, Calatrava, and Santiago appear.

115. *Itinerari*, p. 93.

116. *Llibre*, ch. 165; *Itinerari*, pp. 104–105.

117. *Llibre*, ch. 192; *Itinerari*, pp. 118, 129.

118. *Llibre*, ch. 295.

119. *Itinerari*, pp. 167, 218.

120. *Ibid.*, p. 276.

121. Samper, *Montesa ilustrada*, doc. on II, 822 (Pontons); *Llibre dels feyts*, ch. 446, gives Queralt as one "who held the place of the master of the Temple." On Queralt, who may not have been a Templar himself, see *Itinerari*, pp. 63, 133, 134, 174, 219, 228, 244, 459, 467, 489, 505, 515, 578.

122. *Itinerari*, pp. 400, 473, 480, 496–497.

123. *Llibre dels feyts*, ch. 559; *Itinerari*, p. 536. Berengar of St. Just was master for Aragon and Catalonia in 1283.

124. *Itinerari*, pp. 167, 385. Though the citations for all the men in this paragraph are to the printed sources, names of other provincial masters do not stand out in the Barcelona and Madrid registers. Zapater in his *Cister militante* gives Astrug of "Claramont" in 1239, Bartholomew of Belvis (lt.) in 1276 (p. 110). In Majorca, a situation analogous to that of Valencia, it is interesting to know that there was a series of seventeen commanders from 1234 to 1300, of terms varying from two to ten years, a series of four lieutenants for them (1239–1300) resident for Pollensa, six rectors and vicars in a series from 1252 to 1300 at the church of Pollensa, and four bailiffs (Rotger y Capllonch, *Historia de Pollensa*, I, 44–46).

125. Arch. Cath., perg. 2,441, a local agreement; one cannot be sure that there is nothing earlier. The care with which similar general agreements were preserved, both at the cathedral and in the records of the Orders, inclines one to believe that none was made, though the suppression of the Temple may have led to neglect about documents whose subjects were already covered in other agreements held by the group taking over the properties. The time lapse was similar to that in Majorca a few years earlier; after a rough working agreement had led to difficulties, an arbitration had been arranged in 1240; some of its provisions being ill-defined, renewed quarrels led to a definitive arbitration in 1257 (Rotger y Capllonch, *Pollensa*, I, 35).

126. Arch. Nac. Madrid, Ords. Milits., Montesa, R113, copy on 114; and also in Arch. Crown, James I, Reg. Canc. 11, fol. 167v (June 21, 1259): "magis utile et fructuosum domui"; there had been an oven here in the first place, and its concession was meant to allow room for a cemetery; instead, the Templars after some reflection rebuilt the oven and obtained from the king a confirmation and a monopoly on baking for their section of the city. Their preoccupation with ovens was also noticed by Miret y Sans (*Cases de templers*, p. 257).

127. Arch. Nac. Madrid, *ibid.*, R1 (November 1169): "illud castrum de Xivert, et illud castrum quod vulgo dicitur Or[o]pesa." See too *Colección diplomática*, doc. 112 (July 22, 1233); and "Colección de cartas pueblas," no. XLII, *BSCC*, XIV (1933), 169–170.

128. On Oropesa see notes 67, 80, 127.

129. Arch. Nac. Madrid, *ibid.*, R7 (July 18, 1181): "castrum de Mont-Tornes, quandocumque Deus . . . pervenire concesserit."

130. Arch. Nac. Madrid, *ibid.*, R19 (Nov. 5, 1211): "cum turre . . . et cum omnibus terminis."

131. Miret y Sans, *Cases de templers*, p. 254.

132. Arch. Nac. Madrid, Ords. Milits., Montesa, R20 (May 22, 1213): "de Qullar, quam cito deus illud deus [*sic*] dederit." And see the copy in "Colección de cartas pueblas," no. XXIX, *BSCC*, XI (1930), 355–357; it was given "cum omnibus ecclesiis que ibi et infra termino[s] supradictos construentur et fient vel forte facte sunt, cum hereditatibus et iuribus omnibus mesquitarum et primiciis,

464 NOTES TO CHAPTER TEN

oblacionibus et defuncionibus et aliis ecclesiarum iuribus universis . . . salvo tamen iure episcopali."

133. The Order bought it on March 27, 1303 ("Colección de cartas pueblas," no. XXXII; see above, Chapter IX, note 167 and text). In 1274 Santiago had negotiated for Culla and may briefly have held it. The Hospitallers appear to have had it, or to have claimed it, toward the end of the century.

134. The royal grant of Chivert to Roderick Simon of Luesia (or Llucia, perhaps Lluça castle) is in the "Colección de cartas pueblas," no. XLII (see above, notes 100, 127). The grant to the Temple is in no. XLIV (July 22, 1233), *ibid.*, pp. 172–173. See too Arch. Nac. Madrid, Montesa, R54, where James defends their holding of the "Castrum illud et Villam" against Roderick (Mar. 15, 1236). On Pulpis see below, note 173.

135. Arch. Nac. Madrid, Ords. Milits., Montesa, R25, copies in 26–27 (June 17, 1233): "Alqueriam que dicitur Benahamet, et Alqueriam que dicitur Mantella, que sunt in termino Burriane." The Arch. Crown cartulary has "Benaham" (reg. 310, fol. 46r).

136. Arch. Crown, James I, perg. 495 ("quandam partem ville noviter acquisite"); *Colección diplomática*, doc. 114 (July 25, 1233). "Colección de cartas pueblas," no. LII, *BSCC*, XV (1934), 68–69. Copies too in Arch. Nac. Madrid, Ords. Milits., Montesa, R37–38.

137. Arch. Nac. Madrid, Montesa, R57, and copies on 58–59 (Sept. 15, 1237): "alqueriam nostram que dicitur Cecha que est in Burriana cum terminis et pertinenciis suis, cum introitibus et exitibus, cum melioramentis ibi factis et faciendis, cum pratis, pascuis, herbis, aquis, et lignis." The Arch. Crown cartulary has "Sera," i.e. Serra (Reg. 310, fol. 47).

138. Arch. Crown, James I, perg. 960; cf. *Colección diplomática*, doc. 273; *El archivo*, II (1887–1888), 350.

139. Arch. Nac. Madrid, Montesa, R80, copy on 81 (May 29, 1246): "per alodium proprium, franchum et liberum, turrim et Alcheriam que vocatur Moncada sitam in orta sive termino Civitatis Valencie quam emimus a Petro de Montecatano et Alcheriam que vocatur Carpesa, quam emimus a Bernardo Vitalis notario nostro, et undecim iovatas terre, quas emimus a Guialmono Scriba nostro." See also *Colección diplomática*, docs. 293, 299. Carpesa had been given to Bernard Vidal of Besalú on May 28, 1238; the king recovered it and gave it to the Templars in 1246; they and their successors of Montesa would keep it.

140. Arch. Nac. Madrid, *ibid.*, R92, copy on 93 (Oct. 13, 1248): "quasdam domos infra muros Ville de Liria . . . de una turre ad aliam et continet in se tres Turres duorum murorum."

141. "*Repartiment*" *de Burriana*, p. 63 (Oct. 24, 1249).

142. *Nomenclátor de Valencia*, p. 142.

143. Miret y Sans, *Cases de templers*, p. 341. *Colección diplomática*, doc. 925 (June 23, 1266): "domos . . . et algorfam ipsarum domorum. . . . Quae quidem domos sunt in Murcia in parte Christianorum, secundum quod eas assignavimus et dedimus ordini supradicto, quando in civitate Murcie eramus personaliter constituti. . . . Damus eciam . . . ortum."

144. Arch. Nac. Madrid, Ords. Milits., Montesa, R141 (Aug. 1, 1283): "inde medietatem nobis pertinentem, et collector Templi aliam medietatem."

145. Escolano, *Décadas*, I, 588. The church here belonged to the Segorbe bishop who yielded it to the Valencia diocese in 1277.

146. The Templars have Peñíscola in the *Repartimiento* (see Miret y Sans, *Cases de templers*, pp. 256–257). The castle and town were actually given by a grant of September 15, 1294 (see below, note 148).

147. Arch. Nac. Madrid, Ords. Milits., Montesa, R99 (Sept. 10, 1251): "de hereditate vestra de Maçaroyos et de hereditate . . . subtus cequiam de Moncada," from Simon Peter of Arenós to the Temple, here confirmed. *Nomenclátor*, p. 118, for Benifaraig.

148. Arch. Nac. Madrid, Montesa, R274-276 (Sept. 15, 1294) and R159-160 (Sept. 18, 1294). See Bayerri, *Llibre de privilegis de Ulldecona*, pp. 13, 76-79.

149. *Colección diplomática*, doc. 1064 (Aug. 27, 1250): "quia nobis constat quod fratres templi eiecerunt violenter vos . . . monachos monasterii de Beniffaçano de possessione de Raffalgari quam vos tenebatis . . . restituimus vobis . . ." This is not the Rafelguaraf near Játiva, but a town just across the Tortosa border (no longer existing; see the story below, in Chapter XII, notes 47-48, 60, and text).

150. For Moncada folk, for example, from "leudas, pedagia, vel portagia, seu passagia" (Arch. Nac. Madrid, Ords. Milits., Montesa, R120-121 [Mar. 19, 1268]). Or see the general privilege of James I, extended in 1294, in R156-157.

151. Arch. Crown, Canc., Cart., Reg. 310, fol. 47 (1235).

152. Arch. Crown, James I, Reg. Canc. 10, fol. 82v (July 1, 1258); cartulary, Reg. 310, fol. 54). For the earlier documents, see "*Repartiment*" *de Burriana*, p. 62; *Colección diplomática*, doc. 329 (July 21, 1247). For Almenara and Morella see *Col. dip.*, doc. 380; May 19. On the Templars as bankers and money lenders, cf. the English experience in Parker, *Knights Templars*, pp. 58-80.

153. Arch. Nac. Madrid, Montesa, R68 (Oct. 18, 1238): "illam turrim magnam in Valentia, que est ad portam que dicitur Bebaxachaç cum mure et barbacana et cum omnibus domibus."

154. *Colección diplomática*, doc. 299 (May 29, 1246): "frater Gauterius" signs as commander of "Valencia and Villela"; Miret y Sans argues that the actual commandery perhaps did not exist.

155. See Miret y Sans, *Cases de templers*, p. 156.

156. Bach is in Arch. Crown, James I, perg. 1,787; Ça Corbella is *ibid.*, Peter III, perg. 183. Bergua is *ibid.*, perg. 468. Peyronet is "comendatori Burriane et elemosinario nostro" in Arch. Nac. Mad., Montesa, R132 (1276). See also *Cartoral dels templers de les comandes de Gardeny y Barbens*, ed. J. Miret y Sans (Barcelona, 1899), p. 21.

157. Arch. Crown, James I, Reg. Canc. 16, fol. 249v (June 26, 1271): "patuum ad opus domorum ad portam civitatis domus templi Valencie, [quod: *margin cut*] affrontat in mesquita que ibi est"; and James I, perg. 2,077.

158. A copy of this clarification of October 22, 1238 is among the Order's papers (Arch. Nac. Madrid, Montesa, R69-70: "Cimitaria, Meschite omnes, magne et parve").

159. *Colección diplomática*, doc. 299 (May 29, 1246): "retento nobis iure nostro in duabus partibus decime quam episcopus et capitulum percipit in Ruçafa . . . immo contra episcopum et dictum capitulum . . . ius nostrum libere intentare possimus."

160. Arch. Cath., pergs. 2,437, 2,433 (Jan. 19, 1262: xiv *kals.* February 1262 *an. inc.*).

161. In May of 1282 Peter ordered a farmer of revenues to stop molesting the Burriana Templars for a tithe of their lands or else to take the case before a royal judge (Arch. Crown, Peter III, Reg. Canc. 61, fol. 187).

162. Arch. Crown, Peter III, Reg. Canc. 50, fol. 162v (July 18, 1281): "quam tertiam partem baiulus anni preteriti emparavit."

163. Arch. Cath. Tortosa, cajón Subtesorería, no. 95 (1251); cajón Diezmos, no. 17 (1243); cartulary II, fols. 127 ff. (1263). Samper, *Montesa ilustrada*, II, 822 ff. "*Repartiment*" *de Burriana*, pp. 48-55 (May 14).

164. Arch. Crown, Peter III, Reg. Canc. 42, fol. 230 (Mar. 7, 1280): "instituit unum presbiterim in capella domus Templi in Valencia." See also the documents in Arch. Nac. Madrid, Ords. Milits., Montesa, R134 (Mar. 7, and May 12, 1280).

165. The original grant to William was on April 30, 1238; a copy bearing the date of the transfer to the Temple (Oct. 30) is in Arch. Nac. Madrid, Montesa, R63: "Alqueriam de Barbatur, et domos in Valencia." See also the *Nomenclátor*, p. 155 (May 2, 1238); and *Privilegios reales*, p. 67 (Oct. 30, 1238). On William of (Ça) Portella see *Itinerari*, pp. 44, 54, 131, 174.

166. Arch. Crown, James I, perg. 1,556 (Jan. 29, 1258).

167. Arch. Cath., perg. 1,354 (Sept. 30, 1276).

168. Escolano tells of the tomb and of a chapel from the family (*Décadas*, I, 514). Zanoguera (Sa Noguera) is among the knights summoned by name in 1275 to help the king fight the Valencian Moslems (*Itinerari*, p. 526).

169. See will in Chapter VII, note 59. His knights and esquires are to receive something, and much is to be divided "inter Templarios et alios religiosos."

170. A series of thirteen inventories of movable properties in the Templar houses of Aragon and Catalonia, in 1289-1299, unfortunately include only one Valencian commandery; and they date from the more peaceful last decade of the century ("Inventaris de les cases del temple de la corona d'Aragó en 1289," ed. J. Miret y Sans, *BRABL*, VI [1911], 61-75). Later inventories (1308 ff.) made by order of the king may be seen in "Inventaris inèdits de l'ordre del temple a Catalunya" (ed. J. Rubió et alii, Institut d'estudis catalans, *Anuari*, I [1907], 385-407). There is an inventory of liturgical books and objects of Peñíscola castle (pp. 391, 393-396, 405-406), and for Játiva castle (p. 399); they indicate a good amount of revenue but not great wealth.

171. Arch. Crown, James I, perg. 881 (1242).

172. *Lettres communes de Jean XXII*, VI, 264, no. 26,053 (July 23, 1326): "domos et possessiones in civitate Valentina, ac in de Cervaria, de Peniscola, de Xivert, de Polpiz, de Lescoves, de Cuylla, de Ares, de Onda, de Villafamez et de Perpuxen castris, et in locis de Castrofabib et de Adamiis, ac in de Burriana et de Cuecha villis et in eorum territoriis consistentes, Dertusen., Valentin., et Segobricen. . . . cum caeteris bonis . . . in regno Valentie." The list refers also to Hospitaller lands acquired, but in the main concerns Templar holdings. Cf. with it no. 64,315 (in XIII, 228) of March 30, 1323: "per earum infeudationem" with a yearly rental and share in profits. For Hospitaller ownership of Perpunchent and Villafamés in the thirteenth century see above, notes 82, 83.

173. Arch. Nac. Madrid, Montesa codex, Poblaciones, index and fols. 16-17 (1245); cf. *Nomenclátor de Valencia*, p. 155. The Order gets a third of the produce. See also *Privilegios reales*, pp. 67, 75-76 (where Forcalquier is erroneously made a Templar), 143-144. As an example of Templar settlement policy the later (1287) charter for settling Pulpis is conveniently published in the "Colección de cartas pueblas," no. LXXV, *BSCC*, XXIV (1948), 65-66.

174. *Privilegios*, pp. 9-11, editorial comment. There is a useful Temple cartulary in the Arch. Nac. Madrid (codices, sig. mod. 1,312). No. 50 is a confirmation by Innocent IV of all the castles and properties given them by James I (Jan. 4, 1245): "tots castels, les possessions e los altres bens los cals lo car encrist fiyl nostre Rey Darago noble avos ab piadosa endiscreta voluntat dona axi con les letres . . ." There are formidable privileges (e.g. no. 114), Valencian pre-grants (no. 125), and tax exemptions such as "dalcun logar del regne d[e] Valencia . . . pagar alcunys leudes peatges portages o passatges en alcun logar" (no. 180; Mar. 19, 1267). See also the codex, sig. mod. 1,032. In Arch. Crown see the cartulary in reg. 309 (Liber privilegiorum templariorum); and especially that in reg. 310 (Privilegia templari-

orum), fols. 43–54, for such acquisitions as Chivert, the Gandía market, the Valencia tower, and Carpesa. See also Manuel Magallón, "Los templarios de la corona de Aragón, índice de su cartulario del siglo xiii," *BRAH*, XXXIII (1898), 451–463; and his "Templarios y hospitalarios, primer cartulario en el archivo histórico nacional," *ibid.*, pp. 257–266.

175. *Privilegios reales*, p. 10.

176. *Ibid.*

NOTES TO CHAPTER XI. THE MENDICANT ORDERS

1. In Arch. Crown, James I, Reg. Canc. 13, fol. 171 (May 11, 1264) James sentences a culprit to crusade because of his crime of murder. *Ibid.*, Bulas, legajo VI, no. 17, a letter of instruction to the bishop of Barcelona, who was organizing the Valencian crusade, arranges for the absolution of men who had burned down churches or engaged in trading weapons to the Moors. The rebels of Narbonne are in Pierre Belperron, *La croisade contre les albigeois et l'union du Languedoc à la France, 1209-1249* (Paris, 1946), p. 409. At the end of the great Languedocian uprising (from 1242) thousands were convicted by the Inquisition; but the bishop of Albi got many sentences commuted to crusading in Egypt (1247); see Louis de Lacger, "L'albigeois au siècle de Saint Louis, les évêques Durand de Beaucaire et Bernard de Combret, 1228–1271," *Revue d'histoire ecclésiastique*, LII (1957), 42–43.

2. Ximénez ed., p. 155; Ubieto ed., p. 152. The origins and nature of the Mendicant movement with the premovement and psychology producing it are explored in G. G. Meersseman's *Dossier de l'ordre de la pénitence au xiiie siècle*, Spicilegium friburgense, no. 7 (Fribourg, 1961). On the Mendicant movement see Felix Vernet, *Les ordres mendiants* (Paris, 1933); and on the several Orders in towns of King James which are now French see R. W. Emery, *The Friars in Medieval France, a Catalogue of French Mendicant Convents, 1200-1550* (New York, 1962).

3. Luke Wadding, *Annales minorum seu trium ordinum a S. Francisco institutorum*, 3rd ed. revised, 31 vols. to date (Quaracchi, 1931–   ), I, lxxi, 367, and III, xlvii, 272. *Acta sanctorum*, ed. Jean Bolland *et al.*, 67 vols. to date (Paris, 1863–   ), August, VI, 495–496. León Amorós Payá, "Los santos mártires franciscanos B. Juan de Perusa y B. Pedro de Saxoferrato en la historia de Teruel," *Teruel*, XV (1956), 5–142, especially 28–46. *Episcopologio valentino*, ch. 26. From the Moslem side, see Ibn 'Idārī al-Marrākušī (1173-1232), *Al-Bayān al-mugrib fi-ijtiṣār ajbār muluk al-Andalus wa al-Magrib, Los Almohades*, ed.-tr. A. Huici Miranda, 2 vols. (Tetuan, 1953-1954), I, 321.

4. Morera, *Tarragona cristiana*, II, 480.

5. Further data may be drawn from Anastasio López, *La provincia de España de los frailes menores, apuntes histórico-críticos sobre los orígenes de la orden franciscana en España* (Santiago, 1915); ch. 8 covers the early Valencia story. Pedro Sanahuja does not treat Valencia but offers excellent background in *Historia de la seráfica provincia de Cataluña* (Barcelona, 1959). Vicente Martínez Colomer has a routine chapter on the Valencia foundations in *Historia de la provincia de Valencia de la regular observancia* (Valencia, 1803, ch. 2), as does José Antonio de Hebrera in *Chronica real seráfica* (Zaragoza, 1703-1705; lib. I, c. 3). Only a few of the documents in Ambrosio de Saldes, "La orden franciscana en el antiguo reino de Aragón, colección diplomática," apply to Valencia (see *Revista de estudios franciscanos*, I, 1907, 88 ff.).

6. Moorman, *Church Life*, pp. 387 ff.

7. *Repartimiento de Valencia*, p. 250; the editor Bofarull has transcribed "fratres minores" as Michael Mores. "Frater Illuminatus et fratres minores"

appear on p. 170; "of the See" is *de sede*. The place today is a plaza and street (*Nomenclátor de Valencia*, p. 421). See also *Colección diplomática*, doc. 195 (Jan. 11, 1239). Escolano, *Décadas*, lib. V, *c.* 7.

8. Rodrigo y Pertegás, "Urbe valenciana," p. 329.

9. *Colección diplomática*, doc. 1,129 (Dec. 21, 1260); see too *Antigüedades de Valencia*, II, 22.

10. Arch. Crown, James I, perg. 720 (1238). Cf. *Colección diplomática*, doc. 182; *Episcopologio valentino*, p. 439; *Viage literario*, XVII, 331; Tourtoulon, *Jaime I*, I, 464. "Et domui minorum fratrum eiusdem loci C solidos"; "multa servicia que diu nobis fecit." She appears in a number of property documents in the crown archives, as a person of considerable wealth and power. Her brother En (or Dompnus) Ladrón, a great *rich hom* (the highest feudal class) of Aragon and associate of the king, witnessed the will; he appears a number of times in the king's *Llibre dels feyts*, and signs over thirty documents in the *Itinerari*. Toda's defunct husband was Giles Garcés.

11. Arch. Nac. Madrid, Clero: Valencia, Franciscanas, Concepción, leg. 2,124, arm. 45, fab. 2 (1241).

12. Arch. Nac. Madrid, *ibid.*, St. Vincent, leg. 2,079, arm. 45, fab. 1 (Oct. 26, 1247 *an. inc.*); see Chapter XV, note 101. On Aparicius see *Itinerari*, p. 79.

13. Arch. Nac. Madrid, *ibid.*, leg. 2,079, arm. 45, fab. 1.

14. Armer will in Chapter VII, note 53. He added five solidi for his pastor; the other parishes got twelve pence each; the Merced and St. Lazarus houses received two solidi each, and even St. Vincent's got but ten. The proportion therefore, as well as the placing in the document, indicates the favor in which the donor held them.

15. For the will of Raymond, see Chapter VII, note 56. The queen's is in Arch. Crown, James I, perg. 1,264 (Oct. 12, 1251); also *Colección diplomática*, doc. 410; Tourtoulon, *Jaime I*, II, 437; *Antigüedades de Valencia*, II, 129–130n.

16. Document in Chapter VII, note 62.

17. See document cited in Chapter VII, note 57. Her husband, John Garcés of Mazón (de Mazonis) knight, is to control her Valencian properties as long as he does not remarry.

18. Arch. Cath., perg. 5,012 (Nov. 4, 1256); perhaps seventy solidi more, in an ambiguous item, is left for the anniversary sum. Alternatives to William's name include Frayssinet in Languedoc and the Cid's Fraxino (Fresno de Caracena, near Albarracín).

19. Arch. Cath., perg. 5,980 (Dec. 30, 1257). There is a Bernard Olcina in the *Trobes* of Febrèr, as well as a Léridan and a Barcelonan of the name in the *Itinerari* (pp. 270, 312).

20. Arch. Nac. Madrid, Clero: Valencia, Franciscanas, Concepción, leg. 2,125, arm. 45, fab. 2 (Sept. 14, 1258). "Berengarius domine Rose" may be a clumsy translation for the Berengar Narossa from Tortosa in the *Repartimiento*; he is here a resident of Valencia city. There are several Ros families in James's realms.

21. Arch. Crown, James I, perg. 1,556 (Feb. 28, 1258 or 1259). The name is not uncommon; after Peter's death a Peter of Barberá was involved in a number of land negotiations in the cathedral archives; and a Peter of Barberá in the crown archives was a cloth dealer in 1262.

22. Document in Chapter VII, note 61 (1259).

23. Arch. Cath., perg. 1,334 (Aug. 4, 1261).

24. Arch. Nac. Madrid, Clero: Valencia, St. Vincent, leg. 2,079, arm. 45, fab. 1 (3 docs.), October 2, 1263.

25. Will cited in Chapter VII, note 58.

26. Arch. Crown, James I, Reg. Canc. 18, fols. 88v–90. The lady died on June 20, 1272, and was buried in the Franciscan convent of Narbonne. The registers speak "de illis mille morabatinorum quos eis legaverat domina Berengaria Alfonsi in suo testamento." See also Reg. Canc. 22, fol. 48v (July 9, 1276). It is possible that the delay was owing to legal complications, but the issuance of a promise of payment by the crown suggests a forced loan. The registers have half a dozen documents from about 1258 connected with the Lady Berenguela's financial and feudal business, showing her to be the owner in free and frank alod of a large number of castles, as well as of other important properties.

27. Arch. Cath., perg. 692 (Dec. 28, 1274).

28. Document in Chapter VII, note 55; but the Dominicans were similarly favored.

29. Arch. Cath., perg. 1,362 (Nov. 21, 1279); "eliguo [sic] meam sepulturam in ciminterio bonorum fratrum minorum Valencie."

30. Arch. Cath., perg. 1,357 (Mar. 4, 1279).

31. Document in Chapter VII, note 60.

32. John Baldovini, for example, left them three hundred Jaca solidi; King Peter will order the justiciar in 1282 to clear payment on this (Arch. Crown, Peter III, Reg. Canc. 46, fol. 78v, 13 April 1282).

33. *Gremios y cofradías*, I, 71 ff., docs. 17–20, 28. The dates are from 1329 to 1332, but the organizations had existed earlier, some of them apparently in the third or fourth quarter of the thirteenth century. Thus the charter of the shoemakers recalls that James II had suppressed all guilds, except that named St. James, "inter quas confratriam olim per sutores seu çapaterios dicte civitatis editam et multo tempore observatam noscitur sustulisse." Each group had an altar and patron and, besides meeting regularly, met once a year in the Franciscan convent to eat with the friars. There is no way of knowing if the Franciscans or another group had been their original sponsors; but since the document treats of a reorganization of the same guild, it was probably the Franciscan group. On the brotherhood movement see the general treatment above, in Chapter VII.

34. See Chapter III, note 75 and text on the Segorbe bishop; and Chapter XIII, p. 244 on the Játiva establishment.

35. Pierre Mandonnet has a collection of studies under the general title *St. Dominic and His Work*; tr. M. B. Larkin (London, 1945) where this background material is presented topically; see also his "Frères Prêcheurs," *DTC*, VI, cols. 363–372. M. H. Vicaire's recent definitive work on Dominic and the early years of the Order is now available in English, *St. Dominic and His Times* (New York, 1964); see also his "Dominique," *DHGE*, IV, cols. 592–608.

36. M. M. de los Hoyos, *Registro documental, material inédito dominicano español* (Madrid, 1961), p. 72; with further dates from Morera, *Tarragona cristiana*, II, 883.

37. López, "Confesores de la familia real," p. 146.

38. *Llibre dels feyts*, ch. 87.

39. *Antigüedades de Valencia*, II, 10: "de conventu Valentino Fratrum Predicatorum in nostra memoria sempiterna" (Mar. 16, 1249), and also document of April 11, 1239.

40. *Llibre dels feyts*, ch. 426.

41. *Ibid.*, chs. 236–237.

42. *Itinerari*, pp. 239–240.

43. *Llibre dels feyts*, ch. 69. See Appendix II, "Saints on the Valencian Frontier."

44. Pedro Antonio Pérez Ruiz, *La fe, la historia y el arte en el antiguo convento de predicadores de Valencia* (Valencia, 1952), p. 33. On Fabra, see too the uneven

life in *Biografía eclesiástica completa*, 30 vols. (Madrid, 1848–1868), VI, 38–42. See also *Bullarium predicatorum*, I, 115; Vicaire, *Dominic*, pp. 215, 236, 507.

45. Arch. Crown, Peter III, Reg. Canc. 43, fol. 83 (Dec. 9, 1284) is the Morena episode; but this may be one of many contemporary efforts to force a son out of his Dominican vocation (see Vicaire, *Dominic*, p. 347). Diago devotes a section to Puigventós and his work among the Moslems of Valencia; see his *Historia de la provincia de Aragón de la orden de predicadores* (Barcelona, 1599), chs. 47, 48. Baltasar Sorió has a few words on him in the *De viris illustribus provinciae Aragoniae ordinis praedicatorum*, ed. J. M. de Garganta Fábrega (Valencia, 1950), p. 48.

46. *Itinerari*, p. 133 (Aug. 1, 1238). Arnold, Roderick, and Peter signed. Was Arnold from Barbairan near Carcassonne or from the *conca* of Barberá to the west of Vich? At the same time Gregory, Peter, Arnold, and Roderick signed a related document (Arch. Crown, James I, perg. 729).

47. *Aureum opus*, doc. 12, fol. 4r,v (Nov. 2, 1241). *Antigüedades de Valencia*, II, 8. The older chroniclers of the Order contribute relatively little to our information and even muddy the waters with fanciful stories. Thus, Pablo Vidal in his manuscript history, now in the university library at Barcelona (Anales de la orden de predicadores, 1172–1624), mislocates their first site, has Fabra with cross in hand animating the siegers, puts a Dominican standard-bearer at the head of the victorious procession into the city, and so on. Diago and other authors retail the legend of Fabra's image or ethereal other-self appearing vengefully in the skies during the siege and terrifying the Moslem defenders; see Diago, *Historia de la provincia de Aragón*, p. 158; Escolano, *Décadas*, I, 497.

48. Sarthou Carreres, *Historia de Játiva*, I, 111. See notes 59, 90.

49. *Repartimiento*, p. 167; see also pp. 244, 214. The document of 1239 is in *Colección diplomática*, doc. 197 (April 11, 1239); and in *Antigüedades de Valencia*, II, 10.

50. On October 21, 1273 James confirmed the grant of the site with many details of the boundaries and holdings, "ad construendum monasterium cum suis officinis et ad faciendum ibi viridaria, hortos, ciminterium et ad quelibet alia," i.e. for large improvements on these (Arch. Crown, Peter III, Reg. Canc. 19, fol. 64v). Some chroniclers, confusing the Majorcan with the Valencian situation, make this site the palace of the Moor king; they even have the friars later move to the present St. Nicholas' parish (Pérez Ruiz, *Convento de predicadores*, pp. 21–22). On the modern site, see *Nomenclátor de Valencia*, p. 421.

51. Pérez Ruiz, *Convento*, p. 25. This document of February 10, 1245 was repeated by Bishop Andrew on October 21, 1268. It was supported by a papal privilege of 1257, that no one impede their right of burying any who chose their cemetery (*Bullarium predicatorum*, doc. in I, 133).

52. Pérez Ruiz, *Convento*, p. 21 gives the tradition; note 2 above has the chronicle reference.

53. Arch. Nac. Madrid, Clero: Valencia, S. Dom., leg. 2,107, arm. 45, fab. 1, copy dated 1252: "ecclesiam et alia edificia." St. Dominic lived from about 1172 to 1221.

54. Arch. Crown, James I, Reg. Canc. 21, fol. 4v (July 31, 1271): "quod in platea que nunc est ante domos vestras non fiat aliquo tempore aliquid edificamentum et semper sit ibi illa platea." On the history of this site see also Reg. Canc. 20, fol. 274v (July 21, 1275); and Peter III, Reg. Canc. 59, fol. 128 (Oct. 17, 1282).

55. The location of the Dominican house may be seen in Tosca's map, the pertinent part of which is reproduced by Pérez Ruiz, *Convento de predicadores*, facing p. 30. There is a confirmation of lands held near the Temple, in Arch. Crown,

James I, Reg. Canc. 19, fol. 64v (Oct. 21, 1273). A dispute between a miller and the house, "super . . . decursu acquarum," is recommended to arbitration in Reg. Canc. 16, fol. 258v, May 16, 1271.

56. Teixidor, *Capillas y sepulturas del real convento de predicadores de Valencia*, III, 121, quoting from lost document of May 21, 1257.

57. *Acta capitulorum provincialium ordinis fratrum praedicatorum, première province de Provence, province romaine, province d'Espagne (1239-1302)*, ed. P. Douais (Toulouse, 1894), p. 618 (1275). See also Hoyos, *Registro documental*, p. 22.

58. *Acta*, pp. 612 (1250), 626 (1281). On the other hand, one finds no mention of the Valencian house being established, nor of its progress before mid-century in the wider *Acta capitulorum generalium ordinis praedicatorum (1220-1303)*, ed. B. M. Reichert, Monumenta ordinis fratrum praedicatorum historica, no. 3 (Rome, 1898), except for the notice of two houses founded "in Hispania," in the chapter of 1245 (p. 33).

59. Three houses commissioned in Spain, of which "unam ponendam in Zativa" (Hoyos, *Registro documental*, p. 23). See above, note 48 and below, notes 90-91.

60. Arch. Munic. Val., Sucías codex Conventos, I, 47-49.

61. Bibl. Univ. Val., codex 799, doc. 4: an "ortum," "circa monasterium vestrum." See the study on this early period (1206-1220) by W. A. Hinnebusch, "Poverty in the Order of Preachers," *Catholic Historical Review*, XLV (1960), 436-453, esp. 441, 443-444.

62. Wills in manuscripts cited in notes 10-14, 17-30, and in Chapter VII, notes 53-54, 56, 61-62, 92. In Bertrand's will, "ad faciendos duos arcos in ecclesia eorum"; "in defensione domus versus flumen de Godaloviar"; "ad opus unius breviarii."

63. Teixidor, *Capillas*, esp. I *passim*; each chapel and benefactor is considered at length. On Peter Martyr see text above, p. 95.

64. *Ibid.*, I, 36, 63-65. Pérez Ruiz, *Convento de predicadores*, p. 33. On the Escrivás see below, Chapter XIII, note 19. In Arch. Crown, James I, Reg. Canc. 19, fol. 107v (Feb. 26, 1273), the king owes the friars 4,300 solidi which he consigns to be taken from his Alcira revenues; this may be a legacy, intercepted by the king for some pressing need, as sometimes happened.

65. *Viage literario*, IV, 313-323 (testament).

66. *Gremios y cofradías*, I, 31-33, doc. 7: "concedimus vobis universis et singulis ad catholicam fidem conversis in civitate Valencie habitantibus cuiuscumque artis seu condicionis existatis presentibus et futuris . . . ." The year is 1306; I have taken *seu* as a disjunctive in translating.

67. *Ibid.*, docs. 24, 26 (*an.* 1329). On these two brotherhoods see documents in Chapter VII, notes 91-92.

68. *Colección diplomática*, doc. 476 (April 16, 1250); the king is allowing the (Dominican) bishop to alienate this property and, since it had been a royal gift, to keep the book at the convent in James's memory: "damus vobis venerabili episcopo valentino et precemptori plenariam potestatem, quod locum et lignum que dedimus fratribus predicatoribus Xative, possitis vendere . . . et precium . . . ponatis in una biblia glosata, que semper sit in conventu valentino fratrum predicatorum in nostra memoria sempiterna."

69. See Johannes Vincke, *Zur Vorgeschichte der spanischen Inquisition, die Inquisition in Aragon, Katalonien, Mallorca und Valencia während des 13 und 14 Jahrhunderts*, Beiträge zur Kirchen- und Rechtsgeschichte, no. 2 (Bonn, 1941), esp. pp. 55-56. On the Inquisition in neighboring Tortosa see Bayerri, *Tortosa*, VII, 449-451. On Dominican schools in Valencia, see above, Chapter VI, note 45.

70. Burns, "Journey From Islam" (see Preface). This intriguing subject requires extensive treatment and must be left to a later book.

71. See my "The Friars of the Sack in Valencia," *Speculum*, XXXVI (1961), 435–438. Bibliography on the Order consists of a handful of such articles; G. G. Giacomozzi, "L'ordine della penitenza di Gesù Cristo, contributo alla storia della spiritualità del secolo xiii," *Studi storici dell'ordine dei servi di Maria*, VIII (1957–1958), 3–60; his edition, "Le 'Constitutiones fratrum de poenitentia Jhesu Christi,'" *ibid.*, X (1960), 42–99; R. W. Emery, "The Friars of the Sack," *Speculum*, XVIII (1943), 323–334; his "Note on the Friars of the Sack," *ibid.*, XXXV (1960), 591–595; A. G. Little, "The Friars of the Sack," *English Historical Review*, IX (1894), 121–127; and the articles in Hélyot (III, 421–424) and in Heimbucher (I, 540–541, 612). Cf. again the background in Meersseman's *Dossier*.

72. "Multi hyllari et voce iocunda" (Little, "Friars of Sack," p. 126).

73. *Antigüedades de Valencia*, II, 118. Teixidor wrote in 1767, but the error has not been detected by his modern editor nor by subsequent scholars like Sanchís Sivera. Teixidor cites a document of September 13, 1241, but gives no reference. I have found an original of this document in Arch. Crown, James I, Reg. Canc. 11, fol. 232v; it is written in Aragonese and locates the city's market place with reference to the house of the friars. A Latin version of the document was incorporated into the book of municipal privileges, later published as *Aureum opus*, fol. 18v. The year, however, is 1261 in both, not 1241—a transposition of the Latin "XL" being involved. The date is not September 13 either, but the xiii kalends of September, i.e. August 20.

74. *Antigüedades, ibid.*: "coram domibus fratrum penitentie Ihesu Christi ad portam de buatella"; and cf. document below in note 79. Heimbucher puts them in Valencia in 1251 (*Orden und Kongregationen*, I, 541); it seems unlikely. Emery had pushed the date back only to 1274, and for Játiva to 1272. Giacomozzi follows Emery for Játiva, Heimbucher for Valencia.

75. Soldevila, *Pere el Gran*, III, 444, doc. of expenses at Valencia: "Fratribus de Sacs—x solidos."

76. Arch. Crown, James I, Reg. Canc. 15, fol. 133v (Jan. 28, 1269): "laudamus, concedimus et confirmamus vobis priori et conventui fratrum ordinis penitencie Ihesu Christi domus Xative imperpetuum donacionem quam Raimundus dalila abitator Xative vobis fecit de quondam trocium terre." The name may be a form of Çalila, Sabella, etc.

77. Sarthou Carreres, *Historia de Játiva*, I, 86–87. Beuter thought it should be where St. Mary Magdalene's church stood in his day (*Coronica del reyno de Valencia, primera parte*, p. 219).

78. Arch. Crown, James I, Reg. Canc. 16, fol. 185v (Aug. 1, 1269). "Intelleximus . . . quod Bernarda d'alila quondam defuncta ultima voluntate dimisit . . . filio suo . . . et modo filius suus factus sit sarracenus. Ideo nos ipsum sicut mortuum reputantes per nos et nostros damus et concedimus vobis priori et conventui fratrum penitencie Ihesu Christi domus Xative . . . omnia bona predicta per dictam Bernardam dicto filio suo dimis[s]a ut dictum est . . . pro remedio anime nostre et parentum nostrorum ad constructionem operis ecclesie vestre Xative foro Valencie in aliquo non obstante."

79. *Antigüedades*, II, 118: "quandam partem eiusdem Platee, que est ante introitum Monasterii dictorum Fratrum Penitentie domus Valentie, et extenditur in longum a parietibus dicti Monasterii usque ad inferiorem arcum quarundam domorum Petri Stephani." Anas, for "de Annasio" is conjectural.

80. Will cited in Chapter VII, note 58.

81. Will cited in Chapter VII, note 60.
82. Will cited in Chapter VII, note 55.
83. Will cited in note 24.
84. *Colección diplomática*, doc. 1,385 (Aug. 26, 1272): "ad operi [sic] fratrum penitencie Ihesu Christi domus Xative." Published also in *Thesaurus novus anecdotorum*, ed. E. Martène and U. Durand, 5 vols. (Paris, 1717), I, col. 1,139; and elsewhere. The gift is actually 200 morabatins.
85. Arch. Crown, James I, Reg. Canc. 20, fol. 274v (July 21, 1275): "concedimus vobis Artallo esquerre quod si forte domus ordinis penitentie Ihesu Christi Valentie mutetur vel fratres dimittantur seu deserent ipsum domum iuxta summi pontificis ordinacionem vel ipsum alienaveri[n]t, vos et vestri habeatis et teneatis plateam illam que est ante domos fratrum predicatorum ordinis." Is this a slip of the pen for "predictarum ordinis" (the aforesaid Order)? There was a space also in front of the Dominican house (rented in part, for example, on April 10, 1275 by the king to his chaplain; Miret y Sans, *Itinerari*, p. 516). On May 19, 1276, King James granted the house of the Friars of the Sack at Montpellier to the Franciscans there (p. 532); but a little more than a decade later it was in the hands of the Benedictines of St. Pons de Thomières.
86. Arch. Vat., Reg. Vat. 43 (Honorius IV), fol. 153r, 93v–94r, no. 349 (Feb. 23, 1286). Noted but not published in Prou, *Registres d'Honorius IV*, col. 261, no. 353. A copy of this long document, now lost, was preserved in the convent of the Magdalenes at Valencia, and is published in full by Teixidor (*Antigüedades*, II, 118–119); "non nisi duo vel tres remanserint ex Fratribus."
87. Arch. Cath., perg. 2,920 (Aug. 31, 1278): "ego Raimundus Armerii filius Petri Armerii quondam volens et cupiens intrare ordinem Fratrum Penitencie Jhesu Christi ad honorem illius . . ."; his goods both movable and immovable go to "Geraldo pictori Valencie civi cognato meo et domine Marie uxori vestre sorori mee." His father (above, in Chapter VII, note 53) died in 1251; thus, there seems to be no question here of a calendar confusion.
88. Published by Teixidor from the copy, now lost, in the Magdalenes' archives (*Antigüedades de Valencia*, II, 120). The documents speak of plural "buildings" (*domus*); these would probably be confiscated Moslem suburban residences thrown together into a unit.
89. *Ibid.*: "si vacuae sint . . . alioquin illas cum illas evacuari continget." Emery had advanced the date only as far as to 1286 ("Note," p. 594); actually they may have hung on for some time after 1297.
90. Arch. Vat., Reg. Vat. 43 (Honorius IV), fol. 23r, no. 79 (June 7, 1285); noticed but not published in *Registres* (col. 66, no. 83) by Prou, who corrects the "Villaxacina" to the proper "Villa Xativa" in his introduction (p. xcix); published in *Thesaurus* by Martène-Durand, I, 1,143.
91. Sarthou Carreres has the Dominicans buy the house from the city fathers (sworn officials or *iurati*) in 1291 for 50 "ciclos" (*Historia de Játiva*, I, 111).
92. *Viage literario*, IV, 312–323, item "de pretio domorum ordinis saccorum."
93. See E. A. Foran, *The Augustinians from St. Augustine to the Union, 1256* (London, 1938); and Luigi Torelli, *Secoli agostiniani*, 7 vols. (Bologna, 1659–1682), IV and V. Allied documentation is in the *Bullarium ordinis eremitarum S. Augustini*, ed. Antonio Barberini (Rome, 1628). A survey and bibliography is in the recent "Ermites de S. Augustin," *DHGE*, XV, cols. 787–791. Jaime Jordán has a very uneven and uncritical survey of the early Valencia story in his *Historia de la provincia de la corona de Aragón de la sagrada orden de los ermitaños de nuestro gran padre San Agustín compuestos de quatro reynos, Valencia, Aragón, Cataluña, y las islas de Mallorca y Menorca*, 2 vols. (Valencia, 1704–1712), I, *lib.* II, *c.* 1.

474   NOTES TO CHAPTER ELEVEN

94. Jordán, *Historia*, I, *lib.* I, *c.* 23. He provides biographies of Francis and William Salelles (*lib.* II, *c.* 4).

95. The data on France was gathered by Richard Emery, "Notes on the Early History of the Augustinian Order in Southern France," *Augustiniana* [Louvain], VI (1956), 336–345. The French houses ran in a line along the Mediterranean and thence up to Bordeaux, numbering sixteen by 1300. In 1275 the houses were at Narbonne, Montpellier, Toulouse, Marseilles, Grasse, Aix, Arles, and Avignon.

96. Torelli, *Secoli agostiniani*, IV, 344, cf. pp. 336–337. Arch. Munic. Valencia, Sucías codex Monasterios, I, 9 ff., 18; Conventos, III, 7–8. Jordán, *Historia de la provincia*, I, *lib.* II, *c.* 1.

97. Sarthou Carreres, *Monasterios valencianos*, p. 131 (with a 1250 gift as well). Torelli has "Aquevive nel regno di Valenza" in 1239, citing a lost document of 1260 done by James at Oliva (IV, 344 and V, 648). Cf. Sucías codex Conventos, III, 16–19, but with same document dated 1267. Jordán lists the house as of 1239 but offers no detail.

98. Torelli, *Secoli agostiniani*, V, 201–202 with doc., 336. The Sucías codex, Conventos, suggests that it was founded in 1251 (III, 27). Cf. Traver Tomás, *Antigüedades de Castellón*, p. 313. The phrase in the document, "de novo facere nitebantur," and the revenues suggest long pre-existence.

99. Real Acad. Hist., Miguel Eugenio Muñoz ms. book, Descripciones de . . . las iglesias . . . de Valencia (partly documents, partly "tradition"), fols. 332 ff.

100. Arch. Munic. Val., Sucías, Conventos, III, 31–32. On the Alcoy house see *Nomenclátor*, pp. 43–44, 91. Sarthou Carreres furnishes an excellent photograph of the foundress' skull (*Monasterios valencianos*, p. 216), and more pleasantly her portrait as a motherly lady with a disconcertingly stern jaw (p. 204). Torelli has the house only "della terra d'Alcodio" in Aragon, but dates it from 1270 (*Secoli agostiniani*, V, 220; on Alcira house, p. 758). Jordán lists the Alcira house as beginning in 1274, the Alcoy house in 1300. Sarthou Carreres has the Alcira monastery, a Gothic structure, begin in 1277 (p. 135).

101. Jordán devotes a chapter to this Castielfabib house, St. William's, supposedly begun in 1155 (I, *lib.* I, *c.* 19). Sucías suggests a 1290 foundation here.

102. On the Augustinian dispute with the Carmelites over an earlier date see, besides Torelli (in note 100), *Antigüedades de Valencia*, II, 33–34. Sucías only allows them 1300 as the founding date (Conventos, III, 37) as he does for Alcoy (p. 47). Peter's gift is in Torelli, V, 345 from a 1428 inventory; cf. VI, 210.

103. *Gremios y cofradías*, I, 23–27, doc. 4. *Fabri, miniscalci*, and *argentarii* (blacksmiths, farriers, and silversmiths) were given a brotherhood at the Augustinian monastery to promote union, piety, charity, and the redemption of members in captivity. They could also have "en la Esglea de Sent Agusti de Valencia una lantea la qual crem nit et dia devant laltar del dit bonaventuros Sent Aloy." Nine years later a less specialized confraternity of a hundred laymen was granted to the Alcira house (doc. 10). In 1329 the *agricultores* (farmers) of Valencia city would have their guild approved, under Augustinian patronage (doc. 21); and the *ferrarii* (farriers or smiths; doc. 22), the *aluderii* and *pergaminerii* (skin-dressers and parchment makers; doc. 23) in 1329. These documents of 1329 all refer back to a previous existence of the group ("confratriam olim per . . . editam et multo tempore observatam"), though not necessarily implying a connection with the Augustinians then. The number of brotherhoods and diversity of occupations represented argue a previous popularity of the Augustinians. On the brotherhood movement see the general treatment above in Chapter VII.

104. Arch. Crown, James I, Reg. Canc. 21, fol. 80 (*an.* 1273): "concedimus fratribus heremitis ordinis Sancti Augustini . . . ut in aliquibus civitatibus vel

castris sive locis ... possint libere et absolute ... edificare sibi monasteria in quibus debeant deservire cum voluntate proborum hominum civitatum et villarum ... damus eis licentiam et plenum posse accipiendi domos seu loca alia ... sibi data et emendi similiter."

105. Arch. Crown, Peter III, Reg. Canc. 46, fol. 54v (July 14, 1281): "racione vendicionis per vos nobis facte de quadam hereditate quam quondam Berengarius habebat in termino de Corbera."

106. Jordán, *Historia de la provincia*, I, 190.

107. Morera, *Tarragona cristiana*, II, 851.

108. Arch. Crown, Peter III, Reg. Canc. 44, fol. 204v (Nov. 17, 1281): "possitis habere in quocumque loco extra murum Civitatis Valencie eligeritis causa empcionis, donacionis vel cuiuslibet alterius iusti tituli domos et hereditates ... et hedificare seu construere monasterium vestrum et domos ad salutem fidelium."

109. *Antigüedades de Valencia*, II, 38. Cf. the document described by Esclapés (*Resumen historial*, p. 84); the prior was Arnold de Bachris.

110. *Antigüedades, ibid.* Their residence became the modern provincial museum and their church a parish church (*Nomenclátor de Valencia*, p. 421).

111. *Gremios y cofradías*, I, 33–35, doc. 8; Teixidor has a later copy (*Antigüedades*, II, 37–38).

NOTES TO CHAPTER XII. MONKS AND NUNS ON THE VALENCIAN FRONTIER

1. Philibert Schmitz, *Histoire de l'ordre de Saint Benoît*, 6 vols. (Maredsous, 1942–1956), I, 223–224.

2. *Ibid.* and p. 216.

3. Justo Pérez de Urbel in his *Los monjes españoles en la edad media* (2 vols. [Madrid, 1930–1934], II, 526–597) puts the generalities in vivid detail, and points to the Aragon frontier as the bright spot. The malaise was a Europe-wide phenomenon but it must not be exaggerated; see, for example, the sensible evaluation by David Knowles, who concludes that the Cistercians had remained fairly free of luxury and relaxation of spirit despite internal structural changes (*The Monastic Order in England* [Cambridge, Eng., 1941], p. 689). Moreau praises their vigor and spiritual influence in Belgium at this time, discerning the signs of decay in the later thirteenth century and the real decline in the fourteenth (*Église en Belgique*, III, 404, 415, 419). On the crisis of the monasteries see Schmitz, *Ordre de St. Benoît*, III, 3–5, 116–118. See too the recent article with bibliography, "Espagne cistercienne," in the *DHGE*, XV, cols. 943–970. On the monastic federation and reform movement in Aragon see Philipp Hofmeister, "Die Verfassung der ehemaligen claustralen Benediktinerkongregation in Katalonien und Aragon," *Studien und Mitteilungen zur Geschichte des Benediktiner-Ordens und seiner Zweige*, LXX (1959), 206–235.

4. E.g., on this last point, the complaint of the general chapter in 1267 (*Statuta capitulorum*, III, 55–56, no. 55). James's general connections with the Order may also be reviewed in Ángel Manrique, *Cisterciensium seu verius ecclesiasticorum annalium a condito cistercio*, 4 vols. (Lyons, 1642–1659), IV, index *sub* "Iacobus."

5. See Bernardo Morgades, *Historia de Poblet* (Barcelona, 1948), pp. 67–68; *Llibre dels feyts*, ch. 564. In his wider discusssion of Poblet, Jaime Finestres has a treatise on Benifasá too; see his *Historia del real monasterio de Poblet*, 6 vols. (Barcelona, [1746] 1947–1955), II, 250–288. The Poblet abbot here connected with the Benifasá foundation in Valencia was Vidal of Alguaire (1232–1236); his

predecessor had just become archbishop of Aix in Provence, and his successor as abbot (Simon, 1236-1237) was to be made bishop of Segorbe-Albarracín, his successor in turn (Raymond of Siscar, 1238-1241) becoming bishop of Lérida.

6. Thus the abbey of Escarp (which had a feebler beginning under James's father) was given Corachar near Benifasá in 1230; it was secured from its actual holder in 1235. See the series of documents relating to this property in Arch. Nac. Madrid, carp. 418, 419, 422. An important document from this collection is reproduced in photo and in copy by Agustín Millares Carlo, *Tratado de paleografía española*, 2nd ed. revised, 2 vols. (Madrid, 1932), I, 286, and II, 65 (May 2, 1235). A later document recalls their pacific possession from the time of this original grant (Arch. Crown, Peter III, Reg. Canc. 60, fol. 48, Feb. 11, 1283). Their Alcudia estate appears in a document of June 19, 1246, bounding the property of a knight "Don Drogo miles" (Arch. Cath., perg. 5,970: "quod ortum est ante Monacorum descarp"). Escarp also received Macelmaida in 1237. We hear of one of their vassals in a dispute concerning his land (Arch. Cath., perg. 4,640, Aug. 7, 1257): "ortum vestrum quem vos Bernardus Michus tenetis pro monachis descarp." Their subjects in Valencia seem to have enjoyed immunity from army duty and its fee, because this claim is being investigated in 1280 (Arch. Crown, Peter III, Reg. Canc. 48, fol. 24). See also Chapter IX, note 74. Ripoll monastery held Burjasót from 1238 to 1258. Holy Crosses (Santes Creus) had Valencian properties; King James ordered his officials and subjects in 1263 to recognize these (Arch. Crown, Reg. 12, fol. 85v, June 1). Poblet's holdings are noted in Chapter XV, note 134. On St. Vincent's in monastic hands, see *ibid.*, notes 8-11 with text.

7. Arch. Nac. Madrid, Clero: Castellón, Benifasá, carp. 419, doc. 6 (Dec. 11, 1234); see too *Colección diplomática*, doc. 1,033: "attendentes quod loca religiosa ad laudem et gloriam domini nostri . . . hedifficata, debeant a Regibus et principibus multipliciter augmentari prout divina officia ibi semper et indessinenter celebrentur."

8. Honorio García, "El monasterio de Nuestra Señora de Benifazá en Valencia," *ACCV*, XV (1947), 226. A good account of the early years of Benifasá is given by the same author: "Real monasterio de Santa María de Benifazá," *BSCC*, XXVI (1950), 19-35. And see his "La iglesia del monasterio de Nuestra Señora de Benifazá," *ACCV*, XX (1952), 184-191. There is a cartulary for Benifasá among the codices of the Arch. Nac. Madrid (sig. mod. 871), and two copies of the codex Llibre de la fundació (1586) of Miquel Joan Gisbert (sig. mod. 578 and 896). See also Manrique, *Annales*, II, *an.* 1234, ch. 5; and Finestres, *Poblet*, in note 5.

9. A. J. Cavanilles, *Observaciones sobre la historia natural, geografía, agricultura, población y frutos del reyno de Valencia*, 2 vols. (Madrid, 1795-1797), I, 2.

10. *Itinerari*, pp. 78, 548n. (June 14, 1229). *Colección diplomática*, doc. 120 (Nov. 22, 1233). See Manuel Betí, "Fundación del real monasterio de monjes cistercienses de Santa María de Benifazá," *Congrés I*, p. 414, and Morgades, *Poblet*, pp. 67-68; from 1224 to 1229 the abbot here was Raymond of Cervera, perhaps a relative of King James. For the grants and the pre-grants, see also *Viage literario*, IV, 153-154. Pertinent early documents are in Arch. Nac. Madrid, Clero: Castellón, Benifasá, carp. 418 (*an.* 1226-1233). On an early (1208) settlement attempt by King Peter, see Bayerri, *Tortosa*, VII, 143.

11. Arch. Nac., *ibid.*, document of November 22, 1233: "et castrum et vallem de malgraner et castrum de Fredes et locum et totam terram de Boxar cum suis vallibus et planis et terminis et totam terram de Rossell et Castrum de Capris et castrum de Bel cum suis terminis, que omnia castra et loca singula . . ."

12. *Ibid.*, carp. 422 (Sept. 25, 1254): "ipsum locum . . . cum terminis et pertinenciis suis."

13. *Ibid.*, document of August 13, 1233; related documents *passim*, including the papal confirmation and the agreement of February 20, 1243. See also García, "Real monasterio," pp. 22 ff. At the Arch. Cath. Tortosa, see cajón Benifasá, nos. 2-3; cart. VIII, fols. 127-128.

14. Arch. Cath. Tortosa, *ibid.*, nos. 1, 10, 24, 27; cart., fols. 59-63.

15. Manuel Betí has gathered the story into his small monograph, *Ro[s]sell, pleito que por su dominio sostuvieron en el siglo xiii la orden de San Juan de Jerusalén y el real monasterio de Benifazá*; besides the brief forty-two pages of text, there are fifty pages of documents.

16. John of Malacara or (in García, "Real monasterio," p. 26) John of Cortit. García dates the arrival at nine days after the royal confirmation of November 22, in 1233.

17. Arch. Crown, James I, perg. 1,059 (Oct. 20, 1246): "ad presentes non possint ibi plusquam viginti duo monachi esse." The king had also given houses in the city of Valencia and five jovates of lands in Benimaclet, but these the monastery never got (see the *Repartimiento de Valencia*, pp. 157-158).

18. Knowles, *Monastic Order in England*, p. 223 and n.; Moorman, *Church Life*, pp. 256-257.

19. F. A. Gasquet, *Henry the Third and the Church, a Study of His Ecclesiastical Policy and the Relations Between England and Rome* (London, 1910), p. 268. On the connection of the bishop of Gerona (Berengar of Castellbisbal) with Valencia see Chapter II, note 37 and text.

20. Arch. Vat., Reg. Vat. 21 (Innocent IV), fols. 305r-306v, June 22, 1246; notice in Berger, *Registres*, I, no. 1,992; "mens nostra obstupuit enormitate flagitii."

21. Perg. in note 17: "et acceptamus satisfactionem quam obtulistis spontaneus pro offensa predicta videlicet quod monasterium de Benifassa Ordinis Cisterciensis per vos feliciter inchoatum dotando et edificando, taliter consumetis, ut . . . valeant ibidem quadraginta commode susten[t]ari, et quod fabrice eiusdem ecclesie ducentas marchas argenti impendatis."

22. *Viage literario*, IV, 155, document of January 1251; the move was made on November 1, 1250 (García, "Real monasterio," p. 27).

23. Betí, *Rosell*, doc. 15. Knowles explains all these administrative officials in his *Monastic Order*, pp. 427-431.

24. *Ibid.*, p. 160, documents of 1259 and 1272.

25. *Ibid.*, p. 150. García has Bishop Andrew bless and place the first stone, and on August 15, 1264 ("Real monasterio," p. 34). See also his "Iglesia del monasterio," pp. 184-191.

26. Arch. Nac. Madrid, Clero: Castellón, Benifasá, carp. 425, doc. 11 (May 8, 1273): "opere pl[uri]um sumptuoso noviter fabricari, ad cuius operis consumationem sit subsidium Christi fidelium non modicum necessarium."

27. Enrique Bayerri, in his *Los códices medievales de la catedral de Tortosa* (Barcelona, 1962), believes that Benifasá was making books available to the Tortosa library by the end of the thirteenth century (p. 45).

28. *Itinerari*, p. 551n. (Feb. 11, 1244); it is the subject of a land exchange. On Cistercian wool-growing and farm techniques at this period see David Knowles, "The Agrarian Economy of the Cistercians," in his *The Religious Orders in England*, 3 vols. (Cambridge, Eng., 1950-1959), I, ch. 6.

29. *Colección diplomática*, doc. 427 (July 13, 1252); *Itinerari*, p. 223.

30. Arch. Nac. Madrid, Clero: Castellón, Benifasá, carp. 422, doc. 9 (May 19, 1253): "eorum Grangie de Borriana de Albar et de Bellestar." In the Roman scribe's Albar can be discerned Arberos or Herbés. But it is improbable that the

transcription Borriana can be Burriana; the context calls for a place where winter makes the roads hazardous.

31. *Ibid.:* "a matrice ecclesia adeo sint remote [grangie] quod existentes in ipsis propter viarum discrimina hyemali presertim tempore pro aud[i]endis divinis officio [*sic*] . . . nequeant accedere ad eandem, construendi capellas in eisdem Grangiis licenciam ipsis concedere curarem."

32. Arch. Nac. Madrid, *ibid.*, doc. of January 4, 1252.

33. Arch. Nac. Madrid, *ibid.*, carp. 423, doc. 13 (June 16, 1261).

34. Arch. Nac. Madrid, *ibid.*, carp. 419, doc. 6 (Dec. 6, 1234): "quandam vineam nostram cum terra," and "quendam Cellarium nostrum . . . in Civitate Dertuse."

35. *Itinerari,* p. 549n.

36. *Ibid.,* notes on pp. 550, 552. Arch. Nac. Madrid, Clero: Castellón, Benifasá, carp. 420, doc. 4 (1275); carp. 422, doc. 9 (1247); and carp. 423, doc. 7 (1259) ordering the "alcaydus" of Morella to respect their grazing privileges.

37. Arch. Nac. Madrid, *ibid.*, carp. 423, doc. 11 (June 9, 1261). See Chapter I, note 29.

38. *Nomenclátor de Valencia,* p. 127.

39. Arch. Nac. Madrid, Clero: Castellón, Benifasá, carp. 423, doc. 14 (Aug. 20, 1261); there is a copy under Ords. Milits., Montesa, R119. Cf. Bayerri, *Historia de Tortosa,* VII, 135.

40. Arch. Crown, James I, perg. 2,126; *Colección diplomática,* doc. 1,385 (Aug. 26, 1272): "ad opus operis ecclesie."

41. Arch. Crown, James I, Reg. Canc. 11, fol. 238 (Jan. 2, 1260; fol. 237r is also marked confusingly 238): "ex gratia speciali ob remedium anime nostre."

42. Arch. Crown, James I, Reg. Canc. 12, fol. 51v (May 15, 1262): "recognoscimus et confitemur debere vobis Abbati et Conventui monasterii . . . quattuor millia solidos iaccenses quos vobis damus ex gratia speciali . . . Quos assignamus vobis habendos et percipiendos in redditibus exitibus questiis cenis et aliis iuribus nostris tam decimis primiciis quam quibuslibet aliis Vallis bone et Erbers . . . aldearum Morelle." See the companion document of the same date on this page. There is a copy in Arch. Nac. Madrid, Clero: Castellón, Benifasá, carp. 423, doc. 16 (May 14).

43. Arch. Crown, James I, Reg. Canc. 15, fol. 69r,v (Oct. 27, 1267); this first gift is rather a "concambium et permutacionem," involving minor Lérida revenues. The second gift is in Reg. Canc. 14, fol. 132v (Dec. 16, 1271): "conventui et monasterio benifaçiani monetaticum nostrum . . . in [*a list is given*] aldayis Morelle quas iam a nobis assignatas . . . tenetis cum carta nostra." See too Arch. Nac. Madrid, Benifasá, carp. 425, doc. 2.

44. Arch. Crown, James I, Reg. Canc. 21, fol. 57 (Aug. 26, 1272): "attendentes et considerantes monasterium benefaciani per nos edificatum non habere . . . sufficienciam panis . . . idcirco ut dictum monasterium . . . panis possit habere sufficienciam . . . concedimus vobis . . . imperpetuum totam ab integro partem nostram et iura omnia quam et que percipere debemus in decima totius bladi integriter frumenti scilicet ordei avene millii panicii et adacie . . . in Vall bona et arbers Sobirans aldeis Morelle et in terminis suis." "Sobirans" may be a third town, but I have been unable to find such a place in early Valencia; it may here distinguish between Herbés and Herbesét, or even be construed as modifying both towns. *Sobirà* in Catalan means higher, superior, sovereign.

45. Arch. Nac. Madrid, Clero: Castellón, Benifasá, carp. 422, no. 16 (Nov. 2, 1248).

46. *Colección diplomática,* doc. 1,278, showing that they are receiving this be-

fore 1267 ("racione donacionis quam inde de ipsis habetis a Raimundo Berengarii cum publico instrumento").

47. Arch. Nac. Madrid, Clero: Castellón, Benifasá, carp. 422, docs. 1, 2 (Aug. 7, 1249); docs. 3, 4 are a royal confirmation (Aug. 15); cf. note 60. See too *Colección diplomática*, doc. 1,059.

48. Llibre de la fundació, fol. 84.

49. Bayerri, *Historia de Tortosa*, VII, 274.

50. Arch. Nac. Madrid, Benifasá, carp. 422, doc. of March 20, 1257; also in Arch. Crown, James I, Reg. Canc. 10, fol. 50v. "Laudamus . . . illam donacionem quam G. Bardol vobis fecit de loco qui dicitur Lorabar in termino Burriane." Is this Lombar, or La Llosa?

51. Arch. Nac. Madrid, Poblet cartulary (B-1220), pp. 28-34, doc. 12.

52. Bayerri, *Tortosa*, VII, 533, four gifts; in 1305 the monks will purchase Aldea village (p. 285n.).

53. Arch. Crown, James I, Reg. Canc. 11, fol. 12 (1260 Liria sale). Arch. Nac. Madrid, Benifasá, carp. 425 (1270 land purchase).

54. Moorman, *Church Life*, p. 42.

55. Arch. Nac. Madrid, Clero: Castellón, Benifasá, carp. 423, doc. 2 (Aug. 2, 1258): "Dompnum Iohannem Garces de Ianuis milite[m] dominum de Arberos"; Arberos is Herbés, and the dispute concerns its border with Castell de Cabres.

56. Arch. Nac. Madrid, *ibid.*, doc. 7 (Oct. 3, 1259); cf. *Itinerari*, p. 294.

57. Arch. Nac. Madrid, *ibid.*, carp. 424, doc. 8 (June 10, 1268).

58. Arch. Nac. Madrid, *ibid.*, carp. 425, doc. 9 (Feb. 7, 1272).

59. Arch. Nac. Madrid, *ibid.*, doc. 15 (1274): "super quodam honore qui vocatur Palerols in termino de Benifasa"; "tenebatur facere statica in dicto honore . . ." Is this something in Valderrobres to the northwest of the monastery? And is it the "Patrols" which the monks have here in a document of 1258? On the Pallerols in the Lérida diocese, given to Poblet monastery in 1276, see *Itinerari* (pp. 356, 535) and *Rationes decimarum* (I, 123).

60. The fault here, or at least the open aggression, lay with the Temple. The king writes: "Quia nobis constat quod fratres Templi eiecerunt violenter vos . . . monachos monasterii de Benifaçano de Rafalgari quam vos tenebatis, ideo auctoritate presentis instrumenti restituimus vobis . . . possessionem" (Arch. Nac. Madrid, *ibid.*, carp. 422, doc. 6 [Aug. 26, 1250]). Cf. notes 47-48 and text.

61. See the charter in Chapter IV, note 103.

62. Arch. Crown, Peter III, perg. 261.

63. Vincke, "Patronatsrecht," p. 65.

64. *Statuta capitulorum*, III, 148, no. 51 (*an.* 1275).

65. *Ibid.*, III, 223, no. 23 (*an.* 1282): "per plures annos."

66. J. M. Canivez lists the abbots in his brief notice "Benifasá" (*DHGE*, VII, cols. 1,310-1,312); cf. the list in *Viage literario* (IV, 161). Arch. Munic. Val., Sucías codex Monasterios, I, 44-69 has a list, with some different spellings (Arnold of Manresa, Peter Vilarnau, William of Sarrates).

67. The charter for Benlloc and Albar is cited in Chapter VIII, note 129; that for Fredes is no. XLIX of the "Colección de cartas pueblas" (*BSCC*, XIV, 1933, 339-341 [Dec. 27, 1267] but misdated there as 1266). For Ballestar see the charter cited in Chapter IV, note 103. Other settlement documents may be found in Arch. Nac. Madrid, Clero: Castellón, Benifasá, *passim*. See also *BSCC*, XXXVII (1962), 349 ff.

68. Arch. Nac. Madrid, *ibid.*, carp. 423, doc. 9 (June 9, 1261): "quoddam extremale."

69. *Ibid.*, doc. 13 (June 15, 1261). This refers to the tithe from which the

Cistercians were of course exempt, but reflects the tangle of secular jurisdiction here.

70. Julius Klein, *The Mesta, a Study in Spanish Economic History, 1273-1836* (Cambridge, Mass., 1920), p. 157; cf. p. 150. See pp. 34-36 and *passim* on the merino sheep and on the Castilian wool dominance, so important to the medieval cloth manufacturer. The mesta was the national guild of herdsmen and sheep owners of Castile, formally organized by Alphonse the Learned in 1273 into a single group from the previous flourishing local guilds. Klein has useful observations on the role of these privileges in the reconquest, and on the necessity of checking a privilege against its actual use in the local context (pp. 303-304). Valuable comments on the thirteenth-century stockman's frontier of Castile are in C. J. Bishko's "The Castilian as Plainsman: the Medieval Ranching Frontier in La Mancha and Extremadura" (in the symposium, *New World Looks at its History*, pp. 47-69).

71. Bayerri, *Historia de Tortosa*, VII, 337-342; James confirmed the *lligalo* at Morella in 1270. On the frontier origin of the stockmen's associations see Bishko, "Medieval Ranching Frontier," pp. 58 ff.

72. A "comission de las Cavannas d'Aragon en el Regne de Valencia"; see the "Super officiis Aragonum," ed. J. E. Martínez Ferrando, *Hispania*, IV (1944), 535. The military Orders were also great stockmen in Spain (cf. Bishko, "Medieval Ranching Frontier," pp. 55-56); there are echoes of this concern in the Valencian documents.

73. See doc. of 1259 in note 36; also *Colección diplomática*, docs. 106, 428, 1,037, 1,053; and Arch. Crown, Peter III, Reg. Canc. 38, fol. 93 (Nov. 28, 1276), a quarrel with the king's collector over their rights.

74. *Itinerari*, p. 56 (September 5). Piedra monastery had to pay for their sheep in the Jérica region—see the document in which Teresa Gil Vidaure cancels the bill (*ibid.*, p. 470, September 1272). The Holy Crosses monastery also sent its flocks south. In 1251 this was the subject of arbitration with the diocese because of tithe claims (Arch. Cath. Tortosa, cajón Obispo, no. 95).

75. *Itinerari*, p. 223 (July 13, 1252).

76. See document of 1259 in note 36.

77. Document (Mar. 15, 1298) in José Toledo Girau, *Castell d'Alfandech*, pp. 65-67 but in Catalan translation. See too on Valldigna the same author's "El monasterio de Valldigna, contribución al estudio de su historia durante el gobierno de sus abades perpetuos," *ACCV*, VIII (1935), 74-81; and his "Compendio histórico de Simat de Valldigna," *ibid.*, XXV (1957), 66-92.

78. Arch. Crown, James I, perg. 1,276 (Jan. 1, 1252): "similiter adquisito regno Valencie deo effuso sanguine ad decus totius christianitatis, tribuistis nobis ibi honorem de quo sit semper plena pitancia conventui nostro ad honorem Dei et vestri, in die scilicet sancte crucis madii annuatim." See *Itinerari*, p. 218. The 1249 crown decision including this area as part of Alcira's *terminus* is *ibid.*, p. 199.

79. Arch. Crown, *ibid.*: "vestrum illustre nomen et nobis dulce et carissimum."

80. Arch. Crown, James I, Reg. Canc. 12, fol. 85v (June 1, 1263): "cum omnia bona monasterii sanctarum crucium francha fecerimus et libera ... sicut in privilegio ... continetur et specialiter domos qui nunc sunt in regno Valencie et pro tempore ibidem fuerint institute, videlicet quod de dictis domibus aliqua bona mobilia vel immobilia sive fuerint ista ipsius monasterii vel aliarum personarum, aliqui ... non abstrahant nec abstrahi faciant, immo ipsas domos et bona que ibidem fuerint illabata et inconcussa ... protegant et defendant."

81. Arch. Munic. Val., Sucías codex Conventos, I, 225.

82. *Nomenclátor de Valencia*, pp. 433-435, 54, 90, 99, 272, and *passim*. A con-

siderable documentation on this relatively late foundation is in Arch. Nac. Madrid, Clero: Valencia, Valldigna, e.g. leg. 2,211, arm. 47, fab. 1; running from 1212 to 1255; it is difficult to say just when these early properties eventually came under Valldigna control. In Arch. Crown the Liber patrimonii regni Valentiae gives them "Barc Aliebal" in Alfandech Valley in 1299 (fol. 62v, doc. 2), probably the same as Barig.

83. Arch. Crown, James I, Reg. Canc. 21, fol. 14 (Mar. 3, 1272).

84. Arch. Crown, ibid., but a separate document (Mar. 3, 1272): "ex empcione vel donacione ac largicione fidelium, tot alquerias et alias hereditates et possessiones . . . [ad] mille morabatinorum."

85. Arch. Crown, ibid., another document (Mar. 4, 1272): "concedimus monasterio Gratia Dei quod edificari debet termino de Carlet unum miliare terre," free and frank forever. See too Reg. Canc. 37, fol. 62v (Mar. 8, 1273), doc. of Prince Peter (there is a misbinding in this register, fol. 62 following fol. 70).

86. Statuta capitulorum, II, 294 (an. 1245): "inspectio loci quem confert Ordini dominus rex Aragonensis ad fundandum abbatiam monachorum in regno Valentiae, de Perinacio et de Berola abbatibus committitur, qui ad locum etc., et qui inde etc., et sit filia Scalae Dei." This is not Escala Dei: see note 92 and text.

87. Ibid., II, 305, no. 23 (an. 1246): "negotium abbatiae monachorum quam vult aedificare dominus rex Arragonensis, iterato committitur . . ."; "hoc eis denuntiet."

88. Ibid., II, 319, no. 22 (an. 1247): "negotium . . . usque ad finem debitum prosequantur."

89. Ibid., II, 296, no. 8 (an. 1298): "qui sunt de regno Franciae, Navarrae, Arragoniae, Angliae, et Valentiae."

90. Arch. Crown, James I, Reg. Canc. 21, fol. 21v (April 18, 1272): "attendentes et confidentes devocionem quam vos venerabilis frater Andreas Episcopus Valentinus habetis erga cultum fidei Christiane . . . idcirco nos volentes vestrum laudabile propositum prosequere gratia et favore ad honorem domini nostri Jhesu Christi et gloriose virginis Marie . . . empcionem vel empciones quam vel quas vos facietis a manumissoribus nobilis viri Eximen Petri de Arenoso quondam et a quibuslibet aliis personis in loco vocato Lullen . . ." See too Zurita, Anales, I, lib. III, c. 79. The charter of foundation, given under the general Gerard (1267-1273), is published in Nicolaus Molin, Historia cartusiana ab origine ordinis usque ad tempus auctoris 1638, 3 vols. (Tournai, 1903-1906), I, 349-351. See also Arch. Munic. Valencia, Sucías codex Conventos, II, 1-275.

91. Arch. Crown, Peter III, Reg. Canc. 22, fol. 76v (Dec. 7, 1277): "loco vocato de Luleyll ad edificandum monasterium."

92. See the companion articles on the two in DHGE, XV, cols. 838-848.

93. Arch. Crown, Liber patrimonii regni Valentiae, fol. 56v, doc. 3; cf. Molin, Historia cartusiana, I, 351.

94. Molin, Historia cartusiana, ibid.; cf. Nomenclátor, under Liria. The priory soon expanded, especially with a Gothic church in 1325, acquiring endowments from the rents of Puig. Its principal benefactor was the Lauria family. Eventually the priory accumulated estates, became agriculturally wealthy, and emerged as a cultural center and social-aid bulwark for the local population.

95. Moreau, Église de Belgique, III, 358 ff. See also Moorman, Church Life, pp. 247, 258, 260-261, 310.

96. Examples may conveniently be found in Eileen Power's Medieval English Nunneries (Cambridge, Eng., 1922), an industrious if somewhat uncritical compilation centering upon the weaknesses and problems from 1275 to 1535.

97. Since James's first marriage had been annulled, Teresa was in fact the second

of his two wives. There is a brief but sometimes useful article on her by Julián Avellanes Coscojuela, "Teresa Gil de Vidaure y Jaime el Conquistador," in *Congrés I*, pp. 790–798; the quotation just above is taken from the Cistercian martyrology of 1670, quoted on p. 797. A short archival study of Teresa by R. Chabás, "Doña Teresa Gil de Vidaure," is in *El archivo*, VI (1891), 22–35; on the Valencian properties given her in 1238 see p. 26, and the *Repartimiento de Valencia*, p. 187.

98. *Llibre dels feyts*, ch. 242.

99. The document for the alcazar property is copied in *Antigüedades de Valencia* (II, 133 [April 10, 1255]); the document for the Zaidia is on p. 135 (April 5, 1260). Zaidia represents the feminine equivalent of Cid (*Sa^c̄id*), Lord. There is a reference to its alcazar: "intus Alchaçer Monasterii vocati gratia dei constructi in Çaydia Valencie, sub dominio eiusdem Monasterii" (Arch. Nac. Madrid, Clero: Valencia, Bernardas, Zaidia, leg. 2,075, arm. 45, fab. 1). Later the convent would disappear, to be rebuilt in modern times on the same site (*Nomenclátor de Valencia*, p. 422). See also Escolano, *Décadas*, I, 500–501.

100. *Statuta capitulorum*, III, 16–17, no. 52 (*an.* 1263): "item. inspectio loci in quo fundare intendit abbatiam monialium nobilis domina Teresia Aegidii, de Benefassano et de Scorpion [*Escarp, Lérida diocese*] abbatibus committitur, et Abbas de Benefassano hoc ei denuntiet."

101. Chabás, "Doña Teresa," pp. 31–33.

102. *Antigüedades de Valencia*, II, 138–139.

103. *Ibid.*, pp. 136–137 (Feb. 17 and July 5, 1266): "miramur plurimum qua licentia quo instinctu nobis petitionem obtuleris Deo contrariam, abominabilem angelis, et hominibus monstruosam"; "coniunctionis illicitae pollui participio ex consensu"; "quos ergo Deus coniunxit, Dei vicarius quomodo separaret? absit a nobis hoc scelus." "Tantorum victor hostium, a propria carne sic vinceris, ut divino timore postposito . . . cum multorum scandalo circumducas adulteram et incestu cumulans adulterium, graviter oculos divinae maiestatis offendis."

104. *Llibre dels feyts*, ch. 426.

105. *Statuta capitulorum*, III, 65, no. 44 (*an.* 1268): "incorporatio abbatiae monialium de Gratia Dei in magna Valentia de Scarpio et de Bonifacano abbatibus committitur, et sit filia Cistercii."

106. *Antigüedades*, II, 139 (Feb. 10, 1268).

107. Arch. Nac. Madrid, Clero: Valencia, Bernardas, leg. 2,075, arm. 45, fab. 1. The nun is: "Margarite nepote nostre monache monasterii ordinis nostri."

108. Vicente Ferrer Salvador, "El real monasterio cisterciense de Gratia Dei (Zaidia) en Valencia, aportación a su historia," *ACCV*, XXII (1961), 68.

109. Arch. Crown, James I, Reg. Canc. 15, fol. 95 (April 25, 1268). "Fidelibus suis universis notariis publicis Valencie et omnium aliarum villarum et locorum Regni totius Valencie, ad quos presentes pervenerint salutem et gratiam. Noveritis nos concessisse abb[at]isse et conventui monasterii de Gracia . . . quod possint libere . . . emere quocumque loco . . . hereditates usque ad summam mille morabatinorum, foro Valentie in aliquo non obstante."

110. Arch. Crown, James I, Reg. Canc. 15, fol. 91 (April 16, 1268). "Concedimus monialibus vocate de Gracia quod de novo hedificatur in loco vocato Çaydia termino Valencie presentibus et futuris in dicto monasterio imperpetuum bona omnia quae quondam fuerunt Petri Macioti pelliparii Civis Valentie mobilia omnia et immobilia et totum ius et peticiones quos et quas habemus et habere debemus in dictis bonis, quae quidem bona nobis confiscata sunt, ex eo quod fuerunt relicta indignis personis qui succedere non debebant in eis bonis predictis Petro Macioti. Damus siquidem in hunc modum, quod bona omnia predicta ea

NOTES TO PAGES 227–231

scilicet que immobilia sunt vendantur . . . et ponantur simul cum aliis bonis mobilibus . . . monasterii construendi ad cognitionem operarii eiusdem monasterii." The grounds for such unworthiness are examined in the *Furs, lib.* VI, *rub.* IX, fols. 157 ff.

111. Arch. Crown, *ibid.* (text given there).

112. Arch. Crown, James I, Reg. Canc. 15, fol. 100 (May 12, 1268): "partem et iura omnia nostra quam et que percipimus et habemus ac percipere debemus in molendinis sitis termino Campanarii, in quibus tertiam partem percipit et percipere debet . . ." Cf. *ibid.*, codex Liber patrimonii regni Valentiae, fol. 98r,v.

113. Arch. Crown, James I, Reg. Canc. 16, fol. 242v (May 3, 1271): "concedimus vobis abbatisse et conventui monasterii de gratia termini Valencie quod possitis facere et habere in rambla que est ante ipsum monasterium . . . unum furnum cum suis exigenciis et pertinenciis ad faciendum . . ."

114. Arch. Crown, James I, Reg. Canc. 21, fol. 7v (*an.* 1271). The manuscript is worth transcribing here at length because it is instructive to see the mechanics involved in such a small purchase by a religious group. "Licentiam et potestatem emendi in termino dicte civitatis unam iovatam terre que a nobis ad censum non teneatur, ad opus vinearum . . . Quas iovatas terre ad opus vinearum habeatis vos et conventus dicte monasterii ad ipsum monasterium imperpetuum ad vestras et dicti conventus voluntates perpetuo faciendas. Mandantes firmiter baiulo nostro Valencie ut in predictis vobis nullum impedimentum vel contrarium faciant [*sic*]. Mandantes etiam scriptoribus Valentie universis quod de empcione vel empcionibus . . . faciant vobis cartas licite et secure non obstante foro Valencie in contrarium faciente. Vos enim . . . in carta seu cartis que inde fient confirmamus per nos et nostros, concedimus et laudamus."

115. *Nomenclátor de Valencia*, p. 374.

116. Arch. Nac. Madrid, Clero: Valencia, Bernardas, leg. 2,075, arm. 45, fab. 1, doc. of June 26, 1249: "super quibusdam molendinis sitis in termino Patraix."

117. Document in Chapter VII, note 60. The bequest is to the "monasterii dominarum sancte Clare de Saydia," possibly a scribe's error running the two convents together; the same kind of gift is also left to St. Elizabeth's and to St. Mary Magdalene's.

118. Peter Marqués; see document in Chapter VII, note 55.

119. Ferrer Salvador, "Real monasterio de Gratia Dei," p. 70.

120. *Itinerari*, pp. 470, 532, documents of September 1272 and April 1276: these do not justify Miret y Sans's conclusion that she lived here rather than in Valencia. Cf. also pp. 387, 394, 401, 406, ambiguous references to an earlier period (1266–1267).

121. *Ibid.*, p. 503 (July 29, 1274); *Antigüedades de Valencia*, II, 137–138 and n.

122. Chabás, "Doña Teresa," p. 33 (July 15, 1278).

123. *Antigüedades*, II, 141–142.

124. Morera, *Tarragona cristiana*, II, 846 ff.

125. Andrés Ivars, "Año de fundación y diferentes advocaciones que ha tenido el monasterio de la Puridad o Purísima Concepción de Valencia," *Archivo ibero-americano*, XIX (1932), 439. Cf. *Repartimiento de Valencia*, p. 262 and the reference apparently to the Poor Clare convent of Tarazona on pp. 593, 645. See also Martínez Colomer, *Historia de la provincia de Valencia de la regular observancia*, pp. 33 ff.; and Hebrera, *Chronica seráfica, lib.* I, *c.* 6.

126. Arch. Nac. Madrid, Clero: Valencia, Franciscanas, leg. 2,124, arm. 45, fab. 2: "cum mezquita et era . . . [ex] una parte in cequia, ex alia parte in moraria, ex alia parte in via publica qua itur apud Quart." If the nuns built elsewhere, the property was to revert to Simon Peter's heirs. Sanchís Sivera locates this convent

of La Puridad, from 1239, on the site bounded in modern times (1922) by the streets Rey Don Jaime, Moro Zeit, and Conquista (*Nomenclátor de Valencia*, p. 421).

127. Arch. Nac. Madrid, *ibid.*, document of October 18, 1249. Catherine is "abbess" here but must be prioress, because Tarina continues to appear as abbess. The two Christian names are variants of the same name and can refer to one person, except of course where the two are found together, as in note 126. Is this Catherine the Catherine Berengar who was abbess of the Tarragona convent in 1260 and went then to Majorca to establish that convent? (See Bartolomé Guasp Gelabert, "Unas religiosas clarisas en Mallorca," *AST*, XXII [1959], 56.)

128. Arch. Nac. Madrid, *ibid.*, "dompnus Rodericus de Arandiga"; it is "in carraria de Mezlata."

129. *Colección diplomática*, doc. 1,385 (Aug. 26, 1272): "et dominabus Sancti Damiani . . . domus Valencie ducentos morabatinos."

130. Queen's will cited in Chapter XI, note 15: "alium mantellum meum de amoret violat et supertunicale eiusdem panni."

131. See documents in Chapter VII, notes 55, 56, 57, 58, 60, 61, 62, 92; and in Chapter XI, notes 18, 21, 26. Marqués gives to "monasterio Sancte Helisabet," Peter Armer to the church of "Sancte Ysambelle"; Berenguela provides a "presbyter de meo in Ecclesia dominarum Sancte Elizabet," with burial "in ciminterio dominarum." Ferdinand's will is in Arch. Cath., perg. 5,013 (Oct. 22, 1262); cf. *Antigüedades de Valencia*, II, 130n.

132. *Colección diplomática*, doc. 414 (Mar. 4, 1252): "confirmamus vobis Tarine abbatisse monasterii sancte Elisabet civitatis Valencie siti in Roteros et sororibus eiusdem monasterii in perpetuum, empcionem quam fecistis a Petro Ferrarii draperio Valencie de quodam horto qui est in Roteros et vendiciones et donaciones que . . . de cetero facta fuerint, in tantum videlicet, quantum pendet edificium ipsius monasterii; que omnia habeatis per alodium proprium, franchum et liberum in perpetuum." See *Itinerari*, p. 219.

133. Arch. Cath., perg. 1,375 (July 31, 1288; from Lérida).

134. *Nomenclátor de Valencia*, p. 421; the site is a market today. Cf. Escolano, *Décadas*, I, *lib.* V, *c.* 8.

135. *Repartimiento de Valencia*, pp. 550, 625.

136. *Ordinatio ecclesiae valentinae*, p. 358: "quamdam meçquitam," which may be identical with the house or building above. The eyewitness who reports all this also saw the cathedral ceremony and thus is not confusing St. Mary and St. Mary Magdalene; but he is not certain as to the name, believing it to have been St. Mary Magdalene.

137. *Antigüedades de Valencia*, II, 123-124.

138. Arch. Vat., Reg. Vat. 43 (Honorius IV), fol. 153r, ep. 91 *bis* (July 28, 1286), and attached unnumbered letter to the Dominican master and the Spanish provincial (Aug. 25, 1286). Only a notice of these is given in the *Registres*, no. 588; cf. Prou's list in the introduction, p. civ. See also *Antigüedades de Valencia*, II, 125. A Bernard Riusech appears in the *Repartimiento*; Raymond Riusech, perhaps a relative, was bailiff for the kingdom of Valencia over many years in the thirteenth century.

139. Arch. Crown, James I, Reg. Canc. 21, fol. 4 (July 29, 1271): "concedimus vobis Alandi [*sic*] de Romani . . . et omnibus dominabus ipsius monasterii . . . imperpetuum tantum spacium terre de mercato nostro civitatis Valencie contiguum domibus vestris et ecclesie vestre quantum protenditur portificus vester qui est ante ianuam ecclesie vestre . . ."

140. Arch. Crown, James I, Reg. Canc. 15, fol. 82v (Feb. 29, 1268). See also

Itinerari, p. 409. Cf. the codex Liber patrimonii regni Valentiae, fol. 294v, doc. 9 (undated).

141. Arch. Crown, James I, Reg. Canc. 21, fol. 4 (July 29, 1271), a separate document from that in note 139. The registers of James have a dozen documents on Gía (or Guía) in Valencia, connected with his tax gathering for the crown or with his own purchases of property; his widow was selling his Alcira lands to cover his debts.

142. Wills in manuscripts cited in notes 131, 133; in Chapter VII, notes 53, 55, 56, 60, 61, 62, 92; in Chapter XI, notes 12, 13, 18, 21, 23.

143. Arch. Crown, codex Liber patrimonii regni Valentiae, fol. 136, doc. 4; contrast *Nomenclátor de Valencia*, p. 233.

144. Arch. Crown, Peter III, Reg. Canc. 60, fol. 60 (Mar. 19, 1282). "Venerabili et dilecte priorisse monasterii sancte Marie Magdalene Valencie. Rogamus vos quatenus Agnetum sororem Guillelmi de Sala scriptoris [?] venerabilis Episcopi Valencie recipiatis in sororem et monialem dicti monasterii nostris precibus et amore . . ."

145. *Antigüedades de Valencia*, II, 113–121 *passim*. A refuge would be founded in Valencia in 1345 (cf. II, 235) but would not be a convent.

146. *Ibid.*, p. 124. The document of 1242 (p. 116) may refer to the previous convent (in which case Catherine was prioress at this date) or perhaps to a subjoined ministry or set of tertiaries.

147. *Ibid.*, pp. 151–153.

148. *Ibid.*, p. 152 (May 19, 1298).

149. *Documenta selecta*, doc. 118 (1306) where James II recalls the founding by James I; "accione pia constituit seu construi fecit et dotavit."

150. Arch. Crown, James I, perg. 2,169 (Sept. 10, 1273): "in regno nostro Valencie apud Algeziram." Perg. 2,170 is a copy.

151. Arch. Crown, James I, Reg. Canc. 19, fol. 45 (Aug. 19, 1273). He begins this very long document by announcing "idcirco nos Jacobus . . . monasterium de beata Maria Magdalena in Regno nostro Valentie, apud Algeciram in ecclesia Sancti Bernardi, hedificatum duximus ac eciam construendum."

152. Arch. Crown, James I, Reg. Canc. 20, fol. 329v (Mar. 6, 1275): "licentiam . . . emendi ad opus vestrum, ortum . . . qui etiam affrontat cum . . . monasterio vestro predicti, [et] emendi in termino Algezire centum pedonatas terre nostre ad opus vinearum . . ."

153. Arch. Crown, Peter III, Reg. Canc. 44, fol. 112 (Mar. 15, 1279). Reg. Canc. 44, fol. 168v (Nov. 24, 1279); pergs. of Peter, no. 173, recalling the gifts of James I "super construendo eorum monasterio apud Algeciram," and listing the mills, vines, rents, shops, etc. See also codex Liber patrimonii regni Valentiae, fol. lv, doc. 2.

154. *Rationes decimarum*, I, 256, 262, 267, 268.

155. Document cited in Chapter VIII, note 22.

156. *Documenta selecta*, doc. 225 (July 29, 1314), a request from James II to the Cistercian general chapter to have the Játiva house, "quod illustrissimus dominus Iacobus . . . avus noster dotavit et fundavit," made Cistercian and put under Valldigna. See also *Antigüedades de Valencia*, II, 177–178.

NOTES TO CHAPTER XIII. THE HOSPITALS OF THE KINGDOM OF VALENCIA

1. Jean Imbert, *Les hôpitaux en droit canonique du décret de Gratien à la sécularisation de l'Hôtel-Dieu a Paris en 1565*, L'église et l'état au moyen âge, no. 8

(Paris, 1947), pp. 42 ff., cf. 109 ff. See the canonical position as given by W. Ullmann, "Medieval Hospices," *Month*, CLXXXIV (1947), 46-49. Esclapés has a brief section on Valencian hospitals, to be used with great caution (*Resumen historial*, pp. 125-130). J. R. Zaragoza Rubira's "Breve historia de los hospitales valencianos" in *Medicina española* (XLVII [1962], 152-160) is jejune and of little use for this period.

2. J. H. Mundy, "Hospitals and Leprosaries of Twelfth and Early Thirteenth-Century Toulouse," *Essays in Medieval Life and Thought Presented in Honor of Austin Patterson Evans*, ed. J. H. Mundy *et alii* (New York, 1955), pp. 187, 201, 203n. For England see Moorman, *Church Life*, p. 248n.

3. The Zaragoza hospitals are given in note 68. The six Tortosa hospitals besides the cathedral hospital are in Bayerri, *Historia de Tortosa*, VII, 580-582. For Tarragona see J. M. Miquel Parellada and José Sánchez Real, *Los hospitales de Tarragona* (Tarragona, 1959), esp. on the cathedral hospital, pp. 25 and *passim*. On the Montpellier hospital in James's realms, conducted by a lay confraternity with vows, see Louis Dulieu, *Essai historique sur l'hôpital St-Éloi de Montpellier, 1183-1950* (Montpellier, 1953).

4. González, *Reino de Castilla en la época de Alfonso VIII*, I, 602-625.

5. *Cortes de los antiguos reinos de Aragón y de Valencia*, I, 103.

6. For example King James's document about St. Vincent's in Arch. Crown, Reg. Canc. 15, fol. 12v, *an.* 1265. On the nature of medieval social legislation, its philosophy, institutions, and practice, see Brian Tierney, *Medieval Poor Law, a Sketch of Canonical Theory and Its Application in England* (Berkeley, 1959); hospitals are touched on in ch. 4, esp. pp. 85-87. For Spain this may be supplemented with the more general work of Antonio Rumeu de Armas, *Historia de la previsión social en España, cofradías, gremios, hermandades, montepíos*. See also my "Los hospitales del reino de Valencia en el siglo xiii," *Anuario de estudios medievales*, II (1965), 135-154.

7. *Antigüedades de Valencia*, II, 276-277. Teixidor, lacking our documentation, might still have argued back from the ampler documentation of the fourteenth century.

8. See Armer will in Chapter VII, note 53, and quotation from Willelma will in Chapter XV, note 113.

9. Besides St. Vincent's see, for example, the crown document cited in note 16 for the hospital of St. William in Valencia. A chapel is here granted "pro fratribus et infirmis et domesticis," with no mention of the poor, whereas later in the document only the "poor" who die there are mentioned. Cf. Mundy, "Hospitals," p.191 where inmates of the leprosaries of thirteenth-century France are termed simply "pauperes."

10. *Blanquerna: A Thirteenth-Century Romance*, tr. E. A. Peers (London, ca. 1925), book I, ch. 9 and ch. 10, pp. 79, 81-82.

11. *Ibid.*, chs. 10, 15.

12. Imbert, *Hôpitaux*, pp. 124, 126.

13. *Ibid.*, pp. 138-139.

14. *Ibid.*, pp. 277 ("un veritable service divin"), 124-125. The Benifasá infirmarian and sub-infirmarian are named in a document of 1268 (see Chapter XII, note 23 and text).

15. Rodrigo Pertegás, "Urbe valenciana," p. 307.

16. Arch. Cath., perg. 1,216 (July 25, 1256): "in capite Pontis Civitatis Valentie." The building is gone today but is commemorated in the name of the street there (*Nomenclátor de Valencia*, p. 422). Agustín Sales has some pages on the hospital at the beginning of his *Historia del real monasterio de la Ssma. Trinidad,*

religiosas de Santa Clara de la regular observancia, fuera los muros de la ciudad de Valencia, sacada de los originales de su archivo (Valencia, 1761), pp. 1-5. See also Antoninus ab Assumptione, *Ministrorum generalium ordinis Ss. Trinitatis series* (Isola del Liri, 1936), under Nicolaus, 1231-1257. On the Tortosa Trinitarians see Bayerri, *Historia de Tortosa*, VII, 535-537.

17. Imbert, *Hôpitaux*, p. 218; but cf. Mundy, "Hospitals," p. 187n.

18. Document in note 16. "Noverint universi quod olim Guillelmus scriba tutor filiorum et heredum Guillelmi scribe filii sui quondam defuncti, Cenodoxium seu Hospitale fundaverit ex ultima dispositione ipsius Guillelmi scribe defuncti, in capite Pontis Civitatis Valentie. Et predictum Hospitale tradiderit gubernandum ministro et ordini Sancte Trinitatis." The 1242 date is from Bonaventure Baron, *Annales ordinis Ssmae. Trinitatis redemptionis captivorum fundatoribus SS. Ioanne de Matha et Faelice de Valois, 1198-1297* (Rome, 1684), p. 165.

19. Teixidor's data on the several Escrivás in his *Capillas y sepulturas* (see above, Chapter XI, note 64 with text) is as confusing as that from Sales (*Trinidad*, p. 3). Teixidor has the elder William die in 1260 but the junior William in 1303. Sales has the elder William crusade to Valencia from Narbonne (unfortunately this is from Febrèr's *Trobes*), gives him two sons, Arnold and William, and has young William die childless after founding the hospital. Viciana supplies an essay on the Escrivá family, lords of Paterna from 1239; he claims they came originally from Narbonne as crusaders to Catalonia and subsequently as Catalan crusaders to Valencia (*Segunda parte de la crónica de Valencia*, pp. 130-132). The registers in the crown archives make Arnold, son of William, tutor for the children of his defunct brother William and administrator of his estate; other documents in the registers have William senior dead at least before 1272, and treat of business affairs of Arnold and his son William. See also in Febrèr's *Trobes*: "Del Consell de Estat, è també de Guerra/Era Secretari Guillem Escrivà" (*troba* 218, p. 121).

20. *Antigüedades de Valencia*, II, 55-56.

21. Arch. Crown, Peter III, Reg. Canc. 40, fol. 53 (Dec. 28, 1276): "ad preces venerabilis fratris A. abbatis fontis frigidi, concedimus vobis fratris Petro de Sexeno ministro hospitalis Sancti Guillermi ordinis Sancti Trinitatis domus Valencie quod possitis emere seu retinere ad opus domus vestre seu hospitalis predicti quandam vin[e]am quam na Raynes mulier eiusdem hospitalis dimisit in suo testamento tali tamen condicione quod dictam vin[e]am semper sit de Realenco et fiat pro eadem vobis et nostris servicium sicut pro aliis honoribus realenchi." The testament of Willelma is in Chapter VII, note 60; that of Peter Barberá is in Chapter XI, note 21.

22. Document in note 16: "ipse minister et fratres iamdicti ordinis coram nobis fratrum A. dei gratia episcopo Valentino et capitulo dicte sedis venientes humiliter postularunt ut in fundacione dicti Hospitalis dignaremur eisdem nostrum quidem exhibere consensum et eisdem dare licenciam ibidem oratorium construendi, et in sepulturis et aliis graciam facere specialem." For the English hospitals see Moorman, *Church Life*, p. 15.

23. *Rationes decimarum*, I, 256, 263.

24. *Gremios y cofradías*, I, 35-37, doc. 9; these are the restored *califati*, from 1306, and presumably their predecessors.

25. Arch. Crown, Peter III, Reg. Canc. 43, fol. 99v (Jan. 6, 1285).

26. Arch. Crown, Peter III, Reg. Canc. 56, fol. 33 (Mar. 19, 1285): "ipsi possident duodecim maçmutinas censuales in carregia Valencie," as assigned by the king's judge-delegate.

27. *Antigüedades*, I, 374 (April 13, 1244): "in introitu Hispaniae."

28. Imbert, *Hôpitaux*, p. 218.

29. *Antigüedades*, I, 374; Jacques de Vitry (†1244) is speaking: "fervor charitatis, unctio pietatis, honestatis decor, et severitas disciplinae."

30. Arch. Cath., perg. 1,090 (Nov. 15, 1243): "concedimus vobis dilecto nostro A. Episcopo et capitulo Valencie et conventui Fratrum Ro[n]cidevallis alqueriam sive villam que dicitur Poçol." See also the document of March 15, 1243, in *Colección diplomática*, doc. 264. The hospital sold its share of Puzol to the bishop in 1303.

31. *Repartimiento*, p. 325 (*an.* 1242): "Monasterium Roncidevallium: omnes ecclesias de Roteros"; cf. pp. 534, 591, 645. For the churches, which were widespread, see above, Chapter IV, note 36 and text. Peter's safeguard is in Arch. Crown, Peter III, Reg. Canc. 37, fol. 45v (*an.* 1272).

32. Arch. Cath., perg. 1,316 (Nov. 17, 1243). "Dignum est a nobis eos beneficia grata recipere et nostre partem sollicitudinis eisdem comitere qui redemptoris nostri et universalis ecclesie ac hospitalitatis pauperum noscunter obsequiis fideliter institisse, ut et ipsi nos sibi respondisse pro meritis gaudeant, et alii ex eorum remuneracione presenti ad nostrum et ecclesie obsequium Valentine animosius se accingant. Hinc est quod nos A. et totum capitulum Valentinum, attendentes quod si eis ... manum aliquam provisionis munificam exibemus, illis pocius ex ordinata caritate provide constringimur quorum obsequium ecclesiis et pauperibus omnibus iamdudum noscitur esse gratum."

33. Document in Chapter VII, note 62.

34. *Antigüedades de Valencia*, I, 374 (†1288).

35. Soldevila, *Pere el Gran*, IV, [pt. 2, I], 90, doc. 68.

36. On leprosaries see Imbert, *Hôpitaux*, pp. 149–196; and René Pétiet, *Contribution à l'histoire de l'ordre de St-Lazare de Jérusalem en France* (Paris, 1914), esp. chs. 1, 2, 4. The first leprosaries of Toulouse appear only in the late twelfth century, and seem to have been self-governed both here and in the rest of France (Mundy, "Hospitals," pp. 185, 192, 196). On the hospital of the Order in Tortosa see Bayerri, *Tortosa*, VII, 547, 580 ff.; on leper hospitals in Castile see González, *Reino de Castilla*, I, 616–618.

37. *Antigüedades de Valencia*, II, 281.

38. Peter Armer testament in Chapter VII, note 53 ("item dimito infirmis Sancti Lazari ii solidos"); Barberá will in Chapter XI, note 21 (twelve pence), Jaca will in note 24 ("et leprosis Scti Lazari"). Marqués will in Chapter VII, note 55 (five solidi); Willelma will in note 60 (ten solidi), Abrafim will of 1274 in note 54 ("et infirmis Sancti Lazari xii denarii"), Chicot will of 1279 in note 94 ("infirmis Sancti Lazari"); 1276 will in Arch. Cath., perg. 1,354 (Sept. 30).

39. In 1306 the king gave to "vobis batadors et brunateriis civitatis Valencie" a charter of brotherhood in connection with St. Lazarus hospital, where once a year they were to eat in the patients' building: "domum Sancti Lazari Valencie ... in domo ipsorum infirmorum" (*Gremios y cofradías*, I, 29–31, doc. 6). The two trades apparently designate cloth processers; *bruneta* was a dark cloth imported into Catalonia, and *bata* is a robe.

40. *Rationes decimarum*, I, 256, 263.

41. James gave permission to the "commander" of the hospital of St. Lazarus at Montpellier to marry and live with his family at the hospital, the better to watch over the house and its goods (July 27, 1272). Is this commander the patron, the procurator, the warden, or the head here of a lay brotherhood (*Itinerari*, p. 469)? Bayerri says the Order had been a branch of the Hospitallers until the Lazarists' rejection of celibacy led to separation; this may explain the commander's marriage.

42. *Diócesis valentina*, II, 446. Olmos y Canalda, *Prelados valentinos*, p. 65; on the brotherhood see Chapter VII, notes 95–98 and text.

43. Roca Traver discusses this hospital and is wisely cautious toward the suggestion of Pertegás that it simply continues the Roncesvalles institution ("Real cofradiá de San Jaime," pp. 71 ff.).

44. *Antigüedades de Valencia*, II, 282.

45. *Ibid.:* many others follow, and Teixidor treats of them in the subsequent pages.

46. Arch. Crown, James I, Reg. Canc. 20, fol. 243v (April 18, 1275): "per nos et nostros damus et concedimus tibi P. dahera populatori ville regalis quod possis construere et hedificare in dicta popula [*sic*] hospitalem ad pauperes hospitandos et dare et assignare eidem Hospitali domos et hereditates quas tibi dedimus in ipsa populacione . . ."; this is "dum vita fuerit tibi" and with licence to leave it all his goods "post obitum tuum."

47. Luis Revest Corzo, *Hospitales y pobres en el Castellón de otros tiempos* (Castellón de la Plana, 1947), documentary appendix, section II, doc. 1 (Mar. 4, 1290). Sarthou Carreres gives 1275 as the date of its foundation but cites no document (*Geografía general*, vol. *Castellón*, p. 467). See too Vicente Giméno Michavila, "El antiguo hospital municipal de Castellón," *BSCC*, XIII (1932), 208–213.

48. Document *ibid.*: "in presencia et in posse" of the *iurati* (see p. 38).

49. Arch. Crown, James I, Reg. Canc. 16, fol. 241v (June 21, 1271): "in emendam illius patui terre quod est in Segorbio . . . quod tibi Garcie Anado dedimus ad construendum ibi domos, et postmodum concessimus consilio de Segorbio ad construendum ibi hospitalem, damus . . . aliud patuum terre." The name may be Anadán.

50. Arch. Crown, James I, Reg. Canc. 13, fol. 286v (Jan. 5, 1266): "confirmamus per hereditatem propriam francham et liberam vobis Petro de Sol[er] de Xativa imperpetuum illud alfondicum . . . in Xativa . . . ad opus hospitalis et hospitale ibidem constructum et hedificatum, cum suis pertinenciis . . . a celo in abissum et cum omnibus melioramentis ibidem factis et faciendis." See the *Itinerari*, p. 382; James had given it first to Ferrer of Monzón, now to Peter of Soler. Is this the same one as in the *Repartimiento*, p. 492?

51. *Repartimiento*, p. 345: "hospitale pauperum Xative."

52. In the confirmatory document in note 50.

53. Martínez Colomer, *Provincia de Valencia de la regular observancia*, pp. 40–41.

54. Sarthou Carreres, *História de Játiva*, I, 88, 259 (both claims). Teixidor credits both (*Antigüedades*, II, 63). Sanchís Sivera puts the Murviedro hospital in his *Nomenclátor*, p. 354.

55. Faustino D. Gazulla, "Los mercedarios en Arguines y Algar (siglo xiii)," p. 69. See below, note 116.

56. *Nomenclátor de Valencia*, p. 354.

57. See note 109; its explicit purpose was the care of ransomed captives.

58. Faustino Gazulla, "Don Jaime de Aragón y la orden de Nuestra Señora de la Merced," *Congrés I*, p. 383.

59. *Antigüedades de Valencia*, II, 322: "capellam quam ego construi feci in domibus quas habeo in Alcaria de Fortaleny." *Nomenclátor de Valencia*, p. 232. In 1741 this church would be given by the commander of the Hospital of St. Anthony to the diocesan clergy. On the Antonines see Germain Maillet-Guy, *Les origines de Saint-Antoine, xie–xiiie siècles* (Valence, 1908).

60. *Antigüedades, ibid.*

61. *Ibid.; Nomenclátor*, p. 326.

62. *Repartimiento*, p. 223: "Hospitali pauperum Burriane fr. Michael hospitalario." "Hospitalarius" of itself, of course, could signify an administrative officer of the hospital (see examples in Mundy, "Hospitals," p. 193n.).

63. Thus the will of Peter Abrafim in 1274 speaks of burial "in cimiterio hospitalis sancti Johannis Jherusalemis," and the wife of Blaise Peter has a legacy for "hospitali sancti Iohanis," but these expressions tell us nothing. See also Vicente Ferrer Salvador, "Monasterio de Gratia Dei," p. 497, reference to hospital of St. John. Quote by contemporary in James of Varazze (Jacobus da Voragine), *Golden Legend*, I, 118.

64. *Antigüedades de Valencia*, I, 296, Teixidor's interpretation.

65. Arch. Cath., perg. 4,639 (Dec. 23, 1256).

66. Imbert, *Hôpitaux*, pp. 215–216 and nn.; but for Toulouse see Mundy, "Hospitals," nn. 41, 64, 77.

67. The earliest statutes of the Valencian silversmiths and metal-workers, for example, incorporate this tradition; unlimited care is pledged for the ill member in his own home until he is cured or dead. On this aspect of the brotherhoods in the realms of Aragon see Antonio Rumeu de Armas, *Historia de la previsión social en España*, pp. 65–71, 549–550.

68. Ricardo del Arco, *Zaragoza histórica*, p. 143. A will here in 1218 had legacies for six separate parish hospitals. In Tortosa the cathedral conducted a hospital for the sick at this period (Bayerri, *Historia de Tortosa*, VII, 432). For the Tarragona cathedral hospital see above, note 3.

69. *Viage literario*, V, 313 ff. The conquests below the kingdom of Valencia will have their own hospitals; thus, at Alicante a hospital received a legacy in 1307 of a hundred solidi (*Cláusulas testamentarias relativas a la iglesia de San Nicolás, de Alicante, siglo xiv*, ed. Vicente Martínez Morella [Alicante, 1954], doc. 1).

70. From the grant of land by Bernard Gostanc to the Villarreal hospital see note 47: "pium est et magna karitas subvenire pauperibus Christi qui egeant et indigentiam patiantur."

71. *Furs, lib.* I, *rub.* III, *c.* 112; and *lib.* III, *rub.* IV, *c.* 7: "nos deuem devant tots los altres mantenir sens tota diffuyta en son dret pubils, viudes, homens vells e debils, e aquells als quals deu hom hauer merce quant seran venguts a pobrea o debilitat per cas d'aventura."

72. *Repartimiento*, p. 643, "Loba vetula et paupera"; p. 616, "de duobus pauperibus"; p. 571, "quidam pauper: domus parvissima"; p. 616, "quidam miles pauper"; p. 628.

73. *Furs, lib.* II, *rub.* VI, *c.* 33. On these "miserables" see Tierney, *Poor Law*, pp. 18–19.

74. *Aureum opus*, doc. 49, fol. 16v (*an.* 1255): "ratione pensionis carceragii."

75. Arch. Crown, Reg. Canc. 21, fol. 151v (Jan. 6, 1273 or 1274). This wooden bridge was replaced in the early fourteenth century.

76. Arch. Cath., perg. 5,028 (July 23, 1303). Esclapés gives the date as 1288 (*Resumen historial*, p. 166). Olmos y Canalda, *Prelados valentinos*, pp. 79, 85.

77. Testament of Oller in Chapter XI, note 13 ("inter pannos, lini et lane"; "detur viduis, orfinibus, et pauperibus verecundantibus"); of Jaca in note 24; of Marqués in Chapter VII, note 55; of Chicot in note 94 ("et palleis orphanis maritandis et captivis Christianis redimendis").

78. Muntaner, *Crònica*, ch. 20. King James of Aragon once arranged for alms to be given annually to a thousand poor; the sums were to be drawn partly from Valencian revenues—180 solidi from Valencia city; 20 solidi to each of twenty poor men, from Murviedro; the same respectively from Játiva, Alcira, Gandía, and Beniope (Arch. Crown, James I, perg. 2,242 [Sept. 9, 1275]). Even so unsavory a

thirteenth-century king as John of England sustained an impressive system of crown almsgiving; see C. R. Young, "King John of England: An Illustration of the Medieval Practice of Charity," *Church History*, XXIX (1960), 264-274; see also Hilda Johnstone, "Poor Relief in the Royal Households of Thirteenth-Century England," *Speculum*, IV (1929), 149-157. There was an alms system at the parochial and monastic level in medieval Europe (cf. Tierney, *Poor Law*, ch. 5 *passim*), but only hints of its exercise have survived in our documentation for Valencia.

79. Desclot, *Cronica*, ch. 49. Less important institutions involved in the work of ransoming included the fraternities of craftsmen; on these and the office of the *exea* for official safe-conduct out of Valencia for ransomed or exchanged Moors, see Faustino Gazulla, *La orden de Nuestra Señora de la Merced, estudios histórico-críticos (1218-1317)* (Barcelona, 1934), esp. chs. 1-3.

80. *Colección diplomática*, doc. 520 (Sept. 30, 1255).

81. A document (of doubtful authenticity?) in the Merced codex at Arch. Crown gives a military role to the Order at the siege of Valencia: "quando ego expugnavi et cepi Valenciam contra sarracenorum gentes fortiter praeliastis lancea et sento et multi vestrorum vulneribus mortui ceciderunt" (*Itinerari*, pp. 137-138, Dec. 27, 1239). Gazulla insists on their military role both in the crusade and as garrison; see his evidence in "Jaime I y Merced," pp. 374, 377-378, 380, 384. Vázquez, however, feels that they had few occasions or personnel for fighting. On the ransomer role of Calatrava see González, *Reino de Castilla en la época de Alfonso VIII*, I, 620 ff.

82. Gazulla, "Jaime I y Merced," *passim*.

83. Verlinden, *Esclavage*, I, 832. Gazulla claims he had rescued 1,200 with his personal patrimony alone ("Jaime I y Merced," p. 329).

84. Verlinden, *Esclavage*, p. 537; see also pp. 606 ff. Gazulla, "Jaime I y Merced," pp. 371-373. Guillermo Vázquez Núñez in his *Manual de historia de la orden de Nuestra Señora de la Merced (1218-1574)* (Toledo, 1931) maintains that some of the most important documents for Nolasco's life are late forgeries, including the document of the seals itself and the testimony of Peter Armengol in 1304 (p. ix). An uncritical essay, useful for its industrious compilation of details, is Amerio Sancho Blanco, "San Pedro Nolasco y sus primeros compañeros y la confirmación y constitución apostólica de la orden," *Estudios* [Mercedarios], XII (1956), 233-264; he has a long list of the thirteenth-century ransom expeditions claimed for Nolasco and his early companions, with the numbers freed each time (pp. 246-249).

85. Document cited in note 80: "nos qui eiusdem ordinis patroni et fundatores sumus." See Manuel Mariano Ribera, *Centuria primera*, pp. 57-58; intriguing bits of information on the origins of the Order may be gleaned from this old work, especially in chs. 1 and 2. The masters general from Nolasco on are discussed on pp. 289 ff., and many members from the first century of its history are considered on pp. 430 ff. There are problems with the chronology, but William of Bas seems to have been second master general from 1249 to 1260; Bernard of San Román and William (now in his second term) apparently filled the decade 1260-1270; Peter of Amer governed the Order from 1271 to 1301. William, perhaps a relative of Berengar, may have been master by 1245, "si el document és autèntic" (*Itinerari*, p. 174; cf. also pp. 193, 207, 214, 224, 244, 248). On origins of the Order, especially in connection with the kings of Aragon, see the same author's rambling *Real patronato de los serenísimos señores reyes de España en el real, y militar orden de Nuestra Señora de la Merced, redención de cautivos*, 2 vols. (Barcelona, 1725). See also Gazulla's "Jaime I y Merced."

7—II

86. Arch. Nac. Madrid, Clero: Valencia, Mercedarios, leg. 2,043, arm. 44, fab. 2 (Sept. 16, 1256): "habitum sive signum illud quod decetero deferatis, scutum scilicet signi nostri regni et crucem desuper positam album"; see also the document of June 13, 1251 in *Colección diplomática*, doc. 1,069.

87. King James to Nolasco, letter appended by Gayangos in Forster's English translation of *Llibre dels feyts*, I, 150n. Gazulla, "Jaime I y Merced," p. 371. This document may not be authentic; indeed, wherever Nolasco himself enters the story, it is prudent to be skeptical.

88. See the houses in Guillermo Vázquez Núñez, *Breve reseña de los conventos de la orden de la Merced* (Rome, 1932), esp. pp. 26–32; his edited *Actas del capítulo general de 1317 celebrada en Valencia* (Rome, 1930), esp. p. 10; and his *Manual*, esp. p. 125.

89. *Repartimiento*, p. 189; cf. p. 253; confirmed by the king February 21, 1263 in *Itinerari*, p. 334. The (corrected) date of the grant is July 14, 1238. There is a plaza on the site today, named after them (*Nomenclátor de Valencia*, p. 422). Pope Innocent IV refers to this church in 1245 (*Antigüedades de Valencia*, II, 45). See also Escolano, *Décadas*, I, 498. Despite Teixidor's intense refutation of Esclapés, the Mercedarians do seem to have named their little mosque St. Eulalia's; it so appears in the 1240 document below in note 92. St. Dominic's (or St. Eulalia's) would be the old mosque remodeled; by 1382 St. Dominic's was already reported as "ancient and threatening to collapse."

90. James confirmed to the Barcelona commander six jovates of land in "Naquarella" (probably Andarella) on September 18, 1238, but this was never actually received; it was shortly compensated by Alcira property ("Aliaciria"). See Faustino Gazulla, "Los religiosos de la Merced en la ciudad de Valencia (siglo xiii)," *BSCC*, VI (1925), 1.

91. *Ibid.*, p. 2; see also his "Jaime I y Merced," pp. 377–380.

92. Gazulla, "Merced en Valencia," p. 5. Arnold of Carcassonne or also "de Gasconibus" may really have been prior general; in 1265 he was prior at Lérida. Arnold was prior of Valencia in a document of July 1240 (Gazulla, "Merced en Valencia," p. 5; *Itinerari*, p. 144). Raymond was prior in the document below, in note 109. Sancho Blanco culls Mercedarian names for the realms in his "Nolasco," as does Vázquez in his *Manual*; see also the names involved in the 1317 *Actas del capítulo general en Valencia*.

93. Gazulla, "Jaime I y Merced," pp. 376–377, from a 1260 document.

94. Puig is simply the Latin *podium*, a descriptive designation of the small hill; the Arabic equivalent of this, repeated by the medieval Christian, emerged as Juballa or Capulla or Cebolla—hence Puig de Cebolla or Onion Hill. It also bore the name Puig de Enesa. In old Catalan this hill was "Pug de Sebolla" or "Pug de Sancta Maria."

95. J. Langdon-Davies, citing Narciso Camós, in *Gatherings from Catalonia*, p. 133. On the Puig monastery see Gazulla, "El puig de Santa María," 593–654; and Francisco Boyl, *N[uestra] S[eñora] del Puche, camara angelical de María santissima, patrona de la insigne ciudad, y reyno de Valencia, monasterio real del orden de redentores de Nuestra Señora de la Merced . . .*, (Zaragoza, 1631), fols. 7 ff., 112–113, and *passim*.

96. *Cartulari de Poblet*, ed. J. Pons i Marqués (Barcelona, 1938), pp. 11–12, docs. 29–30, and p. 19, doc. 41; each planned a conquest, a monastery, and burial there. Supplement with *Antigüedades de Valencia*, II, docs. on pp. 48–49. The Cid had made his headquarters here at one time, and it has been called "the Covadonga of Valencia."

97. *Llibre dels feyts*, ch. 237.

98. *Itinerari*, p. 144; *Antigüedades*, II, 46 (July 26, 1240).

99. See Chapter VIII, note 136.

100. *Nomenclátor de Valencia*, p. 354.

101. Arch. Cath., perg. 2363 (Aug. 27, 1240): "sit notum cunctis quod nos Ferrer miseracione divina Electus Valentinus et prepositus Tarrachonensis, volentes et cupientes participes fieri elemosinarum et aliorum merce[de] operum que fuerunt in hordine Fratrum de la merce[de] per nos et successores nostros damus et perpetuo concedimus pro salute anime nostre fratribus antedictis Ecclesiam que vocatur podium sancte Marie."

102. *Ibid.:* "hominum ibi commorancium."

103. Arch. Cath., perg. 2,364 (Sept. 15, 1244).

104. *Nomenclátor de Valencia*, p. 354.

105. Arch. Crown, Peter III, Reg. Canc. 46, fol. 66 (Mar. 9, 1281) for the Bruny gift (Segó is Vall de Segó, also called Valletes de Sagunto). "Ipsi habeant privilegium franquitatis concessum eisdem a domino Iacobo . . . in quo continetur quod totam partem eos [*sic*] contingente[m] de peyta pro alqueriis de Raphalaçeyt et de Valle de Segon quam Guillelmus Brunii eisdem legavit in suo testamento . . . relaxari deberet . . ." See Gazulla, "Jaime I y Merced," p. 383. The testaments are in Chapter VII, notes 53, 54, 60, 61, 94, and in Chapter XI, notes 11, 21.

106. Arch. Nac. Madrid, Clero: Valencia, Puig, has a special section for these Mercedarian benefactions. Maria's gift was to the "domus captivorum Valencie," Dominic's to "domui mercedis captivorum Valencie" (see wills in Chapter VII, note 92 and Chapter XI, note 11).

107. *Colección diplomática*, doc. 520 (Sept. 30, 1255). A four-year quarrel ensued with the previous incumbents. See doc. 1,109; *Itinerari*, p. 248; and Chapter XV, devoted to St. Vincent's.

108. Gazulla, "Merced en Valencia," p. 2.

109. Arch. Nac. Madrid, Clero: Valencia, Mercedarians, leg. 2,043, arm. 44, fab. 2 (Aug. 6, 1245): "semper teneatis Hospitale in Villa Denie ad honorem dei et servicium pauperum captivorum." See also on this document *Itinerari*, p. 174 (July 29, 1245).

110. Faustino Gazulla, "Los mercedarios en Játiva durante el siglo xiii," *BSCC*, IV (1923), 131. See also Sarthou Carreres, *Monasterios valencianos*, p. 270, who puts the foundation in 1248.

111. Gazulla, "Mercedarios en Játiva," p. 131; Arch. Nac. Madrid, Clero: Valencia, Mercedarios, leg. 2,043, arm. 44, fab. 2 (Jan. 4, 1242). The Ondara fort is in Gazulla, "Jaime I y Merced," p. 378.

112. *Itinerari*, p. 193 (Sept. 1, 1248): "quasdam domos in Segorbis [*sic*] contiguas domibus Dominici castellani, et unum ortum."

113. *Nomenclátor de Valencia*, p. 170.

114. Gazulla, "Mercedarios en Arguines y Algar," p. 67 (Mar. 5, 1244). He gave it to St. Peter Nolasco, retaining a fourth of the wine and wheat, and stipulating that a convent of the Order and a church be built, and a chantry provided for the souls of his relatives, himself, and the king.

115. *Ibid.*, p. 68. They may have administered it from 1244, receiving ownership in 1251.

116. *Ibid.*; but possession would have been taken only after his death in 1252.

117. Gazulla, "Mercedarios en Játiva," p. 129 (May 5, 1248; Játiva was conquered in 1244).

118. *Ibid.* (Oct. 1, 1253), a legacy from a canon of Barcelona and Gerona.

119. Gazulla, "Mercedarios en Játiva," p. 137 (June 7, 1237). There were two

altars in the church at the time; its name was changed from "St. Michael" to "St. Michael and St. Bartholomew" (pp. 137–138).

120. *Actas del capítulo general de 1317 celebrada en Valencia*, pp. 34–35: "careat non modicum facultatibus."

121. Sarthou Carreres, *Historia de Játiva*, I, 87.

122. Gazulla, "Merced en Valencia," p. 4 (Mar. 19, 1254).

123. *Ibid.* (April 2, 1255); see his "Jaime I y Merced", p. 383. See too the Murviedro holdings in Arch. Nac. Madrid, Clero: Valencia, Mercedarios, leg. 2,043, arm. 44, fab. 2 (Mar. 4, 1266; and *an.* 1270); the last is "in valle Fecundi termino Muriveteris." These are for the Puig shrine.

124. Gazulla, "Jaime I," p. 384.

125. Gazulla, "Mercedarios en Játiva," p. 136 (Feb. 13, 1292).

126. Gazulla, "Merced en Valencia," p. 3 (Feb. 8, 1245). On oblates or *donnés* see the works cited in Chapter XV, section 2, "Beneficiaries, Staff, Pensioners."

127. Gazulla, "Merced en Valencia," p. 4 (Mar. 28, 1253); see the two documents about them in the appendix to Gazulla, "Puig de Santa María," pp. 647–650, docs. 1, 2.

128. Arch. Nac. Madrid, Clero: Valencia, Mercedarios, leg. 2,043, arm. 44, fab. 2 (Oct. 13, 1268): "dono et offero me ipsum in fratrem ordinis." These were for the support of the Puig shrine; he was a former Léridan, resident in Valencia.

129. Gazulla, "Mercedarios en Játiva," pp. 135–136 (Oct. 2, 1256).

130. *Colección diplomática*, doc. 1,074 (Mar. 12, 1255); *Itinerari*, pp. 244–245: "quod omnes homines ac femine, tam nobiles quam ignobiles tocius terre nostre aut regni, tam milites quam cives . . . possint vobis . . . permutare, dare insuper et legare . . . quaslibet hereditates possessiones ac domos . . . regales vel non regales ubicumque sint."

131. *Ibid.*, p. 518 (May 4, 1275).

132. Gazulla, "Jaime I y Merced," pp. 387–388; "Mercedarios en Játiva," pp. 136 ff., 139; "Merced en Valencia," p. 4. Sarthou Carreres, *Historia de Játiva*, I, 87.

133. Arch. Nac. Madrid, Clero: Valencia, Mercedarios, leg. 2,197, arm. 46, fab. 2 (Aug. 22, 1291): "in podio Sancte Marie, Domos terras et vineas quas habetis in Civitate et diocesi valentini"; "domos terras et vineas quas habetis in Villa Denie"; "Ecclesiam Sancti Dominici sitam in Civitate Valentina cum omnibus pertinenciis suis"; "Domos terras vineas possessiones quas [habetis] in Castris et Villis que Burriana, Xhativa, Algar, Rafalinardha, Rafalatrer[?], Gandia, Cosentanea, Segorb, Mula, Ariona, Almaza, et Beier vulgariter appelantur."

NOTES TO CHAPTER XIV. THE SHADOW OF CASTILE: WARDING OFF THE STRANGER

1. Arch. Cath. Toledo has two contemporary manuscripts of the trial about to be considered; both are in clear, easy script. The original roll is Becerro II de la catedral de Toledo; the bound version is included in the Liber privilegiorum ecclesie toletane. Over a decade ago the Toledo archivist Juan Francisco Rivera announced his project of publishing an edition of the latter, including the trial. See his remarks in "El 'Liber privilegiorum' de la catedral de Toledo y los documentos reales en el contenidos," *HS*, I (1948), 164. Bibl. Nac. Madrid MSS have a fragmentary copy of Tarragona cathedral's lost version, no. 13,028, D-47, fols. 2-21, with the 1248 Valencia statute on fol. 33. Arch. Nac. Madrid has a copy of the Toledo roll, as sig. mod. 1,241, fols. 126–180, Becerro II. Arch. Vat. has its

own, slightly different original; it is often fragmentary, is badly preserved, and was difficult to use. It is filed under Archivum arcis (Archivio di Castel San Angelo), armaria inferiora, arm. I–XVIII, 2,222, Processus causae vertentis inter archiepiscopos toletanum et terraconensem super subiectione ecclesiae valentinae.

F. Martorell has published parts of the Vatican record as "Fragmentos inéditos de la 'Ordinatio ecclesiae valentinae'" in the *Cuadernos de trabajos* of the Escuela española de arqueología e historia en Roma, I (1912), 81–127. R. Chabás gives large samplings of the Madrid library copy in his *Episcopologio valentino* (pp. 375–397, with an index). J. Sanchís Sivera has copied the Madrid archives version into his *Diócesis valentina* (II, 191–412). The director of the diocesan museum at Valencia, Vicente Castell Maiques, has begun collating texts for a critical edition of the whole record; his recent paper at the congress of studies on the realms of Aragon, giving full information on available texts and bibliography, is being published by the Consejo Superior in the proceedings of the congress. For practical purposes citations in this book refer to the defective Sanchís Sivera copy, under its title *Ordinatio ecclesiae valentinae*, since its quality of availability for the reader outweighs its disadvantages of hasty transcription.

2. *Llibre dels feyts*, chs. 339–340.

3. Ramón d'Abadal y de Vinyals lucidly traces the evolution in his *Els primers comtes catalans*, Biografies catalanes, sèrie històrica, no. I (Barcelona, 1958); see part I, chs. 6–8, and part 2, chs. 5–6.

4. J. F. Rivera, "Personajes hispanos asistentes en 1215 al iv concilio de Letrán: revisión y aportación nueva de documentos, datos biográficos," *HS, IV* (1951), 336: "pro terraconensi autem archiepiscopo, quod erat absens, respondit uicensis, suffraganeus eius, pro se et omnibus suffraganeis suis, quorum multi erant presentes, quod to[leta]nus archiepiscopus non erat eorum primas nec tenebantur ei in aliquo obedire." The bishop of Compostela insisted at the council "quod erat falsissimum" that Toledo was "primas Hyspaniarum." The incident, and the speeches connected with it, have long been the subject of heated debate, but the substance can hardly be challenged today; see Stephen Kuttner and Antonio García y García, "A New Eyewitness Account of the Fourth Lateran Council," *Traditio*, XX (1964), 124, 136–138. The council brought together 71 higher prelates, 412 bishops, 900 abbots and priors, legates of the Byzantine and Holy Roman emperors, and 5 kings (including England and Aragon).

5. Gorosterratzu, *Rodrigo Jiménez de Rada*, ch. 10 and *passim*, e.g. pp. 177, 326–327. Some background documentation on the Toledan primacy to 1216 is in the *Monumenta Hispaniae vaticana* (see index *sub* "primacía"). The documentation on Roderick's primatial rights, requested from Rome in 1239, is in Arch. Vat., Reg. Vat. 19 (Gregory IX), fols. 144 ff., partially published by Auvray in *Registres*, III, nos. 5,025 ff.

6. Johannes Vincke has explored this subject in a number of articles and monographs such as his "Kloster und Grenzpolitik in Katalonien-Aragon," and the introductory essay of his *Documenta selecta* (esp. pp. xviii–xix). He finds by about 1300 "nun fast alle Landesklöster und Ordenshäuser durch eigene Provinzen oder Kongregationen zusammengefast" ("Kloster und Grenzpolitik in Katalonien-Aragon während des Mittelalters," *Gesammelte Aufsätze zur Kulturgeschichte Spaniens*, III, 1931, p. 163; cf. pp. 161, 164). The origins of nationalism in the Middle Ages is a thorny question; an able survey is Boyd Shafer's *Nationalism, Myth and Reality* (New York, 1955), ch. 5.

7. "El rey de Castilla no estaba dispuesto, a tolerar que la sede de la cabeza de Castilla dependiese eclesiásticamente de la metrópoli de Tarragona, a la que en otro tiempo perteneció." Urban II ended the dispute by putting it as an exempt

diocese directly under himself. See Demetrio Mansilla Reoyo, "Episcopologio de Burgos, siglo xiii," *HS*, IV (1951), 314.

8. *Crònica*, ch. 23.

9. James demanded that all friars, "qui de nostro dominio non existunt," be replaced by those "de nostro oriundis dominio" (*Documenta selecta*, doc. 77 [Sept. 14, 1297]; the pope finally granted this in 1304; cf. "Kloster und Grenzpolitik," p. 162). The "monachi de dominio regni Castelle" at Piedra he accused of treasonable sympathies, and ordered every one back to Castile (*Documenta*, doc. 85 [Dec. 16, 1299]). The Roda incident is in doc. 39 (Nov. 17, 1284).

10. The king proposed that "ea que, de et sub episcopatu Cartaginensi qui est sub dominio regis Castelle, sunt infra terram regis Aragonum" be detached and put under an Aragonese metropolitan as part of a new diocese of Játiva (*Documenta*, doc. 318 [Nov. 22, 1317]). In the mid-fourteenth century the crown of Aragon would not allow John Gratian to be archbishop in Sardinia because "nullatenus pateremur prelatum . . . nisi Aragonensem aut Cathalanum origine" in a key post (doc. 543). Here too no more than four non-Aragonese friars were allowed in Franciscan or Dominican houses, nor any superior "nisi sit Aragonensis originaliter vel eciam Cathalanus."

11. The only other explanation, one which does not take into account the context of the Valencian and similar contemporary quarrels, is the ingenious theory of Miguel Ferrer Flórez, who sees it as a reassertion of primitive Gregorian Reform ideals before the watching powers of Europe ("Mallorca y la teocracía pontificia," *AST*, XXIII, 1950, 16–30). Innocent IV in 1250 was to do the same for Cartagena, just south of Valencia, because of the bitter fight between Toledo and Tarragona over it. See the similar quarrel of the two over Burgos, and its exemption, above, in note 7. On the word "ordinare," see the *Dictionnaire étymologique de la langue latine, histoire des mots*, comp. A. Ernout and A. Meillet, 2nd ed. revised (Paris, 1939), p. 712; and F. Arnaldi and M. Turriana, "Latinitatis italicae medii aevi . . . ad annum MXXII lexicon imperfectum," *Bulletin Du Cange*, XX (1950), 194 ff.

12. Arch. Vat., Reg. Vat. 22, fol. 214 (July 10, 1245); and in Berger, *Registres*, I, no. 1,378; see the allied prohibition of October 6, 1248 in *Registres*, II, no. 4,185.

13. See note 39 and text.

14. On the ecclesiastical divisions of Spain at this time see the careful descriptions of Mansilla Reoyo, *Iglesia castellano-leonesa*, pp. 98 ff., esp. pp. 103–104. The ecclesiastical structure as elaborated in the taxation lists of the contemporary *Rationes decimarum* are also instructive.

15. These activities and documents are in Chapter III, section 1, "The Metropolitan Founds His Diocese"; see esp. notes 1, 11–14 with text. Quote is from the trial record *Ordinatio ecclesiae valentinae*, p. 409: "sarracenus ecclesias conferre non potuit."

16. Arch. Cath., perg. 2,302 (Oct. 18, 1238).

17. See Chapter III, note 8 and text.

18. Chapter II, note 59 and text.

19. Gorosterratzu, *Rodrigo Jiménez de Rada*, with documentary appendix in pp. 411–469; on the correspondence between the names Jiménez and Simon here see pp. 20, 471; on his work as a historian see ch. 18; on his role at Las Navas see ch. 12; on the two principles see p. 57. A brief, less scholarly biography is Manuel Ballesteros Gaibrois, *Don Rodrigo Jiménez de Rada* (Barcelona, 1936); pp. 159–160 touch upon the trial. See also Gams, *Kirchengeschichte von Spanien*, II, part 2 (see index *sub* "Rodrigo").

20. Gorosterratzu, *Rodrigo Jiménez de Rada*, pp. 324–325. Two bulls of July 19 speak of damage done to Roderick's church during his absence from Spain. A

series of authenticated bulls dated May and June of 1239 were given to agents of Roderick, he himself having left Rome; these concerned his primatial claims and could well have been acquired for use in the Valencia case (p. 326).

21. The document is in Arch. Vat., Reg. Vat. 19 (Gregory IX), included in Gregory's letter, fol. 146, June 27, 1239, and published by Auvray, *Registres*, III, no. 5,041. Cf. the *Ordinatio*, p. 195: "illarum civitatum diocesis, que sarracenis invadentibus, metropolitanos proprios amiserunt."

22. *Ordinatio ecclesiae valentinae*, p. 196: "de utriusque partis procuratorum assensu."

23. Arch. Vat., Reg. Vat. 19 (Gregory IX), fols. 102v–103r; published in *Registres*, III, no. 4,815. There are late copies in Bibl. Nac. Madrid and in Arch. Cath. The concluding portion of the document, only partially published by Auvray, reads: "efficaciter moneatis ut pia meditatione considerans quod in celestes thesauros congeritur quidquid ad laudem et gloriam divini nominis deputatur, futuro episcopo et cathedrali ac aliis ecclesiis Civitatis predicte dotes ita congruentes assignet ut sicut olim sic et in posterum munificam in prosperis divine sentiat dexteram maiestatis."

24. Arroniz seems to be Aranjuez, to the northeast of Toledo. On John Pérez see note 72. On Vidal see text, p. 280. Oloron, at that time subject to the viscount of Béarn, is west of Lourdes and southwest of Pau; in 1858 it incorporated with the bourg of Ste. Marie, below on the plain and across the river, into modern Oloron-Ste-Marie. John was bishop here from 1231 to 1246.

25. *Ordinatio*, p. 198 and see p. 398. The monastery of St. Mary of Fitero was just to the southwest of Fitero between Pamplona and Tudela, in the diocese of Tarazona. It had one of the largest and most important of the Cistercian churches in Spain; Roderick Simon of Rada may have begun it when bishop of Osma.

26. Gorosterratzu, *Rodrigo Jiménez de Rada*, pp. 328–329, 277. This background is given fully in José Goñi Gaztambide, "Los obispos de Pamplona del siglo xiii," *Príncipe de Viana*, XVIII (1957), 41–237.

27. *Ordinatio*, pp. 329–330. Roderick arrived at the end of November. On December 30, 1239 he was at the fortified town of Brihuega, a holding of the see of Toledo. But this absence was during a lacuna in the trial, when evidence was being gathered; nor was Brihuega very far from Tudela; so Roderick may well have returned to the scene later, at least from time to time. He was certainly present and active again at the final stage (see below, note 73 and text).

28. See note 104 and text.

29. Morera, *Tarragona cristiana*, II, 275.

30. Arch. Vat., Reg. Vat. 25, Alexander IV, fol. 19v (Feb. 12, 1257); noted but left unpublished by Bourel de la Roncière in the *Registres*, II, no. 1,749: "ecclesia valentina magnis sit debitis obligata."

31. *Aureum opus*, doc. 56, fol. 17v (July 7, 1258). As it affected the realms of King James, some background to this legal movement may be found in Tourtoulon, *Jaime I*, II, chs. 6, 7, and (for Valencia itself) 8; see also Miret y Sans, "Escolars catalans al estudi de Bolonia en la xiiia centuria," pp. 155, *passim*. See above, Chapter VI, note 6 and text.

32. Doc. quoted in Chapter VII, note 31.

33. Dubois, *The Recovery of the Holy Land*, tr.-ed. W. I. Brandt, Columbia University, Records of Civilization series (New York, 1956), pp. 141–142, with supporting quotations from his *Summaria*.

34. There was some transfer of ownership in the reshuffling, so that for example a reduced number would include new acquisitions. See Mansilla Reoya, *Iglesia castellano-leonesa*, p. 110; on Oreto, p. 71. Background on the Visigothic dioceses

may be found in the rather summary work of Luis Duart, *Obispados godos de Levante, aportación a la historia eclesiástica del reino de Valencia* (Madrid, 1961); and in a more general way in Zacarías García Villada, *Historia eclesiástical de España*, 3 vols. as 5 (Madrid, 1929–1936), III, ch. 9, and map on p. 215.

35. *Ordinatio ecclesiae valentinae*, p. 410: "fabulosam." The trial was to bring out that the bishops of old Valencia had regularly appeared in many Toledo councils but not at those of Tarragona.

36. See the Vatican copy in Martorell, "Fragmentos inéditos," p. 92.

37. Luis Vázquez de Parga has a critical study of the Wamba document, *La división de Wamba, contribución al estudio de la historia y geografiá eclesiásticas de la edad media española* (Madrid, 1943); its use in this trial is discussed on p. 46. It was also used in confirming the boundaries of the Zaragoza diocese in Aragon (1158).

38. *Ordinatio*, pp. 213–214: "impertinens," "alicubi sic, alicubi non sic."

39. *Ibid.*: "regnum Valentie est pars illius provincie que dicitur Aragonia sive Arago."

40. *Ibid.*, p. 232: "fuisse ingresum possessionem meçquitarum Valentie auctoritate illustris Regis Aragonum, qui civitatem et regnum occupavit." The Abbot William above was suggested by King St. Ferdinand III in 1239 as papal negotiator with the empire; he will be used in this capacity in 1243, and created a cardinal in 1244.

41. Mansilla Reoyo, *Iglesia castellano-leonesa*, p. 93n.; the author considers this the strongest part of Tarragona's case for Valencia.

42. *Ordinatio ecclesiae valentinae*, p. 233: "rex Aragonum potuit conferre et contulit ecclesias in diocesi Valentie constructas Archiepiscopo Terraconensi ratione [privilegii] domini Pape regibus Aragonum concesse."

43. *Ibid.*, p. 405. Cf. p. 410: "nec me movent libri nec monumenta ex parte domini Toletani producta cum non publica sit sed privata."

44. *Ibid.*, p. 407: "presumptio iuris pro possessore faciat." Other forms of the original argument come up: "favorabiles sint [leges] rei quam actores" in civil and canon law; and the possessor is preferred "cum promptiora sint iura ad solvendum quam ad condempnandum" (p. 411).

45. *Ibid.*

46. This applied only when reconquest was obviously possible by the negligent bishop; his neglect must previously have been called to his attention by a convention of neighboring bishops, so as to give him a chance to do better (*ibid.*, p. 408).

47. See note 19. In fact, his biographer feels constrained to defend this fierce aspect of his character (*Ordinatio*, pp. 391–392).

48. *Ordinatio*, p. 409: "multa mala contulit sarracenis"; "pro viribus."

49. *Ibid.*, p. 235: "expoliavit . . . vel spoliari mandavit . . . vel ratam habuit spoliationem."

50. *Ibid.*, p. 409 (Anastasius, Urban); cf. Chapter IV, note 124 and text.

51. Martorell, "Fragmentos inéditos," p. 88. The phrase only appears in this one version, a *passio* incorrectly attributed to Prudentius and based upon the *acta* of St. Vincent's martyrdom.

52. *Itinerari*, pp. 353–354.

53. *Ordinatio ecclesiae valentinae*, pp. 249–250: "precaventes ne effranatam multitudinem testium recipiatis contra canonicas sanctiones"; "occupavit meçquitam maiorem de mandato regis . . . mandavit fieri tria altaria . . . recepit claves meçquite . . . apposuit custodes . . . consecravit eadem [altaria]"; similar questions are provided concerning the other claims.

54. *Rationes decimarum*, II, 103, 120. It is possible, though not likely, that he is

the "Stephenus de Ariberti clericus" who witnessed the 1279 Zaragoza accounts (p. 91). He should not be confused with the Tarragona citizen, Stephen Giles Tarín, who signed an important political document in 1260 and received a broad tax-exemption for life from the king in 1265, but who died in 1276 (*Itinerari*, pp. 307, 364, 531).

55. *Ordinatio*, p. 252: "ne dum de hoc diceptaretur, contingeret processum negotii retardari"; "in quantum de iure debet esse salvum."

56. *Ibid.*, p. 336, e.g.: "in fine aliud folium conglutinatum cum tabula."

57. *Ibid.*, pp. 336-339. The Toledan or Visigothic script preceded the French script which, though it was in Catalonia in the ninth century, was carried into Spain especially by the Cluniac monks at the end of the eleventh century.

58. *Ibid.*, p. 340: "non erat tantae scientiae"; p. 345: "post captionem civitatis Valentie audivit quod erat controversia . . . super ea, et alias nesciebat quod esset fama sed aliqui dicebant . . . Toletane et aliqui quod Tarraconensi, sed plures dicebant de Toletana"; p. 346: "decem anni, vel parum plus, vel parum minus"; p. 347: "que est in provincia toletana"; p. 348: "de quatro arriba"; p. 349: "sed qui erant non recordatur, et si recordaretur non diceret"; "si recordaretur, diceret"; "antequam rex Aragonum veniret ad obsidendum Valentiam et post."

59. *Ibid.*, p. 350: "ex quo fuit Valencia opsessa." "Dominicus dictus abbas" is in the *Rationes decimarum* in 1279 for this diocese (II, 78). Peter Ferdinand's own bishop, who also claimed Segorbe diocese in the kingdom of Valencia, was Toledo's agent within the crusading army of King James (see Chapter III, section 1, "The Metropolitan Founds His Diocese").

60. *Ordinatio*, p. 350: "quod Valentia erat in conquista regis Aragonum, et quod ecclesia debebat obedire ecclesie Toletane"; "quod cum Valentia caperetur, quod esset suffraganea Toletana." This was said "a quodam magno viro de Maioribus terre."

61. *Ibid.*, p. 358: "quidam obediebant et quidam non, et dicebatur per civitatem a magnatibus quod spectabat Valentia ad archiepiscopum Toletanum et ab aliis quod spectabat ad Terrachonensem." The word "magnates" probably bears its technical meaning here: men of high feudal station, the barons and great knights on the crusade.

62. For example, the witness who recalls: "et plus regebat se exercitus pro eo quam [*sic*] pro episcopo [Albarracensi]" (*ibid.*, p. 260: cf. p. 356).

63. *Ibid.*, p. 365: "audivit multotiens et a multis quod Valentinus erat suffraganeus Archiepiscopo Toletano, et etiam murmurabantur dum erant in exercitu Valentie quia Toletanus non veniebat ad exercitum."

64. *Ibid.*, pp. 287-288.

65. E.g.: "de Romana [littera] . . . nec videbatur littera multum antiqua"; "debebat multum apreciari"; "antiquum et bonum"; "satis antiquus."

66. *Ibid.*, p. 276: "presentes erant non iurati."

67. *Ibid.*, p. 280: "in superiore parte remansit aliquantulum de cera"; p. 284: "per leges suas adiurati"; p. 275: "quamvis presens esset, noluit aliquid dicere quid sibi videbatur de libro, licet super hoc a nobis requisitus"; p. 285: "post aliquantulam moram"; "quod credebat ipsam bonam villam, et aliquando fuisse civitatem"; "nunquam fuerat civitas sed villula."

68. E.g.: "repperitur 'Iohannes' et reperiuntur due 'ss' . . . sed in tribus aliis . . . non sunt ibi due 'ss'" (*ibid.*, p. 291); "ibi locus vacuus sine rasura, et capax tante scripture vel maioris" (p. 293).

69. *Ibid.*, p. 375: "ita bene sicut credit Deum esse."

70. *Ibid.*, p. 372: "ipse non fuit in fundatione predicte ville"; pp. 297-298: "nos autem iudices non vidimus istud privilegium [originale] nec scimus utrum sit

transcriptum, quia non vidimus bullatum nec sigillatum, nec scimus nec credimus quod publica manu sit roboratum, nec scimus utrum ab aliquo instrumento sit extractum"; p. 314: "operam collatiendi librorum"; p. 315: "fuisse civitatem et sedem episcopalem et ibi fuisse episcopum et credit quod ab initio fuit vocata Valentia"; p. 317: "ad ostium domus ospicii eorum"; p. 321: "rex Bambe fuit multum presumptuosus et abutens potentia . . . sua circa ecclesias"; "olim plures fuerunt Valentie."

71. *Ibid.*, p. 324: "et cum fuisset diutius disputatum," or "eadem die esset diu allegatum a partibus" (*ibid.*, p. 324).

72. *Ibid.*, p. 329: "propter plurimas ecclesias quas habet"; "ad Sedem Apostolicam appellamus"; p. 329–330 (Gregory). There is record of a dispensation in 1234 by Gregory IX, by which he could hold an extra benefice; other dispensations may have come later. (See Mansilla Reoyo, *Iglesia castellano-leonosa*, p. 246 and doc. in n. 288.) On John Pérez of Arroniz see above, note 24.

73. *Ordinatio*, p. 330: "instaret ora ferendi sententiam"; p. 388: "legite cum eo, legite cum eo"; "ambobus legentibus sic pronunciaverunt sententiam"; p. 333: "de bonorum iurisperitorum consilio sententiando, adiudicamus ordinationem ecclesie valentine archiepiscopo Toletano"; p. 388: "quod absit." See also the transcript by Fita in "Don Pedro de Albalat," pp. 342–345. On the metropolitans being present see pp. 388, 392; and cf. note 27.

74. *Ibid.*, p. 335: "longam recitationem facti et iuris"; p. 393: "inter se verba habuerunt" (cf. pp. 391–392); p. 395: "ad ostium camere"; "quidam qui intus erant, in camera, clamabant ne vox Raymundi . . . audiretur"; "per quoddam foramen ostii"; "dixit quod valeret appellatio et valere poterat [*sic*]."

75. Both S. Martino ai Monti and S. Lorenzo in Lucina are in Rome. On May 14, 1240 Cardinal Sinibald noted the appeal by Tarragona (see Gorosterratzu, *Rodrigo Jiménez de Rada*, p. 330 and docs. of March and December on pp. 464–465).

76. *Ibid.*, pp. 388, 384, 386, 399.

77. *Diócesis valentina*, II, 430 and n.; Martínez de la Vega cited a bull of February 15, 1240 (*ibid.*).

78. One of the surviving documents may have been misinterpreted; if there was a document now lost, it too was misread, as the events about to be narrated show.

79. *Episcopologio valentino*, p. 397.

80. Gorosterratzu, *Rodrigo Jiménez de Rada*, p. 331.

81. H. K. Mann, *The Lives of the Popes in the Middle Ages*, 18 vols. (London, 1906-1932), XIII, covers Gregory's pontificate well except in connection with Aragon. The political history of the papal state and the changing policies of the popes are examined in detail by Daniel Waley, *The Papal State in the Thirteenth Century* (London, 1961).

82. Mann, *Lives of Popes*, vol. XIV, is a detailed but overly sympathetic biography of Sinibald; Ernst Kantorowicz, *Frederick the Second, 1194-1250*, tr. E. O. Lorimer (New York, 1957), supplies useful detail but from an overly hostile viewpoint. By the pious he is presented as a hero, by the German nationalist as a villain. On his legal side see Mann, pp. 14-17nn. The Ancona March, a critical post which he governed from 1235 to 1240, will be held by the bishop of Valencia from 1291.

83. Document dated from Calatayud A.D. 1239 but actually incarnational (1240), inserted into the *Ordinatio ecclesiae valentinae*, p. 389. Was he a relative of the canon Bernard of Soler at Valencia cathedral, who was also papal subdeacon, notary to the king, and apparently judge-ordinary in Cerdagne from 1263?

84. Gorosterratzu, *Rodrigo Jiménez de Rada*, pp. 327–338; on p. 326 the date 1241 is incorrect. A bull of April 24, 1239 had confirmed his primatial rights, and

he left Rome for Spain shortly afterward; he may therefore have crossed the Tarragona province just after the provincial council of 1239. On August 25 he would be invited to return to Rome for the ecumenical council of 1241.

85. *Collectio maxima conciliorum*, V, 189. *Episcopologio valentino*, pp. 370-371n. Cf. *Diócesis valentina*, II, 418-419n.; Morera, *Tarragona cristiana*, II, 277-278.

86. See note 90; it speaks of Toledan rights "que sibi competere poterant ex indulgentia sedis apostolice speciali" (what is the exact force of "poterant" here?), and notes that a complaint could have been entered at Rome. The quote below is: "apud Valentiam quam ad suam asserit provinciam pertinere."

87. *Viage literario*, XIX, 330-331. For Gorosterratzu on the bulls see above, note 20. For the papal rebuke see note 90.

88. Mann, *Lives of the Popes*, XIII, 305, quoting a pamphlet of that year; this seems to have been a stock epithet for Frederick (see Kantorowicz, *Frederick*, pp. 593, 546). See also Waley, *Papal State in the Thirteenth Century*, pp. 146 ff.

89. Kantorowicz, *Frederick*, p. 549.

90. Arch. Vat., Reg. Vat. 20 (Gregory IX), fol. 68v (April 16, 1241). The document is published by Auvray in the *Registres*, III, no. 5,978, also in the *Episcopologio valentino*, pp. 371-372n., and in *Diócesis valentina*, II, 419n.

91. Arch. Vat., Reg. Vat. 20 (Gregory IX), fol. 87v (July 14, 1241): "cum non potuisset liquere de meritis causae." Auvray notes the document (*Registres*, III, no. 6,086), and Gorosterratzu publishes it (*Rodrigo Jiménez de Rada*, pp. 466-467, doc. 164).

92. *Ibid.*: "coram ipso papa compareant." Peter Guarner is of "Burdegala." On Peter Albert see *Itinerari*, pp. 125, 179, 279, 319 (*an.* 1236-1262).

93. Arch. Vat., Reg. Vat. 21 (Innocent IV), fol. 3v: "testes recipiant ac diligenter examinent." The document is noted by Berger (*Registres*, I, no. 17), and published by Gorosterratzu (*Rodrigo Jiménez de Rada*, p. 466, doc. 165) and in the *Bullarium ordinis praedicatorum*, I, 119-120.

94. *Itinerari*, p. 167. *Llibre dels feyts*, chs. 343 ff., 348. For the treaty see *Colección diplomática*, doc. 269; it was also signed by Archdeacon Martin of the Valencia cathedral.

95. Gorosterratzu, *Rodrigo Jiménez de Rada*, pp. 392-393.

96. Olmos y Canalda discusses the date (*Prelados valentinos*, p. 59). See also *Diócesis valentina*, II, 415; Escolano, *Décadas de Valencia*, I, 285; Fita, "Don Pedro de Albalat," p. 34. The metropolitan council held at Valencia on May 8, 1240 has Ferrer's signature as bishop-elect. For Castellbisbal's life see above, Chapter II, note 37 and text; for Ferrer see *ibid.*, notes 38-50 and text. The April 1239 papal document is in Chapter VIII, note 4.

97. Arch. Cath., perg. 1,308 (Oct. 21, 1240): "nos Ferrarius dei gratia sedis Valentie electus."

98. *Diócesis valentina*, II, 429; *Viage literario*, XIX, 127.

99. As early as June 23, 1240, appearing as elect but signing as bishop (Arch. Cath., perg. 2,309). In perg. 2,330 he has "nos F. dei gracia Episcopus Valencie," yet the date is March 4, 1240 (cf. *Diócesis valentina*, II, 430); and later (Aug. 27, 1240), in an agreement with the Mercedarians, he has again become "electus valentinus."

100. Gorosterratzu, *Rodrigo Jiménez de Rada*, pp. 47, 55.

101. *Ibid.*, p. 163.

102. *Ibid.*, p. 53.

103. Arch. Cath., perg. 2,310 (June 14, 1242) when the metropolitan was reviewing the organization of the Valencian church. *Diócesis valentina*, II, 440 for the council and necrology.

104. *Cartulario de "Sant Cugat" del Vallés*, ed. J. Rius Serra, 3 vols. (Barcelona, 1946–1947), III, 501–502, doc. 1,385 (Feb. 22, 1244): "camerarius Terrachone." On William of Soler see *Itinerari*, docs. on pp. 222, 261.

NOTES TO CHAPTER XV. ST. VINCENT'S: CROWN OF THE IDEOLOGICAL RECONSTRUCTION

1. *Itinerari*, p. 319 (Mar. 17, 1262), a later privilege by James: "monumentum sive locum in quo beatus Vincencius fuit positus in tormento."

2. Arch. Crown, James I, Reg. Canc. 12, fol. 79v (May 17, 1263): "quia fides nostra talis est quod dominus Ihesus Christus ad preces speciales [?] Sancti Vincentii nobis civitatem et totum Regnum Valentie subiugavit et eripuit de posse et manibus paganorum."

3. See, for example, the short letter of King Peter ordering municipal authorities to defend St. Vincent's (Arch. Crown, Peter III, Reg. Canc. 59, fol. 40v [July 22, 1282]). A chapter is devoted to St. Vincent's in *Diócesis valentina* (II, 149–170), brief, jejune, and not free from serious inexactitudes of detail. Much the same ground had been previously covered by Chabás in his *Episcopologio valentino* (chs. 5–6). Underlying both is the work of Teixidor in the *Antigüedades de Valencia* (II, ch. 4, and I, 403–410); he devotes considerable attention to correcting the inexactitudes of Escolano. Jaime Finestres includes a dissertation on St. Vincent's in his *Historia del real monasterio de Poblet*, III, diss. 2. Sarthou Carreres touches only slightly on the place in his *Monasterios valencianos* (pp. 21 ff.). Two codices of St. Vincent documentation in Arch. Nac. Madrid deserve notice: (1) the medieval collection of thirteenth-century materials, Privilegia et scripta S. Vincentii Valencie; and (2) the compilation by P. F. Lluch in 1763, Repertori de tots los privilegis, y gracies reals, ê indults ô bulles apostolics, i demes escriptures y papers que se encontren en lo arxiu de este real priorat de San Vicent.

4. Arch. Nac. Madrid, Clero: Valencia, St. Vincent, leg. 2,079, arm. 45, fab. 1 (April 17, 1239): "beati Vincencii martiris qui iuxta Civitatem Valencie martirio extitit coronatus."

5. On Vincent see the *Bibliotheca hagiographica latina antiquae et mediae aetatis*, ed. the Bollandists, 2 vols. (Brussels, 1898–1901), II, 1,247–1,250; and the life as understood by contemporaries of King James I, in Jacobus da Voragine's *Golden Legend* (I, 114–117).

6. Doc. in González, *Castilla en la época de Alfonso VIII*, II, 162–165 (*an.* 1167), but see I, 102, with the more probable 1179 date.

7. Arch. Nac. Madrid, Codices, Repertori, fol. 43, grants of 1177, 1212.

8. Arch. Nac. Madrid, Codices, Privilegia, fol. 1 (era 1270): "apud Valenciam laudabilem civitatem." See the *Antigüedades de Valencia*, I, 406–407 and II, 272; *Colección diplomática*, doc. 106; *El archivo*, IV (1890), 292–293 (Mar. 19, 1232). Miret y Sans argues that the date (era 1270) is a scribal error for era 1271, our 1233 (*Itinerari*, p. 101). See the confirmation of this charter, under changed circumstances, in Arch. Crown, Peter III, Reg. Canc. 44, fol. 190 (Aug. 26, 1280). St. Victorian began as St. Martin of Asán (ca. 506) in the diocese of Huesca (now of Barbastro) between the rivers Esera and Cinca; it emerged again at the beginning of the eleventh century to become one of the most powerful Aragonese monasteries; see A. Lambert, "Asan," *DHGE*, IV, cols. 867–870; *Répertoire topo-bibliographique des abbayes et prieurés*, ed. L. H. Cottineau, 2 vols. (Mâcon, 1939), I, 169–170, *sub* "Asan," with bibliography.

9. *Itinerari*, p. 128 (July 9, 1237). On James's patronage see, for example, the document of January 7, 1254 (p. 235). Sanchís Sivera notes the existence of a

grant to the monastery "Crassensis" but confuses this with St. Victorian itself, and even supposes that its abbot Bernard is to be identified with Bernard the first prior at St. Vincent's (*Diócesis valentina*, II, 151–152 and n.). On Lagrasse see the *Répertoire des abbayes*, I, 1,334–1,335; on its jurisdictional penetration into the realms of Aragon and its importance there, see Vincke, "Kloster und Grenzpolitik," pp. 141–143, 156.

10. Bibl. Nat. Paris, MSS Latin, no. 5,455, Chartae monasterii S. Mariae crassensis, no. 7 (June 20, 1238). "Gregorius episcopus servus servorum dei, Dilectis filiis Abbati et Conventui de Crassa Carcassonensis diocesis salutem et apostolicam benedictionem. Cum a nobis petitur quod iustum est et honestum tam vigor equitatis quam ordo exigit rationis ut id per sollicitudinem officii nostri ad debitum perducatur effectum. Eapropter dilecti in domino filii nostri iustis postulationibus grato concurrentes assensu, Triginta Iovatas terre circa ecclesiam Scti Vincentii prope Valentiam quas Carissimus in Christo filius noster [Jacobus] Rex Aragonum Illustris vobis ut asseritis pia et provida liberalitate donavit, prout in eiusdem litteris asseritis plenius contineri ac alia bona vestra sicut ea omnia iuste ac pacifice possidetis vobis et per vos monasterio vestro auctoritate apostolica confirmamus et presentis scripti patrocinio communimus. Nullo ergo omnino hominum liceat hanc paginam nostre confirmationis infringere vel ei ausu temerario contraire. Si quis autem hoc attemptare presumpserit, indignationem omnipotentis dei et beatorum Petri et Pauli apostolorum eius se noverit incursurum. Datum Laterani, xii kalendas Iulii, pontificatus nostri anno duodecimo."

11. James confirms Lagrasse holdings for example in 1229 and 1265 (*ibid.*, no. 6 [Jan. 25, 1229]; and Collection de Languedoc [Doat], 67, fol. 33 [Sept. 22, 1265]). There was a charter of protection issued by James I on January 6, 1254 (*Itinerari*, p. 235). On Languedoc Benedictinism in the thirteenth century cf. R. W. Emery, *Heresy and Inquisition in Narbonne* (New York, 1941), pp. 115–116; and cf. note 142. Bernard was "multipliciter diffamatum de vitio incontinentiae."

12. *Ordinatio ecclesiae valentinae*, p. 369. Sanchís Sivera speaks of St. Vincent's hermitage as being in Boatella (*Diócesis valentina*, I, 285), but it was in the Rayosa of King James's day, just south of Boatella. Part of the old site of the church and shrine is now occupied by the nuns of St. Thecla (cf. *Nomenclátor de Valencia*, p. 422).

13. *Ordinatio*, p. 832. The witness, John the Painter [Pintor] of Teruel, says: "milites armati erant ibi cum eo [episcopo] quia alias non esset ausus celebrare ibi."

14. Arch. Vat., Reg. Vat. 19 (Gregory IX), fol. 68r, ep. 365 (Jan. 9, 1239); noted by Auvray in *Registres*, II, no. 4,705; published in *Documenta selecta*, doc. 6.

15. The project is referred to in Prior Bernard's document of 1240 cited below in note 23.

16. Arch. Vat., Reg. Vat. 19 (Gregory IX), fol. 68v, ep. 366 (Jan. 9, 1239); Auvray, *Registres*, II, no. 4,706. *Le Liber censuum de l'église romaine*, ed. L. Duchesne and P. Fabre, 3 vols. (Paris, 1901–1952), I, 214–215 and note. M. Michaud has a long discussion of the nature and historical evolution of this exemption, with much incidental information, in his "Censuum, liber," *DDC*, III, cols. 234–253. See too the papal document of April 17, 1239 in the Arch. Nac. Madrid above in note 4; documents of protection for St. Vincent's from Pope Innocent are cited in note 24.

17. Arch. Nac. Madrid, Clero: Valencia, St. Vincent, leg. 2,079, arm. 45, fab. I, doc. of March 20, 1259. Besides the direct exemption proper to St. Vincent's, the monastic groups controlling it brought their own. This date seems more

plausible than that of March 19, 1239 for a metropolitan statute of similar import, connected with a dispute over burial rights, *ibid.*, Codices, Poblet cartulary, doc. 2.

18. *Diócesis valentina*, II, 163 (until 1835); Finestres, *Poblet*, III, 69.

19. Finestres, *Poblet*, III, 73 (the "Fiesta del Centenar").

20. Escolano, *Décadas*, I, 527; this was the street of St. Vincent from St. Martin's church; heavy traffic eventually broke up and destroyed the paving. Chabás ridicules the tradition, however.

21. For example in *Colección diplomática*, doc. 894: "in via publica que vadit ad Sanctum Vincencium."

22. Muntaner, *Crònica*, ch. 23. When leaving the city, on their way north to the council of Lyons, the Castilian royalty also visited another Valencian shrine of note, Our Lady at Puig (on Puig see Chapter XIII, section 4, "The Knights of Mercy, Ransomers").

23. Arch. Nac. Madrid, Clero: Valencia, St. Vincent, leg. 2,079, arm. 45, fab. 1 (July 2, 1240); in *Diócesis valentina*, II, 154n.

24. Arch. Nac. Madrid, Codices, Repertori de San Vicent, fol. 15v, doc. 2 (June 5, 1242); Clero: Valencia, St. Vincent, leg. 2,079, arm 45, fab. 1 (April 28, 1245 and September 10, 1246).

25. Arch. Crown, Bulas, leg. IX (Innocent IV), no. 34 (Nov. 29, 1247): "secularis ecclesie."

26. *Diócesis valentina*, II, 163. Teixidor says James built a new church here this early (*Antigüedades de Valencia*, II, 272).

27. *Colección diplomática*, doc. 520 (Sept. 30, 1255): "predictum monasterium et ecclesiam, . . . domum . . . cum hospitali ibidem edificato et constructo"; this seems more definite than the wording in the papal document ("ius patronatus quod in ecclesia sancti Vincentii et hospitali iuxta Valenciam") above in note 14 where an official foundation plus an inchoate beginning might satisfy, especially since the latter document does not deal with St. Vincent's alone. On the financial difficulties, see text p. 295.

28. *Antigüedades de Valencia*, II, 276 (1255 explanation to new administrators); previous phrases are samples from other documents.

29. The work for orphans is mentioned only much later, in a document of 1357, though as an established and primary work of St. Vincent's ("infantium expositorum educationis"). Whether this tradition extended backwards seventy-five or a hundred years it is impossible to say. Earlier (1338) a municipal functionary called the Father of Orphans had been created to seek out and collect orphans and abandoned children (*Diócesis valentina*, II, 160-161 and n.).

30. The supply of medicines at St. Vincent's is spoken of in a document of 1269. The separate infirmaries for men and women are in the legacy quoted in note 113. The *infirmi* are noted in a number of documents, one of which divides the personnel of St. Vincent's into clergy, corodians, servants, and ill (quoted in note 158); *servitores* is a wider term than "servants" or "staff" (see Chapter II, notes 101–102 and text). The first three classes belong to the "house" of St. Vincent's, the ill to "its hospital." Both *peregrini* and *pauperes* are mentioned as residents, in the papal document of 1239 cited in note 16.

31. Susan Wood, *English Monasteries and their Patrons in the Thirteenth Century* (London, 1955), pp. 3, 90–92, 107–111, 114–115. Cf. Moorman, *Church Life*, pp. 46–47, 269–271, 356. See the thorough treatment of corodies in Jean Marchal's *Le "droit d'oblat," essai sur une variété de pensionnés monastiques*, Archives de la France monastique, no. 49 (Ligugé, 1955), esp. chs. 1, 2, 6; on p. 176 corodians by purchase; on pp. 20 ff. the needy pensioners. Further background, mostly on allied practices in Spain, may be found in J. Orlandis Rovira, "Traditio corporis et

animae: la 'familiaritas' en las iglesias y monasterios," *AHDE*, XXIV (1954), 95–279.

32. *Antigüedades de Valencia*, II, 276–277: "nos et successores nostri possimus ibi instituere et destituere Portionarios de Domo et Familia nostra ad nostrum arbitrium, loci facultatibus iam dicti pensatis."

33. Arch. Nac. Madrid, Clero: Valencia, St. Vincent, leg. 2,080, arm. 45, fab. 1 (Mar. 30, 1266); cf. codex Repertori de San Vicent, doc. 11 and *Itinerari*, p. 385.

34. This is stated as a general principal for all pensioners here in Martin's document and in the specific case also of Raymond; cf. Arch. Crown, Liber patrimonii regni Valentiae, fol. 300, docs. 14, 19 (and below, notes 45, 46, 50).

35. Document in note 33: "hactenus est consuetum."

36. Arch. Crown, James I, Reg. Canc. 15, fol. 78v (Jan. 26, 1267): "pro ut alii porcionarii eiusdem hospitalis."

37. Arch. Crown, Peter III, Reg. Canc. 39, fol. 212v (June 25, 1277): "Petrus dei gratia, etc., attendentes quod tu Andreas Almerich domino Iacobo inclite recordationis Regi Aragonum patri nostro plura servitia intulisti essendo [eundo?] in domo sua, ideoque damus et concedimus et assignamus tibi in tota vita tua porcionem victus et vestitus . . . consuetam." *Victus* may be "board" or "living" or "pension," though perhaps only "food"; probably the double term was a legal convention.

38. Arch. Crown, James I, Reg. Canc. 16, fol. 244v (July 15, 1271).

39. Arch. Crown, James I, Reg. Canc. 12, fol. 62v (June 1, 1262); "cum carta nostra."

40. Arch. Crown, James I, Reg. Canc. 15, fol. 90 (April 10, 1268). "Per nos et nostros damus et concedimus tibi P. de Amaldano diebus omnibus vite tue victum et vestitum in domo seu hospitali Sancti Vincentii Valencie. Mandantes Rectori seu procuratori dicte domus seu dicti hospital[is] presentis videlicet et futuris quod de cetero habeant pro portionario dicte domus seu dicti hospitalis et tibi provideant dum vixeris in victum et vestitum prout aliis porcionariis dicte domus sive dicti hospitalis facere tenentur. Et quod hoc non mutent aliqua racione. Datum Valencia iiii Idus Aprilis." Amaldán may stand for La Ametlla (de Mar) near Tarragona; the name Ametlla (or Samenla) is found both in the *Repartimiento* and the *Llibre dels feyts*, but not this man.

41. Arch. Crown, Peter III, Reg. Canc. 40, fol. 42 (Nov. 11, 1277): "noverint universi quod nos Petrus dei gratia Rex Aragonum damus et concedimus in beneficium personale tibi Petro de Foresio in tota vita tua racione servicii quod nobis diu fecisti, victum et vestitum in domo sancti vincencii valencie . . . sicut uni de porcionariis dicte domus." A Peter of Fores, crossbowman to Prince Peter, received a building site from him near Valencia in 1273; the same name appears in the *Repartimiento*. Possibly the Peter of Fores who is justiciar of Gandía from 1279 to 1281 is a son or relative.

42. *Antigüedades de Valencia*, II, 277: "quod solvistis et satisfecistis mihi . . . pro Portione mea."

43. Arch. Crown, Peter III, Reg. Canc. 60, fol. 18 (Jan. 25, 1282): "assignavit . . . quandam porcionem Solarmunde mulier de domo sua tum propter servicium quod eidem . . . fecit quando nutrivit et lactavit per aliquod tempus Petrum fratrem nostrum tum etiam quia pauper est et indigens."

44. Arch. Crown, James I, Reg. Canc. 15, fol. 90v (April 15, 1268). "Concedimus tibi Bernardo de Calatayub victum et vestitum in hospitali Sancti Vincentii Valencie diebus omnibus vite tue. Ita quod in dicto hospitali habeas victum et vestitum dum vixeris prout alii porcionarii eiusdem hospitalis habent et habere debent. Mandantes prioribus . . . presentibus et futuris . . ."

45. Arch. Crown, Peter III, Reg. Canc. 40, fol. 30v (Oct. 24, 1277).

46. Arch. Crown, Peter III, Reg. Canc. 44, fol. 172 (Mar. 18, 1279). See also Liber patrimonii regni Valentiae, fol. 300, doc. 14, where the name is Raymond of Turrisella; Toralla, Torayla, Torrella, Toroella, Turricela, Torrohella, Turriles, etc. are variants of a name common to a number of families in contemporary documents.

47. The story may be reconstructed especially from Arch. Crown, Peter III, Reg. Canc. 46, fol. 119v (Nov. 17, 1283).

48. Arch. Crown, Peter III, Reg. Canc. 40, fol. 93 (April 15, 1278); the previous grant is now to be diminished. A document of April 15 (*ibid.*) grants him also two hundred solidi a year from crown rents in the city of Valencia.

49. Arch. Crown, Liber patrimonii, fol. 300v, doc. 22.

50. Liber patrimonii, fol. 300, doc. 19 (Nov. 17, 1285). The corody came from King Peter, Martin being poor at the time; this document from Alphonse III in 1285 is confirming the gift.

51. Arch. Crown, James I, Reg. Canc. 12, fol. 91 (June 26, 1263): "prout aliis porcionariis ipsius monasterii." A part of the document is cut away, down the left side.

52. *Antigüedades de Valencia*, II, 275: "continue quinque Presbiteros . . . et quinque alios Clericos inter Diaconos et Subdiaconos, Ordinis vestri"; they were to pray for the souls of the king and his ancestors.

53. Arch. Crown, James I, Reg. Canc. 10, fol. 100 (July 4, 1258): "damus et concedimus et affirmamus tibi G. Aymerici clerico diebus omnibus vite tue victum et vestitum in domo sancti vincencii Valencie que habeas sicut unus de aliis clericis dicte domus." See the allied document in Reg. Canc. 19, fol. 84 (Dec. 17, 1273).

54. Arch. Crown, James I, Reg. Canc. 10, fol. 144v (Sept. 15, 1259): "damus concedimus et assignamus in presenti . . . Grossi presbitero in beneficium personale . . . victum et vestitum in monasterio sancti Vincentii de Valentia." He was to have an income equivalent to that of the other clerics in service here.

55. Arch. Crown, James I, Reg. Canc. 10, fol. 132 (Mar. 16, 1259). "Concedimus tibi Bernardo de Calvis [Caldis?] presbitero victum et vestitum in monasterio Sancti Vincentii de Valencia diebus omnibus vite tue [*sic*]. Ita quod de cetero . . . recipias in dicto monasterio victum et vestitum sicut alii canonici eiusdem loci . . ." Cf. *Itinerari*, pp. 141 (Dec. 29, 1239), 493 (Jan. 27, 1274).

56. Arch. Crown, James I, Reg. Canc. 13, fol. 196v (July 1, 1264): "damus [et] concedimus tibi Ferrando de Vilella clerico diebus omnibus vite tue portionem cotidianam in monasterio Sancti Vincentii Valentie."

57. Arch. Nac. Madrid, Clero: Valencia, St. Vincent, leg. 2,080, arm. 45, fab. 1 (Mar. 30, 1266). Also in the codex Privilegia S. Vincentii, fols. 2r–3v. Cf. *Itinerari*, p. 385.

58. Arch. Crown, James I, Reg. Canc. 16, fol. 181 (June 29, 1269). Copy in Arch. Nac. Madrid, *ibid.* The "scolaris" of the first document, called "scolarius" in the second, may be a scholarship boy chosen from the cathedral school; it was a common minor benefice in Spain then. Sanchís Sivera puts him down as a sacristan, probably due to a misreading (*Diócesis valentina*, II, 156). For other *scholares* in Valencia at this time, see above, Chapter VI, note 47. The document assigns each priest-canon: "singulis annis de cetero unusquisque" eighty solidi "pro vestitu"; but "scolarius quadraginta solidos [habeat]". See note 64 and text, on this scholar's subsequent career.

59. Arch. Crown, James I, Reg. Canc. 13, fol. 286v (Dec. 21, 1265): "per nos et nostros damus et concedimus tibi G. de Piaria [Apiaria?] clerico Canoniam monasterii Sancti Vincentii Valencie . . . dum vixeris annuatim victum et vestitum."

60. Arch. Crown, Reg. Canc. 16, fol. 231v (Feb. 12, 1270). "Concedimus vobis Guillelmo de Apiaria presbytero capellaniam nostram quam nos in altari Sancti Iacobi Ecclesie Sedis Valentie duximus statuendam. Et tunc Capellanie erat Capellanus Jacobus de Terolio [?] nunc defunctus. Et vos in capellanum nostrum eiusdem capellanie constituimus toto tempore vite vestre. Ita scilicet quod vos in tota vita vestra sitis capellanus eiusdem capellanie et celebretis in dicto altare Sancti Iacobi assidue divina Officia ad honorem eiusdem sancti et in remedium anime nostre. Et sic habeatis dictam capellaniam quamdiu vita fuerit vobis . . . Et habeatis et recipiatis vos et quos volueritis loco vestri singulis annis decetero in tota vita vestra illos quadraginta et quattuor morabatinos alfonsinos annuales quos eidem Capellanie quam ipsam hedificavimus assignavimus super quibusdam operatoriis nostris sitis in Civitate Valencie. . . ."

61. Raymond of Apiera and the lawyer Francis of Apiaria were substantial citizens in the new realm; an A. de Apiera had been a vassal of the viscount of Béarn, and both G. and Ferrer de Apiaria (later a magistrate of Valencia city) are in the Valencian *Repartimiento.* Apiaria would be Piera, involved in St. Vincent's story in 1286 (see below, note 133 and text); its Carthaginian name had been Apiara.

62. Document in note 58.

63. Arch. Crown, Peter III, Reg. Canc. 46, fol. 121 (Nov. 19, 1283). Published in *Documenta selecta,* doc. 30.

64. *Ibid.;* "sicut alii presbiteri"; see above, note 58. Did he own the Játiva buildings, apparently an expensive property, which passed from William Bernard to Count Denis of Hungary in 1276 (Reg. Canc. 39, fol. 58, docs. of Feb. 3)?

65. Arch. Nac. Madrid, Codices, Repertori de San Vicent, fol. 4v, doc. 19 (Oct. 1, 1290).

66. Arch. Nac. Madrid, Clero: Valencia, St. Vincent, leg. 2,079, arm. 45, fab. 1 (Jan. 7, 1244); also in Poblet cartulary, doc. 6; and in Codices, Privilegia S. Vincentii, which misdates it as 1264. *Itinerari* discusses another dating problem for this document—1244 against 1243 (p. 165). See the *Colección diplomática,* doc. 265. *Repartimiento de Valencia* has, under 1244: "Sanctus Vincentius: castrum et villam de Quart et alqueriam de Ladea." On Cuart see *Nomenclátor de Valencia,* though it should not assume the rector here was a religious (p. 202). Aldaya (Ladea, Ladera, Rahalladea, Raalludea) and Cuart are also in the Repertori manuscripts, fols. 22, 24, 39 ff.; the 1303 extension of jurisdiction for Cuart is on fol. 5r, doc. 23; a 1282 rental by the prior here is on fol. 121v, doc. 2.

67. Arch. Crown, Liber patrimonii, fol. 300, doc. 12 (July 13, 1279).

68. Arch. Nac. Madrid, Repertori de San Vicent, fol. lv, doc. 4; in *Colección diplomática,* doc. 265 (Jan. 7, 1244) and doc. 520 (Sept. 30, 1255). Cf. *Itinerari,* p. 248. Momblanch y Gonzálbez, *Historia de la Albufera,* pp. 43-44.

69. Arch. Crown, James I, perg. 1,346: "salva tamen Ecclesie Sancti Vincentii decima."

70. Arch. Nac. Madrid, Clero, Valencia, St. Vincent, leg. 2,079, arm. 45, fab. 1 (Sept. 12, 1244): "Castrum et villam Castilionis de Burriana et cum alqueriis."

71. The Privilegia S. Vincentii dates this 1264 (fol. 1); the Repertori gives it as 1245; cf. the Poblet cartulary. The *Itinerari* refers to the 1244 grant, and has the pertinent documents for Prince Peter; see esp. pp. 169-170, 194. Traver Tomás' *Antigüedades de Castellón,* though it has a chapter of general background on this century, does not advert to the problem (cf. pp. 35-44); nor are the articles of Betí, García, Martínez Ferrando, and others concerning Castellón origins more helpful here. On Montornés see below, notes 75-77, with text.

72. *Itinerari,* p. 308. The 1255 transfer document is cited below in note 127.

73. Arch. Crown, James I, perg. 1,059 (Oct. 20, 1246): "tot et talibus posses-sionibus dotetis ut reddituum sexcentarum marcharum argenti annuatim habeat complementum."

74. Arch. Crown, Liber patrimonii regni Valentiae, fol. 77, doc. 2 (Sept. 13, 1259).

75. Arch. Nac. Madrid, Repertori de San Vicent, fol. 43. *Colección diplomática*, doc. 1,290 (June 15, 1268): "ius feudatarium totum et dominium et potestatem." And confirmatory document 1,296 (Nov. 6, 1268). Arch. Crown, James I, Reg. Canc. 17, fol. 98 (Mar. 5, 1268–1269): "prout in dicta carta," says Prince Peter, "lacius dignoscitur contineri." See too the document infeudating castle and town for the monastery's gain, in Arch. Nac. Madrid, Clero: Valencia, St. Vincent, leg. 2,079, arm. 45, fab. 1 (Nov. 9, 1268). St. Vincent's was still in possession in 1281, when Peter Simon was ordered to deliver the castle to the new prior, Bernard the abbot of St. Victorian (Arch. Crown, Peter III, Reg. Canc. 50, fol. 162 [July 31, 1281]). King Peter confirmed the gift of Montornés again in 1280 (codex Repertori, fol. 43). See also the Poblet cartulary in Arch. Nac. Madrid, fols. 16A to 16E. The "signum crucis" purchased is in the Repertori, fol. 44, doc. 4 (April 1, 1264).

76. Arch. Crown, Liber patrimonii, fol. 77, doc. 4.

77. *Itinerari*, p. 154 (1242): "quod est ante Castilionem Burriane"; cf. p. 198, and on the other Montornés pp. 73, 207, 223, 389.

78. Arch. Nac. Madrid, Codices, Privilegia, fols 3r–4r, and Repertori, fol. 3r, doc. 12 (June 13, 1276); Arch. Crown, James I, Reg. Canc. 22, fol. 42; see the Liber patrimonii, fols. 19v, 26or, 299v. "Concedimus . . . monasterio . . . castrum nostrum et villam de Almoneçir situm in Regno Valencie," and "turrem et al-queriam de Siyllana [Suylana in Privilegia, Soyllana in Repertori, Sullana in Liber patrimonii] . . . et turrem et Alchariam de Beniçeron [Binazeron, Binasexon]." Sanchís Sivera incorrectly gives this as Benidorm and misdates it 1273 (*Diócesis valentina*, II, 157); a settlement charter was granted here, October 22, 1277 (*Nomenclátor de Valencia*, p. 391). Benisa was a hamlet with tower stronghold annexed.

79. Arch. Crown, Peter III, Reg. Canc. 40, fol. 95 (April 20, 1278): "castrum de Chirello quod est domus sancti Vincentii." The prince here orders the procu-rator of St. Vincent's to pay the castellan Arnold his salary. On Chirivella see Chapter X, notes 37, 44 and text. Both Chirello and Cortes are in a document of 1280: see below, note 159.

80. Arch. Crown, James I, Reg. Canc. 21, fol. 97v (Jan. 1, 1273); this was in the Cuart grant and included a rent by the users to the monastery: "viginti et octo [*or* septem: "xxti et viijem"?] cafizas ordeorum quas pro cequiatico percipit ab illis qui rigant de cequia antedicta."

81. Arch. Crown, James I, Reg. Canc. 16, fol. 162v (May 9, 1269). See *Colección diplomática*, doc. 1,319, from the municipal archives there. "Per nos et nostros damus et concedimus vobis dilecto et fideli nostro Iacobo de Rocha procuratori hospitalis sive monasterii Sancti Vincentii Valencie et vestris successoribus procu-ratoribus ipsius monasterii et ipsi monasterio imperpetuum ac etiam statuimus quod . . . annuatim celebrentur nundine in villa castilionis de Burriana . . . et durentur per decem dies . . ."

82. Traver Tomás, *Antigüedades de Castellón*, p. 42 (Villareal fair of 1273 and others).

83. Arch. Crown, Peter III, Reg. Canc. 41, fol. 104 (July 12, 1279); the road from Valencia to Requena was involved: "intellecto quod transeuntes per caminum Regne quod est per ortam de Quart dampnificent dictam ortam . . . volumus ut dictum caminum predictum transeat per villam de Quart."

84. Arch. Nac. Madrid, Repertori de San Vicent, fol. 2r,v, doc. 8 (Mar. 19, 1261).

85. Arch. Crown, James I, Reg. Canc. 14, fol. 130 (Dec. 10, 1271): "in villa castillionis . . . cenam"; see the Liber patrimonii regni Valentiae, fol. 299v, doc. 9.

86. Arch. Nac. Madrid, Repertori, fol. 6v, doc. 35.

87. *Repartimiento de Valencia*, p. 287: "totum bestiare Sancti Vincentii possit pascere per totam dominationem regis franchum sine carnagio et herbagio monetatico." See also the travel toll and market dues for their Castellón subjects in *Colección diplomática*, doc. 1,283 (Jan. 13, 1264); and on the hospitality tax and coinage fee of Cuart and Aldaya, doc. 265 (*an.* 1244).

88. Arch. Crown, Peter III, Reg. Canc. 40, fol. 93 (April 15, 1278): "super tabula nostra pensi Valencie."

89. Arch. Crown, James I, Reg. Canc. 12, fol. 79v (May 17, 1263); Liber patrimonii, fol. 299r, doc. 5; Arch. Nac. Madrid, Codices, Repertori, fol. 2v, doc. 9.

90. *Antigüedades de Valencia*, II, 276.

91. Arch. Nac. Madrid, Clero: Valencia, St. Vincent, leg. 2,079, arm. 45, and leg. 2,078, arm. 45, *passim*.

92. Arch. Nac. Madrid, Repertori, fol. 61r, doc. 1.

93. Arch. Crown, James I, Reg. Canc. 12, fol. 55 (June 10, 1262) for the Patraix property. Arch. Nac. Madrid, Repertori, fol. 121v, doc. 2 (1282).

94. Arch. Nac. Madrid, Privilegia, fol. 5r,v. Sometimes St. Vincent's was overzealous in collecting fees and had to be rebuked (Arch. Crown, Peter III, Reg. Canc. 43, fols. 81v, 114v [Dec. 9, 1284 and Jan. 27, 1285]).

95. Arch. Nac. Madrid, Clero: Valencia, St. Vincent, leg. 2,079, arm. 45, fab. 1 (Aug. 17, 1260); Poblet cartulary, doc. 10; Repertori, fol. 2, doc. 7; *Itinerari*, p. 304.

96. "Repàs d'un manual notarial del temps del rey En Jaume I," ed. Joan Segura, in *Congrés I*, p. 325, doc. 36 (1241).

97. See Chapter XI, note 11: "hospitali pauperum."

98. Arch. Nac. Madrid, Clero: Valencia, St. Vincent, leg. 2,079, arm. 45, fab. 1: "Martinus de Cecilia et Domina Madona uxor eius . . . duos Sacerdotes seculares." Also in Repertori, fol. 181 (Aug. 12, 1242), confirmed by the king again in 1260. The two priests comprised the benefice named after the Holy Spirit. Each was to get 60 solidi for "vestitum," and sustenance such as the other canons here got. The Repertori has Martin of Cilia, but Martin of Sicily was an important person who appears in the *Repartimiento*; in 1258 after his death King James paid his widow 740 morabatins to purchase their castle of Argensola (*Itinerari*, p. 271).

99. *Antigüedades de Valencia*, II, 275. Atrosillo (Otrocello, Troxillo, Datrocillo, etc.). In the *Llibre dels feyts* the king begins a small feudal war for his interests, talks with him at the moment of victory on Majorca, and entrusts captured Bayren to his care (chs. 15, 67, 310–314). He was at the siege of Valencia. His wife Sancha was the daughter of the baron Lope de Alvaro; his brother Gil was lord (from 1250) of Montclús; he himself had lands at Pina, then at Ança, and at Huesa and elsewhere with knight service "sicut ricihomines Aragonum nobis tenentur servire." See also *Itinerari*, docs. of 1232–1257, pp. 99, 112, 122, 131, 139, 164, 180, 181, 194, 220, 248, 259, 551.

100. Arch. Nac. Madrid, Codices, Repertori, fol. 43v, doc. 1.

101. Will cited in Chapter XI, note 12; copies in Arch. Nac. Madrid, Poblet cartulary, doc. 9, and St. Vincent's codex, Repertori, fol. 43v, doc. 2 (1247):

"apparicius porterius domine Yoles Regine Aragonum . . . in cimiterio Sancti Vincencii Valencie . . . honorifice." Yoles (Hyolenz, Yolanda, etc.) is Violante of Hungary, queen of Aragon.

102. Will cited in Chapter XI, note 13: "Petrus Allerii draperius Valencie"; the prior is to conduct the corpse there and bury it "honoriffice"; "si obiero in Regno Valencie."

103. Will cited in Chapter XI, note 15: "item duos mantellos de seda, qui fuerunt domini regis, dimito ecclesie sancti Vincencii de Valencia, cui eos reservabam."

104. Will cited in Chapter VII, note 56. Also in 1251, Peter Armer willed: "pauperibus hospitalis eiusdem loci ad refficiendum eos v solidos" (cited in Chapter VII, note 53).

105. *Antigüedades de Valencia*, II, 278. He was a settler at Peñíscola (*Itinerari*, p. 210, Jan. 28, 1251).

106. Will cited in Chapter VII, note 62. On the word "opus" see text, p. 98.

107. Will cited in Chapter XI, note 21: "item dimitto operi Sancti Vincentii Valencie ii sols."

108. Arch. Nac. Madrid, Clero: Valencia, St. Vincent, leg. 2,079, arm. 45, fab. 1 (B. of Teruel). Because no notary was present at the first draft, litigation was going forward before the justiciar of Valencia.

109. A confirmatory document regarding those goods left to St. Vincent's for a chaplaincy was issued by the crown in 1263 (Arch. Crown, James I, Reg. Canc. 12, fol. 119v). "Confirmamus et concedimus . . . domo et monasterio beati Vincentii de Valentia stabilimentum quod Go. de Jacca notarius et Civis Valentie . . . mandavit in ecclesia et monasterio predicto de quadam capellania pro remissione peccatorum suorum . . . Concedentes imperpetuum quod prior et monasterium habeant teneant et possideant hereditates censualia possessiones et omnia alia que dictus G. dimisit dedit et assignavit p[ro] constitutione et stabilimento dicte capellanie p[er] hereditatem propriam francham et liberam prout praestamentum ab eodem G . . . continet sine aliqua retentione nostra et nostrorum et cuiuslibet alie persone." Also in Arch. Nac. Madrid, Codices, Repertori de San Vicent, fol. 2v, doc. 10; cf. fol. 43v, doc. 3 (1263). See will above in Chapter XI, note 24.

110. Arch. Nac. Madrid, Clero: Valencia, St. Vincent, leg. 2,079, arm. 45, fab. 1 (docs. of Nov. 12, 1262 and April 15, 1264 by Arnold of "Podio Monzo" and "Podio Monsone"). See the documents of the same date in Arch. Crown, James I, Reg. Canc. 12, fols. 35v and 73v (April 22 and Nov. 12); and the codex, Liber patrimonii regni Valentiae, fol. 299r. This does not seem to be the Arnold of Monzón, bailiff for the kingdom of Valencia below the Júcar River, who died about 1267 or 1268—unless there is question of two men, perhaps father and son, both dying in the same decade.

111. Arch. Crown, James I, Reg. Canc. 12, fol. 73v (Nov. 12, 1262) confirms the legacy: "attendentes piam et laudabilem ordinationem quam Arnoldam de Podio monço fecit in suo testamento in quo legavit hospitali Monasterii Sancti Vincentii . . . omnes honores et possessiones quas habet apud Exativam excepto Regali quod est prope murum ipsius ville . . . et mandavit quod in Capella dicti hospitalis institueretur unus presbyter qui celebraret ibi divina officia . . . et haberet honores predictos."

112. Arch. Nac. Madrid, Codices, Poblet cart., doc. 12, "quousque sit nutritus" (copy of 1272).

113. Willelma, cited in Chapter VII, note 60: "duos lectos paratos pannorum unum videlicet domui ubi iacent homines infirmi et alium domui ubi iacent femine infirme."

114. Arch. Cath., perg. 1,354 (Sept. 30, 1276); her name too was Willelma.

115. See note 157.

116. Will of Xicot or Jicot cited in Chapter VII, note 94: "vicinus et habitator parrochie Sancti Bartholomei Valencie."

117. Arch. Crown, Peter III, Reg. Canc. 44, fol. 229v (May 2, 1282); Teixidor gives this as Araost (*Antigüedades*, II, 276). Cf. also codex, Liber patrimonii regni Valentiae, fol. 300, doc. 16.

118. As is later noted by King Peter (Arch. Crown, Peter III, Reg. Canc. 50, fol. 223v [Jan. 3, 1282]): "fuit deposita quondam caxia in domo vestra [Templi] in quo sunt privilegia . . . domus sancti Vincencii"; in connection with a legal dispute over St. Vincent's, the king now ordered this box brought from the Temple and unsealed in his presence: "coram nobis defferi faciatis et in presencia vestri faciemus ipsam aperiri." On the Templars in thirteenth-century England as depositaries, see Parker, *Knights Templars in England*, pp. 59-63.

119. See Chapter VII, note 21; cf. Chapter VIII, note 21.

120. *Rationes decimarum*, II, doc. in appendix, pp. 320-321; cf. pp. 31-32.

121. *Itinerari*, p. 146.

122. E. G. Hurtebise, *Guía histórico-descriptiva del archivo de la corona de Aragón en Barcelona* (Madrid, 1920), p. 8.

123. *Llibre dels feyts*, ch. 304.

124. See note 158 and text, for 1279 farming. Cuart is farmed for five years at 15,000 solidi in Arch. Crown, Reg. Canc. 46, fol. 180 (April 10, 1284). For Castellón-Montornés see Arch. Crown, Liber patrimonii, fol. 301, doc. 29; see the even higher figure in Arch. Nac. Madrid, Repertori de San Vicent, fol. lv-2, doc. 5.

125. Arch. Crown, Peter III, Reg. Canc. 41, fol. 11 (Nov. 3, 1278): "quod desistat," "si quid fecit clericis domus sancti vincencii super ordinacione vestium suarum et quod non intromittat se in ordinacione dicte domus."

126. Arch. Crown, Peter III, Reg. Canc. 59, fol. 40v (July 22 and 23, 1282): "capiendo clericos ipsius domus et alia plura gravamina inferendo."

127. *Colección diplomática*, doc. 520 (Sept. 30, 1255); cf. codex Repertori, fol. 43: "nos qui eiusdem ordinis patroni et fundatores sumus . . . concedimus . . . in perpetuum predictum monasterium et ecclesiam, locum sive domum sancti Vincencii cum hospitali ibidem edificato et constructo." Cf. above, Chapter XIII, note 85.

128. *Ibid.*: "volentes insuper monasterium . . . in melius reformari." Sanchís Sivera, *Diócesis valentina*, II, 154; Teixidor, and Briz, in *Antigüedades de Valencia*, II, 273. Cf. *Itinerari*, p. 248.

129. Gazulla, "Don Jaime I de Aragón y la orden de Nuestra Señora de la Merced," p. 380 (Feb. 1257): "maligno spiritu ducti Magistrum et fratres ordinis de mercede per provincias et loca multipliciter diffamarunt a qua diffamacione personam nostram non relinquerunt immunem dicentes publice, et firmiter asserentes quod predicti . . . monasterium habuerunt a nobis pecunia mediante." Cf. *Itinerari*, p. 255.

130. Arch. Crown, Reg. Canc. 10, fol. 143 (two documents of Sept. 10, 1259, connected with the recent decision). And see *Itinerari*, p. 292; *Colección diplomática*, doc. 1,109 (same date); *Antigüedades de Valencia*, II, 273. Cf. also the list by Amerio Sancho Blanco of unedited bulls of Clement IV (1266-1267), in the *Catalogus documentorum ordinis Beatae Mariae Virginis de Mercede quae in archivo coronae Aragoniae asservantur* (Rome, n.d.), p. 16.

131. Arch. Crown, James I, Reg. Canc. 15, fol. 12v (*an.* 1265): "quod cum domus Sancti Vincencii Civitatis Valencie propter plurimas vacuas et inutiles ac immoderatas expensas quas priores et dicte ecclesie domus eiusdem fecerunt acthenus [*sic*] in ipsius domus maximum detrimentum, domus ipsa in suis sit

redditibus diminutta et debitis honerata"—the exact nature of the king's gift is illegible, obscured by damp or by water-damage.

132. Arch. Crown, James I, Reg. Canc. 15, fol. 33v (Oct. 1266), a pardon for the notary: "per nos et nostros absolvimus et difinimus atque remitimus vobis Petro Pauli notario publico Valencie omnem petitionem . . . pro eo scilicet quod vos sine licentia nostra suscepistis et confecistis appellationem pro clericis domus seu hospitalis sancti Vincentii Valencie . . . ad summum pontificem . . . in preiudicium nostre iurisdictionis."

133. Arch. Nac. Madrid, Codices, Repertori de San Vicent, fol. 3r, doc. 13 (April 3, 1286). Cf. above, note 61.

134. *Ibid.*, fol. 3v, doc. 16; codex *Privilegia S. Vincentii*, fols. 5v–8r (Dec. 12, 1287). See Arch. Crown, *Liber patrimonii*, fols. 300–301, doc. 26, confirmed by James II (June 2, 1293). The *Répertoire des abbayes* incorrectly assigns St. Vincent's to Poblet from 1237 (II, 3,274, 2,917). Poblet already owned property on its own account in Valencia; besides the grants in connection with Benifasá, it received in 1238 buildings in Valencia city and four jovates in Mislata (Repertori, fol. 1). The quote here is "in suburbio Valencie." Teixidor has some odd argumentation concerning the diminution of hospitality at this period, and its functioning only by freewill legacies; there is no real evidence for either thesis (*Antigüedades*, II, 277–278).

135. Arch. Nac. Madrid, Codices, Poblet cartulary, 19d.

136. Arch. Nac. Madrid, Repertori, fol. 4r,v, docs. 17–18 (May 24, 1289).

137. *Ibid.*, fol. 16r, doc. 8 (April 1, 1297).

138. Arch. Crown, *Liber patrimonii regni Valentiae*, fol. 301v, doc. 31.

139. *Furs*, lib. I, rub. IX, c. 4. And the document of March 17, 1262 about "causa extrahendi inde aliquem vel aliquos homines vel personas qui ibi fuerint propter maleficia perpetrata" (*Itinerari*, p. 319). See too Arch. Nac. Madrid, Clero: Valencia, St. Vincent, leg. 2,079, arm. 45, fab. 1 (April 20, 1255); and Codices, cartulary of Poblet, doc. 11 (1261); also the privilege of March 17, 1262 in *Itinerari*, p. 319.

140. Arch. Nac. Madrid, codex *Repertori*, fol. 6r, doc. 30; the Poblet abbot as administrator of St. Vincent's agreed to surrender asylum.

141. Arch. Crown, James I, perg. 2,287 (July 20, 1276): "opus Sancti Vincensi quod nos emparavimus et facimus fieri ita quod fiant quinque domus similitudinis illius domus que iam est ibi facta . . . unum claustrum in Corrallo prope Ecclesiam . . . unum Dormitorium aliquantulum longius sicut fit et construitur in Domibus ordinum . . . [parietes in orto] ob hoc ut nemo possit ibi entrare . . . lectum nostrum et cortinas . . ." The full will is published in Tourtoulon, *Jaime I*, II, app. 21, and in excerpted sections in *Diócesis valentina*, II, 157n.

142. Prior in document of 1240 cited above, in note 23; documents of 1243 and 1244 cited in *Antigüedades de Valencia*, II, 275. On the Lagrasse abbot of dubious reputation, who resigned in 1255 there, cf. above, note 9 and text. Teixidor actually puts a single prior from 1243 to 1284, confusing the first Prior Bernard with the abbot of St. Victorian who assumed the priorate much later.

143. Arch. Crown, Bulas, legajo IX (Innocent IV), no. 34 (Nov. 29, 1247), papal confirmation. Sanchís Sivera dates this incorrectly as 1248, and by copying "est" for "ut" rather obscures the meaning (*Diócesis valentina*, II, 155n.). Pension in Arch. Crown, James I, Reg. Canc. 10, fol. 143 (Sept. 13, 1259). Rental doc. in Arch. Nac. Madrid, Repertori, fol. 121, doc. 1 (1253).

144. Arch. Nac. Madrid, Clero: Valencia, St. Vincent, leg. 2,079, arm. 45, fab. 1 (July 8, 1258), making Berengar "speciale et generale procuratore," over "omnia negotia." Another document here, but misplaced under a later dating as 1239, is of

June 25, 1259, allowing Berengar as prior to survey and check all Burriana properties: "licentiam ... sogueandi omnes hereditates et possessiones terminorum Castillionis de Burriana," with special reference to the holdings of St. Vincent's. Documentation involving Berengar as prior of St. Vincent's may also be found in Arch. Crown, James I, Reg. Canc. 10, fol. 132 (Mar. 16, 1259); Reg. Canc. 11, fol. 187 (Dec. 18, 1260); Reg. Canc. 12, fol. 35v (April 22, 1263) and fol. 79 (May 17, 1263). The Zamora will of 1267 gives him as prior (Arch. Nac. Madrid, Codices, Poblet cart., doc. 12).

145. Ricardo del Arco copies the inscription in full in his *Sepulcros de la casa real de Aragón* (Madrid, 1945), p. 180. Miret y Sans's opinions are in *Itinerari*, pp. 17, 428–429, and chart facing p. 545. The partial epitaph is "Petrus de Rege canonicus et sacrista istius sedis, qui fuit filius ilmi. domini regis Petri Aragonum." See also text, p. 34.

146. *Itinerari*, p. 429: "nos Petrus frater domini regis Aragonis et sacrista ilerdensis." The name "de Rege" (or Rey, Rex, Reg, Reig) was held by other men; thus a Peter de Rege was master of works in the repair of the royal palace at Barcelona early in the next century; a P. dez Rech, citizen of Valencia, was carried into slavery by the Moors at that same time; a Bartholomew Reg was building near the port of Valencia in 1271; a Bononato Rey was a merchant on the coasts of Aragon in 1312; and an Alphonse Pérez de Rege was involved in an inheritance case at Játiva in Valencia in 1271. Serious search would undoubtedly turn up other holders of the name, and of approximations to it.

147. See document in note 151 (June 13, 1274).

148. Arch. Crown, James I, perg. 2,287 (July 20, 1276) and perg. 2,289 (July 23, 1276); both published in Tourtoulon, *Jaime I*, II, apps. 21, 22: "P. de Rege Sacrista Ilerde." *Llibre dels feyts*, ch. 563; cf. ch. 489. *Itinerari*, pp. 17, 41, 368, 535, 539n. Soldevila, *Pere el Gran*, I, 419 and n. On Peter de Roca see Arch. Crown, James I, Reg. Canc. 13, fol. 264 (April 9, 1265), Reg. Canc. 14, fols. 61 (July 25, 1264) and 79 (Feb. 6, 1266), Reg. Canc. 15, fols. 97 (April 30, 1268) and 99v (April 9, 1268), and Reg. Canc. 17, fol. 48 (June 30, 1268).

149. *Rationes decimarum*, I, 107, 145; and cf. II, 54.

150. Arch. Crown, James I, Reg. Canc. 16, fol. 185; also in Arch. Nac. Madrid, codex Privilegia, fol. 4r (July 21, 1269). "Concedimus vobis Petro de Rege Canonico Illerde et Valentie prioratum domus sive Hospitalis sancti Vincentii Valentie in Regimen ac administracionem ipsius domus sive Hospitalis ac prioratus in tota vita tua." He is to care for affairs as have the previous priors. Places held by St. Vincent's—"tam christianis quam Sarracenis presentibus et futuris" are to acknowledge him as prior and pay to him the customary revenues. An example of later documents is Reg. Canc. 22, fol. 42 (June 13, 1276): "vobis Petro de Rege priori."

151. Arch. Nac. Madrid, Privilegia, fol. 4v, documents of Gregory's first and third years. The second dispensation is also in Arch. Vat., Reg. Vat. 37, Gregory X, fol. 141 (June 13, 1274), published in Guiraud, *Registres*, doc. 370.

152. Arch. Crown, Peter III, Reg. Canc. 44, fol. 190 (Aug. 26, 1280). See also fol. 225 (two docs. of April 10, 1282); and Reg. Canc. 50, fol. 162 and 162v (two docs. of July 31, 1281). Biela may be Bielle in the Pyrenees or perhaps the commune of Biella near Vercelli or Biel near Huesca.

153. Arch. Nac. Madrid, Clero: Valencia, St. Vincent, leg. 2,080, arm. 45, fab. 1 (Jan. 24, 1282). Royal confirmation of his election is in *Documenta selecta*, doc. 14 (Nov. 22, 1276). On Peter March, or Marqués, see the documents in *Itinerari*, pp. 213, 231, 233, 299, 303, 307, 327, 343, 362, 390, 455, 510. His last testament, favorable to religious institutions in Valencia, is cited above in Chapter VII, note 54 (June 4, 1275). Five solidi were left to St. Vincent's. He asked to be buried

in the cathedral close of Valencia, near his brother; his wife was still living in 1275.

154. On Peter's 1285 restoration see Arch. Crown, Liber patrimonii regni Valentiae, fol. 301, docs. 20–21; the Poblet transfer is given below; the pension and sale document is in Arch. Nac. Madrid, Privilegia S. Vincentii, fols. 8v–11r. Owing to the difference in incarnational and nativity calendars, one cannot be certain that Peter did not sell his rights in January 1287 and then under his abdicated title of prior join in the December 1287 agreement between Poblet and Alphonse III; he is in both documents, for 19 kals. of January 1287 and for pridie idus in December 1287.

155. See document in note 144 (with quotes). The multiple ownership of revenues, by tenants and farmers, is suggested in a document of 1283 (cited in note 63) to the prior "et quibuscumque aliis tenentibus domum sancti Vincencii."

156. Cf. Arch. Crown, James I, Reg. Canc. 17, fol. 98 (Mar. 5, 1268), and Reg. Canc. 16, fol. 162v (Jan. 25, 1268). On Sarroca see above, Chapter II, note 109. James blames the priors in the document cited in note 131 above.

157. Arch. Crown, Peter III, Reg. Canc. 40, fol. 103 (May 7, 1278): "concedimus vobis Berengario de Conquis et quibuslibet aliis qui mutuaverint ad opus ecclesie Sancti Vincentii sive ad missiones et expensas domus et hospitalis Sancti Vincentii quod illud quod vos et ipsi ad opus predicte ecclesie faciendum . . . habeatis et recipiatis de redditibus hospitalis." The name probably does not derive from Cuenca but from Conques-en-Rouergue in Languedoc.

158. Arch. Crown, Peter III, Reg. Canc. 42, fol. 158v (Oct. 21, 1279); "et provideas clericis, porcionariis, et servitoribus dicte domus et infirmis hospitalis eiusdem, bene et condecenter prout ordinatum est per dominum Iacobum inclite recordationis patrem nostrum et hactenus est melius . . . consuetum."

159. Arch. Crown, Peter III, Reg. Canc. 48, fol. 184v (Nov. 18, 1280); exclusive of Chirello and Cortes this time. Cf. Reg. Canc. 49, fol. 33v (Feb. 18, 1280–1281).

160. Arch. Crown, Peter III, Reg. Canc. 44, fol. 125 (April 10, 1282); cf. Liber patrimonii, fol. 300, doc. 15. Reg. Canc. 59, fol. 189, 189r,v (two docs. of Dec. 19, 1282): "ad restituendum . . . domum Sancti Vincencii et castrum de . . . Quart et alia bona."

161. Arch. Crown, Peter III, Reg. Canc. 46, fol. 121 (Nov. 19, 1283); published in Documenta selecta, doc. 30. King Peter recalls that Peter had recently assigned a priest to one of the crown chaplaincies there, Peter "tunc tenentem dictam domum sancti Vincencii." With both Prior Peter of the King and Procurator Berengar of Conques opposing the claims of Abbot Bernard at this time, Peter may have administered both offices for the crown.

162. Arch. Crown, Peter III, Reg. Canc. 43, fol. 21v (two docs. of Aug. 15, 1284).

163. A document of 1283 ordered Berengar of Conques to stop delaying his payment of the 10,000 solidi (Reg. Canc. 61, fol. 121, May 3, 1283); "ex parte nobilis dompni Ferrandi fratris nostri propositum extitit coram nobis quod vos non solvitis . . . illa decem millia solidorum quos sibi vel procuratori suo tenebamini solvere quolibet anno de redditibus domus Sancti Vincentii Valencie, quare mandamus vobis . . ." See the similar document of May 6, on fol. 122. Prince Alphonse in November 1282 spoke of the crown grant to Ferdinand of "decem mille solidos regalium quos idem Ferrandus debet percipere et habere in redditibus domus Sancti Vincencii et monasterii Sancti Victoriani" and other places each year (Arch. Crown, Peter III, Reg. Canc. 71, fol. 127v [Nov. 14, 1282]). Another document (ibid.) tells us he was studying at Paris ("qui stud[et] parisiis"). See too the document in Documenta selecta, doc. 29 (Oct. 6, 1283). Ferdinand was

to be allowed to seize St. Vincent's priorate and the revenues of St. Victorian if the yearly sum was not paid. The Paris studies would consume only a small part of this money; in 1308 James II could send his illegitimate brother John to the University of Montpellier for two thousand solidi.

164. Arch. Crown, James I, perg. 2,148 (Mar. 27, 1273); cf. Liber patrimonii, fol. 287v, doc. 6, excluding lands held by St. Vincent's in the Tortosa diocese from the king's agreement to reduce his tithe-share from a half to a third. In the Valencia diocese the tithe question was only finally settled with the bishop in 1308 (*Diócesis valentina*, II, 160). After an earlier accommodation, St. Vincent's remained in control of a number of ex-mosques and Moslem cemeteries (cf. Arch. Nac. Madrid, Codices, Repertori de San Vicent, e.g. fols. 22v, 24).

NOTES TO CHAPTER XVI. CONCLUSION

1. Joan Fuster, *Nosaltres, els valencians* (Barcelona, 1962), p. 150; see also pp. 17 ff.

2. Ibn Khaldûn, *The Muqaddimah; an Introduction to History*, tr. Franz Rosenthal, Bollingen Foundation series, no. 43, 3 vols. (New York, 1958), I, esp. ch. 2, secs. 22–23, and ch. 3., sec. 5. In ch. 3, sec. 9, he speaks of the civil troubles which demoralized Moslem Valencia just as King James was planning his conquest.

INDEX

INDEX

(For the spelling of names see pages x–xi, 321–322. Persons are indexed under surname where possible, or by the second of two Christian names; names within parentheses are variants or corrected forms; "de" is rendered "of" for medieval names.)